Methods of Teaching Business and Distributive Education

Third Edition

Harm Harms, Ed.D.

Professor, Department of Business
East Texas Baptist College
Marshall, Texas

B. W. Stehr, Ed.D.

Professor, Department of Business Education
Northern Illinois University
DeKalb, Illinois

E. Edward Harris, Ed.D.

Professor, Department of Business Education
Northern Illinois University
DeKalb, Illinois

X81

Published by

SOUTH-WESTERN PUBLISHING CO.

CINCINNATI   WEST CHICAGO, ILL.   DALLAS   NEW ROCHELLE, N.Y.
BURLINGAME, CALIF.   BRIGHTON, ENGLAND

This book is intended to be useful to in-service teachers of business subjects, to college and university teachers of methods courses in business, and to students enrolled in methods courses.

The Third Edition is designed to provide, for beginning teachers, practical help in solving the many problems of classroom teaching. This edition not only reemphasizes the use of procedures that have been proven successful by teachers throughout the nation, but also introduces new and promising developments in methods and materials of instruction in business. For example, this edition presents material on learning systems, on behavioral objectives, and on techniques of evaluation consistent with innovations in education methodology. The approach to providing solutions to the problems of teaching experienced by new teachers and those already in the profession is realistic. Step by step the user of the textbook is provided with examples, diagrams, and specific material to aid in the task of teaching and providing a learning atmosphere conducive to learning. In each major section of the textbook, all phases of the teaching task, from initial planning through evaluation, are presented in detail.

The volume is an extensive and complete revision of the Second Edition. Chapters 8, 9, 10, and 11 are entirely new, representing teaching methods and procedures in the distributive subjects, the cooperative plan, the project plan, and youth organizations. The first two chapters serve as an introduction to teaching, the authors recognizing that a successful teacher must possess a sound foundation in (1) current and projected aims of education and (2) the psychology of the learning process and approaches to planning.

The authors are indebted to many college and high school teachers, to state and national education officials, and to businessmen who contributed their time to test and comment on the manuscript as it was being developed. Grateful acknowledgment is extended to the authors and publishers whose materials are cited in the book. Special recognition must be given to the business students at both East Texas Baptist College and Northern Illinois University for their criticism and constructive comments which were extremely valuable in developing various parts of the manuscript.

Harm Harms
B. W. Stehr
E. Edward Harris

TABLE OF CONTENTS

Chapter 1

MODERN BUSINESS EDUCATION AND THE ROLE OF THE TEACHER

TRENDS IN EDUCATION FOR BUSINESS

Current changes in the American educational scene require that all business teachers understand the role of education for business and economic literacy in the framework of the total school curriculum. Education for business appears at times to be dependent on a mechanistic approach which places maximum stress upon acquiring routinized skills to the exclusion of decision-making and problem-solving that are primary requisites to success in a complex society.

The results that are demanded of an educational system cannot be obtained unless all parts of a system are scrutinized carefully. Quite often, preparation for a vocation is neither pre-planned nor developed. Conversely, education for business is planned occasionally without regard for the total educational needs of the students. O. J. Byrnside, Jr., Executive Secretary of the National Business Education Association, recently stated:

> Business education programs are part of the total education program and will become an even more important part. Coordinated efforts on the part of business educators, school administrators, and guidance counselors will be necessary to bring about needed change. A high-quality program must be developed. Both the academic and vocational aspects of the present program need to be carefully examined

and possibly adjusted to better fulfill the needs of today's students. . . Business education cannot be divorced from the problems that are certainly a part of general education and a part of vocational education.[1]

Various attempts have been made in the literature of education to picture the old and new philosophies of education. The "little red schoolhouse" of the turn of the century is a good example of the old. In penmanship and art, one was taught to copy. In fact, most students never arrived at a stage of schooling involving any creative endeavor. In the little red schoolhouse, pupils learned virtually nothing about physical fitness, and mental hygiene was not yet born. Children ate much but not well of the educational offerings. Facts in school had little meaning, no purpose—just so much to be learned because is was "good for you." Attempts at English composition were so stilted, because of severe criticisms of spelling, grammar, and punctuation, that rarely did anyone dare to strike out on his own. In botany, the class was forbidden to talk about anything that was in the least familiar; plants or trees of a domestic nature were taboo. The time was spent on Latin terms that frighten one even now, while the home orchard and flower gardens died for want of knowledge of plant culture.

The class followed Caesar through many a campaign, but failed to learn the meaning of a few of the common prefixes. These students studied the minutest crystals in geology, but they learned nothing to help them appreciate the wonderful outcroppings of the Grand Canyon or even those in the backyard of the school. They learned names of states and their capitals, but they learned not a word about the influence of geography on the lives of people. They learned dates in history, but they found nothing to help them function as economic citizens in a free society.

American Education in the Decade of the 1970's

A change is taking place in education, a change of revolutionary proportions that can be identified as a trend—a general tendency or inclination in a certain direction. The past

---

[1] O. J. Byrnside, Jr., "Business Education—Unlimited Opportunities for All: An Editorial," *Business Education Forum*, 24 (December, 1969), p. 2.

half century has been notable for its accomplishments in the education of the mass population of the United States. Since October 4, 1957, the date of the Russian Sputnik, the problem of American education has been how to make the most effective use of the technological and scientific resources of the nation. We want to sustain and enhance our present standard of living, yet cope with the Kremlin in the race for space. The educational system now strives for depth, as well as breadth, in the total educational development of youth. They must not only cultivate the ability to earn a living for themselves and their families, to participate as members of their communities, but must also become prepared to fit into the total framework of society as free, independently-thinking, and functioning citizens.

Typical of the concern for the direction of education, particularly at the secondary school level, is the view expressed by Professor Irwin Widen:

> Recent years have brought tremendous advances in the state of our technology. We have zoomed into the air age and have blasted off for the space age. Yet, as has been wisely pointed out, a rocket ship is no more useful to man than an ox cart if he does not know where he wants to go.
>
> As it has to other fields of endeavor, technological progress has come to education. Our school buildings have become more functional, our teaching and administrative practices more efficient, and our public-relations techniques more astute. Still, with education as with transportation, advanced means do not of themselves guarantee the attainment of worthy ends.
>
> What should be the ends of education and what means are appropriate to such ends? These are the basic questions that confront our profession.[2]

Two major philosophical issues in education in the United States today are pointed out by Dr. John H. Fischer, President of Teachers College, Columbia University:

> In our society, what is the special function of the school? This is the query which, often unnoticed and ignored, underlies the heated discussions about quality in education. It is

---

[2] Irwin Widen, A review of *Democratic Educational Theory* by Ernest E. Bayles (New York: Harper, 1960) in *Phi Delta Kappan*, 41 (June, 1960), p. 403.

pointless to ask whether a school is doing its work well until we have agreed on what its work is.

There is a *second* question on which you will have to clarify your own thinking and be prepared to offer a responsible opinion: How shall we conduct schools so as to nurture most fruitfully the individuality of the students? The implications for schools are broad and deep, confronting us immediately with paradoxes. For one of the principal aims of education is to make people alike. In pursuit of this purpose we teach children their mother tongue, a common alphabet, a system of symbols to express quantitative ideas and mathematical processes. But the coin has another side, for while the common characteristics of people make a community possible, it is their uncommon qualities that make it better. *Variety, innovation, leadership, and progress come only from individuality.*[3]

Special directions of emphasis for our educational resources are a part of the educational scene. In his writing on usefully constructed school programs for the education of the economically disadvantaged, Robert J. Havighurst, of the University of Chicago, points out special difficulties of this group:

Economically disadvantaged children have difficulty in the school system for two reasons:

1. Their family environment limits their perceptual, conceptual, and linguistic experience in their early years, thus preparing them poorly for school. . .

2. Teaching methods in the schools have not been well-adapted to the learning styles of economically disadvantaged children. . .[4]

It is necessary to "tune in" to the needs of the modern child of society and to "tool up" for the kind of educational program which will benefit this citizen of our world. Byrnside further extends the thought of careful attention to the clientele of the modern school:

---

[3] John H. Fischer, "Our Changing Conception of Education," *Phi Delta Kappan,* 42 (October, 1960), pp. 16-17.
[4] Robert J. Havighurst, "Curriculum for the Disadvantaged," *Phi Delta Kappan,* 51 (March, 1970), p. 373.

Although much attention has centered on the gifted and the talented, the exceptional learner, the alienated and disaffected, and the disadvantaged and the handicapped, there is an even greater majority which must be considered. The learning problems of the average student have not yet been adequately researched and met, and therefore, must be considered in our plans for the future.[5]

Implications for Education for Business

To make a living is a prime desire and struggle of man, and history records the efforts of men and nations to achieve sound economic status. The ability of men in modern business to operate and manage the large and complex concerns does not come from self-initiative and "boot-strap pulling" alone. Our business world has become too complex. Eyster senses this when he writes:

> Vocational and technical education is of great importance to people, to society, and to the economy of the nation. Opportunities to earn a livelihood without pre-service preparation for an occupation are decreasing rapidly. Manual and skilled labor jobs in many instances are being replaced by technological procedures. The link between man and productive labor is education. Education makes individuals eligible for holding a job in a given field of employment.[6]

Growth in knowledge and ability must be attributed in great measure to well-directed programs of education for business in both secondary and post-secondary schools. Education for business in these institutions represents a major expression of the concern of a nation for the economic competence of its youth. Leon P. Minear, of the U.S. Office of Education, writes:

> For generations Congress has felt that education was the melting pot, the backbone of our society. Our forefathers came to these shores from many countries. Within a generation or two the public school system made us a people with a common culture. Congress still looks upon education,

---

[5] Byrnside, *loc. cit.*
[6] Elvin S. Eyster, "Business Education Shares in Solving Problems in Vocational Education," *Journal of Business Education,* 24 (December, 1969), p. 92.

and vocational and technical education in particular, as the device to bring all elements of our society into accord.[7]

Education for business has a manifold purpose. It consists of the total activity which is planned, organized, and evaluated in order to prepare youth to meet the technical and economic needs of a complex society. It is a program of instruction, counseling, guidance, and service which seeks, through a variety of planned experiences, to provide for and improve the part that each young person will eventually fulfill in his social and economic surroundings. Education for business seeks to develop youth beyond the capability of obtaining and holding an initial job.

The business education curriculum is a particular and distinct part of the total school program. It should be viewed as such and developed on that basis. It includes the formal aspects of educational effort as these are developed in the classroom under the heading of instruction; personalized efforts to inform and counsel the individual pupil; and general information and guidance activities developed on a group basis. Implied in the total business education effort is the utilization of all of the learning activities possible for the purpose of providing realistic and functional business education experiences.

The responsibilities that rest on the business curriculum were recently restated and reaffirmed by a major association for the improvement of business education in the high schools, the Policies Commission for Business and Economic Education: [8]

> Major statements of the purposes of education in America have identified a need for business education. Business education achieves its goals through—
>
> Specialized instruction to prepare students for careers in business.
>
> Fundamental instruction to help students assume their economic roles as consumers, workers, and citizens.

---

[7] Leon P. Minear, "Role of Business Education in National Manpower Program," *Business Education Forum*, 24 (January, 1970), p. 3.

[8] Policies Commission for Business and Economic Education, "This We Believe About Business Education in the Secondary School," *Business Education Forum*, 25 (October, 1970), p. 8.

Background instruction to assist students in preparing for professional careers requiring advanced study.

In an effort to satisfy the needs of all students, secondary schools should provide sound programs of business education that provide instruction for and about business.

WE BELIEVE THAT

. . . Business education is an effective program of occupational instruction for secondary students desiring careers in business.

. . . Business education has an important contribution to make to the economic literacy of all secondary school students.

. . . Business education is desirable for students who plan programs requiring post-secondary and higher education in the field of business.

PROGRAM DEVELOPMENT

Careers in Business

The occupational program should be related to the needs of business. Therefore, the business curriculum must be flexible and sensitive to changes in business.

WE BELIEVE THAT

. . . Every secondary school should provide opportunities for students to prepare for careers in business.

. . . The time devoted to preparation for business occupations should depend upon the student's abilities, interests, and personal qualities.

. . . The sequence of learning experiences should be planned so that the student will achieve his highest occupational competency upon completion of his program.

. . . Instructional equipment and facilities should be comparable to those found in the businesses where students are likely to be employed.

. . . In-school laboratories that simulate business conditions can be an effective means of providing business education.

. . . On-the-job experience through cooperative education can be an additional effective means of providing business education.

. . . An advisory committee should be involved in planning programs leading to employment in business.

. . . Certificates of occupational proficiency should be awarded to students who develop employable competencies. Proficiency certificates should be recognized as evidence of competency by employers or employment agencies.

. . . Every secondary school should have a youth organization for business students.

Roles as Consumers, Workers, and Citizens

The consumers, workers, and citizens should know how to interpret economic issues which affect them and how to manage their economic affairs efficiently.

WE BELIEVE THAT

. . . Opportunities must be provided for secondary school students to develop an understanding of how our business system operates.

. . . Programs that develop economic understanding should be planned cooperatively with other departments of the school that are concerned with economic education.

. . . Any requirements relating to the development of personal and social economic competencies should be reciprocally recognized by the respective departments of the school.

GUIDANCE

The diversity and comprehensiveness of the business program requires that guidance services be available to all students.

WE BELIEVE THAT

. . . Occupational information and assistance in interpreting that information should be available to all students.

. . . Every student should be assisted in establishing an awareness of his own interests and capabilities so that he may plan his career.

. . . The secondary schools have a direct responsibility to provide occupational counseling, placement, and follow-up of students enrolled in the business programs.

There is good reason to believe that extensive activity in business and economic education in the nation's schools will continue unabated. In addition to the philosophical bases indicated above, a multitude of practical problems in business and industry continue to demand the best effort of those who follow the pennant of business education. The increase of paper records, for example, in the past twenty years, while being expedited through the use of machines, has placed a drain on the available top-level manpower.

It is the present-day climate of thought and need for serious appraisal of educational practices that causes us to study critically the business education curricula. If ours is indeed the space age, the school must accept the challenge to contribute generously to the preparation of youth for life in a complex and ever-changing world. Ruben Dumler, past president of the Mountain-Plains Business Education Association, commented on this need:

> Sometimes all of us become very complacent because we feel that everything *at present* is going along very nicely. Actually, teachers are always working in the future, and, above all, for the future; therefore, they must be concerned with the future.[9]

A significant amount of interest at the national level has developed in education for business. National legislation serves as a major point of reference for those who would understand clearly the extensive effort in behalf of the vocational and economic education of youth in our nation.

The Future in Education for Business

Projections into the future are a necessary and essential part of sound program planning. While a number of excursions into the future have been made for business education, one of the most recent and comprehensive was made by Marguerite Crumley, State Supervisor of Business Education for the State of Virginia:

> My first prediction is that, as in the past, business educators will be able to take in stride the changes that the future will bring. . . .

---

[9] Ruben Dumler, "The Future of Business Education," *The Balance Sheet,* XLI (April, 1960), p. 339.

I predict that the NOBELS research project now under way will revolutionize business education in much the same way that the new math, new English, and new physics have revolutionized those fields. . . .

I predict revolutionary changes in office machines. . . .

I predict the decline of the standard textbooks as we have known them. . . .

I predict the use of more sophisticated teaching aids especially designed for small and large groups and independent study. . . .

I predict more innovations in instructional methods based on the laws of learning and changes in school organization. . . .

I predict that the program of office occupations education will be sufficiently diverse in curriculum construction and offered in a variety of schools to accommodate the manpower needs of society and to meet the wide range of abilities and interests of students. . . .

I predict that typewriting will at last become a common tool of communication—as common as the pen is now. . . .

I predict that we in business education will be spending more of our efforts on teaching basic business and economic understandings, office systems and procedures, and more efficient applications of skills to office situations. . . .

I predict the continued phenomenal growth of adult and continuing education offered by the public high schools. . . .

I predict that the business teacher of the future will be a true *professional*—and an educational leader. . . .[10]

Nowhere is the thought for the need to develop teachers to meet these trends and challenges more appropriately expressed than by T. James Crawford, past president of the National Association for Business Teacher Education:

The prime challenge for the 1970's, however, will be the development of master classroom teachers. Though impressive emphasis will continue to be placed on curriculum, facilities, research, and materials, the big payoff for business

---

[10] Marguerite Crumley, "Business Education in Transition—Tomorrow," *Business Education Forum*, 24 (February, 1970), p. 3.

education in the years ahead will reside in the capacity of its individual teachers to demonstrate increased teaching competence. The extent to which classroom teachers learn to (a) incorporate research evidence, (b) utilize the hardware of technology, and (c) structure innovative procedures in meaningful programs designed to increase their personal teaching power will determine, in large measure, the future of business education as a profession. As the teaching stature of individual business teachers increases, the total image of business education will be enlarged to impressive proportions. Increasingly, the strength of business education programs will be determined more by the strength of its teachers than by adaptations of vehicles of instruction.[11]

THE IMPACT OF RECENT FEDERAL LEGISLATION

"Too Much Stress on College—An Official Report," "Vocational Education Neglected," or "More Vocational Training Essential" have been typical headings for newspaper editorials and magazines throughout the country in recent years. Why? Facts presented in two reports [12 & 13] by the National Advisory Council on Vocational Education to the Secretary of Health, Education, and Welfare, such as the partial list below, served to arouse the public:

1. Each year the ranks of the school dropouts increase by three-quarters of a million young men and women.

2. Schools fail to educate nearly 25 percent of the young men and women each year who turn 18 for the eight out of ten job opportunities which do not require a college education.

3. The federal government invests $14 in the nation's universities for every $1 it invests in vocational education programs; yet, turns around and spends as much as $12,000 per person in remedial programs to get unemployables off the welfare rolls.

---

[11] T. James Crawford, "At the Start of a New Decade," *The Balance Sheet*, LI (January, 1970), p. 195.

[12] National Advisory Council on Vocational Education, *First Annual Report* (Washington, D.C., July, 1969).

[13] National Advisory Council on Vocational Education, *Second Report* (Washington, D.C., November, 1969).

4. Local school districts concentrate on college-preparatory and general programs in reckless disregard of the fact that high school is the last formal type of education for 60 percent of our young people.

5. Young people are making inappropriate choices because they are victims of the national yearning for educational prestige.

6. The number of jobs which unskilled workers can fill is declining rapidly. The number of jobs requiring a liberal-arts college education, while growing, is increasing far less rapidly than the number demanding a technical skill.

7. In the 1980's, it will still be true that fewer than 20 percent of our job opportunities will require a four-year college degree.

These and other facts were contained in the reports which were released at a time when our country was deeply concerned with racial unrest, violence, and unemployment of youth. The reports came during a time when Americans were discarding an estimated $18 billion worth of repairable items because of the complexity of modern appliances and the scarcity and high cost of the repairman.

Challenges for Business Educators

How would business educators respond to such factual information? How did Congress respond? Congress responded by passing unanimously the Vocational Education Amendments of 1968. Congress authorized a total of $3,180,050,000 for vocational education for the 1969-1972 four-year period. The mandates of Congress are quite clear in Public Law 90-576.

John A. Beaumont, formerly with the U.S. Office of Education and a consultant to the National Advisory Council, said:

Educators should take seriously these mandates because they indicate very definitely a dissatisfaction with some of the current procedures in the educational institution. It is apparent that the continued support of the educational institutions by the Congress and the public may in large measure depend upon the reaction (that is taken by the educational institutions) to this legislation.[14]

Business educators now face a challenge that will have more impact on their beliefs, concepts, philosophies, curriculum designs, and instructional strategies than anything faced previously. The aspiring educator should feel relieved that he does not have to learn all about the Smith-Hughes Act of 1917, the George-Deen Act of 1936, the George-Barden Act of 1946, and the Vocational Education Act of 1963 before he can intelligently discuss federal legislation affecting education for business. Because, for all practical purposes, the Vocational Education Amendments of 1968 supercede all prior legislation in vocational education.

The foreword to the 1968 General Report of the Advisory Council on Vocational Education, which was published in *Vocational Education: The Bridge Between Man and His Work,* may serve to highlight the challenge that is facing educators in business:

> Vocational education faces a unique challenge in the years ahead—a challenge rooted in the social and economic welfare of people. In the contemporary social scene, with its large city problems, the ghettos, school dropouts, and a variety of disadvantaged groups, the need for vocational education stands out clearly. Never before in its history has vocational education had such an opportunity to reach out to the total population and serve the groups that society has passed by.
>
> Under the influence of the 1963 legislation, vocational education has grown rapidly. This rate of growth must continue so that more of the youth in high schools and in post-high school institutions have an even greater opportunity to prepare for the world of work. Preparing students for the transfer from school to work requires a greater variety of educational preparation for work and demands new levels of integration of general and vocational knowledge and skills. Similarly, expansion of programs for employed and unemployed workers, including retraining, must take into account the personal needs of individuals as they attempt to adjust to the occupational changes by technology.

---

[14] John A. Beaumont, "Emerging Trends and Direction," (Paper presented at Business Education Conference, Northern Illinois University, DeKalb, Illinois, July, 1969).

New dimensions, ideas, and experimentation must mark the departure into the future. In no way have we explored the limits of the potential of vocational education. A cultural and skills learning corps, with a focus upon youth, can provide the motivation and idealism from which one derives a sense of purpose. Many youth need a new home environment which is conducive to their self-employment before great strides can be made in their occupational planning. Concepts of work must be generated early in the educational career of youth so that they have first-hand information against which to match their talents and desires. Their total educational experience must have increasing emphasis upon the world of work.[15]

Vocational Education Amendments of 1968

John A. Beaumont, discussing the intent of Congress in establishing each of the provisions of Public Law 90-576, said:

Role of the Citizen

Vocational education has a long history of citizen involvement, particularly in its use of advisory committees. At the local level, especially, these committees have been a key to success or failure of occupational training and resultant placement. Congress appears to be reinforcing this principle of quality vocational education. It has placed in the Amendments a number of requirements that will assure a broader use of lay talents as well as those of professionals in the vocational education movement.

The National Advisory Council is charged with an equally broad range of duties. It will advise the Commissioner on the preparation of general regulations for vocational education programs, and the administration and operation of such programs. It is charged with reviewing vocational programs supported by the legislation, reporting its findings and making recommendations to the Secretary of Health, Education, and Welfare for transmittal to Con-

---

[15] U.S. Department of Health, Education, and Welfare, Office of Education, *Vocational Education: The Bridge Between Man and His Work,* OE 80052 (Washington: U.S. Government Printing Office, 1968).

gress. It will also have the duty to conduct independent evaluations and publish the results.

Citizen involvement is mandatory also at the state and local levels. To receive grants, each state must establish a State Advisory Council to be appointed by the Governor (or by the State Board of Vocational Education in states where members of this Board are elected).

No specific requirements are established for local advisory committees. Community involvement in the application for funds at the local level is, however, made clear in the State Plan requirements. The State Plan must show policies and procedures which will assure that applications from local educational agencies have been developed in consultation with various community interests—representatives of schools, students, parents, manpower needs, etc.

The urgent demand for community and lay participation in education is thus clearly recognized in P.L. 90-576. Vocational educators have the know-how and experience to move rapidly into a leadership position in the involvement of the citizen in the educational process, and the student will be the gainer as a result of giving the citizenry a broader role in vocational education.

Search for Innovation

Encouraged by the report of the Advisory Council on Vocational Education, Congress included in the Amendments a series of provisions which will insure a sensitivity to change in the labor market, a response to the needs of various segments of the population, and the development of innovative procedures and programs. These provisions are:

* An allotment to the Secretary of Labor to finance national, state, and local studies and projections of manpower needs.
* The appointment of the National Advisory Council and State Advisory Councils charged with evaluation and the making of recommendations.
* The emphasis on planning at state and local levels in the development of state plans.
* The provisions for research at both national and state levels.

* The proposal for special funding of exemplary programs and projects.
* The provisions for demonstration schools as part of the residential vocational education program.
* The emphasis on making cooperative education a major dimension of all vocational education.
* The provision for curriculum development.
* The provision for teacher education, particularly the exchange programs.

The implication is plain that vocational education must respond to social change. Prevailing practices must be subject to continuous evaluation and vocational educators must demonstrate the courage to experiment with new and different concepts. Only thus can vocational education become a viable institution in which men are not made prisoners of their own procedures but remain free to pursue their goals.

Vocational Education in the Mainstream

This legislation tends to place vocational education in the mainstream of education. It places an emphasis on the development of occupationally-oriented curriculum. It is presumed that the entire program of the school will be made more relevant to the student by the use of understandable goals, which relate directly to his occupational objectives; and further by the use of methodology which permits the student to participate in activities which easily relate to established occupational goals. The general or academic curriculum will be organized in such a manner as to have direct application to the goals of the student. The schools and junior colleges of the 70's would provide an opportunity for youth to learn more about the work of the society in which he lives. Through broad clustering of occupations the student will have an opportunity to pursue, through classroom and other experiences, studies which will help him to learn some of the skills and understandings about the broad cluster of occupations in which he experiences interest. As he moves through the curriculum to higher levels, he would have opportunities to specialize in areas of particular interest. The important thing would be that the total program of studies would be directed toward an understandable objective; and thereby, would have relevance to the student and his concerns.

As one educator has said, we must recognize the importance, particularly to a large segment of our population, of attaching significance to a series of short-range goals and objectives of increasing difficulties rather than the long-range objectives of the present educational institution which become lost in the minds of the students.

The legislation takes a new approach toward specific grants in aid. While the bulk of the authorization is devoted to the total program of vocational education, the Congress saw the need to establish specific authorization for certain activities which they believed should become major functions of the vocational education program.

Research Emphasis

This act continues the research emphasis of the 1963 Act. However, there is a major difference in that half of the funds available for research are given directly to the states for research which is considered important to the needs of a particular state. Now instead of having to climb the long trail to Washington for research funds, funds should be available at the state level for the studies and research which will help to improve the instructional program for youth and adults.

Exemplary Programs

The National Advisory Council strongly recommended the inclusion of authorizations for what they termed "exemplary programs." Considerable emphasis in this program is given to the needs of occupational orientation in the elementary schools and to the need for occupational guidance at all levels. We know little about what should be done in the field of vocational education in the elementary schools and junior high schools. Little has been done to experiment with programs in the elementary schools and junior high school levels to bring these pupils face to face with the world of work in our society.

The authorization under this proposal is in a sense similar to the research authorizations in that 50 percent of the funds are to be retained by the Office of Education and 50 percent are to be used by the state in initiating exemplary programs. These grants should help us to find new directions for bringing the elementary and junior high school program more directly into the vocational education mainstream.

Residential Schools

The residential school authorization, which was initiated in the 1963 Act, is continued in this legislation. This is a particular authorization that should be pushed by the educational profession because there are many places where a residential school might be the ideal way to serve certain disadvantaged or handicapped young people. There is a great deal to be learned about residential schools. There has been experimentation in several states and the Job Corps has operated a number of such schools. We still know little about taking young people out of one environment and putting them into another as a means of supplementing their education.

Consumer and Homemaking Education

Congress has seen fit to include consumer and homemaking education in the vocational amendments as a separate part. These activities, while not oriented to occupational development, are a most important area of concern for our society. What new directions should be taken in order to bring this expertise into focus and make it a part of the total program? New directions here are essential if this part of the Act is to serve its major purpose, "giving greater consideration to improving social and cultural conditions and needs especially in economically deprived areas."

Cooperative Vocational Education

The National Advisory Council found that cooperative education had an outstanding record in achieving gainful employment. The Council's findings in the field of distributive education encouraged them to include this particular part in the legislation.

There are many ways in which the cooperative approach can be used in vocational education. We haven't really scratched the surface in finding ways to give students an opportunity to participate in a work-oriented situation that supplements classroom preparation. We have tended to stay with one pattern of half-days in school and half-days on the job when a little innovation and vision would find hundreds of ways of using this method in preparing students to enter the world of work. It is really most discouraging to find so little use of this concept in the junior colleges.

Work Study Programs

The authorization for the work study programs has been continued in this Act. There are tremendous opportunities for finding jobs that students can fill in order to earn the funds that they need to support themselves in school. Look for new ways and opportunities to help students through a work study program to continue their education.

Curriculum Development

This legislation for the first time authorized funds for curriculum development. These funds are retained by the Office of Education but are available as grants for colleges and universities and state boards or other nonprofit agencies and institutions. This particular authorization should lead to the development of curriculum laboratories throughout the nation.

Educational Professional Development

The Congress is concerned with the lack of interest in vocational educators on the part of those administrators who are responsible for the Educational Professions Development Act program. Therefore, in this act they amended the Higher Education Act of 1965 to include a provision for vocational educators. Plans and procedures should be developed to secure such funds for needed preparation of vocational education teachers and leaders. One aspect of this act, which should be looked into particularly, is the provision for developing cooperative arrangements with industry or business or government for giving teachers an opportunity to improve and update their knowledge of the field in which they are teaching. This has long been a dream in vocational education and is now part of the legislation.

Unequivocal

The concern of Congress for a redirection of vocational education which will have an impact on all education is forcibly expressed in the following statement in House Report No. 1647 by Congressman William H. Ayres of Ohio:

> There should be a renewed sense of urgency about the need for a modern structure of occupational education which will meet the needs of the total population.

We simply must not permit millions of young Americans to grow into adulthood without salable skills and opportunities for further training that will be needed in a fast changing job market. We may think that we have troubles now, but if our total educational system does not shape up to the demands of these times, we are facing a real tragedy.

Meeting these needs will require a great deal more than additional money. In my judgment, we must use existing resources more intelligently. This cannot be done without broad public understanding of and support for the goals of job-oriented education. If most people continue to feel against all reason and experience that the most important goal of education is a college degree and that any career objective not requiring the degree is a measure of failure, the cause is lost. It may be lost unless the educational community is prepared to abandon some ingrained attitudes and narrow interests which are impeding change when it is most in order.[16]

Implications for the Teacher

Public Law 90-576 provided that state and local plans will be developed for submission to the appropriate agencies. These plans will vary from community to community and state to state. However, the basic challenges presented in the Vocational Education Amendments of 1968 are stimulating. Listed below are some of the implications for business educators:

1. Business educators will find themselves involved in occupationally oriented programs where there is no dichotomy between academic and vocational education.
2. Teachers will have an opportunity to initiate and participate in research, exemplary, and curriculum development projects.
3. The curriculum will be adjusted to accommodate a wider range of occupational opportunity and a larger number of students.
4. Teaching strategy and scheduling of instructional time will be designed to encourage individualized instruction.

---

[16] John A. Beaumont, *loc. cit.*

5. Better quality curriculum guides and instructional materials will be made available through various agencies.
6. Consumer economics will receive increased attention at all levels of education.
7. Teacher education programs will place increased emphasis on in-service training of various types.
8. Fellowships will be available for teachers desiring to move into leadership roles.
9. Teachers will be encouraged to innovate and explore new approaches in occupational education.
10. Programs using cooperative and project instructional plans will receive increased financial support and encouragement.

Business educators are in a strategic position to respond to the challenges presented by the passage of the Vocational Education Amendments of 1968. Congress has provided the financial support and encouragement to make it possible for business educators to provide excellence and opportunity for youth and adults.

THE MODERN BUSINESS TEACHER

The businessmen and businesswomen of the future who hopefully will guide an economically literate society do not "happen" automatically as a consequence of a program of studies in business. They are the result of a planned, organized, and evaluated effort by those who are qualified to teach, to counsel, to guide, and who have a major responsibility for doing these things. The teacher, as a professional person, holds the primary responsibility for the education of these future leaders and workers.

The Role of the Modern Business Teacher

The role of the teacher in the program of education for business cannot be minimized. Unlike the administrator, principal, or supervisor, the teacher is part and parcel of the daily experience of the students. By his example, understanding, and the impact of his personality, he becomes second only to the parents as the major force in the young person's educational experience. The teacher brings to the business education program valuable training and experience in matters concerning business and economic education. He understands the vocational interests of youth and the significant values of business concepts which contribute to development of an economically and vocationally able member of society. His training in business qualifies him to function well in matters relating to the counseling and guidance of students in occupational and vocational choices in business.

The Business Teacher as a Member of a Profession

A necessary element for the growth of any school program in business is the capability of the business teacher to function effectively in his role. He is a specialized instructor who must be able to adapt his instruction to the economic and vocational needs and interests of his students. He should, by his own appearance and example, afford firsthand evidence of the meaning of competence in business. He has a demanding responsibility which, when fulfilled, will greatly enhance the effectiveness and value of a school program.

Competence in teaching, particularly as applied to new teachers entering the field, is a crucial factor resulting from these factors:

1. A depth and breadth of knowledge related to teaching responsibilities.

2. A knowledge of children and young people and the ability to work with them in developing the best learning situation possible.

3. A knowledge of current curriculum methods and the opportunity to work with them.

4. A knowledge of the duties and responsibilities inherent in the whole teaching situation.[17]

Top level performance in teaching, whether in business or in other learning areas, involves a need to recognize the

[17] Genevieve Starcher, from an address given before the West Virginia Association for Student Teaching, Marshall University, Huntington, West Virginia, November, 1962.

characteristics of a profession. Such a definition has been set forth by Lieberman:

1. A unique, definite, and essential social service.
2. An emphasis upon intellectual techniques in performing its service.
3. A long period of specialized training.
4. A broad range of autonomy for both the individual practitioners and for the occupational group as a whole.
5. An acceptance by the practitioners of broad personal responsibilities for judgments made and acts performed within the scope of professional autonomy.
6. An emphasis upon the service to be rendered, rather than the economic gain to practitioners, as the basis for the organization and performance of the social service delegated to the occupational group.
7. A comprehensive self-governing organization of practitioners.
8. A code of ethics which has been clarified and interpreted at ambiguous and doubtful points by concrete cases.[18]

Mentioned above is the axiom of professional ethics. A Code of Ethics was adopted by the NEA Representative Assembly in 1966. The four divisions of the Code deal with the classroom teacher's commitment to the student, to the community, to the profession, and to professional employment practices. Other than the parents of the young person, the teacher exerts the most important influence on the young people in his classes. To the extent that the teacher adopts as a personal tenet and implements a code of ethics in his teaching, the school will serve as an agency through which avenues to vocational and economic success are made possible to students.

Schools are changing, not only physically, but in terms of the youth that are served. There is a movement toward new and more flexible ways of using time and talent in the schools, a making possible of pupil-tailored instruction that has been talked about for many years. Don Davies, Associate Commissioner of Education, refers to a changing concept of teacher education:

---

[18] Myron Lieberman, *Education as a Profession* (Englewood Cliffs, N.J.: Prentice-Hall, Inc., 1956), pp. 1-6.

As our schools move toward equalization, individualization, and humanization, educators are increasingly confronted by the notion that educational institutions should shoulder the responsibility for the learning successes or failures of their pupils. This concept links student performance with teacher performance. It implies educational goals. It forecasts the measurement of achievement. It means, in effect, that schools and colleges will be judged on how they perform, not by what they promise.

This approach to education requires something very basic: It means changing ourselves and all of the people who have anything to do with running and serving the schools. It means changing the institutions that control education—the colleges and universities, State departments of education, local education agencies, the Federal agencies responsible for developing education programs—by changing the concepts and attitudes of the people who control them. We need people and institutions capable of continuous change, renewal, and responsiveness to the needs of children who come from different backgrounds and have a variety of hangups as well as talents.[19]

The Business Teacher as a Manager of the Learning Situation

The level of excellence in teaching is due in large measure to the competence of the business teacher within the learning situation. Guides to self-examination which can be applied are those related to personal qualities, managing the lesson, and evaluation of class reaction. In detail, these are listed below:

PERSONAL QUALITIES

1. *Appearance.* Shows good judgment in care and appearance of hair, skin, and nails; wears neat and appropriate clothing; exhibits good standing and sitting posture in front of class and during class period.
2. *Posture.* Exhibits confident and pleasant manner in front of class; avoids annoying and distracting mannerisms in voice and body movements; is able to put class at ease.

[19] Don Davies, "Come Out From Under the Ivy," *American Education*, 6 (March, 1970), p. 29.

3. *Voice*. Has pleasant voice tone and sufficient volume without shrillness; compensates for varying classroom conditions (outside noises, hall noises); articulates correctly; avoids monotony in use of voice.

4. *Vigor*. Shows alertness through personal appearance; is enthusiastic toward the day's tasks.

5. *Good Use of English*. Uses language correctly and effectively; avoids poor use of word endings.

MANAGING THE LESSON

1. *Knowledge of Material*. Shows clear command of the technical subject matter of the lesson; is able to relate background material to supplement textbook facts when necessary and desirable.

2. *Preparation (including materials)*. Prepares lesson plans well; has supplementary materials ready for use; does not have to rely heavily on prepared notes.

3. *Care of Physical Environment*. Checks as often as needed on ventilation; employs seating arrangement appropriate for the method used; makes use of bulletin boards and other display areas for course enrichment; is aware of chalkboard in relation to glare and lighting conditions; provides for efficient use of classroom in succeeding periods (for the next teacher coming in) through checking of furniture arrangement, erasing of chalkboard, replacing of audio-visual equipment to proper location.

4. *Use of Illustrative Materials*. Uses appropriate charts, chalkboard drawings, and other visual aids; shows evidence of practice in the use of the chalkboard.

5. *Ability to Question*. Shows knowledge of the use of the question in teaching; makes sure that student questions and answers are heard by all; avoids rephrasing student questions and answers in "own words"; shows that key questions were planned for in lesson plan.

6. *Control of Pupils*. Knows when and how to use authority; does not attempt to "top" student comments or use sarcasm; plans classroom procedures and handling of materials so that confusion does not arise; applies control through knowledge of pupils and backgrounds.

7. *Ability to Motivate Pupils*. Directs class session so that pupils recognize the worth of the situation; uses devices

and materials to gain student interest; recognizes the necessity for change of pace in procedure.

8. *Provision for Individualization.* Shows awareness of need for differentiated assignments when appropriate; provides opportunities for some participation by most of the students in some way; is sensitive to problems in which students are interested; reflects concern for individual differences in lesson plan.

9. *Appropriateness of Method Used.* Recognizes and uses psychological principles in the conduct of lesson; shows awareness of the fact that teaching methods must vary with given situations.

10. *Achievement of Stated Objectives.* Conducts lesson to permit achievement of objectives outlined in lesson plan; recognizes the need for occasional deviation from planned approach in order to achieve objectives; avoids wandering from both the subject and the planned lesson for no apparent reason.

11. *Time Routine (including summary).* Begins class promptly; has routinized housekeeping details; provides time, when appropriate, for a drawing together (summary) of the material presented; plans sufficiently enough to be able to handle the "unexpected."

12. *Evaluation of Pupil Understanding.* Sees and exhibits an understanding of objectives in relation to pupil progress; has a variety of means to check on pupil progress during lesson; shows understanding of the relationship of testing to the whole picture of evaluation; sees pupil evaluation in relation to directing student achievement; lists key evaluative points on lesson plan; is able to judge pupil progress is relation to individual growth and improvement; shows familiarity with methods of group evaluation and testing.

13. *Assignment.* Exhibits in lesson plan key points of *what, why, how,* and *when;* makes assignment at appropriate time; gives time to necessary assignment development during class period; is careful that assignment is not interrupted by end-of-class bell.

14. *Ability to Give Clear Directions.* Is responsive to student reaction to ambiguous or unclear directions; anticipates beforehand possible directions that might be given during class; avoids waste of class time resulting from repeating directions several times.

EVALUATION OF CLASS REACTION

1. *Participation.* Conducts class so that students show eagerness to participate; cautions against the limitation of participation to three or four pupils; keeps participation relevant to the subject under discussion; encourages students to show respect for viewpoints of other students and for effective discussion.

2. *Interest and Attention.* Guards against apathy and boredom (sometimes reflected through reading of material for other classes); motivates students so they are willing to work to the end of the period and do not disrupt the conduct of the class.

ASCERTAINING THE QUALITY OF A PROGRAM IN EDUCATION FOR BUSINESS

If it can be made clear what schools are to accomplish, it should be a fairly simple matter to organize an educational system and curriculum to attain the desired goals. Evaluation of a program in order to effect improvement implies that a set of criteria has been established in order to provide a measurement. Dr. Eugene Wyllie of Indiana University points out that:

> Before changes in curriculum, instructional practices, course content, or other facets of a departmental program leading to improvement in business education programs can take place, an objective appraisal of what conditions and practices (both strengths and weaknesses) currently exist must be made.[20]

What are the elements of a *good* program in education for business? Wyllie has developed a self-evaluation instrument to enable staff members to assess their programs. A section of this instrument dealing specifically with the teacher and the directions for evaluation are stated on the following pages: [21]

---

[20] Eugene D. Wyllie, *An Evaluation Plan for Business Education Programs in High Schools,* Monograph 109 (Cincinnati: South-Western Publishing Co., 1963), p. 1.
[21] *Ibid.,* pp. 27-29.

SECTION IX. STAFF

A. The business teacher has the necessary personal qualifications
which enable him to become an effective teacher.
Specific Evaluative Rating Scale for Items Below

++ Good — condition exists or practice is made extensively
 + So So — condition exists or practice is made to some extent
 0 Weak — condition exists or practice is very limited
 — Void — condition does not exist or practice is missing, *but
   needed*
 — — Bad — condition or practice is not desirable or applicable
   to your school situation

	Check List	
	Indiv.	*Entire*
The business teacher	*Teacher*	*Staff*
1. presents a good personal appearance	——	——
2. projects his voice well and has a pleasant speaking voice	——	——
3. uses impeccable grammar (both in speaking and in writing)	——	——
4. possesses good mental and physical health ..	——	——
5. is accepted socially by his professional colleagues and the community	——	——
6. possesses qualities of integrity, fairness, and moral fitness	——	——
7. accepts new challenges and responsibilities willingly	——	——

GENERAL EVALUATION:

The personal qualifications of the business teacher are (draw a circle around number that expresses your general evaluation)	*Individual*	*Entire Staff*
	5 — excellent	5 — excellent
	4 — very good	4 — very good
	3 — adequate	3 — adequate
	2 — poor	2 — poor
	1 — inadequate	1 — inadequate

B. The business teacher has a background of work experience related
to his specific teaching field.
Specific Evaluative Rating Scale for Items Below

++ Good — condition exists or practice is made extensively
 + So So — condition exists or practice is made to some extent
 0 Weak — condition exists or practice is very limited
 — Void — condition does not exist or practice is missing, *but
   needed*
 — — Bad — condition or practice is not desirable or applicable
   to your school situation

	Check List	
	Indiv.	*Entire*
The business teacher has had	*Teacher*	*Staff*
1. secretarial, sales, or managerial experience ..	——	——
2. recent work experience (within past five years)	——	——
3. work experience which was closely related to his specific teaching field	——	——

The distributive education coordinator has had

4. store supervisory experience	——	——

GENERAL EVALUATION:

The work experience of the business teacher is (draw a circle around number that expresses your general evaluation)	*Individual*	*Entire Staff*
	5 — very extensive	5 — very extensive
	4 — extensive	4 — extensive
	3 — adequate	3 — adequate
	2 — limited	2 — limited
	1 — none	1 — none

C. The professional preparation of the business teacher is of the quality and nature which enable him to become an effective teacher.

Specific Evaluative Rating Scale for Items Below

++ Good — condition exists or practice is made extensively
 + So So — condition exists or practice is made to some extent
 0 Weak — condition exists or practice is very limited
 — Void — condition does not exist or practice is missing, *but needed*
 — — Bad — condition or practice is not desirable or applicable to your school situation

	Check List	
The business teacher	*Indiv. Teacher*	*Entire Staff*
1. has a bachelor's degree and meets the state's minimum certification requirements	———	———
2. has a background of college courses in business administration and economics in addition to courses in business education	———	———
3. has had special methods courses in addition to a general methods course	———	———
4. who teaches the skill subjects has a thorough knowledge of the psychological theories of skill development	———	———
5. who teaches the skill subjects possesses proficient skills in the subject he teaches	———	———
6. who teaches the distributive education courses has had college courses in salesmanship, retailing, and advertising in addition to his distributive education courses	———	———

GENERAL EVALUATION:

The professional preparation of the business teacher is (draw a circle around number that expresses your general evaluation)	*Individual*	*Entire Staff*
	5 — excellent	5 — excellent
	4 — very good	4 — very good
	3 — satisfactory	3 — satisfactory
	2 — poor	2 — poor
	1 — unsatisfactory	1 — unsatisfactory

SUMMARY

This chapter is, in effect, a summary in itself. We have attempted to set forth the trends in American education and in education for business through the use of historical perspective. The past speaks well of business education in the

United States. The future is beset by challenges and opportunities for the business teacher to meet and use for the advancement of vocational and basic business understandings.

How successful the teacher's classroom experiences will be will depend greatly on his insight into the learning process, discussed in Chapter 2, and on the assimilation and implementation of sound methods in teaching, which are the subject matter of this book.

SELECTED BIBLIOGRAPHY

American Vocational Association. (Selected publications with articles relevant to implementing legislation.)

American Vocational Journal. (Selected issues with articles relevant to implementing legislation.)

Beaumont, John A. "Emerging Trends and Directions." Paper presented at the Business Education Conference, Northern Illinois University, DeKalb, July, 1969.

Brown, Kenneth W. "Business Education—The Secondary School Dumping Ground?" *Journal of Business Education,* XLVI (March, 1971), pp. 228-229.

Byrnside, O. H., Jr. "Business Education—Unlimited Opportunities for All: An Editorial." *Business Education Forum,* 24 (December, 1969), p. 2.

"Career Education, Equipping Students for the World of Work." *Nation's Schools* (December, 1971), pp. 35-48.

Crawford, T. James. "At the Start of a New Decade." *The Balance Sheet,* LI (January, 1970), p. 195.

Crumley, Marguerite. "Business Education in Transition—Tomorrow." *Business Education Forum,* 24 (February, 1970), pp. 3-4.

Davies, Don. "Come Out From Under the Ivy." *American Education,* 6 (March, 1970), pp. 29-31.

Dumler, Ruben. "The Future of Business Education." *The Balance Sheet,* XLI (April, 1960), p. 339.

Emerging Content and Structure of Business Education, Eighth Yearbook of the National Business Education Association.

Washington, D.C.: National Business Education Association, 1970.

Eyster, Elvin S. "Business Education Shares in Solving Problems in Vocational Education." *Journal of Business Education,* XXIV (December, 1969), pp. 92-93.

Fischer, John H. "Our Changing Conception of Education." *Phi Delta Kappan,* 42 (October, 1960), pp. 16-19.

Havighurst, Robert J. "Curriculum for the Disadvantaged." *Phi Delta Kappan,* 51 (March, 1970), p. 371-373.

Lieberman, Myron. *Education as a Profession.* Englewood Cliffs, New Jersey: Prentice-Hall, Inc., 1956.

Marland, Sidney P., Jr. "Career Education Now." Speech given at the convention of the National Association of Secondary School Principals, Sam Houston Coliseum, Houston, Texas, January 23, 1971.

_____ "Career Education—300 Days Later." *American Vocational Journal,* 47 (February, 1972), pp. 14-17.

Minear, Leon P. "Role of Business Education in National Manpower Program." *Business Education Forum,* 24 (January, 1970), pp. 3-6.

National Advisory Council on Vocational Education. *First Annual Report.* Washington, D.C., July, 1969.

National Advisory Council on Vocational Education. *Second Report.* Washington, D.C., November, 1969.

Policies Commission for Business and Economic Education. "This We Believe about Business Education in the Secondary School." *Business Education Forum,* 25 (October, 1970), pp. 8-9.

Starcher, Genevieve. An address given to the West Virginia Association for Student Teaching, Marshall University, Huntington, West Virginia, November, 1962.

U.S. Department of Health, Education, and Welfare, Office of Education. *Career Education,* OE 72-39. Washington: U.S. Government Printing Office, 1971.

U.S. Department of Health, Education, and Welfare, Office of Education. *Vocational Education: The Bridge Between Man and His Work,* OE 80052. Washington: U.S. Government Printing Office, 1968.

Widen, Irwin. A review of *Democratic Educational Theory* by Ernest E. Bayles (New York: Harper & Row, 1960) in *Phi Delta Kappan*, 42 (June, 1960), pp. 403-405.

Wyllie, Eugene D. *An Evaluation Plan for Business Education Programs in High Schools*, Monograph 109. Cincinnati: South-Western Publishing Co., 1963.

Chapter 2

THE LEARNING PROCESS AND PLANNING FOR INSTRUCTION

We generally concede that it is of primary importance to have before us a plan or pattern of action before starting a job. Architects prepare a complete set of blueprints, including detailed specifications, before they begin to build. Aircraft engineers work for many months, even years, in the planning and designing of a new type of plane. So it must be in creating the situation for learning. Considering that a plan is essential when dealing with raw materials that are inanimate, which can be fabricated and shaped in whatever mold the designer or builder wishes, think how much more necessary it is when dealing with the human mind.

HOW LEARNING TAKES PLACE

Before a teacher can intelligently begin to build this plan for learning experiences, it is necessary for him to understand certain basic concepts that underlie the process by which a human being learns. Educators have defined learning as any activity that develops the individual and makes his later behavior different from what it otherwise might have been. This is sometimes referred to as a desirable change in the behavior of the human being. We are not always sure just what this "change in behavior" means or how to "make it happen." Bernard attempts to define desirable learning in this way:

. . . We may say that learning is the *modification of behavior*. This process involves many changes in perception and behavior. Improvement is usually involved.

. . . In this respect two observations are pertinent. First, not all modification of behavior is learning. Without learning anything new, one may be able to lift heavier weights because of muscular development. One may, however, *learn* some "tricks" in lifting without acquiring stronger muscles. The loss of an arm modifies behavior, but the loss itself is not learning. The person, though, may *learn* to compensate for the loss of his arm.

Second, modification does not necessarily result in improvement—at least in terms of values. Pupils may learn to dislike school, but their adjustment is not improved thereby. Criminals learn to violate accepted legal and moral codes and may become experts at it, but their behavior is, in terms of values, not improved. With these limitations in mind, we may now define learning as *the modification of behavior through activity and experience which improves modes of adjustment to the environment*.[1]

This statement by Bernard indicates that a change in behavior *can*, and probably will, be effected by the teacher, but not necessarily in the right direction. Nor do we find that even when a desirable change in behavior has somehow been accomplished that it will become permanent. Just when it seems that students are in full command of a process and can apply it with ease, they seem to slack off and forget whatever it is they apparently "learned."

Psychological Guides to Learning

The needs, interests, attitudes, and capabilities of pupils are of fundamental importance. To ignore them is to provide a classroom exercise, or "performance," that will be certain to result in indifference by the pupil and frustration on the part of the teacher. To implement learning, good teaching is required. Good teaching is based on sound psychology. A reasonable understanding of how persons

---

[1] Harold W. Bernard, *Psychology of Learning and Teaching* (New York: McGraw-Hill Book Co., Inc., 1954), pp. 121-122.

learn has been established by psychologists through constant study and experimentation. The 30 psychological guides to good teaching developed and compiled by Columbia University Professors Mort and Vincent represent one of the most complete references to the place of psychology in teaching and learning. Research on a wide scale would tend to repeat item after item of this basic listing:

1. *No one learns without feeling some urge to learn.* It may be fear, need, inborn drive, curiosity, mystery, challenge, importance, or personal attachment—or any other motivating force. The force has to be there, and the more the force wells up out of the person himself, the more the person will learn of his own accord.

2. *What a person learns is influenced directly by his surroundings.* If you want a person to learn something, make that thing a part of his environment so that he may see it, live with it, be influenced by it.

3. *A person learns most quickly and lastingly what has meaning for him.* The pupils do not always see the meanings the teacher sees. An act takes on meaning from its outcome—what the act produces. To produce a thing he wants or can see the value of, a person is likely to master the skill necessary.

4. *When an organism is ready to act, it is painful for it not to act; and when an organism is not ready to act, it is painful for it to act.* This means that some time must be spent in preparing learners to learn, that physical action is as much a part of school as mental action.

5. *Individuals differ in all sorts of ways.* When you get a group of people together to do anything, some will be better than others. It is easy to see that some people are taller than others, less easy to see that in dozens of abilities that relate to success in learning any class will show a vast range of difference.

6. *Security and success are the soil and climate for growth.* No one can learn well when he doesn't belong—any more than a plant can grow without roots in the soil. No one can succeed on failure.

7. *All learning occurs through attempts to satisfy needs.* What people do, consciously or not, they do because of

need; and as they do, they learn what to do to satisfy need.

8. *Emotional tension decreases efficiency in learning.* Before the skills and facts of teaching come friendliness, security, acceptance, belief in success. Without these, tensions are procured. Constant, monotonous attention to any one thing is also a producer of tension.

9. *Physical defects lower efficiency in learning.* A sound mind in a sound body. For greatest efficiency in any kind of teaching, physical health comes before mental vigor.

10. *Interest is an indicator of growth.* We don't teach to get interest, but if interest isn't present, the teaching isn't prospering.

11. *Interest is a source of power in motivating learning.* When you are interested in a thing, you are in it and feel a part of it. A teacher who doesn't hook his teaching to whatever pupils feel they are already a part of is not making the greatest use of the powers he has at his command.

12. *What gives satisfaction tends to be repeated; what is annoying tends to be avoided.* Practice makes perfect only when it is the right kind of practice. Learning is efficient if the pupil tries to master what fits his abilities and gives satisfaction.

13. *The best way to learn a part in life is to play that part.* This is the apprenticeship idea. Upon leaving school, the parts in life which pupils play are not completely new to them if they have practiced those parts in school.

14. *Learning is more efficient and longer lasting when the conditions for it are real and lifelike.* Attitudes, habits, skills for life are best learned when the activities of school are like those of life. Methods of teaching should be as much as possible like those one uses in actual living.

15. *Piecemeal learning is not efficient.* We learn facts and skills best when we learn them in a pattern, not as isolated bits of subject matter. The facts and skills that we learn become part of a pattern when we learn them in relation to their use—as part of a project, job, or other enterprise.

16. *You can't train the mind like a muscle.* There is no body of knowledge that is the key to "mind-training." There is no set of exercises that will "sharpen the wits" as a

grindstone will sharpen steel. This means: don't isolate the things you want to teach from the real setting in which they belong.

17. *A person learns by his own activity.* He learns what he does; he gains insight as he learns to organize what he does. Within certain limits, the more extensive a learner's activity, the greater will be his learning.

18. *Abundant, realistic practice contributes to learning.* Learners need much practice in the many intellectual, creative, and social acts which we want them to master.

19. *Participation enhances learning.* Participation is essential to any complex learning. Complete participation is important—from planning to checking results.

20. *Firsthand experience makes for lasting and more complete learning.* Learners need experience between reading and hearing about something secondhand and the kind of knowledge and insight that comes from firsthand experience.

21. *General behavior is controlled by emotions as well as by intellect.* Far more than a place to train only the mind, the modern school is concerned with training the emotions, too.

22. *Unused talents contribute to personal maladjustment.* Not only are unused talents a waste to society; they form a core of dissatisfaction to the individual. Frustrated talent can lead to many kinds of neurotic symptoms.

23. *You start to grow from where you are and not from some artificial starting point.* It is unrealistic to assume that pupils can move through the grades of school like taking the steps on a ladder jumping from step to step. It is impossible to move a pupil on from some point or grade standard that he has not yet achieved.

24. *Growth is a steady, continuous process, and different individuals grow at different rates.* It is impossible for a class of first-graders to move along all together until they come to the twelfth grade. Each individual learns, but at his own rate. His growth is steady; he does not leap from grade to grade.

25. *It is impossible to learn one thing at a time.* It is impossible to turn everything else off while learning two times two. The learner as a whole responds to his setting as a whole and takes in many things besides two times

two. Learning by problems, topics, and projects, replacing learning by bits, makes capital of this fact.

26. *Learning is reinforced when two or more senses are used at the same time.* One-cylinder learning sticks only to reading or only to listening. Pupils learn better if they see with the eyes, touch with the hands, hear with the ears, heft with the muscles, at the same time they are seeing with the mind's eye.

27. *The average pupil is largely a myth.* Grade standards are an average which every pupil is expected to achieve. But any standard that you can set will be too difficult for some, too easy for others. The achievement of a group scatters over a wide range—only a few are at the "average" point. A far greater number are scattered above and below the average.

28. *If you want a certain result, teach it directly.* Your pupils are not born with the skills you want them to have; nor can we always depend upon other teachers to teach pupils to our satisfaction. If your pupils do not know what you want them to know, the most efficient thing to do is to teach it to them.

29. *Children develop in terms of all the influences which affect them.* Not only the 180 days of school, but the 365 days of living in school, home, and community go to make a person what he becomes.

30. *It has been said that a person learns more in the first three years of his life than in all the years afterward.* However this may be, it is certain that the early years of home life are very important. Accordingly, to improve its effectiveness, a school must do what it can to improve the educational setting of the home.[2]

According to Mort and Vincent,[3] these guides can be used in a number of ways: to judge the *variety* of the teacher's practice, to judge the psychological *validity* of his practice, to *test* new practices, and to *justify* his practice.

Setting the Stage for Teaching and Learning

If business education is to be effective, the conditions of learning must be favorable, and the aims of the program

---

[2] Paul R. Mort and William S. Vincent, *Introduction to American Education* (New York: McGraw-Hill Book Co., Inc., 1954), pp. 303-330.
[3] *Ibid.*, p. 306.

must be clearly recognized. Curiosity must be aroused and appropriate information provided for the students. Given these primary bases of approach, the efforts of the teacher will bring tangible results of great value to the pupils and a justifiable sense of satisfaction to the teacher.

Goal Setting

To set goals requires considerable judgment if this is to be significant. Goals set by students themselves are more effective, but students need guidance in setting goals. The atmosphere of teacher-student cooperation is in great part created by the adroit direction of the teacher. Teachers sometimes lose class cooperation and fail to supply that needed stimulus because they do not take time to understand those whom they teach. To achieve top-level interest, students must be encouraged to take an active part in constructing the plan of action for the course. Too many complications? This is perhaps true, but it depends on whether a teacher is interested in setting up "good-looking" course outlines and in developing a model "paper" course or in helping pupils to learn. In other words, the teacher's plan should be tentative; the final plan for class direction should be developed by both the students and the teacher.

The classroom teacher who attempts this kind of learning situation must be sold on this approach, which, if successfully carried out, achieves a better quality of classroom control and motivation. The teacher's role is to help the class see what alternatives there are, to analyze them, to help the class see the consequences of the choices, and then to outline a plan together. For example, Rainey points to a definite increase in interest in basic economics courses through the use of an "Inventory of Business and Economic Concepts" in which even the poorest students can volunteer information and opinions.[4] (See Chapter 7 for details.) Through the use of this plan, the students play an active part in the direction of the class, which results in a feeling of contribution and satisfaction necessary for learning to take place.

---

[4] Bill G. Rainey, "Stimulate Economics Students with Supplementary Aids," *Business Education World*, XXXVIII (May, 1958), pp. 26-27.

Relating Goals to Students' Abilities

Because of increasing attention to individual needs of youth being given in modern-day education, many youngsters are in school who might otherwise have dropped out. The resulting situation is a standard classroom full of pupils with mixed abilities to learn. Quite frequently this is a major motivational problem. A haphazard approach in planning learning materials for such groups will inflate the ego of some pupils and neglect others.

It is the teacher's task to help pupils make adjustments to their learning problems and to refrain from assigning projects, tasks, and performances beyond their abilities, or to make work so general that the superior students lose interest. In either case the result is a feeling of frustration for all. A student will often strike out in an attempt to ward off this frustration, resulting in a possible disciplinary problem. The process of growing up is not easy, particularly in the adolescent years. The classroom teacher represents authority; the judicious use of this authority in the classroom is underscored by Young in her study of delinquency problems:

> All delinquents are trapped in their painful and dangerous conflict over authority. In brief, they treat the world as they have been treated. When adults use their superior strength to break the will and spirit of a child, rather than support and direct that life force toward maturity, the child has only two alternatives: to submit and be crushed, or to fight blindly, bitterly, and destructively.[5]

PLANNING INSTRUCTION

Success in any venture is best assured by planning. Accidental success is possible, but rather infrequent. Mere planning does not guarantee success, but it does assure consideration of the factors and conditions regarded as most essential to success.

It may be said that we are living in a planning age. Planning is required to make group action intelligent. Procedures in political, social, economic, industrial, and business

---

[5] Leontine R. Young, "Delinquency from the Child's Point of View," *The Presidio* (November, 1960), p. 16.

realms follow specifications established by careful thought and long-range planning. In public affairs, planning boards and planning commissions—local, state, and national—are becoming more numerous. It is true that much of our civilization "just grew" like Topsy, but we are now realizing the great potential and effectiveness of programs based upon design and plans.

Since the principal business of the school is to facilitate learning, little justification seems necessary for emphasizing instructional planning. The primary reason for instructional planning is that teaching is a creative rather than a mechanical type of activity. Students change from year to year, and new classes coming on are different. Each day and every lesson brings new situations which are entirely new. Not only do students change, but both society and business constantly undergo modification. The constantly shifting panorama of business and educational scenes, and the learning situation, can be effectively met only by adequate instructional planning.

The modern point of view and philosophy regarding education places planning at a premium. Teaching has become recognized as a creative activity, wherein the teacher serves as the *director of learning* and not merely a dispenser of facts and information.

The planning required for designing a curriculum is presented in Chapter 8. A system for individualized instruction through the use of large group, small group, and individual teaching techniques is presented in Chapters 9 and 10. Therefore, planning for instruction in this part of the chapter will be devoted to the following: (1) unit planning, (2) daily planning, and (3) formulating objectives.

Unit Planning

One of the first steps a teacher usually takes after accepting a position in a school system is to find out what he is supposed to teach. In some school districts and individual schools the curriculum has been carefully designed and courses of study for each of the subjects have been made.

If curriculum and courses are available, they should be discussed carefully with appropriate school officials. Business educators will, on rare instances, even find units of study which have been designed for all teachers to follow. However, the typical business teacher will find that he has to start by making a tentative list of the units he expects to teach in a course.

A *unit* has been defined as a means of organizing instructional material into larger, related, and unified patterns of instruction in order to achieve important educational objectives. A chapter or a large block of material in a textbook does not necessarily constitute a unit. In addition, a distinction must be made between a *resource unit* and a *teaching unit*. A resource unit is constructed by teachers for the use of teachers. It includes more suggestions than any one teacher could possibly use, and provides the raw materials for teaching units or for daily lesson plans. An individual teacher may, of course, prepare a resource unit, but many of the advantages of cooperative thinking are lost. A teaching unit is usually prepared by the individual classroom teacher, or with the help of his class, for use in a particular class. For example, a unit in the general business course might be "Understanding Insurance and Its Uses."

After selecting the units of study for a course, the next step is to set up a tentative time budget for each unit. Hopefully, well in advance of the actual construction of unit plans, the teacher will know the type of students with whom he will be working and the nature and extent of instructional resources and materials which are available. Chances are good that even with the best pre-planning, the first unit planned and taught may well be a most frustrating experience. A teacher really can't know his students until he has had an opportunity to study school records, discuss them with the guidance staff, and work with the students for a period of time.

The time devoted to the preparation and implementation of a unit plan will pay rich dividends in terms of time saved in daily planning and overall teaching effectiveness. Some values of unit planning are listed below:

1. A better continuity in learning is possible. Teachers and students are able to attack problems and topics requiring longer periods of time than one or two regular class periods. There is continuity in a theme or problem that can be explored for days or weeks until possible solutions are found, as contrasted with segmented, piecemeal approaches that often characterize the daily-lesson teaching from a single textbook.

2. Unit planning incorporates a great variety of learning activities, such as speaking, researching, listening, planning, and reporting. These are specifically provided for in relation to the objectives stated for the unit. A *time block* anticipated for teaching the unit makes such broad planning possible. The segmented, day-by-day approach does not always permit this variety of student activities.

3. Unit planning makes use of a great many different kinds of learning materials and instructional technology.

4. Better opportunities to plan for individual differences are available through unit organization. A well-planned unit includes activities which offer students a variety of choices to better utilize all the talents in a class.

5. There are more opportunities for student participation when unit planning is used than if planning is done on a day-to-day basis. Students are presented with more frequent opportunities to share ideas.

6. There is greater likelihood that every student will experience *some* achievement when activities are not limited to the verbal type, often the only avenue of participation in the day-by-day teaching approach.

7. There is a better chance that students will make use of other learning from their total school program. For example, reports by individual students or by committees will bring speech course training into use.

Basically, the unit plan outline consists of the following seven major divisions:

1. Setting and overview
2. Content outline
3. Instructional objectives
4. Learning activities
5. Instructional materials and media

6. Evaluation

7. Bibliography

Figure 2-1 is a copy of a guide for preparing a unit plan, given to business teachers-in-training to follow when designing their first plans. Methods instructors may have their students duplicate unit plans so that class members have a number of plans to launch their teaching careers.

Daily Planning

Daily planning is necessary if teaching is carried on according to a unit plan. Unit planning does not take the place of daily planning, but paves the way for it. Students, while studying a unit, will be conscious of the unit as a whole, but they must work on it one part at a time. While they are guided by the comprehensive and significant goals of the unit, they must be conscious of the most appropriate next steps. A secretary typing a report does not work on all parts of a report at once, but rather prepares one part at a time. Similarly, the teacher viewing what remains to be done, faces the task of deciding the next steps.

Plans for each instructional time period should vary with the different stages of the unit. Initiation, development, and culmination of the unit require different plans. The plans will vary in objectives, activities, procedures, and materials. For example, the daily plan for a demonstration lesson would differ significantly from the plan for a day which was to be devoted to group discussion. Likewise, daily plans for individual and small group techniques are not the same as group instruction plans. However, every daily plan should indicate a clear sense of direction, make provision for adequate content and activities, provide a proper sequence with other lessons, make provisions for individual differences, and include provision for evaluating or checking results.

The most commonly used plan for conducting classroom instruction is called a *lesson plan*. The lesson plan represents a detailed analysis of a particular activity described in the unit plan. Various forms have been developed by teachers

A GUIDE FOR PREPARING A UNIT PLAN

1. Prepare a setting and overview (unit title, subject, grade level, and time planned for unit). (See page 49.)

2. List the general and enabling objectives of the unit.

3. Prepare a content outline of the total unit based on stated objectives.

4. Construct a unit pretest. Identify correct answers. Identify the objective or objectives for each question.

5. Plan a detailed introduction to the unit. This should be your means of motivating students to want to learn during the unit.

6. Prepare a list of suggested teaching activities—initiatory, developmental, and culminating.

7. Plan individual student, committee, and class unit assignments. Be specific in your written directions.

8. Construct a bibliography of both student and teacher materials listed under such headings as:

   a. books
   b. magazine articles
   c. free materials
   d. inexpensive materials
   e. monographs
   f. programmed learning materials

   Include a complete bibliographical entry of each for future reference and use (author, title, publication [if magazine article], publisher [if book], date, and page numbers).

9. List films, filmstrips, and other visual aids available for the unit. Identify the source and complete address. Describe the contents briefly (40-60 words), if possible.

10. Draw or construct a unit bulletin board.

11. Draw or construct a summarization poster covering the major concepts of the unit.

12. Construct a final test on the unit. Include at least several of the following types of questions:

    a. true-false
    b. matching
    c. multiple choice
    d. completion
    e. classification
    f. essay
    g. performance

    Identify the objective or objectives for each question. Identify the correct responses for each question.

FIGURE 2-1

to fit their individual teaching styles. However, the real test of an effectively developed lesson plan is whether the teacher can actually teach from the prepared guide. All too frequently student teachers prepare one form of a lesson plan to satisfy their university supervisor, and then teach from another guide. Aspiring teachers should find a lesson plan format which serves as a guide for planning their instruction.

Elements of a Daily Plan. Most good lesson plans for conducting group instruction include the following elements:

1. Preliminary information, such as name of subject and grade level, unit title, descriptive lesson title, date and time of day, and special reminders.

2. Specific behavioral objectives stated in terms of expected student performance. The daily plan should include specific behavioral objectives stated in very precise terms.

3. Materials needed by both teacher and students to implement the lesson. Typically, only those materials which require special planning are listed.

4. Introduction to the daily plan is carefully designed. Rich dividends result from efforts which are made in preparing the students, providing for continuity, clearly explaining expected student performance (objectives), organizing the learning activities, and motivating learners. A number of techniques may be used to refresh the memory of students and stimulate interest. The following are a few of these techniques: (a) raise provocative questions, (b) review previous lesson and have students relate their experiences to what was learned, (c) give a brief demonstration, (d) tell an interesting anecdote, or (e) have one or more students do something unusual. Without a memory-jogger and mind-stimulator preceding the body of the lesson, the net result may be an unresponsive class and a frustrated teacher.

5. Presentation and application or "what" the students will learn. The "what" portion of designing learning experiences must be carefully considered in conjunction with the "how" planning phase of teaching. The concepts, generalizations, or competencies which are to be learned must be carefully delineated and placed on the daily plan in a logical order. As the content is being listed, the teacher must carefully consider the strategy he will follow in helping the students to learn. Care is exercised in order that the daily plan does not become so detailed that it is impossible to use effectively in a teaching situation.

The lesson plan is not a prepared speech, but a memorandum to guide the teacher's thinking. Ideally, the plan should outline or list key points to identify the lesson content. Keep in mind, however, that the nature of the learning that will take place dictates the form of the daily plan.

6. Learning activities on "how" the students will learn. The "how" part of teaching is what identifies a good teacher. Some people have the mistaken idea that all a teacher has to do is talk, and if the students listen they will learn. Nothing could be further from the truth. The professional teacher not only has a command of the subject matter or discipline which he is teaching, but also a vast array of properly designed teaching techniques which he uses with precision. The master teacher has learned his trade through hard work, study, and experimentation.

The "how" portion of the daily plan will vary considerably with the type of planned learning activities. For example, a group discussion should always be based upon a few key questions prepared in advance, while a demonstration may require an outline of step-by-step procedures to follow. The amount of detail required depends on such teacher factors as the familiarity with the material being presented, previous experience in teaching the same lesson, total teaching experience, and memory. Some teachers prefer to jot down a number of items to refresh their memory while others make relatively few notations.

Time is really the most important commodity that teachers have. It must be used carefully to assure maximum student achievement. Therefore, time should be carefully planned and indicated in designing both unit and daily plans.

7. A provision for follow-up activities is made in most daily plans. Formal or informal techniques for evaluating expected student performance in terms of the stated objectives are frequently used. For example, a review using some type of team competition may be conducted, or an actual performance test may be administered. An assignment should be given or other means provided for summarizing what was learned and setting the stage for the next period of learning.

Assignments should be given carefully if the teacher expects the students to perform them well. An effective assignment is one that is designed to achieve at least three purposes: to contribute to the achievement of the objectives of the unit or daily plan, to motivate students to learn, and to provide a basis for directing students in the learning process. Normally assignments should be given so that the students know the following: (1) exactly *what* is to be done, (2) *why* it is to be done, (3) *how* it is to be done, and (4) *when* it is to be completed.

Ideally, assignments should be given as they develop naturally from ongoing learning activities. The teacher should be alert to avoid making assignments when the class dismissal bell is ringing. Short assignments may be given orally, written on the chalkboard, or shown with an overhead projector. Long assignments generally should be duplicated for distribution to the students. A guide for completion should be provided with complex assignments. When a teacher assigns work that is to be completed over an extended period of time, it is helpful to develop a plan for securing student progress reports at periodic intervals.

The professional teacher analyzes both daily and unit plans to determine successes and failures. A short period of time devoted to post-analysis can be of major assistance in improving teaching. Notes may be made to contribute to the improvement of the unit or daily plan the next time it is used, or to suggest improvements for teaching in general.

Preparation of a Daily Plan. Daily plans may have a variety of forms, developed by teachers to fit individual teaching styles; school districts, too, are designing more such forms. Some teachers make up to two or three forms to fit their style of teaching. They duplicate a supply of the forms so that their planning is simplified. As the forms are prepared for each day, they are inserted in a ring notebook, together with the unit or other planning guide. This system facilitates both current and future planning. Once the system is established, planning becomes a creative rather than a laborious activity.

The basic format used in preparing the preliminary information, objectives, and materials portions of the lesson plan is usually quite similar in any form. An example of the basic format is the following:

Descriptive Lesson Title:	Name of Unit:
Name of Teacher:	Subject:
Grade Level:	Date and Time of Day:

Objectives:

Special Materials:

Reminders:

Some teachers use a two column format for planning the "what" and "how" portion of the plan, while others use three or four divisions. Examples of typical headings are shown for two, three, and four column lesson plans.

Time	Presentation and Application	Techniques for Teaching

Time	Content	Method

Time	What Will Students Learn	How They Will Learn

Time	Content	Teacher Activity	Student Activity

Time	Content	Teacher Activity	Student Activity	Evaluation

The provision for indicating follow-up activities varies considerably. Side headings such as summary, evaluation, assignment, and post-analysis are frequently placed on the daily planning guide. The skeletal lesson plan guide on page 51 illustrates one form which can be used for daily planning.

Student teachers in business education are usually expected to type an original and one carbon copy of their daily plan. The carbon copy is given to the supervising teacher in advance so that the student teacher can receive assistance on what appears to be illogical or inappropriate

Descriptive Lesson Title:	Name of Unit:
Name of Teacher:	Subject:
Grade Level:	Date and Time of Day:
Objectives:	
Special Materials:	
Reminders:	

Time	What Will Students Learn	How They Will Learn
7 min.	Introduction:	
	New Materials:	
10 min.	I.	
15 min.	II.	
5 min.	III.	
10 min.	Evaluation:	
8 min.	Assignment:	

Post-analysis:

teaching strategy. Local school policy determines the procedure to be followed in preparing daily plans for experienced teachers. Some school districts require non-tenured teachers to turn in complete daily plans for the next week every Friday afternoon.

Formulating Objectives

An instructional program can be defined as a sequence of pedagogical steps designed to bring the learner to a particular level of performance evidenced by certain competencies or ways of behaving. These competencies and behavioral expressions are the instructional objectives of the program.

The importance of defining instructional objectives as an initial step in the planning of instruction has long been emphasized.

Planning is facilitated when an outline is prepared. An outline provides a means of breaking down a larger topic into smaller parts. It also provides the planner with a way of going from the general to the specific. The following educational objective outline enables the teacher to break down his instructional program and proceed from the general to the specific:

I. General Objective
  A. Enabling Objective
    1. Specific behavioral objective
    2. Specific behavioral objective
    3. Etc.
  B. Enabling Objective
    1. Specific behavioral objective
    2. Specific behavioral objective
    3. Etc.
  C. Etc.

General and Enabling Objectives. Statements which describe expected student learning outcomes in broad terms may be referred to as general, terminal, overall, or primary objectives. Teachers using the unit or competency plan approach to teaching formulate their general objectives with a great deal of care. Listed below are examples of general objectives: [6]

1. The student will have ability to relate good grooming and good health to productive job performance.
2. The student will have the ability to relate the values of good customer relations to successful business.
3. The student will comprehend the effect of competition in the American private enterprise system.

---

[6] Many of the objectives listed in this chapter are taken from Lucy C. Crawford's *A Competency Pattern Approach to Curriculum Construction in Distributive Teacher Education,* OE-6-85-044 (Blacksburg, Virginia: Virginia Polytechnic Institute, 1967).

The objectives state, in general terms, just what the students need to achieve. Once the general objectives have been formulated, it is then necessary to break them down into enabling objectives.

Enabling objectives are actually sub-divisions of the general objective or objectives. It is almost meaningless in terms of instructional planning to merely state general objectives without providing a way of achieving the stated objectives. For example, the general objective "students will comprehend the effect of competition in the American free enterprise system" should be further developed by the teacher by adding the following enabling objectives:

1. The students are able to recognize the effect of competition on the search for new ideas.
2. The students are able to identify the values of competition.
3. The students are able to explain competition as a regulator of economic activities.

General and enabling objectives are carefully stated in the unit plan. They are usually not stated in the daily lesson plan. Specific behavioral objectives are carefully prepared and provide the basis for daily planning.

Specific Behavioral Objectives. Business educators have long been sensitive to the utility of stating objectives in terms of expected student performance. However, it was not until the concepts authored by Robert F. Mager and Kenneth M. Beach [7] were received and applied by educators on the local level that a full-scale interest in performance objectives became evident.

A meaningful specific instructional objective should satisfy three important criteria. The objective should identify or describe:

1. Expected student performance, or what the student will be doing when he demonstrates that he has attained the objective.

_____
[7] Robert F. Mager and Kenneth M. Beach, Jr., *Developing Vocational Instruction* (Belmont, California: Fearon Publishers, 1967).

2. Conditions under which the student will be expected to demonstrate or show his achievement of the objective.
3. Evaluative criteria, or what are the minimum standards of performance expected of the student.

These three items constitute the basic structural components of an objective or a learning activity guide that should be used in a lesson plan. To assist in the preparation of specific behavioral objectives, the following guidelines are provided:

1. Objectives should be worded in terms of changes expected in the pupil, rather than as duties of the teacher, since attainment of objectives must in any case be evaluated in terms of pupil changes.

2. An objective should be put in terms of observable changes in the pupil between the beginning and end of his experiences in a defined segment of the educative process. Unless we can tell whether pupils are changed, we shall have difficulty in justifying the objective, however worthy it may appear on philosophical grounds.

3. The terminology of the objective should be clear; its meaning should be defined in terms that pupils, parents, and other teachers can appreciate. Obviously, such clarity often requires much thought and discussion.

4. To prevent confusion and to facilitate ready identification of the objective, each statement should refer to only one objective.

5. Objectives should be grouped for use in guiding pupil activities, in organizing units of work, and in constructing evaluation devices. That is, specific objectives should be grouped under the objective that is general to them.

Teachers in education for business design specific behavioral objectives to describe (1) knowledges, (2) skills, and (3) attitudes. Benjamin S. Bloom has developed a list of verbs to assist in describing behaviors dealing with recall or recognition of knowledge and development of intellectual abilities and skills:

COGNITIVE VERBS

Verbs used to indicate behaviors in the cognitive domain:

1. *Knowledge*

   to define
   to distinguish
   to be familiar with
   to understand
   to recall
   to recognize
   to acquire
   to be conscious of
   to develop
   to outline
   to identify
   to know

2. *Comprehension*

   to understand
   to translate
   to prepare
   to comprehend
   to interpret
   to grasp
   to distinguish
   to conclude
   to predict
   to estimate
   to differentiate
   to recognize
   to explain
   to summarize
   to demonstrate by example
   to see implications, effects,
      and consequences
   to paraphrase
   to indicate
   to make predictions

3. *Application*

   to apply
   to employ
   to relate
   to predict
   to use

4. *Analysis*

   to distinguish
   to discriminate
   to analyze
   to detect
   to recognize
   to infer
   to categorize
   to choose
   to discover
   to select

5. *Synthesis*

   to create
   to propose
   to integrate
   to plan
   to design
   to synthesize
   to formulate
   to perceive
   to organize
   to prepare
   to develop
   to compile
   to incorporate
   to visualize

6. *Evaluation*

   to select
   to judge
   to assess
   to compare
   to appraise
   to distinguish
   to evaluate
   to decide
   to determine

FIGURE 2-2

David R. Krathwohl has developed the following list of verbs to assist describing changes in interest, attitudes, values and development of appreciations and adequate adjustment:

AFFECTIVE VERBS

Verbs used to indicate behaviors in the affective domain:

1. *Receiving*

    to be aware of
    to be conscious of
    to recognize
    to be sensitive to
    to tolerate
    to accept
    to listen to
    to attend to
    to appreciate
    to prefer
    to be alert to

2. *Responding*

    to comply with
    to obey
    to volunteer to
    to practice rules
    to respond with interest
    to perform
    to cooperate with
    to contribute to
    to ask
    to participate
    to enjoy
    to acquaint
    to engage in
    to assume responsibility
    to accept responsibility
    to find pleasure in

3. *Valuing*

    to feel (to feel strongly about)
    to be loyal to
    to be devoted to
    to examine
    to value
    to prefer

4. *Organization*

    to relate
    to form judgments
    to weigh
    to identify characteristics
    to find out and crystalize

5. *Characterization*

    to change behavior
    to revise judgments
    to face facts and conclusions
    to approach problems objectively
    to develop a conscience
    to develop a philosophy of life

FIGURE 2-3

In addition to assisting the teacher in writing objectives, the cognitive and affective verbs can serve as a guide for planning learning experiences, test items, and course curriculum evaluation. If a teacher finds that all his objectives contain verbs listed in the knowledge level, he can make an effort to design learning experiences which are at a higher level in the cognitive domain, such as analysis, synthesis, or evaluation. During the process of evaluating a course or curriculum, the teacher may determine that students should be developing a number of attitudes which are not presently being taught, or that attitudes are not being planned at a high enough level.

RELATIONS BETWEEN THE
COGNITIVE AND AFFECTIVE DOMAINS

1. The cognitive continuum begins with the student's recall and recognition of *Knowledge,*

2. it extends through his *Comprehension* of the knowledge,

3. his skill in *Application* of the knowledge that he comprehends,

4. his skill in *Analysis* of situations involving this knowledge, his skill in *Synthesis* of this knowledge into new organizations,

5. his skill in *Evaluation* in that area of knowledge to judge the value of material and methods for given purposes.

1. The affective continuum begins with the student's merely *Receiving* stimuli and passively attending to it. It extends through his more actively attending to it.

2. His *Responding* to stimuli on request, willingly responding to these stimuli, and taking satisfaction in this responding,

3. his *Valuing* the phenomenon or activity so that he voluntarily responds and seeks out ways to respond,

4. his *Conceptualization* of each value responded to,

5. his *Organization* of these values into systems and finally organizing the value complex into a single whole, a *Characterization* of the individual.

FIGURE 2-4

The three structural parts of a specific behavioral objective are listed below:

1. Conditions under which the student will be expected to demonstrate or show his achievement of the objective.

2. Expected student performance, or what the student will be doing when he demonstrates that he has attained the objectives.

3. Evaluative criteria, or what are the minimum standards of performance expected of the student.

The following are examples of specific behavioral objectives coded to indicate the structural parts to which they relate:

1. Given the amount of a sale and the amount tendered by a customer,
2. the student will make change and count it back to a customer,
3. without error.

---

1. Given a list of fifty numbers and a ten-key adding machine,
2. the student will add the numbers,
3. with 95 percent accuracy in a period of 30 seconds.

A quick look at the cognitive verb list will indicate that both examples require application level learning. Use the lists of cognitive and affective verbs to determine the type of learning described in the next two examples:

1. Given a human relations case problem,
2. the student will determine the facts and describe them in writing,
3. with 80 percent accuracy in a period of five minutes.

---

1. Given the roles of a supervisor and an irate client in a role-playing situation,
2. the student will recognize the true problem and assume responsibility for solving it,
3. by scoring at least 10 points on a 15 point rating scale.

Teachers who prepare specific behavioral objectives have been pleased with the results. They find that by telling their students in advance what is expected of them, a majority of the students are challenged to reach or exceed the minimum goals. The behavioral goal type instructional system requires effective student-teacher dialogue. This is particularly true if instruction is to be individualized. Students want to know what performance is expected, under what conditions they will perform, and what criteria will be used to evaluate their performance.

Teachers find that by writing down exactly what student outcomes they are trying to achieve, their teaching improves. The process of analyzing the content and behavior to be taught helps teachers to structure more carefully their teaching in logical order. Once the logical order of teaching is determined, the teacher can devote his attention to the selection of the best media for presenting instruction.

Teachers who know what their students should learn, and are able to communicate to them the importance of what is to be learned, will find that specific behavioral objectives are a real asset in increasing student performance. Evaluation also becomes a much easier task because both the student and teacher know the criteria for evaluation; it has already been specified in the objective itself.

Specific behavioral objectives should be used in designing all types of individual, small group, and class instruction. The same principles apply to all three instances.

SUMMARY

When one attempts to teach another, the situation of *intent to learn* is immediately posed. Do the pupils really want to learn, or are they forced into the situation by the society in which they live? It is entirely possible that they may prefer to be doing something other than school work. If so, how can we, as teachers, go about changing these preferences, that is, to create an atmosphere for learning?

All of the reliable background on the education of youth indicates that learning takes place when there is a desire to learn. It is the task of the teacher to raise his sights above the mechanics of lesson planning to look at the more fundamental factors of what makes the human organism react and change behavior in a way that we deem desirable. Learning takes place when pupils understand, enjoy, and are interested in the activities with which they are confronted.

The business teacher girds himself for this challenge by a purposeful study of the following factors, particularly as related to the teaching of skills:

1. *Motivation*. The many factors involved in the motivation of learning have the purpose of creating a dynamic urge that will irresistibly impel the learner to *want* to learn and to translate this desire into action. The major factors to be

considered in creating adequate motivation are: (a) to recognize and provide for individual differences; (b) to set realistic and attainable goals, determined through teacher and teacher-pupil planning; (c) to provide incentives, whether intrinsic or extrinsic, the major point being that they help achieve the goals of the course; (d) to recognize the effect of physical surroundings upon the human organism in a learning situation; and (e) to know that success is what "makes the world go 'round" for the student. A student needs to experience success as an encouragement for further experimentation and goal-seeking.

2. *Sound procedures in lesson planning.* Once the stage is set by providing the motivation, well-planned lesson materials and procedures must follow. Many descriptions of "what to do" are given in the following chapters.

3. *Practice.* It has been stated often that practice does not necessarily make perfect. The practice must be of the right kind and based on the best we know about psychology applied to practice. Techniques of successful practice involve: (a) understanding the principles of practice applied to skill—this includes conditions under which practice should be conducted, speed and accuracy, distribution of practice, and the effect of mental set; (b) consideration of the factors of whole learning and part learning; (c) recognition of learning plateaus and making adjustments to meet apparent lack of progress. Plateaus are a common occurrence and can be overcome readily in most cases if the teacher is familiar with the causes and common characteristics.

The principles outlined in this chapter constitute a list on which there is almost universal agreement in education. Many of these principles pertain especially to skill development and should be considered a "must" in the teaching equipment of the business teacher.

SELECTED BIBLIOGRAPHY

Ammermann, Harry L., and William H. Melching. *The Derivation, Analysis, and Classification of Instructional Objectives.*

Alexandria, Virginia: George Washington University, Human Resources Research Office, 1966.

Banathy, Bela H. *Instructional Systems*. Palo Alto, California: Fearon Publishers, 1968.

Bernard, Harold W. *Psychology of Learning and Teaching*. New York: McGraw-Hill Book Co., Inc., 1954.

Bloom, Benjamin S., and David R. Krathwohl. *Cognitive Domain*, Handbook I of *Taxonomy of Educational Objectives*. New York: David McKay Co., Inc., 1956.

Bloom, Benjamin S., *et al*. *Affective Domain*, Handbook II of *Taxonomy of Educational Objectives*. New York: David McKay Co., Inc., 1964.

Crawford, Lucy C. *A Competency Pattern Approach to Curriculum Construction in Distributive Teacher Education*, OE-6-85-044. Blacksburg, Virginia: Virginia Polytechnic Institute, 1967.

Huffman, Harry A. *A Taxonomy of Office Activities for Business and Office Education*. Columbus, Ohio: Ohio State University, Center for Vocational and Technical Education, 1968.

Mager, Robert F. *Developing Attitude Toward Learning*. Palo Alto, California: Fearon Publishers, 1968.

_____. *Goal Analysis*. Belmont, California: Fearon Publishers, 1972.

_____. *Preparing Instructional Objectives*. Palo Alto, California: Fearon Publishers, 1962.

_____, and Kenneth M. Beach, Jr. *Developing Vocational Instruction*. Palo Alto, California: Fearon Publishers, 1967.

_____, and Peter Pipe. *Analyzing Performance Problems*. Belmont, California: Fearon Publishers, 1970.

McAshan, H. H. *Writing Behavioral Objectives*. New York: Harper & Row Publishers, 1970.

Mort, Paul R., and William S. Vincent. *Introduction to American Education*. New York: McGraw-Hill Book Co., Inc., 1954.

Rainey, Bill G. "Stimulate Economics Students with Supplementary Aids." *Business Education World*, XXXVIII (May, 1958), pp. 26-27.

Simpson, Elizabeth Jane. "The Classification of Educational Objectives, Psychomotor Domain." *Illinois Teacher of Home Economics*, X (Winter, 1966-67).

Young, Leontine R. "Delinquency from the Child's Point of View." *The Presidio* (November, 1960), p. 16.

Chapter 3

TYPEWRITING

BASIC CONCEPTS

The teaching of typewriting is more than just giving timed writings! A foreign student doing graduate work was forced to learn how to type because he could not find an American typist who could do the job that his thesis required: German, Latin, Greek, etc. He took a standard university-level course in typewriting. Upon his return to Germany, he wrote a letter commenting on his educational experiences. "Of all the subjects I took," he wrote, "I acquired the most from my typing class. I learned much about English, of course, but I also received an insight into the way American business operates, its economics, its office procedures, etc." The teacher who taught the class was just doing the routine job he had always done. Typing teachers should not hesitate to "give out" as occasions present themselves. What good is it for teacher-training institutions to require rich backgrounds of its teacher-trainees, if they do not use that material to enrich classroom lectures and demonstrations when they get out on the job?

At a business teachers' convention in Chicago, a teacher from a small midwestern high school made this remark: "Typing is the only business subject offered in our high school. It is the only classroom contact our students have with the world of business. In teaching this typing course, I feel I have a privilege and a responsibility."

There are many interesting things that could be written about typewriting. Volumes have been devoted to the subject. Since this is a methods book and since we have very little space, the material presented here will have to do for the most part with the *how* of teaching typewriting. Although this chapter is aimed particularly at the beginning teacher, experienced teachers might find this material useful for a quick review. Teachers of methods courses might also want to use these suggestions as a springboard for their discussions on typing.

There was a time when school boards thought that they had fulfilled their responsibility if they erected a glass partition between a "regular" classroom and the typing room. The teacher thought he had done his job if he succeeded in preventing wholesale bedlam and sabotage of the machines. Slowly over the years the idea evolved that typewriting, too, had to be taught—and taught vigorously.

Before we go any further, it might be well to take a good look to see the position typewriting has assumed in today's complex educational program. Jerry W. Robinson surveyed 18,000 American high schools to get the answer for us.[1]

Typing remains a popular subject in the American high school. It is taught, for the most part, in the regular comprehensive high school, where the classes meet five days a week for about 50 minutes. The class size is about the same as other high school classes. Many schools report that as high as 70 percent of the students in the entire student body take at least one semester of typing. It will continue to be popular, for 85 percent of the schools reporting say that they plan "no change" in the number of semesters offered.

Many different makes of typewriters are being used, about 10 percent of them electric. Blank keyboards are slowly going out of style.

Many schools provide the textbooks, usually one book per typewriter. Teachers prefer a book containing a full two-years' work, rather than separate books for each year. Not all teachers use workbooks. Many seem to prefer supplemental material for speed tests, short problem exercises, etc.

In spite of the rapid development of the computer and all that it means to business education, teachers now in

---

[1] Jerry W. Robinson, "Profile of Typewriting Instruction in American Secondary Schools," *Practices and Preferences in Teaching Typewriting*, Monograph 117 (Cincinnati: South-Western Publishing Co., 1967), pp. 1-9.

training will do well to prepare themselves for the challenge as it now exists, for that is the way they are likely to find it when they take their first jobs.

BASIC PRINCIPLES ESSENTIAL TO TEACHING TYPEWRITING

Many authors have compiled their own lists of principles. They differ little in substance. (See pages 106-114 for examples.) Even though there is some overlapping, it helps to look at these basic concepts from several different angles. It helps, too, to see that most of the authorities agree upon what is really essential in the teaching of typewriting. These principles have to do, for the most part, with beginning or first-year typing, although they would apply perhaps with equal force to advanced typing, sometimes called production typing or problem-solving.

Although it would be difficult to hold the point of view that there is one best way of teaching any subject, there are certain basic facts regarding presentation and procedure that psychologists and research workers have discovered and validated. These the typing teacher simply cannot afford to ignore.

First-Day Procedures

It is recommended that the typing teacher have a first-day procedure with which he is familiar, one that is psychologically sound, and one that he knows will get results. Such a lesson plan should contain provisions for the following:

1. Some type of work to occupy the class until everyone gets in his assigned place and the group settles down to business. This we call the "pre-first day," or a period when we are stalling for time. It is the period before the real teaching starts. If the first day is somewhat chaotic, the teacher should not plan to do anything other than organizational details: books, seating arrangement, supplies, etc. Time may be found for teaching position of the hands on home row, the carriage return, insertion of paper, and,

perhaps, the home row drill. This will put the class in excellent shape for the first day of real teaching, yet it will not disturb things if a few should come in late.

2. During the first real teaching day, the students should actually operate the typewriter, producing meaningful copy.

3. There should be vigorous demonstration on the part of the teacher to set the mood and pattern for the day. (See page 82 on how to make a demonstration table during one class period.)

4. Before the end of the period students should be typing meaningful copy in good rhythm at 40 wpm or better. (Refer to page 81 to see how this is done.)

5. During rest intervals on this first day, the teacher should sell the subject of typewriting. Students need to realize the tremendous significance of typewriting in the modern business office. A good typist can get a job practically any time and any place.

6. Students should leave the first class with a feeling of excitement over the experience. They should be eager for more. They should have the feeling that typewriting is easy and that they are going to enjoy learning it. The technique outlined on page 81 goes a long way towards accomplishing this objective.

7. The teacher should make no attempt to keep the students from looking at the keys. He might praise those who, toward the end of the period, can write the exercise in good form with complete independence of the machine, that is, without taking eyes from the copy when stroking, returning the carriage, etc.

8. Nothing whatsoever should be said about making errors. Emphasis should be on good work habits, rhythm, correct stroking, proper placement of hands, relaxed position of the body, and manipulation of the carriage throw. No attempt should be made to learn the parts of the machine that do not enter into the presentation.

9. All typewriters should be in good working condition. Margins should be uniformly set. The teacher should attend to such things before class time. The teaching period on

this first day is too valuable to devote any of it to machine adjustments or repair.

Transition to Text

Since under the authors' method the textbook is not used the first day, the teacher should have a definite procedure to take care of the transition from the first-day exercise to the text. The teacher may tie in the "if-it-is-in-the" approach with any standard keyboard method. (See page 81.)

Mixed Classes and Individual Differences

A class in which all students are absolute beginners is quite a rarity. Even though the subject is listed as Typing I, or Beginning Typewriting, the experienced teacher knows that he will not only find students who are approaching the keyboard for the first time, but also those who already know the keyboard and many who type quite well. It is the teacher's job to so organize the class that the real beginners will not be discouraged and the others will not be bored. Even if the class is quite homogeneous at the beginning, it will not stay that way very long. The factor of individual differences is always with us. (See page 84 for procedures for handling several groups in one class.)

First-Year Typing Objectives—Standards

There are only two basic sets of objectives the teacher needs to keep in mind: (a) objectives for beginning typewriting, and (b) those for advanced or production typing. There was a time when a great deal of space was devoted to delineation of specific objectives for personal-use typing. Now it is generally agreed that any good course in introductory typing will also meet the needs of those who wish to use the skill for personal use.

The objectives of first-year typing should be live, meaningful, and accepted by both teacher and student. When introducing new teachers to beginning typing situations, department heads find it helpful to go over the course outline with them carefully. Considerable time might well be spent on the section marked "objectives" to make sure that these objectives are not just so many words, but that the teacher sees them as guide lines or road markers which will help him steer his course throughout the term. The teacher should go over these objectives occasionally with the students so that they, too, may see where they are going, what they have to do to get there, and why the route they are taking is the best route.

Just as students want to know how they are getting along, so the typing teacher wants to know how *he* is doing. Because of the many variables both in objectives and in local circumstances, it is difficult, and perhaps not even desirable, to have a nationwide set of absolute standards. Such standards would discourage some, for they would present unrealistic aspiration levels; for others, it would mean doing less than they could.

On page 86 a general set of objectives is outlined, and on page 107 some specific sets of standards are given. From these the teacher can set up his own set of standards to meet his own particular situation.

Motivation and the Desire to Learn

The teacher's job is one of motivation, building up energy-packed capsules of desire, then directing that energy effectively to accomplish worthwhile student-accepted objectives. He should not be afraid to use every ace in the deck if necessary to create the desire to learn. Business, industry and government capitalize on the value of using awards and rewards in order to motivate workers to higher achievement. Why should we do less in our typing classes?

If he is going to learn to type, the student must *want* to learn. Through any motivation device at his command, intrinsic or extrinsic, the teacher must create a desire on the part of the student to want to learn. This flame should be kept burning brightly through a variety of interest-stimulating devices. (See page 87 for devices.)

Quotas or goals for which to shoot are motivation devices that probably go as far back as recorded history. The teacher should help her typing students to set realistic immediate and long-range goals. The aspiration levels of students differ. Good students are likely to underestimate their abilities; poor students usually attempt too much. This leads to failure, failure leads to frustration, and frustration means no learning.

"Actuating" is another term used quite often when we are thinking about motivation. Terry defines it as follows:

> Favorable actuating efforts are normally obtained by treating employees as human beings, encouraging their growth and development, instilling a desire to excel, recognizing work well done, and insuring fair play.[2]

Terry thus sets a good standard toward which typing teachers might work.

Speed and Accuracy Development

The techniques involved in building speed and the methods that produce the best accuracy results are two different things. Speed and accuracy cannot be stressed in the same breath. While pressing for higher speeds, the teacher might temporarily forget about accuracy; when working for accuracy, he should forget about speed. *As typing power develops, the two will finally merge into one.* (See page 91 for some speed-building programs that have been effective. Pages 92-98 contain several other excellent speed and control development techniques.)

Here are some points that should be taken into consideration when trying for higher speeds and for better control:

1. On straight-copy typing, speed scores are reliable. At any time, any place, dependable scores are usually obtainable.

2. Accuracy scores are not reliable. They differ from time to time and from place to place. No single test is dependable.

---

[2] George R. Terry, *Principles of Management* (Homewood, Illinois: Richard D. Irwin, Inc., 1968), p. 426.

3. In a speed development program, it is best not to say anything about accuracy in the beginning. Introduce this factor gradually.

4. The most important factor in the speed-building program is the will or the intent to learn. We practice because we *want* to learn; we do not necessarily learn because we practice.

5. Eliminate all unnecessary details. Concentrate on one thing at a time. If you don't need it, don't use it.

6. Always work with meaningful wholes. These should be as close to the professional level as possible. The most meaningful situations are generally the most natural and the most businesslike.

7. The teacher should keep hold of the reins at all times in order to regulate the intensity of the practice effort.

8. Warm-up drills are as essential in typing as they are in sports or in any manipulative activity. The organism needs time to adjust itself both mentally and physically. However, one should not get so concerned with the warm-up that he forgets there is a game going on.

9. Developing any skill requires a great deal of practice. They say it takes one thousand mental and physical adjustments to hit a golf ball. Perhaps that is why Arnold Palmer often practices as much as eight hours a day. Musicians often practice from four to eight hours a day. Typing students might make some progress just by thinking about it—it has been done in some cases—but by and large, to make worthwhile improvements, the students have to do a great deal of typing.

10. Forgetting is normal. Plan for it; review accordingly.

Knowledge of Progress

The teacher should provide a continuous answer to the question "How am I doing?" Knowledge of progress is one of the essentials of skill building. Without the knowledge of where he was yesterday and where he is now, how can the student possibly be interested in where he is likely to be tomorrow? (See page 110 for an example of a progress chart.)

Success Is Crucial

Obtainable goals having been established, the teacher should set the stage so that every student in the class experiences success in reaching these goals. All students should succeed in *something*. There is no better stimulus to skill building than success. SUCCESS IS CRUCIAL! A teacher reports that a student in one of his classes was most discouraged, for she was at the bottom of the class. The teacher was hard pressed to give her something in which she could succeed. The key came entirely by accident. One day the teacher noticed that the girl had developed expertness in returning the carriage. She was asked to make a special demonstration. From that day on she was a new person; her progress was rapid. She, too, had found something in which she could succeed.

Evaluation in Beginning Typewriting

The teacher should have a sound plan for evaluating (grading) his students. The evaluation technique ought to have a direct tie-in with the objectives of the course. When students share in setting up the instrument by which they are to be evaluated, the entire procedure acts as a powerful motivating force. If a student is surprised by the mark he receives at the end of the term, it may be an indication that the lines of communication between teacher and student have broken down. (See pages 98 and 99 for evaluation plans that have won considerable acceptance. Also see page 110 for a suggestion on cutting down paper work.)

Quality of Typing

What constitutes good typing? Many office managers have been irritated by letters that are just good enough to pass inspection but not poor enough to be rewritten.

Such supervisors find it hard to criticize because the office worker himself has not been trained to distinguish between the finer shades of typewritten copy. Too often a sheet of typewritten material, which contains no errors (wrong letters), loses its effectiveness because of uneven intensity of stroke, capitals that are above the line of writing, fingerprints, keys that need cleaning, faulty alignment, poor syllabication, uneven lines, smudgy erasures, and because the material is not well arranged on the page. Typing teachers should, therefore, make sure that they themselves observe good typing standards.

Classroom Organization

There is a philosophy of education which suggests that schools be a living example of democracy in action. Typing teachers should provide opportunities for experience in democratic procedures by effecting a proper classroom organization. Not only will proper organization help students to experience the meaning of democracy, but it will make the whole job easier for the teacher. The typing teacher is the expert who points out right directions, time-saving devices, proper techniques, and who builds enthusiasm. He is the coach, standing on the side lines directing the work of the class in the most efficient manner possible. Early in the term students should be given an opportunity to elect officers: a chairman, a secretary, and various assistants. A librarian should be given charge of books and typing tests to facilitate handling of papers, tests, and the like. If this becomes burdensome, the librarian can have several assistants. There should be a class statistician to check attendance, and a person whose duty it is to supervise bulletin boards. There might also be a supervisor of maintenance—a person whose special duty it is to see that classroom property is protected, that waste is cut to a minimum, that the room is properly lighted and ventilated, and that inventories are checked regularly.

The class as an organization can pass on many things to be done during the semester. An agreement as to the methods to be used and standards to be achieved will make the term's work a student project. The typing teacher should be familiar with several good classroom organization systems and then choose a plan that best meets the needs of the class. Whatever the details, the student should not be deprived of the opportunity to exercise his initiative —to show that he is dependable and to demonstrate his poise by taking an active part in the work of the class.

It is only by setting the stage so the learner may take the first step that the teacher can hope to lead his students toward more difficult objectives. Acting as chairman of a classroom organization may give the student confidence to try for an office in some social organization, which again may lead to class presidency, and later on, perhaps, to leadership in a business organization.

The Typing Assignment

Typing assignments should correlate with the course objectives. The nature of the assignment will depend on the local situation. If all the work is done during the typing period, and if everything is completed in the teacher's presence, the assignments are of necessity brief and simple. If the class meeting is short in comparison with the total practice time (adult evening programs for example), the assignment must be more specific. An introduction to the work might well be given in class before the students are left to go on their own initiative. (See page 111.)

Before making the assignment the teacher might wish to ask herself such questions as:

1. Is this assignment realistic? Can the average student complete it in the time available?

2. Is it meaningful, not just busy work? Can the student see that this work is helping him achieve the objectives of the course?

3. Is it interesting? Sometimes the assignment can be reshaped so as to tie in with a local happening or a current event.

Dependability in Proofreading

Students and beginning office workers need a shock of some kind before they catch the full significance of this statement, which was seen in a New York office:

ARE YOU POSITIVE IT'S CORRECT? SOMEONE IS GOING TO MAKE SOME PRETTY IMPORTANT DECISIONS TOMORROW ON THE BASIS OF WHAT YOU TYPE TODAY!

The joint meeting of the board of regents and the budget committee of a certain university was about to start. The chairman called the meeting to order. One of the businessmen, used to dealing with figures, startled everyone by saying, "Gentlemen, we might as well go home. There's a mistake here someplace. These figures don't jibe. This throws everything off." The originals from which the typist had worked could not be obtained immediately. The chairman had to call for an adjournment until the discrepancies could be cleared up. The whole matter was carefully investigated. Everything was traced to some careless typing and haphazard proofreading. (See page 101 for information about proofreading.)

Composing at the Machine

One day the authors visited an executive who is a good typist and uses the typewriter extensively. The executive was writing something in longhand. "Have to make a speech," he said. "Yes," was our reply, "but why the longhand?" "You know," said he, "I've just never learned to think at the machine. As soon as I touch the keys, my thoughts leave me. Just can't get going." "Come to our typing class for a week," we told him, "and we guarantee you will be able to think as you type."

Ability to compose at the machine does not correlate with straight-copy typing skill *unless something is done about it*. How, then, does one learn to think at the machine? (See page 102 for details.)

PRODUCTION TYPING

"Now they are on their own. I have taught them all I know," said one typing teacher with pride as she completed her work with a first-year group of typing students. This is all too common a concept: that we do our real teaching in Typing I, that we have done our job if we have brought the class up to 50 or 60 wpm on straight copy. Many, however, would differ with the above statement and say that when we get to this point, our work is only just beginning.

The authors now continue to present basic concepts of good typewriting, but here the attention is focused primarily on production typing and problem-solving. The following are some broad guidelines that have crystalized in the thinking of the writers after many years of experience in the classroom.

BASIC PRINCIPLES AND GUIDELINES

1. Emphasize the fact that "This is it!" This is the time the students have all been waiting for—the time when they are going to *do* things with the typewriter. The beginning, straight-copy, skill-building period is over.

2. The training period now coming up is one of *realism*: "This is the way they do it in the modern office." "This is what the typist actually does when she is on the job." "In all our work during this semester of production typing, let's imagine that we are actually in an office; think office, talk office, dress office, and work office."

3. During typing, the students often took a long time to do a job—they had to learn how. Now they have to do these jobs both well and efficiently. One manager heard his secretary make this statement: "I'm going to get this letter perfect if it takes all morning!" This story was told to a production typing class. They saw nothing wrong with the situation; in fact, they thought it was a commendable attitude.

Let us recognize, however, that there *is* something wrong with that picture. The firm is paying for that letter. It is costing too much. In production typing the student needs to be reminded that it is *output* that counts—usable, high-class output, but not perfection. Errors will have to be kept to a minimum, neat corrections will have to be made efficiently.

4. Endurance is something that must be considered in advanced typing. "She flopped on the bed as soon as she came home and hasn't moved since," was one mother's remark when a teacher called to see how well the daughter

had survived her first day on the job. Such a reaction is not uncommon. In school the student types for a brief period and then takes a break. She gets little opportunity to condition her mental and physical faculties for an eight-hour day.

In advanced typing everything possible should be done to develop stamina, staying power, and endurance. This means that the student must be taught to work with as little tension as possible and in a rhythm that can be maintained for hours at a time without undue fatigue.

5. Advanced typing offers an excellent opportunity for the student to experience *joy* in work well done. As each new series of contracts is negotiated, it becomes evident that the prime goals of life seem to be more money, more leisure, and shorter working hours, whereas just the opposite is true. Man's greatest happiness lies in his work and achievement, a responsibility accepted and successfully accomplished. Work is not something to get away from as soon as possible so that we can do something else. We live in a job economy, an average job worth $100,000. Unless we are happy in that job, our efforts are in vain.

Multiple-Job Efficiency

"The average new employee," commented office manager Elmer Rule of the Nationwide Insurance Company, "does well if you keep her on a certain job for a long time. She soon learns that operation and becomes quite proficient at it. But, if you interrupt her routine typing work and ask her to do something special, there is usually a great deal of fumbling around before she gets going. Assignments which should take only about ten minutes may take as much as a full hour." (See page 103 for sample five-minute-limit multiple-job projects.) Exercises of this kind serve as good introduction to production typing and problem-solving.

Letter Typing as a Problem-Solving and Production Exercise

One means of gaining production power in handling letters is to set up attainable learning stages.

Stage 1. The student reviews what he has learned about letter typing so far in the course—it will be mostly copy work from standard samples, no particular problem involved. Typing books have letter exercises which give the word count so that they can be used both as a speed building assignment and for letter format review.

Stage 2. The student is asked to make small changes, such as dates, prices, order numbers, etc., in letters with which he is familiar.

Stage 3. The problem aspect is now emphasized. Changes are asked for that involve judgment and close attention to details.

Stage 4. The letter-per-hour-exercise is introduced. From letter booklets prepared in Typing I, students now see how many mailable letters they can type in an hour's time. Some teachers set the clock for one-half hour and then double the results. In this way the project can be handled during a regular typing period. Where circumstances permit, the full hour is preferred.

Stage 5. The student is now ready to do actual office projects involving letters that are to be mailed. (See page 104 for an example.)

Typing on Printed Forms

There have been many studies endeavoring to find out just how a typist spends her time when on the job in an average office. These lists sometimes contain a score or more of daily activities. Straight-copy typing, when listed, usually comes near the bottom. Typing on some style of business form comes near the top. More will be said about this in connection with office practice. Suffice it to say here that the typist should be familiar with a large number of business forms, know their purposes, and be able to use them in on-the-job situations.

Evaluation of Advanced Typing—Standards

A ninety-year-old gentleman celebrating his birthday made this remark: "I've got one foot in heaven. I'm still enjoying things here on this planet, but I've got my eyes on the next." Students who have reached the advanced stage of training in typing may still have one foot in the classroom, but the other is already in the office. For months they have been hearing their teachers say, "This is the way it is done in the modern office." Films and field trips have conditioned them to what they may expect. It is only logical, therefore, that when we think of typewriting standards and evaluation, we should think in the terms of the businessman. Harlan B. Miller, of the Institute of Life Insurance, for example, has this to say:

> How does a businessman look at typewriting? To put it succinctly, he looks at the typed material which is placed on his desk with just two questions in mind: (a) Is it clean and accurate? (b) How long did it take the typist to complete the job? The first question probably carries more weight than the second since the speed with which a manuscript or letter is typed has no significance unless it meets the quality standards which apply to that particular job.[3]

Advanced typing is a time for realism. It is here that students make the transition from routine straight-copy typing to production and problem-solving. Except in rare instances in which a rough draft is all that is required, the office typist will make all the necessary corrections as she goes along. She will proofread material before taking it out of the machine and thus be able to make further immediate corrections if necessary. It is at the advanced typing stage, therefore, that erasure tests should become the rule. (See page 112 for a variety of standards—excellent material to help teachers with their grading and evaluation problems.)

MISCELLANEOUS OBSERVATIONS

Learning Plateaus

"Plateau" is a polite word for "rut." Plateaus should be avoided if possible and dealt with vigorously when they do appear. Plateaus can often be avoided by anticipating their causes early in the program.

---

[3] Harlan B. Miller, "A Businessman Takes a Look at Typewriting," *Business Education Forum*, 14 (November, 1959), p. 9.

Inexperienced teachers sometimes introduce the "i" and "e" one after the other, thus setting the stage for juxtaposition troubles later on. Teachers often pay little attention to correct techniques in the beginning, thinking that they can fix those things up later on. They talk a great deal about accuracy and use all sorts of special "accuracy building" drills. We now know that such drills do very little good in the first place, and they can do much harm in developing tension plateaus. If it were possible to set up the perfect learning situation and to put into operation all the psychological principles of learning, no doubt we would have a progress curve closely resembling the normal learning curve —no plateaus whatever.

Holding Power

The real test of a typing teacher's ability comes in connection with an adult evening program. High school classes are usually captive audiences; students have no other choice. In adult evening programs, it is different. If they like it, they stay; if they don't, they leave. Some evening class teachers hold almost all of their students to the very end; other teachers lose from 50 to 75 percent each term. Students' reasons for dropping may be something like these: "Oh, I am having my mother give me speed tests." "I couldn't see that I was getting anywhere." "It's not worth the long drive." "At first I came only when I thought the teacher would give us something new; finally, I quit altogether."

Something new! That's the magic word. The magic formula for holding students is nothing else than to give them something new, something that they won't want to miss, *each evening.* This will, of course, involve careful planning, but perhaps that's just the difference between the superior teacher and the average teacher.

Independence of the Machine

One of the earmarks of an advanced typist is that he is completely familiar with his machine; he can make the typewriter talk. Just as a musician must know the notes and a dancer the steps before any thought can be given to interpretation, so the typist must have complete mastery of his machine before he can really tackle advanced-level typing projects. The building of this proficiency, if the student comes lacking in it, is one of the first duties of the teacher of advanced typing.

An example in point: A typing teacher noticed a student using the space bar in connection with a rough draft tabulation project. In reply to the question, "Why don't you use your tabulator stops?" she said, "I never feel sure of myself with them. This has to be just right."

Factual Information

A student on a cooperative office education program became disturbed over her employer's impatience with her many questions. He had just told her that at the rate she was interrupting his work with questions which he thought she should be able to answer, he ought to be getting half of her pay. Her remark was, "Well, does a typist have to know *everything*?" "No," she was told, "but you should know how to spell, know basic punctuation, know something about word usage, know fundamentals of artistic design and page format, know enough about English to catch routine slips of the boss, and you should know the hundred and one little things in connection with capitals, underscoring, use of footnotes, and so forth." "My," said she, isn't that just about everything?" Well, if it is, then the typist has to know everything. The ability to type 60 wpm is of little value if much time is lost while scouting about the office for the answer to some little detail that should be a part of one's basic fund of knowledge in office procedures.

Tricks of the Trade

Even though it has been said (and correctly so) that the teaching of typewriting is more than dishing out a bag of tricks, nevertheless, there are many tricks of the trade that add to the efficiency of the typist. True, these "tricks" are by no means the cornerstone of a typing course, but once a good foundation has been laid, many of these little short cuts can be thrown in along the way as interest-getting devices without hampering the overall training program. In learning a foreign language, one limits himself at first to the simple way of saying things; but later on, when he "feels his oats" so to speak, he can begin using delightful local idioms, which add color to the language. So it is with these efficiency or short cut techniques—they add spice to the day's work.

TV and the Typing Teacher

Practically all of the business subjects in one form or another have been taught successfully by television. The procedures are too new and our space too limited for a complete analysis of all the problems. The important thing to recognize is that here is a technique that requires specific training. Just what this is and how it is done is described elsewhere in this text.

TEACHING TECHNIQUES AND PROCEDURES

First-Day Procedures

The following detailed procedure has been found effective and in accordance with the psychological principles of learning mentioned in Chapter 2.

After the students are seated and have been supplied with paper, the teacher gives a brief demonstration of how to put the paper in the machine and how to take it out. Classmates are usually eager to help those who have difficulty. The position of the hands on home row is briefly illustrated.

The teacher now writes the word "if" on the board and asks students to feel for the right keys. Classmates help to see that the right fingers are used. At the movable demonstration table, the teacher types the word, setting both the visible and the sound pattern. Cardboard instead of paper in the teacher's machine will help accentuate the sound. Right thumb is mentioned in spacing. After a few moments of practice on "i-f-space," members of the class are asked to demonstrate how nearly they can approach the quick, flash-like pattern established by the teacher.

After the word "if" has been developed, the word "it" is placed on the board. Since the students are already familiar with "i," the "t" is the only new element. There is sufficient contrast not to cause confusion. Other words are written in like manner until "if it is in the" have been introduced. By the end of the first period students will be writing this phrase rapidly and in good style. On the second day this phrase can be reviewed together with a formal introduction to the text. The sound-and-word-pattern techniques may be continued regardless of the particular approach suggested by the text. This introductory procedure is suggested here simply to assure good basic typing techniques with a snappy, quick, get-away stroke right from the beginning. It is important that the mental process back of the physical manipulation be conditioned to act quickly.

Space does not permit us to point out the many psychological factors that have been built into this simple "if-it-is-in-the" approach. One thing is certain, if the first day has been properly utilized, students will go home with the satisfaction of having actually typed something. They eagerly await their next experience. How different the above procedure from the method used when one teacher took his first course in typing. The class sat before the covered typewriters, just itching to get their fingers on the keys, but that privilege was denied them until the third day. By that time enthusiasm had died down considerably, even though the class did know something about the history of the typewriter.

Vigorous demonstration is now an accepted part of the teaching of typewriting. Now and then there are excuses for not demonstrating. "I have tried for two years to get a demonstration stand for our typing room," complained one teacher. To show teachers how easy it is to build a good demonstration stand, we usually make one right in the classroom in connection with each typing methods class. On one occasion we found an old discarded table top. From this we cut two square pieces, one 15 x 15 inches and another 20 x 20. One student bought four swivel casters at the dime store. A 4 x 4 from a nearby woodpile supplied the upright. We nailed the square blocks to the top and bottom of the 4 x 4. Then we put the casters in the four corners of the larger block. The entire operation took less than a class period; the cost was about one dollar.

After an initial good beginning, the alert typing teacher continually seeks better answers to such questions as "How can I best achieve the objectives I have set for this class?" "Are these objectives still sound?" "Do we still want to do what we planned to do in the beginning?" "Can our skill-building techniques be improved?" In mathematics, history, and science, solutions themselves determine the correctness of the method; but in skill subjects a student may use a wrong technique day by day without being aware that there is a better way. Here it is not so much the right answer as it is the right way to operate the machine.

It is the duty of the teacher, therefore, to help each individual student find the best methods to reach his particular goal. The teacher is a technician, a coach, a specialist called in to serve in the capacity of an efficiency expert.

As soon as the class is in action and things are running smoothly, it is time to check on details. Is the table high enough to enable the student to lower the wrist to secure the correct, comfortable position illustrated in the typing text? (As mentioned in connection with equipment, the table is a relative proposition. It is more often too low than too high.) Are students using the right fingers? Is the stroking executed with a snappy, get-away touch? Is the carriage returned quickly with proper technique?

The whole method of learning would indicate that the keyboard should be learned as quickly as possible. Some teachers introduce students to the entire keyboard the first day; others take as long as four weeks. The average time, however, is ten to twelve class periods. Most textbooks introduce words, phrases, and sentences in the first few lessons. Context material in short paragraphs may be used for timed writing practices by the end of the first week. By this time the class routine is fairly well established, and plans for the semester organization can get under way.

Lessenberry, Crawford, and Erickson give the following suggestion for the first period:

Teaching the Lesson. The students want to get their fingers on the typewriter and make it work. Don't let class organization, clerical work, or interruptions keep you from beginning to teach as soon as the students are assembled. Omit explanations that can be given as appropriately in the next lessons. Reserve the "pep talks" and the motivating examples until a later time. Demonstrate everything you want to do; capitalize on their initial enthusiasm, and keep them typing—and they won't be able to resist learning to type.[4]

Additional suggestions for first-day procedures are given on pages 65-66.

Transition to Text

Some teachers using the "if-it-is-in-the" approach follow up with the three-letter words found in the first few lessons of almost every text. These words can be used in connection with the "if-it-is-in-the" group in meaningful phrases and sentences and so continue the pattern established during the first few days. One teacher reports excellent results by using rhythm records in 4/4 time for the three-letter words. The drill would then be "f-u-r-space," etc. After a short time the basic concept of rhythm in typing is established. From then on the goal will be an even flowing, "keep-that-carriage-moving" type of rhythm, rather than the metronomic style.

As stated before, there are many different opinions when it comes to teaching the keyboard. All agree that it should be covered in a relatively short time. (See pages 106-107 for definite recommendations.)

Handling Different Groups in One Class

Of the many millions of people who inhabit this globe, there are no two exactly alike. To be different, therefore, is the normal state of affairs. "I am so used to having different levels of ability in my typing classes," said one typing teacher, "that I do something about it the very first time the class meets." Assuming that all machines are in

---

[4] D. D. Lessenberry, T. James Crawford, and Lawrence W. Erickson, *Manual for 20th Century Typewriting* (8th ed.; Cincinnati: South-Western Publishing Co., 1962), p. 36.

good working condition and margins set, the authors recommend the following:

1. Absolute beginners, those who do not know the keyboard or are so rusty they need a review, are seated in the front of the room; the rest, in the rear.

2. If space is available, it helps to have a vacant row of seats separating the beginners from the others. The nonbeginners are now given a 5-minute timed writing. They are instructed to check their papers as soon as they finish. This allows about ten minutes of uninterrupted time to spend with beginners on the "if-it-is-in-the" approach.

3. After ten minutes of intensive work paced by the teacher, the beginners are far enough along that they can continue on their own for a few minutes, which allows time for a quick appraisal of the 5-minute test results. From this information the next step is planned.

4. Generally, a half dozen or so of the nonbeginners stand out above the rest. They are ready for some form of production work. If there is an out-of-the-way corner available, that's the place for the production workers. A problem that needs very little explanation is all ready for them. In a minute or two they are busy at work.

5. The remainder of the nonbeginning group now take another timed writing to see if they can do better. The real reason for this second writing is to provide time for the teacher to work with the beginners. There are now three groups: beginners, advanced, and the rest which we will call intermediates. All this in a "beginning" class!

6. The beginners are now far enough along for the teacher to help them with various phases of technique. After all those in the front of the room thoroughly understand the assignment for next time, they work by themselves for the remainder of the period.

7. The beginners are busy with their next day's assignment, and the intermediates are selecting the better of the two tests they have just taken. The teacher then visits the advanced group and goes over the objectives for the term and with the students decides on a specific job for next

time. A special short job keeps them "gainfully employed" until the end of the period.

8. The intermediates are now next in line for final attention. With the teacher they decide on a good place to start in the text—letter writing, for example.

9. The opening and closing remarks are always to the group as a whole. After the first few sessions, there are many exercises on which all three groups can work at the same time: short one-minute tests, warming-up exercises, discussions on office procedures, factual information, and so forth. By working together as a group at the beginning and at the end, there is a feeling of class unity, even though the students are working at different levels.

Of course, the teacher always breathes a sigh of relief when the first class is over, and no wonder. It is a most challenging experience. To keep three distinct groups happy and usefully busy every minute for the very first time they come together is no mean accomplishment. From then on the teacher will have to study carefully the needs of each group and come to class with definite plans and materials to take care of these needs.

Objectives

The objectives of beginning typewriting might well be summarized as follows:

1. ATTITUDE—the *desire* to want to be a good typist.
2. GOOD WORK HABITS—right position at the machine, proper stroking, efficient handling of materials, proper spacing of attention and effort, neatness, a minimum of lost motion; in other words, correct techniques.
3. KNOWLEDGE FACTORS—the proper "know-how." A part of typing efficiency is the ability to exercise quick and accurate judgment in connection with the many writing details. The proper procedure here is simply *to know* what leading authorities have decreed as the best practice.
4. QUALITY AND CONTROL. It is during this stage of his development that the student should formulate a concept of what constitutes good typing, should subscribe to an acceptable standard, and should overcome the usual

inhibitions, fears, and indecisions which so often hamper the beginning typist.

5. SPEED. Although basic speed patterns are emphasized from the very first day, nevertheless, speed is here placed near the end in this list of objectives. Without the foregoing four objectives, a speed-building program is not likely to succeed. Most of the speed-building devices given in this text alternate short pressure spurts with reinforcement periods for control. Eventually these two merge into one—the total skill necessary to meet modern office standards.

6. PERFORMANCE—the ability to do. Producing practical results with the typewriter, especially on a production basis, should be reserved as an objective of advanced typing. Nevertheless, many things can be done during this year to get students ready for production typing.

By the time students have completed the first half of their typing program, they should be able to set up simple letters from printed copy, should be able to arrange copy attractively on different size forms, should be able to do many of the "5-minute jobs" suggested as "pre-production" material, should be able to do some composing at the machine, and should be able to do simple tabulation.[5] Some authorities feel that a degree of pressure in connection with production projects should be applied even in beginning typewriting.[6]

Interest-Generating Devices

Devices and "teaching tricks" are in disrepute. This has come about, perhaps, by the fact that many beginning teachers do not have a clear concept of what constitutes a good teaching device. Too many devices are in the nature of busy work or just "having fun" exercises. A good device is one that stirs the imagination, generates additional interest, heads directly towards the target, and inspires a host of concomitant learnings along the way. When students have progressed to the point where they can handle

[5] Harm Harms, "Standards for Beginning Typewriting," *The Journal of Business Education*, XX (February, 1945), p. 23.
[6] *Practices and Preferences in Teaching Typewriting*, Monograph 117 (Cincinnati: South-Western Publishing Co., 1967).

problem situations, the teacher will have no difficulty in finding an interest-creating exercise if the text does not supply the needed material. Actual work exercises brought in from the community are sure-fire interest-getting devices. (For some high-powered devices to get speed with control, see pages 91-98 on speed building.)

Speed and Accuracy Development

Speed and accuracy are two important component factors in achieving our typing objectives. Business educators have come a long way since the day when the teacher with an eagle eye insisted on absolutely perfect copy with no erasures. The new attitude is more in harmony with actual conditions. The modern typing student emulates the good work habits of efficient stenographers and typists. Certainly they erase, but they maintain a proper balance. Too many erasures destroy efficiency. Accuracy is still of great importance, but it cannot be achieved by overemphasizing it to beginning students any more than one can achieve happiness by telling a person to go out and be happy without making it physically possible for him to do so.

The concept of accuracy should be introduced gradually. First, it might be suggested that the student do as well as he can; next, that he work on his exercise until he is satisfied with it. Carefully and adroitly the teacher can instill higher standards so that the students themselves will not be satisfied with copy containing more errors than necessary at their present stage of development. As a further step, papers having few errors may be placed on display— the teacher need not wait for perfect papers to do this. A desire for accuracy can also be introduced by having the students type five successive one-minute timed writings in an effort to see how many out of the five they can type with one or no errors. Each one-minute timed writing represents a new challenge.

The word "control" is gradually being substituted for accuracy. The aim is to help the student to so direct his energies that he can manipulate the typewriter with relatively few unintentional and undesirable results, actions, or responses. When the will is capable of exerting this influence with effective measures, the typist is said to have control.

Good control involves more than striking the right keys. Errors in technique are frequently more serious and attended with more far-reaching ill results than errors involving the wrong keys. Blackstone was thinking of such errors when he said:

> Of course the student may, by slowing down, type a word correctly. That word needs additional practice too. To mark such words for technique practice, the student may strike the diagonal key after every word that slows him down. After typing the exercise through, he should practice each word that was incorrectly typed and each word that was slow.[7]

Some of the early methods books often devoted as much as an entire chapter to drills and devices for getting rid of certain kinds of typing errors. This type of remedial work can be overdone. One teacher remembers having a girl in his class who seemed to have no control whatever—seldom wrote a line without several errors. Psychologists and research workers labored over her in vain. Yet one day, to the teacher's surprise, she typed an entire page without an error, with no other incentive than a banana split that was offered to the class as a stunt. When asked for an explanation, the student's simple, but significant, remark was "Guess this is the first time I really wanted to be accurate."

The price of speed with control is first of all an intense desire on the part of the student to achieve such a goal. This often means lower speeds for the moment, more attention to techniques, and more practice.

Few experienced typists type with perfect control. Errors do creep in. The perfect copy requirement for beginning students is giving way to a more natural situation in which the student does the best he can about accuracy while striving for rapid stroking with good form and with relaxation.

Simply to tell the student, "Don't be tense—relax," is about as useful as telling the groom not to be nervous or the young applicant that he must have poise. Something must be done about it. To secure relaxation the typing

---

[7] E. G. Blackstone,"How to Speed Up Typewriting Instruction," *The National Business Education Quarterly,* 12 (December, 1943), p. 65.

teacher must help the student by positive means. Relaxing is not so much physical as it is mental. Relaxation and poise go together. Poise is the result of anticipating conditions—familiarizing one's self with coming experiences and the elimination of the element of fear. In order to help him relax, the student should know exactly what is expected of him. The job must be easy enough so he can do it without great difficulty. The student should bear in mind that results from the very beginning are not so important. All that is desired just now is a bundle of good work habits: comfortable position at the machine, quick, snappy stroking, skillful carriage return—all with an air of confidence that permits daring and encourages speed.

The word "tense" as used above refers to that type of nervous condition which produces cold hands, overly taut muscles—a general condition associated with fear and not the tension mentioned by Dvorak and others, where tension is discussed as a readiness of the body to meet the problem at hand. "The new situation of struggling with a typewriter which you desire to operate is bound to heighten the tension of your muscles somewhat, so that you are ready to act. What is called your 'interest' is simply the degree of this bodily tension." [8]

Lessenberry [9] admonishes teachers to talk less about making errors and more about improving technique.

The Page Club as an Accuracy Builder

The literature of business education contains many devices intended to promote accuracy. The following is one device that can be used in almost any typing class. The daily lesson material may be used for copy.

Any student writing a page without a mistake during a fifteen-minute segment of the regular typing period becomes a member of the Page Club. His name is placed on the membership scroll. Since it will be some time before many in the class can do this, a preliminary chart is set up showing the greatest number of consecutive perfect lines (seventy

---

[8] August Dvorak, *et. al., Typewriting Behavior* (New York: American Book Company, 1936), p. 89.
[9] D. D. Lessenberry, "The Teaching of Typewriting," *Sixth Yearbook of the National Commercial Teachers Federation* (Bowling Green, Kentucky: National Business Teachers Association, 1940), p. 455.

spaces) each student has been able to write. Line by line they thus progress toward Page Club membership. This device is flexible and can be used in connection with almost any material. Other awards may, of course, be substituted. In actual practice office workers need not labor under such a strain, since erasures may be made when necessary. However, the ability to write a paragraph or page with a high degree of accuracy is often quite an asset. Techniques of this kind are often found in certain employment tests.

Speed-Building Devices

A student at the Vocational Arts Center, Columbus, Ohio, volunteered to try a special technique known as guided writing (developed by Lessenberry) to see how much improvement in speed could be made in one month's time. The routine consisted of a daily series of five-minute timed writings. Five interval timers were used. The first was set for one minute, the second for two, the next for three, etc. The copy was marked to indicate where the student wished to be at the end of each minute. Goals were set at the beginning of each day's work. Frequently it meant slowing down on a particular test and the establishment of higher goals on the next try. By using this device exclusively, the student increased her speed from 61 words a minute to 111. On the 96-word level several tests were written without errors. The highest record of 111 gross words a minute on a five-minute test contained 1.2 errors a minute.

The Skyline Drive. There is no magic or secret formula for increasing typing speed. A review of the training routines used by champion typists indicates that the program is made up of: warming-up drills to secure independent, individual finger action; timed writings in which the candidate always seeks higher levels; and much practice.

The literature of business education contains many devices helpful in a speed development program. The device illustrated on page 93 has been named "The Skyline Drive." It consists of an individual chart for each student. These may be posted on the bulletin board or kept by the typist.

In the illustration the uppermost line is the Skyline Drive. It represents the maximum speed at which the student is able to manipulate the typewriter. Any drill material that makes for maximum speed is used, no error limit. The typewriter is set for a seventy-space line. To compute their speed, students simply count lines—fourteen words for each line. Line No. 2 represents the results of one-minute timed writings with a control of one error a minute. The bottom line indicates the speed of five-minute timed writings with an accuracy standard of one error a minute.

Such a chart gives the student a whole series of incentives. The upper line proves to him that he can move his fingers fast enough to write at the speed indicated. With a little effort he can write the material, as indicated by line No. 2, at that speed also. In like manner the speed of line No. 3 can be brought up to that of line No. 2. This entire speed-building routine need take no more time than twelve minutes of the class period. A little additional time may have to be allowed for scoring.

Speed drills	2 min......(The Skylines)	
3 one-minute, 1 error a minute	3 {	Student selects the best out of three trials and records results on his Skyline Drive Speed Chart.
1 five-minute speed test	5	
Free time	2	
	12 min.	

Local conditions will determine whether to have this twelve-minute speed-building program at the beginning or at the end of the period and whether to have it only on certain days a week over a longer period rather than intensively every day for a special speed-building drive.

A Speed and Accuracy Builder. Some of the most effective speed-building devices are also the least complex. The speed-and-accuracy-building paragraphs [10] on pages 94-95 are good examples of such devices. One of the authors conducted an experimental class, made up of high school juniors, in which these paragraphs were introduced after two weeks' work in the text. With no previous knowledge

---

[10] The origin of the drill paragraphs is not certain. The authors have used them for years, changing the content frequently to include items of local interest.

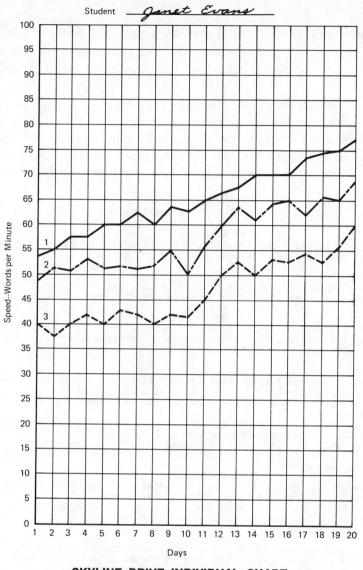

Student *Janet Evans*

Speed--Words per Minute

1

2

3

Days

SKYLINE DRIVE INDIVIDUAL CHART
A four-week program to increase speed in typing.
KEY
1. Skyline Drive
2. One-minute timed writings—one error per minute
3. Five-minute timed writings—one error per minute

of typing this class developed an average speed of 42 words
a minute in eight weeks. The instructions to the student
were simply that he type the first paragraph over and over
again until he could type it in one minute without error. If

accomplished, he had typed 25 words a minute and was ready to begin on the next one. Incentives in the form of prizes were used to spur the class on to greater efforts.

Calling-the-Throw Drills. This device is advocated by Lessenberry and is now quite widely used. After the student has found the line of copy he can write in just ten seconds, the teacher calls the throw by a signal, or the word "return." The student places the current date to the left of

SPEED-AND-ACCURACY-BUILDING PARAGRAPHS

25 Words

You can build speed and accuracy at the same time if you will just give all the time to drill asked of you by your teacher.

30 Words

Each day you are to give, at the very least, five minutes of practice to these lines; all the extra time you can give now will count much for you.

35 Words

You are required to type this set of drill lines every day until you can type the entire group of lines with no errors. Give every bit of spare time to this sort of typing.

40 Words

As soon as you can type accurately and within one minute the lines on which you are now working, you are to proceed to the next drill. This drill has five more words than the one you have just written.

45 Words

By the use of this easy program you will not fall into any habit of slow, lazy stroking. You will be trying each day to raise your stroking rate. You will also be striving for good typing that is free of mistakes of all kinds.

50 Words

In typewriting, as in other skill subjects, you must keep right at it. There are no short cuts in learning to type well. You may be sure I would have found them if they existed, for I am a firm believer in doing things with the least possible physical effort.

55 Words

You may have noticed by this time that fewer and fewer easy words are being used in these special lines. The stroke intensity is made higher in each drill. You know, of course, that we find the stroke intensity by dividing the total number of strokes by the actual number of words in the drill.

60 Words

If you can possibly do so, type these special drills outside of the regular class period in the typing room. As you write in your class period, strive to maintain a smooth, continuous rate. Do not permit your stroking to lag as you type your assignments, such as letters, manuscripts, or legal papers. Keep your typing rate at its best.

65 Words

It has been said that the only reason for the existence of this machine of keys, cogs, and levers known as the typewriter is its power to increase speed in the writing of business letters and all sorts of legal and business papers. That statement is quite true, but there must also be added to this factor of speed the valuable quality of accurate typing.

SPEED-AND-ACCURACY-BUILDING PARAGRAPHS--CONCLUDED

70 Words

As simple as this paragraph drill may seem to you, it is most effective. It is a strange fact that we mortals seem to believe that any exercise must be difficult if we are to accomplish anything through its use. That belief is far from the truth. Actually, a simple exercise on the typewriter, repeated over and over, is one of the most effective ways of building speed and accuracy.

75 Words

At any time during your typing you find yourself making certain types of errors, do not fail to give special attention to the stroke combinations or words that cause you difficulty. Remember that it is just about ten times as easy to form a bad typing habit as it is to overcome that habit. That is something to think about whenever you are tempted to become careless and to neglect practice on difficult stroke combinations.

80 Words

A fact not often recognized is that a limited understanding of word meanings and syllable-division rules can cause a delay in the typing of letters or straight copy. As a general rule, the more difficult the copy, the slower the typing rate. Copy containing many words with double letters is spoken of as very "slow" copy. Not even an expert can type much over seventy words a minute on double-letter sequences, no matter how much he may drill.

85 Words

I once heard a young man who had reached the sixty-word rate in typewriting. He found that he was hopelessly "stuck" at between sixty and sixty-two words a minute. Drill and type as he would, he seemed to be unable to get beyond this speed level of sixty words. In despair he appealed to an expert trainer of typists. The expert gave him a series of simple paragraphs which progressed gradually in length, just as do these paragraphs you are typing.

90 Words

In two months he built up his rate to a speed of one hundred words a minute. He was able to write the hundred-word paragraph accurately in one minute. The expert also gave the young man many special timed writings and forced him to write each business letter at his very best rate, timing him on every letter. On the advice of his teacher, the boy entered the amateur class of the state typing contest. This young typist won his event easily, typing more than eighty words a minute for fifteen minutes--without a single error.

95 Words

Each day this young man typed away at the sixty-five word copy. He wrote for at least five minutes, timing himself on each writing of the drill. It was not long before he wrote the paragraph accurately within one minute. He then took the next copy of seventy words and typed it each day from five to ten times. Finally, he was able to write the seventy words in one minute. All this special speed writing was done during the daily practice period, along with other forms of typing.

100 Words

When you reach this speed, you are far above the average in your rate and typing ability. Careful study and thoughtful checking of thousands of typists have pretty well shown that the average student will be able to type at least sixty words a minute; that is, if he stays with his daily practice until he reaches the approximate limit of his stroking ability. When you are able to type this paragraph of one hundred words within one minute, you will have pretty good evidence that you can type between seventy and eighty net words a minute for ten minutes.

the line he can write fluently in ten seconds. He is urged to write just one stroke faster the next time.

There are many variations of the calling-the-throw drill. The student may be asked to write the line on which he is

CALLING-THE-THROW DRILL

Return carriage every 10 seconds.

		WPM
	1. Avoid waste motions.	24
	2. Know your typewriter.	25
	3. You must try to learn.	26
	4. Keep your wrists level.	28
	5. Relax and you can write.	29
	6. Keep the carriage moving.	30
	7. Try to write with fluency.	31
	8. Keep your eyes on the copy.	32
	9. Check your errors carefully.	34
	10. Avoid excessive wrist motion.	35
	11. Never linger on the space bar.	36
	12. Avoid glancing at the keyboard.	37
	13. Analyze your own typing problem.	38
	14. Keep both feet flat on the floor.	40
	15. Throw the carriage; don't push it.	41
	16. Don't sit too close to the machine.	42
	17. Keep your elbows close to your body.	43
	18. Type steadily; avoid jerks and stops.	44
	19. Speed and accuracy are both essential.	45
3/1	20. Type for accuracy as well as for speed.	47
	21. Take your fingers from the keys quickly.	48
3/2	22. Sit as far back in the chair as possible.	49
	23. Never practice doing anything incorrectly.	50
3/5	24. Strike the keys with a quick, light stroke.	52
	25. Concentrate on the material you are writing.	53
	26. Type only as fast as you can type accurately.	54
	27. Do not let your thumb linger on the space bar.	55
	28. Strike the space bar with the right thumb only.	56
3/15	29. Do not erase over the center of your typewriter.	58
	30. Learn to follow directions quickly and precisely.	59
	31. Do not take your eyes from the copy while writing.	60
3/17	32. Listen for the bell to ring at the end of the line.	61
	33. Know how to insert your paper quickly and correctly.	62
3/19	34. Do not let an error upset your feeling of confidence.	64
	35. Learn the use of every feature on the machine you use.	65
3/21	36. Take an interest in typing if you expect success in it.	66
	37. Use your little fingers as pivots to hold home position.	67
3/23	38. No pupil ever learned to type by merely wishing he could.	68
	39. It is as easy to fix good habits as it is to fix bad ones.	70
	40. Insert paper with the left hand; turn it in with the right.	71

41. But the extra time you can give now will count much for you.	72
42. Give every bit of spare time to typing with few or no errors.	73
43. You are to type this drill each day until there are no errors.	74
44. Your instructor will help you to use your practice time wisely.	75
45. You will be striving for good typing that is free from mistakes.	77
46. Each day you are to give five minutes of practice to these lines.	78
47. This drill has five more words than the one you have just written.	79
48. The beginner must create high standards of performance for himself.	80
49. Yes, you can build just about any skill you are willing to work for.	82
50. Every typing room should hold approximately twenty-seven typewriters.	83
51. In typewriting, as in other skill subjects, you must keep right at it.	84
52. Practice these drills outside the classroom when it is at all possible.	85
53. As simple as this paragraph drill may seem to you, it is most effective.	86
54. Accuracy improvement should be sought steadily through the typing course.	88
55. Speed and accuracy may be built at the same time with sufficient practice.	89
56. I once knew a young man who had reached the sixty-word rate in typewriting.	90
57. You may have noticed by this time fewer and fewer easy words are being used.	91
58. In two months he built his speed up to one hundred accurate words per minute.	92
59. A simple exercise on the typewriter is a most effective way of building speed.	93
60. Have the front of the frame of your typewriter even with the edge of your desk.	95
61. The beginner should have appropriate materials with which to drill and practice.	96
62. When you reach one hundred words per minute you are above average in your typing.	97
63. Learners should not be forced or made to practice when they are disgusted with it.	98
64. You will be able to type accurately and proceed to the next drill in seven minutes.	99
65. If you have a desire to be an expert typist, practice often--as most top typists do.	100
66. On the advice of the teacher, the boy entered the amateur class of the state contest.	101
67. Rhythm is still an important factor in the development of typewriting speed, for most.	102
68. Students must use their own resourcefulness and initiative in trying to solve problems.	103
69. The typist is stimulated to try new ways of reacting as he finds the old unsatisfactory.	104
70. Speed drills are made primarily to automatize responses and increase strokings for speed.	105

(*) This page contributed by Mary Ann McClelland.

working six times a minute without an error. If he can do so, he may move on to the next line. This is an excellent device for developing control.

Evaluation

Sample evaluation summary sheets follow on this page and page 99.

Name_____   Date_____

EVALUATION SUMMARY SHEET
Beginning Typewriting

This evaluation is made in consideration of the following course objectives:

Acceptable speed and control: 50 to 60 wpm gross, 5-minute test, one error per minute.

A solid foundation of good typewriting techniques: stroking, complete command of machine, rhythm, manipulative techniques.

Factual information: knowledge of format and design, basic punctuation, word usage, spelling, and other such factors.

Foundations of production: letter styles, stencils, masters, manuscripts, business forms, etc.

Quality: neat appearance, well-balanced page setup, strikeover, erasures, clean type.

Work habits: work station organization, attitudes, operational efficiency.

This is not what is required to pass the course, but what is expected of a good typewriting student.

ITEMS AFFECTING FINAL TERM GRADE	SCORE POINTS
Gross speed: average of best 3 out of 5 trials on 5-minute tests, based on competency achieved during last month of term _____ x 2	
Control: average errors a minute on the above 3 tests (0-.5=100; .6-1.0=80; 1.1-1.5=60; 1.6-2.0=40)	_____
Typewriting technique: (teacher's estimate, percent of 100)	_____
Typewriting technique: (student's own estimate)	_____
Factual information: average of tests taken during term	_____
Factual information: score on final examination	_____
Quality: score based on bulletin board scale (Samples on display range from 20 to 100)	_____
Work habits: teacher's estimate	_____
Preproduction items--20 points for each classification of items completed up to standard.	
Letters, two basic styles _____	
Stencils _____	
Master _____	
Rough draft _____	
Tabulation, simple _____	
Tabulation, complex _____	
Form letter project _____	
TOTAL	_____
Summary score of other special items during term	_____
TOTAL SCORE FOR TERM	_____

LETTER GRADE FOR TERM_____

EVALUATION SUMMARY SHEET
Advanced Typewriting

This evaluation is made in consideration of the following course objectives:

Acceptable speed and control: 60 to 70 wpm gross, 5-minute test, one error
     per minute.
Good techniques are assumed. If deficiencies are not corrected during the
     first month, penalty involved.
Factual information: same standards as beginning typewriting. If defici-
     encies are not corrected during the first month, penalty involved.
Quality: since only usable copy will be considered, it is expected that the
     quality will be in keeping with standards in a modern office.
Production: this is the principal objective of the course.

This is not what is required to pass the course, but what is expected of a
     good typewriting student.

ITEMS AFFECTING FINAL TERM GRADE	SCORE POINTS

Gross speed: average of best 3 out of 5 trials on 5-minute
     tests based on competency achieved during last month of
     term. (Tests with more than one error a minute will not
     be considered, except in speeds above 60 wpm.) _____x 2   _____
Number of mailable letters per hour (130-150 words) _____x 10   _____
Number of pages of manuscript (without footnotes) per hour,
     double spaced _____x 10   _____
Number of invoices per hour _____x 10   _____
Number of 5-minute projects in an hour _____x 10   _____
Other projects _____x ?   _____

OUTPUT FOR TERM

Total output in mailable letters during term _____x 5   _____
Number of 5-minute projects successfully completed _____x 5   _____
Other production achievements _____x ?   _____

- -

Score made on National Business Entrance Typing Tests
     (Teacher will make subjective evaluation.)   _____
Rating on major projects: outside business jobs, for example   _____

TOTAL SCORE FOR TERM   _____

LETTER GRADE FOR TERM_____

Quality of Typewritten Material

Scrapbooks containing samples of excellent typing done
by experienced operators can be used as classroom reference material. Rating charts similar to the well-known
handwriting scales can be posted. The letters on such a
scale would range from very good to very bad. The first
letter on the scale should be a model of neatness, of beauty
of design and arrangement, and of rhythm. The poorest
is usually characterized by these defects: poor placement
(the message is usually crowded near the top of the page,

leaving over three fourths of the sheet blank), the lines are uneven, letters are out of alignment (especially the capitals), the touch is uneven (some impressions dark, others hardly visible), the page gives clear evidence that keys need cleaning, some errors have been corrected by smudgy erasures, and there are many strikeovers. A letter of this type may be of very poor quality and still not have a single error of the kind usually checked in typing classes. Teachers themselves should be able to recognize good typing and should be able to demonstrate the technique by means of which such results may be obtained. Students should be asked to rate their daily work by means of this scale and label their work according to the numbers on this chart before handing in their typewritten material.

Another important objective of beginning typing is to develop in the student a sense of what constitutes good form in typing. The student should be able to arrange the material on the sheet attractively. The typing should be clear and even, and the entire job should have an appearance of neatness. Such basic work habits will provide a foundation upon which advance skills may be built. One businessman reports hiring a secretary who could type "well up in the 60's." Her only fault was that her capitals were out of alignment. He called this to her attention, assuming that a day or so would eradicate the trouble. Finally, after weeks of admonition, she was transferred to another department because she seemed unable to eliminate this difficulty. An elaboration of the word "form" by the teacher will often help to inspire students toward better design.

Handling of Papers and Materials

Office managers in charge of the flow of work put much emphasis on proper placement of paper and supplies. First-semester typewriting is an excellent time to teach effective handling of materials. At the first opportunity this matter can be investigated as a class project, and by experimentation a plan can soon be found that is most efficient for the job at hand. Modern typing texts give specific directions concerning the proper way to insert paper, handle envelopes when addressing, the best carbon paper technique, etc. The teacher should see to it that there is provided a standard place for textbooks and for supplies (paper, erasers, etc.) so that they may be distributed quickly at the beginning of the period and assembled quickly at the close of the period.

Making Assignments

"Aller amfang ist schweer," says an old German proverb, "all beginning is difficult." The secret of making successful assignments is, therefore, to help the student make that beginning, both mental and physical.

On the opening day the students have been working with the "if-it-is-in-the" exercise. In making the assignment the teacher asks them to polish up that which they already know. "Work on it until you are satisfied with it: good rhythm, even touch, good all-around technique, and fair speed." In tabulation assignments or other problem exercises assigned for homework, it helps to just run through the skeleton, so to speak, using x's instead of numbers to give the idea of placement.

Even if typewriters for homework are not available, a great deal can be accomplished through mental gymnastics. A famous golfer once said, "The night before a game I play the course, mentally, just as I plan to play it the next day."

Proofreading

The authors had occasion to watch some typists at work in a local office. "Would you give me a hand, Lucy?" said Betty. Without hesitation, Lucy stopped her work and went over to Betty's desk. Betty handed Lucy the material she had just typed. Lucy followed the script carefully while Betty read from the original. This was not a hasty, let's-get-this-thing-over type of operation. Each one was very serious. When they came to figures, important names, or unusual constructions, Betty read them to Lucy; then Lucy read back again from her copy. On one occasion Lucy said, "Doesn't make sense to me, but maybe it's okay." Betty pushed the intercom button: "Is this really what you want?" Evidently it was, for they went on with their proofreading. When the job was done, Lucy went back to her desk and continued her work. Not a moment was lost. That this was not a new operation could be determined by the routine which indicated that each one knew just what to do. The girls had established a technique of helping each other when it came to the important job of proofreading.

In our typing classes we often let proofreading go without careful checking. Students take a quick look to check their errors, and that's it. Some have learned not to check too carefully. "Why penalize yourself?" said one who evidently knew the score.

We need an entirely different approach. For a change we might not consider the errors at all but have the student's grade depend on his proofreading ability. This type of thing should be preceded by some drill in *how* to proofread, what to look for, etc. Does it follow the copy? Does it make sense? These are the two basic considerations. Names, dates, and figures are particularly important. When it comes to grammar, punctuation, spelling, and word usage, it is not so much a matter of following copy as it is to have the transcript follow good standard usage. There should be one person in every office who is an authority on such matters. Such persons often win quick recognition. Teachers should encourage their students to aim for such a mark.

Composing at the Machine

The following are some techniques that teachers have found useful in teaching students how to compose at the typewriter. The exercises are presented in order of difficulty and are intended as suggestions to encourage the teacher to develop her own interesting, apply-to-the-situation material.

1. My name is ....
   I like typewriting because ....
   After school I plan to ....
2. One student tells a short story. The other students then type the story in their own words, or their reaction to it.

3. Students write letters to friends, typing as much as they can in five minutes. There is no pressure, no check-up on typing quality.
4. The body of a letter is given. Students add a first paragraph thanking the recipient for the order, and a closing paragraph of their own choosing. No check-up on quality.
5. An actual letter needing reply is presented to the class. After a discussion as to what the reply should be, each student types one in his own words. The best letter is put in the mail.

Multiple-Job Projects

The idea of these projects is to train students to move quickly from one job to another with a minimum of confusion. One booklet [11] that more than meets the needs of the most enterprising teacher contains 130 projects. If the booklet is not readily obtainable, the teacher can easily make up her own problems. Care should be taken to make them short so that the average typist can do each job in five minutes or less. Listed below are a few suggestions, each of which can be done easily in five minutes by a student whose gross speed is 40 wpm or more.

1. Type a message on a postal card, address it, and put it in the mail.
2. Same job, but use a double postal card with proper information.
3. Type a short letter from a form letter, making necessary fill-ins.
4. Same job, but make carbon, address envelope, put letter in mail.
5. Type a Ditto master, double space, half page of material.
6. Take above master and run off ten copies; file master.
7. Type stencil, same length as above Ditto—same message can be used.
8. Run off ten copies of above stencil; file stencil.
9. Type invoice of six items, extend, and total.
10. Check figures of ten invoices done by other students.

---

[11] Ruth I. Anderson and Leonard Porter, *130 Basic Typing Jobs* (Englewood Cliffs, New Jersey: Prentice-Hall, Inc., 1960).

11. Arrange work station for project involving carbons, letter-heads, envelopes, etc.; get everything in working order.
12. Make five actual phone calls telling date of certain meeting.
13. Choose partners to help, then proofread two pages of material, checking dates and figures with original.
14. Take a short letter from dictation, transcribe, one carbon, place on teacher's desk for signature. Dictation time not included in the five minutes. (This, of course, is for those who are in transcription.)
15. Take a message to the principal, get a reply, be back in five minutes.

There is practically no end to projects of this kind. Problems of this nature tie in nicely with what happens to be in the school news at the moment, for example, school party, dance, fund drive, and so forth. When these projects are first introduced, it is well not to say anything about a five-minute limit. Record the time it takes each student to do the job assigned. There is great satisfaction for both teacher and student to see a half-hour job shrink to fit the five-minute schedule. It is not unusual to have a student cut her time down from 45 minutes to the standard five minutes. One teacher referred to minutes as "man-hours" and then tabulated the man-hours saved each day.

Letter Typing

Another type of activity that comes near the top of any list of duties is that of typing letters from some basic form. For the most part, the fill-ins or changes that have to be made are of routine nature; however, they can become quite involved. Here is an area that furnishes excellent opportunities for production typing. Letters-per-hour standards are easy to establish. The teacher might want to begin his letters-per-hour projects by having the students do straight copy work from a duplicated set of standard-length letters in order to ascertain the number of mailable copies a student can produce in an hour's time. After the students become familiar with this practice, the problem can be made more realistic by having them fill in addresses, prices, etc., on a letters-per-hour basis.

A class agreed to do a thousand letters for a local civic club charity drive, provided their executives would check the letters for mailability. This they willingly did—and did carefully. The letters that were returned as not mailable were then posted on the bulletin boards. One exceedingly rapid typist did 60 letters. Over half of her letters were returned. No comments were necessary. This did more to improve quality of output than anything else the class might have attempted. Such experiences are the type of thing needed in connection with production typing: much repetition, careful supervision—all in an atmosphere of business-like meaningfulness.

Printed Forms Add Realism to Typing

At a meeting of office executives in Columbus, Ohio, one teacher made the statement that it was difficult for the average typing teacher to get his hands on enough actual business forms so that they could be used in sustained production projects. To this the office manager of a large insurance company replied, "Because so many old forms are being discarded in connection with computerized installations, I venture to say that there are more forms being taken to the city dump than you could use in a year's time." And right he was! During the following week several pick-up trucks stopped at the teacher's building. The drivers wanted to know where to leave "these forms." Two years later the supply had still not been exhausted. In the meantime, thousands of these discarded papers had found their way past the typewriter platen, and, hopefully, given the students an idea of the many types of forms used in offices today.

RESEARCH AND OPINIONS OF EXPERTS

In this part of the chapter we consider some of the research and some opinions on a variety of aspects in the teaching of typewriting. As in other chapters, it is difficult to choose what quotations to use, particularly when several educators express themselves forcefully on the same subject.

Basic Principles

Many writers have given us basic principles to observe in the teaching of typewriting. Dr. Erickson of the University of California advises teachers to consider the following skill learning factors in planning instruction:

1. Active learner participation
2. Specific tasks or goals
3. Simple-to-complex learning progression
4. Motivation
5. Difficulty of the task
6. Tension or anxiety
7. Feeling tone
8. Interest and success
9. Knowledge of results
10. Reinforcement
11. Transfer
12. Evaluation [12]

Teaching the Keyboard

Over the years, Lessenberry has been consistent in his position that the keyboard should not be introduced too quickly—in too large learning segments. The following is his philosophy:

The lessons for teaching the letter keyboard should be organized to avoid the "too much, too soon" danger than comes from trying to cover the keyboard too quickly and the "too little, too late" boredom that comes from introducing the keyboard too slowly.[13]

Typewriting teachers have stated their preference for teaching no more than 2 or 3 new keys a lesson, for covering the entire letter keyboard in 2 or 3 weeks, and for providing

---

[12] Lawrence W. Erickson, "Modes of Instruction and Their Meaning," *Practices and Preferences in Teaching Typewriting*, Monograph 117 (Cincinnati: South-Western Publishing Co., 1967), pp. 12-14.

[13] D. D. Lessenberry, "The Rationale for a Widely Used Sequence of Introducing the Letter Keyboard," *Practices and Preferences in Teaching Typewriting*, Monograph 117 (Cincinnati: South-Western Publishing Co., 1967), p. 17.

periodic review lessons to consolidate the learning as it accumulates.[14]

Four basic principles guide the determination of the sequence of initiating control of the letter keys:

1. Ease with which the reach-stroke can be made by the beginning student so that good stroking facility can be developed at once.
2. Frequency of use of the letter so that a wide range of words can be used for practice.
3. Adjacent keys not to be taught as new reaches in the same lesson (except in the first lesson when teaching the home keys).
4. Keys to be controlled by the same finger, opposite hand, to be taught in different lessons, if possible; and where taught in the same lesson, the sequence to be such as to require different direction for the finger movement.[15]

Standards—Beginning Typewriting

A teacher, in response to a challenge, once brought a class of junior high summer school students up to 40 wpm in eight weeks just to see if it could be done. The 40 wpm represents class average gross on a five-minute straight-copy test with not more than one error a minute. There were 30 students in the class. We must develop basic speed as rapidly as possible—up to 50 or 60 wpm—so we can get into production and problem-solving with basic skills that we can really exploit.

Russon and Wanous [16] give us the following straight-copy standards for the various levels of typewriting instruction. The scales are for 5-minute tests, with one error per minute.

The following scale is for the first semester of a high school typewriting course: (GWAM)

$$\frac{45+}{39-44} \qquad \frac{A}{B}$$

---

[14] *Ibid.*
[15] *Ibid.*, p. 18.
[16] Allien R. Russon and S. J. Wanous, *Philosophy and Psychology of Teaching Typewriting* (2nd ed.; Cincinnati: South-Western Publishing Co., 1972).

$$\frac{32\text{-}38}{22\text{-}31} \qquad \frac{C}{D}$$

The following scale may be used for the second semester of a high school course: (GWAM)

$$\frac{49+}{42\text{-}48} \qquad \frac{A}{B}$$
$$\frac{32\text{-}41}{25\text{-}31} \qquad \frac{C}{D}$$

If a third semester is offered, the following scale may be used: (GWAM)

$$\frac{52+}{47\text{-}51} \qquad \frac{A}{B}$$
$$\frac{40\text{-}46}{35\text{-}39} \qquad \frac{C}{D}$$

For the first semester of college typewriting course, the following scale may be used: (GWAM)

$$\frac{45+}{41\text{-}44} \qquad \frac{A}{B}$$
$$\frac{36\text{-}40}{30\text{-}35} \qquad \frac{C}{D}$$

The speed levels at the end of the second semester of a college typewriting course are as follows: (NWAM)

$$\frac{58+}{52\text{-}57} \qquad \frac{A}{B}$$
$$\frac{46\text{-}51}{40\text{-}45} \qquad \frac{C}{D}$$

For a complete discussion of standards with suggestions of all kinds, the reader is urged to consult Chapter II of Russon and Wanous.

When we are typing to build speed, we should concentrate on speed, using all the know-how at our disposal to do the job; when it is control we are after, then we should put our control-getting devices into action. Later, at a less intense level, the two can be blended into a "cruising speed" operation. West compared typing straight-copy skill with performance-on-the-job type of activity and found the following:

> The characteristically near-zero relationship between speed and errors in straight copy work for those at intermediate levels of skill suggests that the factors that account for fast stroking are different from those that bring about accurate stroking—a finding which suggests that any attempt to build stroking speed and reduce errors at the same time will meet with limited, if any success. The two features of performance are apparently based on different underlying factors.[17]

West discovered another interesting fact. Errors are unpredictable. A person may make many errors on one test and few on another. He may make few errors today and many tomorrow. The errors a person makes on any given single timed writing may or may not be an indication of his typing control. However, speed measured at one time is likely to be as good an index of this person's true speed as speed measured at some other time. "Gross stroking speed is the only measure of straight-copy proficiency with genuine stability and predictive power."[18]

West also says:

> ". . . The low reliability of error scores, it may be added, is another reflection of the great complexity of the factors that have to do with straight-copy accuracy and suggests, as well, that practically everything we have at present by way of accuracy-development materials and procedures is of doubtful value."[19]

---

[17] Leonard J. West, "Some Relationships Between Straight-Copy Typing Skill and Performance on Job-Type Activities," *The Delta Pi Epsilon Journal*, 3 (November, 1960), p. 18.

[18] *Ibid.*, p. 21.

[19] *Ibid.*, p. 22.

Knowledge of Progress

Tonne, Popham, and Freeman [20] offer the following suggestion for indicating knowledge of progress in typewriting speed and control:

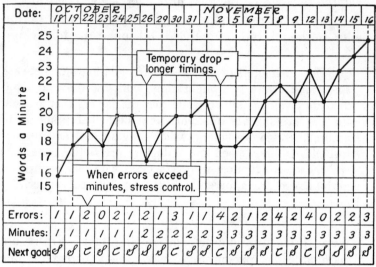

Date:	OCTOBER 18	19	22	23	24	25	26	29	30	31	NOVEMBER 1	2	5	6	7	8	9	12	13	14	15	16
Errors:	/	/	2	0	2	/	2	/	3	/	/	4	2	/	2	4	2	4	0	2	2	3
Minutes:	/	/	/	/	/	/	2	2	2	2	2	3	3	3	3	3	3	3	3	3	3	3
Next goal	S	S	C	S	C	S	S	S	C	S	S	S	C	S	S	S	C	S	C	S	S	S

Graph: Words a Minute (15–25). Labels: "Temporary drop – longer timings." and "When errors exceed minutes, stress control."

Courtesy Rowe, Lloyd, Gregg Typing, New Series, p. 41

TYPEWRITING PROGRESS RECORD

Evaluation

Stewart lists the following suggestions for handling paper work in typing. These have been rephrased to save space.

1. Check students at work rather than the work of the students.
2. Collect only a small percentage of papers for grading.
3. Evaluate some papers with the students during the class hour.
4. Have students proofread and check many of their own papers.
5. Save time in marking and recording work by checking one major detail at a time on all papers.

[20] Herbert A. Tonne, Estelle L. Popham, and M. Herbert Freeman, *Methods of Teaching Business Subjects* (3rd ed.; New York: Gregg Division, McGraw-Hill Book Co., Inc., 1965), pp. 96-97.

6. Systematize the handling of make-up work.

7. Sample student papers instead of doing them all.[21]

Quality in Typewriting

In a study made at Ohio State University, Fleser found the following concerning quality:

Businessmen tend to agree that the following four errors are serious and cause a letter to be unmailable: letters in a word slightly out of line, failure to space between words, incorrect division of a word at the end of the line, and presence of spaces within a word. Business teachers agreed with the businessmen that these four errors were serious.

Businessmen considered these four errors as minor errors: uneven left-hand margin, crowding of letters, inconspicuous strikeover, and too many spaces between words.[22]

Assignments—Priming the Pump

An assignment well made is a lesson half learned. Tate and Ross favor priming the pump:

As four semesters of typewriting are cut to three or two, a great deal of production projects will have to be done outside regularly scheduled classes. . . . Did it ever occur to us that perhaps the practice of outside work in typewriting fell into disrepute because we did not handle it right? Did we plan our classwork so that students were adequately briefed to do such assignments effectively? Did we assign them problems, or did we assign them so many perfect lines of this and that? Did we really habitualize sound techniques before we gave them the responsibility of doing outside projects? Did we explain to them that proper work habits are just as necessary for homework as for classwork? Did we follow up with production tests in class? [23]

---

[21] Jane Stewart, "Managing Paper Work in Typewriting," *Business Education Forum,* 15 (November, 1960), p. 17.

[22] Clare Honaker Fleser, "The Effect Upon Mailability of Ten Typewriting Errors as Judged by Businessmen and Business Teachers" (Master's thesis, Ohio State University, Columbus, 1959). Reported in *The National Business Education Quarterly,* 29 (Fall, 1960), p. 28.

[23] Donald J. Tate and Kenton E. Ross, "College Teachers Take a Look at Typewriting," *Business Education Forum,* 14 (November, 1959), p. 19.

Standards—Advanced Typewriting

Most typing methods books and introductions to regular typing texts give detailed sets of standards. Some indicate a certain letter grade if the student makes a given number of words a minute on a test. Recently in connection with production work there has been a tendency to relate the output standard to the student's basic typing speed.

Douglas, Blanford, and Anderson use the following in relating output to basic typing speed. The following standards are suggested for various types of production jobs:

a. Typing letters	2/3 to 3/4 the basic typing rate
b. Addressing envelopes	50 percent of basic rate or minimum of 2 envelopes a minute (120 to 150 an hour)
c. Typing rough drafts	40 to 50 percent of basic typing rate
d. Manuscripts with footnotes	40 to 50 percent of basic typing rate
e. Manuscripts without footnotes	60 to 75 percent of basic typing rate
f. Tabulations	25 to 50 percent of basic typing rate
g. Stencils	4 single-spaced stencils an hour
h. Transcription from voice recording machines	25 words a minute
i. Typing form letters with envelopes (medium length)	10 an hour [24]

Things My School Didn't Teach Me

Forkner quotes a young office worker and lists all the things she wishes the school had taught her. Here are a few of them:

---

[24] Lloyd V. Douglas, James T. Blanford, and Ruth I. Anderson, *Teaching Business Subjects* (2nd ed.; Englewood Cliffs, New Jersey: Prentice-Hall, Inc., 1965), p. 179.

1. The Use of Previous Reports. I wish I had learned to take that previous report, place it in the typewriter, set my tab stops according to the plan of the report, and then typewrite my report.

2. The Importance of Proofreading. I wish I had learned the importance of it while in school.

3. The Importance of Number Competency. I wish I had learned how to typewrite numbers at a better rate than I was able to do.

4. The Skill of Reading, Editing, and Correcting Material. Another job I have had to do for which I felt I should have had better preparation was the job of typewriting materials from rough draft and at the same time being expected to make sense out of what I was typewriting.

5. The Importance of Erasing Skill. It was suggested to me on the job that I could turn out a great many more letters in an hour if I did not take time to make corrections on the carbon copies.

6. Proper Organization of Materials. I guess one of the most bothersome problems I had to solve when I took this job was how to arrange the materials on my desk so that I would not lose time in assembling papers for typewriting.

7. Acceptable Production Standards. My supervisor pointed out to me that I had addressed less than one envelope a minute, whereas an experienced operator could do 120 to 180 an hour. I needed to analyze the steps I took in addressing each envelope and see if I could improve my rate.

8. How to Analyze a Typewriting Job. I think I would have been spared some embarrassment and certainly I would have been a higher producer if my typewriting teachers had insisted that I analyze each problem I had to do in a step-by-step procedure.

9. Problem-Solving Experiences. I believe teachers teach too little real thinking in typewriting classes. I find I am continually thinking now about whether I can find a better way to do what I have to do.

10. The Value of Repetitive Practice. One final suggestion—would it not be possible for advanced typewriting classes to have more outside work so that students would get

more experiences on actual work that someone is going to use?[25]

SUMMARY

"As a man thinketh in his heart, so is he." Unless the student feels deep down in his heart that he wants to learn to type, the teacher labors in vain. If the student has taken the first step, that of really wanting to learn the subject, then, to be successful, he must have, or the teacher must create within him, a host of other wants or desires: he must *want* to write with good rhythm, to have good control, to acquire advanced speeds, to be neat, to produce good quality, to learn those factual details without which his speed will do little good, and he must want those basic techniques that the expert has found to be essential.

Having made sure of these wants, the teacher needs but to show him the way and provide the right guidance, encouragement, and materials to make it possible for him to do the job.

SELECTED BIBLIOGRAPHY

Anderson, Ruth I., and Leonard Price. *130 Basic Typing Jobs.* Englewood Cliffs, New Jersey: Prentice-Hall, Inc., 1960.

Blackstone, E. G. "How to Speed Up Typewriting Instruction." *The National Business Education Quarterly,* 12 (December, 1943), p. 65.

Clem, Jane E. *Techniques of Teaching Typewriting,* 2nd ed. New York: Gregg Division, McGraw-Hill Book Co., Inc., 1955.

Douglas, Lloyd V., James T. Blanford, and Ruth I. Anderson. *Teaching Business Subjects,* 2nd ed. Englewood Cliffs, New Jersey: Prentice-Hall, Inc., 1965.

Dvorak, August, *et al. Typewriting Behavior.* New York: American Book Co., 1936.

Emerging Content and Structure of Business Education, Eighth Yearbook of the National Business Education Association. Washington, D.C.: National Business Education Association, 1970.

---

[25] Hamden L. Forkner, "What I Wish I Had Learned About Typewriting," *Business Education Forum,* 13 (November, 1958), p. 7.

Erickson, Lawrence W. "Teaching the Number Row." *The Journal of Business Education*, XXXII (October, 1956), pp. 23-25.

Fleser, Clare Honaker. "The Effect Upon Mailability of Ten Typewriting Errors as Judged by Businessmen and Business Teachers." Master's thesis, Ohio State University, Columbus, 1959. Reported in *The National Business Educational Quarterly*, 29 (Fall, 1960), p. 28.

Forkner, Hamden L. "What I Wish I Had Learned About Typewriting." *Business Education Forum*, 13 (November, 1958), p. 7.

Grubbs, Robert L., and Frederick J. Gaskin. "Typewriting: The Individualizers in Typewriting Instruction." *Business Education Forum*, 26 (February, 1972), pp. 44-45.

Harms, Harm. "Standards for Beginning Typewriting." *The Journal of Business Education*, XX (February, 1945), p. 23.

Hoffer, Barbara. "Television in the Beginning Typewriting Class." *The Balance Sheet*, LII (March, 1971), pp. 252-253.

Lamb, Marion M. *Your First Year of Teaching Typewriting*, 2nd ed. Cincinnati: South-Western Publishing Co., 1959.

Lessenberry, D. D. "The Teaching of Typewriting." *Sixth Yearbook of the National Commercial Teachers Federation*. Bowling Green, Kentucky: National Business Teachers Association, 1940, p. 455.

Lessenberry, D. D., T. James Crawford, and Lawrence W. Erickson. *Manual for 20th Century Typewriting*, 8th ed. Cincinnati: South-Western Publishing Co., 1962.

Lindsay, Vaughnie J. "Psychological Concepts for Motor Skill Development in Typewriting." *The Delta Pi Epsilon Journal*, 3 (May, 1969), pp. 21-32.

Lloyd, Alan C. "Building More Speed in Advanced Typewriting." *Business Teacher*, 46 (January-February, 1969), pp. 8-9.

_____. "Typing: Performance Goals and Typewriting." *Business Education Forum*, 25 (February, 1971), pp. 48-50.

Miller, Harlan B. "A Businessman Takes a Look at Typewriting." *Business Education Forum*, 14 (November, 1959), p. 9.

Rhodes, George S. "A Plan to Boost Numbers Typing Skill." *The Journal of Business Education,* XLVI (February, 1971), p. 218.

Robinson, Jerry W. "Skill-Comparison Activities in Typewriting." *The Balance Sheet,* L (February, 1969), pp. 244-250.

Robinson, Jerry W. (ed.). *Practices and Preferences in Teaching Typewriting,* Monograph 117. Cincinnati: South-Western Publishing Co., 1967.

_____. *Strategies of Instruction in Typewriting.* Cincinnati: South-Western Publishing Co., 1972.

Stewart, Jane. "Managing Paper Work in Typewriting." *Business Education Forum,* 15 (November, 1960), p. 17.

Tate, Donald J., and Kenton E. Ross. "College Teachers Take a Look at Typewriting." *Business Education Forum,* 14 (November, 1959), p. 19.

Terry, George R. *Principles of Management.* Homewood, Illinois: Richard D. Irwin, Inc., 1968.

Tonne, Herbert A., Estelle L. Popham, and M. Herbert Freeman. *Methods of Teaching Business Subjects,* 3rd ed. New York: Gregg Division, McGraw-Hill Book Co., Inc., 1965.

Tonne, Herbert A., and Louis C. Nanassy. *Principles of Business Education,* 4th ed. New York: Gregg Division, McGraw-Hill Book Co., Inc., 1970.

Valencia, Artilano A. "Flexible-Modular Lab Arrangements in Typing." *Business Education World,* XLIX (May, 1969), pp. 9-11.

Wanous, S. J. "The Need for Motivation in Typewriting." *Business Education Forum,* 12 (November, 1957), pp. 11-13.

_____, and Allien R. Russon. *Philosophy and Psychology of Teaching Business Subjects,* 2nd ed. Cincinnati: South-Western Publishing Co., 1972.

West, Leonard J. "Some Relationships Between Straight-Copy Typing Skill and Performance on Job-Type Activities." *The Delta Pi Epsilon Journal,* 3 (November, 1960), p. 18.

Winger, Fred E., and Russell J. Hosler. "Seven Guides for Typing Drills." *Business Education World,* L (January-February, 1970), pp. 16-20.

Chapter 4

SHORTHAND

BASIC PRINCIPLES OF TEACHING SHORTHAND

"There won't be any shorthand tomorrow," said a dictation-transcription machine salesman twenty years ago. The echoes of that prediction have continued until today. Gibson, for example, says:

> The teaching of shorthand will be affected, too. . . . Most dictation will be done on dictation machines of one type or another. . . . But of even greater consequence to typists and stenographers, and to accountants and book-keepers, may be the growing practice of sending paper and magnetic tapes, cards, or other media by mail in place of a printed copy.[1]

It seems that in 1889, Thomas A. Edison predicted that the end of shorthand was not far away because of the invention of the phonograph.

But there are other points of view. Tonne says:

> It would be not only unwise but contrary to all the evidence to assume that shorthand will drop to a negligible subject in the secondary schools. All the evidences of job needs as found in the newspapers and employment agencies and the eagerness with which even marginally competent stenographic students are hired indicates the contrary.[2]

---

[1] E. Dana Gibson, "Automation and Business Education," *Business Education Forum*, 14 (January, 1960), p. 13.

[2] Herbert A. Tonne, "The Present and Future of Shorthand," *Business Education Forum*, 15 (October, 1960), p. 11.

It seems that the demand for shorthand has not decreased in the "soaring sixties." At a recent (1970) meeting in Houston of business teachers and representatives of the U.S. Employment Service, the following statement was made:

> We have almost given up trying to do anything about calls for shorthand writers; the demand is so great and the supply is almost nonexistent.

The present trend of one-year shorthand programs does little to better the situation. Zoubek [3] lists survey after survey to show the desperate need for shorthand writers. Wanous quotes the *Wall Street Journal* stating that the shortage of stenographers and secretaries is one of the most serious manpower problems faced by American business today. [4]

For the most part, teachers are doing a good job in the teaching of shorthand. For the most part, also, at one time or another, about everything that needs to be said to enable a teacher to do a good job has been said. Now and then, however, the experienced teacher does not apply the knowledge that is available, while the beginning teacher has not yet had an opportunity to digest and use the materials that are available.

The purpose of this chapter is, therefore, to give a quick review of the old war horses, the time-tested principles and techniques of good shorthand teaching—psychologically sound and philosophically in line with desirable objectives. The reader will no doubt agree with all of them. The authors once compiled a bibliography of 600 references on shorthand and transcription. A sampling of 100 readings from this list showed that approximately 95 percent, either by direct statement or by the tone of their writings, indicated that they favored the principles listed in this chapter.

If the teacher uses these, he can't go far wrong in teaching shorthand. If he follows these, he need not fear a supervisor or visitor who might wish to observe his class. There

---

[3] Charles E. Zoubek, "Shorthand on the Way Out, Hardly!" *Business Education World*, XLI (November, 1960), p. 3.

[4] S. J. Wanous, "Let's Break the 'Egghead' Stranglehold on Business Education," *The Balance Sheet*, XLII (November, 1960), p. 104.

are a thousand details that the perfectionist might want to consider—one can never learn them all—but any teacher can shape his teaching to conform to the basic principles listed in the following sections. Should he omit very many of these basic guide lines, it doesn't matter how many details he does right; he will still be wrong. If he *does* conform to these principles, he will, in our opinion, do a good job of teaching shorthand.

Shorthand is Easy to Learn

The often-used first-day statement of the "tough" instructor, "Students, you are not going to find this course easy. In my classes I expect——," has no place in a shorthand class. Our purpose is not to show the students how much we know and how little they know; rather it is to show them that with the usual amount of study and practice in a brief time they, too, will be writing as well as we do. If the teacher sets the stage so that the students go home from the first lesson actually writing more rapidly than they can in longhand, he has won the first round. (See page 143 for the story of a class that went home after the first session of shorthand bragging that they had written 60 wpm.)

Students Must Experience Success

A shorthand teacher once had the diabolical urge to see what would happen to a new class if he arranged matters so that not a single student would experience success during the first meeting of the group. It was a night-school course in transcription—stenographers and secretaries from downtown who had come to the university to brush up their shorthand. The teacher took a letter from some text, a letter that had been used to illustrate *what not to use* in the early stages of transcription. There were over 50 error possibilities in the letter. The material was dictated at about 100 wpm. "After all," said the teacher, "this is an advanced class, the office is paying you for writing shorthand, so one can assume that you know *some* shorthand."

The bell rang before they completed their assignment and, incidentally, before the teacher could tell them it was just an experiment. A more depressed group would be hard to find. "Oh, well," thought he, "I'll fix it up with them when they come on Thursday. Then I'll give them something they *can* do, brag them up, everybody will be happy, and we'll go on from there." The trouble was that, even though they had paid their fees, only half of the class came back. Phone calls and explanations were of no avail. The damage was irreparable!

It is the teacher's business to so set the stage that each student will experience some measure of success, without which there can be but little progress. "Nothing succeeds like success" is a trite expression, but many of us have learned from experience that *success is crucial!* How the teacher can make sure that every student finds some degree of success will be shown later in the chapter.

Success does something to the human organism. It turns the pessimist into an optimist. It changes the frown to a smile. It throws into the blood stream of the tired, listless person a new supply of energy and produces effects that are often startling. In United States Steel, Andrew Carnegie paid Charles M. Schwab one million dollars a year to manage the business because Schwab had that peculiar ability to bring out the best in people. He recognized their successes in little things, and soon they were able to achieve success in big things. The clever teacher, the good teacher, knows how to tap this reserve.

Students Must Read, Read, Read

Another principle that has been documented almost to the point of excess is that reading in shorthand is *most important.* (See page 167.) What shorthand teacher is not familiar with the "reading approach" introduced by Leslie! Current practice differs as to the amount of class time that should be given to it, but all agree that in the learning of shorthand, reading *is* important. There are cases showing that shorthand was learned almost entirely by reading alone. Businessmen are requesting shorthand writers who can read back fluently because more and more revision work is being done while the material is in the shorthand stage.

How the teacher can get his students to do homework in reading and how he can check the reading of an entire class in three minutes and yet have each person read are taken up under techniques in developing good reading habits on page 146.

All Students Must Make Progress

It is not unusual for an instructor who is teaching an adult evening class in shorthand for the first time to exclaim, "There are some students in this class who have had shorthand before! I thought these were supposed to be beginners! What shall I do?"

In his 20 years of post-high school shorthand teaching one of the authors has had only one class in which *all* the students were absolute beginners. At all other times—college, business college, adult vocational programs, day, evening—the classes were mixed. Whether teachers like it or not, this seems to be the *normal* state of affairs. If a teacher of an adult shorthand group should happen to have a homogeneous class, he should consider it a bit of heaven and then get ready for the next inning in which he will most certainly have to have effective techniques that will enable him to handle two and even three groups at the same time and do a good job. (See page 147.)

Words Must Be Presented in Contextual Form

The cruelest thing a teacher can do to a shorthand class is to give the students a list of words, tell them to "learn them," and dismiss the class. It is the teacher's job to make learning easy—students can do it the difficult way without the teacher. The teacher's knowledge of psychology should make him an expert on how the human organism learns to recognize and write new words. He should be eager to organize his class so that a given body of material is learned with the least effort, in the shortest time, and is retained the longest. In shorthand it means learning brief forms and other new words in context.

In the section on techniques, illustrations are given showing how this can be done. In addition, these very techniques can help to boost shorthand class morale, help the students with their English, give variety and interest to the program because the dictation material used has to do with the things that are current and of interest to the student. (See page 148 for techniques on presenting brief forms in context.)

Daily Realization of Progress

The growth in shorthand power is often so gradual that the student is not aware of the progress he is making. He becomes discouraged and has a feeling that he isn't getting anywhere. It's like riding in an airplane. It is difficult to realize while soaring at 35,000 feet in a jet that the plane is traveling at 600 miles an hour; but when the jet comes in for a landing, and we see the trees and houses whiz by, we become aware of speed. So it is with shorthand. We need to give our students landmarks by which they can estimate their speed, by which they can tell the progress they are making. (See page 149.) Only by knowing where he is now can the student set proper aspiration levels for himself for tomorrow.

On page 149 a procedure is outlined whereby it is possible for a teacher to check the progress of his students in such areas as fluency in reading, speed in taking dictation, knowledge of new vocabulary and brief forms, and the quality of the students' shorthand notes. The motto is: Check-up daily, but test only when necessary.

Provide Effective Daily Classroom Procedures

In business and industry each day's work is somewhat different, but the working pattern remains the same; that is, until new research establishes a better way of doing the job. In the classroom the student should be familiar with the way things operate so that he can get down to business as quickly as possible. There should be no question as to the "machinery" of the skill-building lesson. (See page 168.)

A teacher should be able to justify every minute of his classroom teaching time. Each three-, five-, or ten-minute segment should do a specific thing, and the teacher should know what it is he wants to do with that time. (See page 152 for a sample lesson with justification for each segment of the period.)

No matter what the plan of operation used in the classroom, the keynote to remember always, according to Himstreet,[5] is participation, stimulation, variation, and co-operation. These four words, with all the meanings that have been attached to them, in the hands of an enthusiastic and vitally alive teacher are certain to produce results.

Successful Teaching Requires an Enthusiastic Teacher

Some people are naturally enthusiastic. It matters not what the subject, they have that effervescent urge to say something, and they want the world to know it. People often make fun of a person who rides a hobby, who is forever talking about the merits of his subject-matter area. We may have to tone him down at a faculty meeting and make him settle for half of his original demands, but he is liked. It is easy to whittle down a man's enthusiasm, but it takes dynamite to build it up in a person who does not have it. A teacher must have enthusiasm. A shorthand teacher should not be afraid of overselling his subject. Sharpe, to quote just one of a hundred who have written on the subject, says, "Few things promote success in the teaching of shorthand more than enthusiasm and interest on the part of the teacher." [6] Enthusiasm is not high pressure.

Psychologists agree that when too much pressure is applied to the human organism, one can expect all sorts of defense mechanisms to go into action. When a person can no longer cope with a situation, he blames others, becomes belligerent, crawls into his shell, etc. That applies to both student and teacher.

---

[5] William C. Himstreet, "Shorthand Can Be Taught in Less Time," *Business Education Forum*, 9 (October, 1954), p. 17.

[6] Hollie W. Sharpe, "A Few Essentials for Teaching Shorthand and Transcription Successfully," *Business Education Forum*, 11 (October, 1956), p. 17.

If an administrator notices that a teacher who was enthusiastic is daily becoming less and less so, he should begin to look around. Dwindling enthusiasm, like a falling barometer, is a sure sign that something is wrong. "It could be," a University of Maine graduate student once remarked, "six classes, a study hall, two committees, a club, a ticket taker at basketball games, those never-ending duplicating jobs, parent-teachers' meetings, and—enthusiasm, did you say? Why, I'm thankful if I can drag this carcass from class to class!"

Chalkboard Demonstrations Must Inspire Confidence

A foreman once remarked to a student who was working his way through college, "Why do you pass yourself off as a carpenter when you can't saw a straight line?" No person has a right to pass himself off as a shorthand teacher if he can't write shorthand and write it well. Many of the techniques recommended in this chapter presuppose that the teacher can read and write shorthand fluently. If a teacher is not satisfied with his writing ability, we suggest that he work through a set of tapes or other recorded dictation.[7] Better still, he should work through the series and write the copy on the chalkboard, thus learning the shorthand and developing the ability to demonstrate at the same time.

Many teachers suffer through years of inadequate presentations when they could be masters of the situation by several months of concentrated effort. The teacher who knows his shorthand can take his nose out of the book and enjoy teaching. Douglas, Blanford, and Anderson sum the matter up as follows:

> It is not enough for the shorthand teacher to tell the students how to write shorthand or even to write isolated outlines on the board. He should be able to demonstrate to his students the art of taking dictation.[8]

---

[7] Mary Ellen Oliverio, "Selected Aids for Shorthand Transcription," *Business Education Forum*, 12 (January, 1958), p. 29.

[8] Lloyd V. Douglas, James T. Blanford, and Ruth I. Anderson, *Teaching Business Subjects* (2nd ed.; Englewood Cliffs, N.J.: Prentice-Hall, Inc., 1965), p. 200.

Transcriber's Shorthand Need Not Be Perfect

Mistakes are a natural part of the shorthand classroom experience. "Nontechnitis" applies to both the teacher and the student. A teacher in this frame of mind will expect his students to make certain deviations from the standard book shorthand. Research has established that a person can make a 95 percent correct transcript from 71 percent correct shorthand notes. Perfect shorthand is not an absolute must in doing a good job. In a teaching atmosphere reflecting this point of view, students will be encouraged to call attention to irregularities in the teacher's chalkboard shorthand. The teacher should welcome students' comments and center the discussion around some "do's" and "don't's" of correct shorthand. It might be said, however, that a teacher's shorthand should not be sloppy and should, perhaps, deviate not more than 5 percent from the norm. This has to do with contextual material; words and phrases and preview material should, of course, be accurate. If the teacher is relaxed and enjoys teaching, the students will relax and enjoy learning.

A word of caution is in order here. It has been one teacher's experience, obtained from dictating to many different stenographers and secretaries covering a span of over 20 years, that one just can't write "any old way" and get away with it. When the chips are down, when the material is difficult, the "who-cares,-just-so-you-can-read-it" steno finds herself in deep trouble. In the classroom it has been found that when the student drops below 75 percent of the standard, she begins to get into difficulty. (See Dr. Pullis' study cited at the end of this chapter.)

Classroom Atmosphere Should Be Free From Fear

It does not help much if we tell our students, "Relax, don't be nervous!" and then proceed to do the very things that cause tension: overemphasize grades, test when we should be teaching, dictate new material without proper preview, show by our actions that we are tense ourselves (not properly prepared, perhaps), maintain a hard-boiled, you-get-this-or-else expression throughout the period. There are hundreds of other ways to create tension, but failure to have a proper appreciation of the principle stated on page 125 is perhaps the greatest fear developer of all.

Students Must Want to Learn

Volumes have been written on motivation. All this material points to the same conclusion: Unless a student really *wants* to learn a certain subject, our best efforts are likely to be in vain. As shorthand teachers, we need to pull all the stops to create enthusiasm for shorthand and an urge to learn it. We can create a desire to learn shorthand by having some of our graduates visit the class and talk about their work; we can point to ads in the newspapers listing good jobs for shorthand writers; and we can show them what a joy it is to be able to write shorthand as we make frequent demonstrations on the board. But by putting into practice the basic principles of good shorthand teaching and learning, the teacher will have done all that is generally necessary to keep the fires of enthusiasm burning at full blast. "If the teacher enters the classroom promptly, full of enthusiasm and energy, the class tends to respond in an alert, vigorous manner." [9]

Accelerated Final Learnings Require Great Effort

Learning takes time to jell. New material can be learned thoroughly the day it is presented, but at the expense of terrific effort; however, this same material can be learned with much less worry and pressure if learned partially the first time and then reviewed for several days until the new vocabulary becomes a foundation that the student can use for the next assignment.

How often do teachers become exasperated on a Monday when the students seem to have forgotten everything taught them on Friday! At such times it is difficult for teachers to realize that this forgetting, too, is normal. Like it or not, that's the way the human organism works. Just as the same dress often looks new because of a different

---

[9] *Ibid.,* p. 201.

collar and accessories, so the same vocabulary will sparkle with new interest when presented on another occasion in context with a different theme.

According to the principles that Dale Carnegie expounds, it should be possible to match the names and faces of every person in one's class on the *very first day.* Anyone who has tried it, however, knows that the mental effort it takes is hardly justified by the achievement; for without effort, one knows the names anyway by the end of the first week. If a teacher is reluctant to tax herself to this extent, why should she expect it of the shorthand student?

Students Should Use Their Own Shorthand

To be effective, learning must have real, experiential meaning to the student. In the discussion of contextual learning, the use of the student's own material for dictation purposes is suggested. To add additional interest and to underscore the idea that shorthand is something he can use in daily living, the student should be encouraged to take advantage of his own shorthand whenever possible: Use it to outline assignments or duties to be performed during the day, to make up grocery lists, to keep a diary, and to take class notes. The fact that these notes will be partly in longhand does not matter. As time goes on, the longhand will disappear.

Just as learning how to compose at the typewriter is valuable to the typing student, so is learning how to think in shorthand important to the shorthand student. There is something fascinating about transferring thoughts from the brain to the shorthand notebook. Letters written in shorthand often are more fluent, have better style, and are far more interesting than those written in longhand. One veteran shorthand writer has observed that after several hours of composing in shorthand, his own ability to take dictation has also improved. Research in this area may bring to light something of value to the shorthand teacher.

Eliminate Learning Blocks

It is indeed a fascinating sight at a football game to watch the blockers take out the opposition so that the runner may have an open path for his touchdown drive. The effective shorthand teacher removes all possible learning blocks in order that the student can proceed at the most efficient rate to his touchdown—to become a good shorthand writer.

In his zeal to do a good job, or because of a lack of knowledge of how the organism learns, a teacher may often block the student's progress and cause many additional, unnecessary drives. In some cases he may prevent the touchdown altogether. We are referring to such learning blocks as fear and tension, too much emphasis on accuracy, too much attention to unusual words, drawing versus fluency in writing, too difficult dictation material, poor work habits and poor handling of writing tools, much criticism and little praise, and in general allowing the students to form patterns not tolerated by the professional—habits the student will have to break when he reaches a certain level of proficiency or be content to remain on a mediocre plateau.

We are fortunate that it is the nature of the human organism to grow, to mature, to learn, to develop. If left alone, if no impediments are placed in its path, learning follows a curve about like that pictured below.

If a block is allowed to remain in the path of a learner, the block will tend to slow the curve from its natural devel-

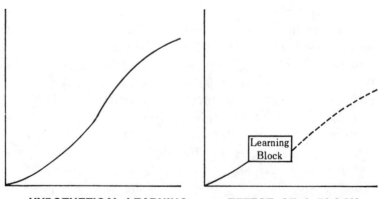

HYPOTHETICAL LEARNING CURVE

EFFECT OF A BLOCK ON LEARNING CURVE

opment. It is the duty of the teacher to anticipate blocks and to eliminate them before they do damage.

Provide a Democratic, Efficient Classroom

In a well-organized classroom, students share in the responsibility to get the work done. A teacher who insists on doing everything himself robs his students of an opportunity of getting practice in democratic action. In one school the teacher had placed an extra desk in a front corner of the room. Each week a different student took his turn at being chairman for the week. Sitting at this desk gave the student an idea of what it might be like to hold an important secretarial position. In addition, this teacher appointed a class secretary. The chairman and secretary assisted with the routine work of the classroom.

Assignments Should Tie in With Objectives

An assignment that does not clearly make a contribution to the basic objectives of the course as the student sees them is apt to cause resentment. The student has a right to know where he is going and that all the energy he is asked to expend is helping him to get where he wants to go. Therefore, the assignments should not only be clear and meaningful to the student—in writing on the board, if possible—but should also show how this work will contribute to the next day's work.

An interesting variation is to have the students themselves make the assignment. On such occasions students are likely to challenge each step with "Is that necessary?" or "Why do we have to do that?" If the questions cannot be answered, the work has no part in the assignment. On the farm in the winter time it is customary to pour some water in the top of the pump to get it started. This is called "priming the pump." In shorthand, too, we need to "prime the pump"—an assignment that starts the students on their work for tomorrow, gets them in the mood, and makes a valuable contribution to the learning demands for the next lesson. (See page 169 on making assignments.)

Spelling in the Beginning is Important

Although it may be difficult to find the exact psychological principle undergirding this concept, there seems to be something in the spelling aloud of shorthand words in the beginning stages of the course that conditions the organism to the fluent writing of sounds according to certain principles found later on in the course. This spelling builds an association between the sound of the word and the kinesthetic action required in writing. What actually goes on, we do not know. We do know that spelling aloud in the proper setting, with the proper associations, does facilitate the writing from sound and does pay dividends later when the student is required to take new-material dictation. (See page 170 for opinions of others about spelling as a shorthand learning technique.)

Use the Gestalt Approach

A photographer once took a picture of a lady in a blue dress. When he showed her the finished product, her remark was, "There's something wrong with your camera. That's not the color of my dress. Why, look at that collar, it looks pink; it should be white." She was thinking of the dress as it appeared to her in the mirror. When the picture was taken, she was standing near a bright red door. The dress "borrowed" some of the red from the door. So it is with shorthand. Every character taught borrows something from its surroundings. Whenever possible, the teacher should give the character the "setting" it will eventually have. Then, if the student wishes to remove the letter from this setting for a minute to give it careful scrutiny, all well and good; but the beginning and end should find the new letter in a suitable environment. The letter "A," for example, should not be presented just as "A," but as it looks in "Mary," or better still, in "Mary made a cake."

Have a Systematic First-Day Procedure

All lessons should be well planned, but the first-day outline should involve some extra-special planning. Everything used should be sure fire. This is no time for experimenting. The method a teacher wishes to employ on the first day depends, of course, on his belief regarding the various approaches. If he believes in an extreme version of the reading approach, his first lesson will perhaps follow quite closely the suggestions given by Leslie; if he believes that reading and writing should go hand in hand right from the start, then he will need a different first-day plan for his class. A sample first-day lesson plan that might be of help to the reading-and-writing approach teacher is presented on page 143, "Shorthand Is Easy."

Use Care in Selecting Material for Dictation

Almost any material found in textbooks today is suitable for reading purposes, provided it is used in the lesson for which it is intended. Great care, however, must be used in selecting material for dictation. At this stage, it should be familiar, easy, meaningful to the student, and well previewed. An observant teacher will be constantly on the alert for anything that might act as a brake to fluent writing. Generally speaking, the most frequently used words should be introduced first. Most textbook writers have taken this into account in the organization of their materials. The teacher should not be tempted to introduce uncommon words of his own just because they happen to illustrate the principle being used at the moment.

In his first attempt at teaching shorthand, a teacher located all the words he could find illustrating the "ulate" principle. The list was a dandy. He was proud of it. He was happy, too, to see the principal when he came in. He was well prepared that day. That is, he *was* happy until the principal said, "Even if they all live to be a hundred, they still won't use all those words!" How quickly the principal had put his finger on a weak spot in this man's teaching.

Don't Teach Rules for Rules' Sake

At a recent convention a veteran business teacher told this story: "When Dad sold the old home place, he asked me to get a trunk which dated back to my high school days. In it I found evidence of the method my teacher had used in shorthand many years before. I found two notebooks: one labeled *Rules*, the other, *Dictation*. It seemed that I had failed miserably in the part of the course having to do with *Rules*, whereas I did fine in *Dictation*. I also found the final examination paper. The section having to do with rules was marked 'F.' On the back of the paper was the following comment by the teacher: 'I am passing you in this course, although perhaps I should not. In ability to take dictation you are good, very good; and your transcription, I must say, is also good; everything else, however, is bad, very bad.' "

Gregg himself once said, "When I first taught shorthand, I, too, made much ado about rules. Then gradually I began doing less and less with them. The less I did, the more fluent became the writing of my students." For many years now the authors have said little about rules. When a student asks a question where a statement of a rule will help, it is given. When the rule will help tie together a list of words on the board, there is no objection to using the rule. If a student is having difficulty and a rule will help, the rule is used.

Evaluation Should Relate to Objectives

In adult classes, some of the best students are often the auditors. They have no grade to worry about; they simply want to learn to write shorthand. They usually reach their objective and are happy about it. Most school systems, however, require teachers to give each person a mark of achievement for the course. This is not too difficult if certain principles of evaluating progress are kept in mind.

Testing should do as little harm as possible to student progress. Students should be learning and reviewing even while being tested. Testing should be in terms of the objectives set up for the course. Business teachers, as well as those in the general academic area, have often been accused of pointing their teaching toward one objective and then testing for another. Formulating a fine set of objectives is easy; even teaching in the hope of attaining these objectives is also relatively easy; but evaluating these higher-level learning outcomes is often difficult. It has been said that the more important the outcome, the more difficult it is to measure or evaluate. Perhaps that is why we often concentrate on trivia when it comes to evaluating our work. Results of tests should, therefore, be weighed in accordance with the importance of the element in question. For example, a score on a word list is of less importance than ability to take dictation and transcribe.

Students should have a share in planning the evaluation procedure. An example of an evaluation procedure and justification for each part is given on page 154.

ADVANCED SHORTHAND AND TRANSCRIPTION

At one time students with instruction in only basic shorthand went directly into office work. When it became obvious that these graduates were inadequately prepared, schools began to offer arrangements which included practical dictation. From these humble beginnings emerged modern transcription instruction: well-developed terminal programs, experienced teachers to handle them, and a wealth of materials designed to produce the best possible results.[10]

The present trend is to give more time to transcription and less to basic shorthand. Teachers are competing with one another in their race to teach the basic principles as rapidly as possible. In practice, the time allotted to each is about equal. If there is a two-year course, the first year is devoted to basic shorthand and the second year to advanced shorthand and transcription. In some cases—assuming that the students can type—there is no break at all. Transcription is started the first day that the shorthand class meets.

Although there are some "quickie" systems now on the market that are sold primarily for their personal-use appeal, there is a general agreement that shorthand cannot be justified for personal use. It follows, therefore, that a basic course in shorthand without that vital second part—transcription—cannot be justified. The purpose of devoting so many hours of intensive study to shorthand fundamentals is that the skill may be used in transcription.

---

[10] "Transcription" refers here to the process of producing usable typewritten copy from shorthand notes.

Transcription Must Be Taught

Transcription must be taught, not just "timed." The fact that a subject so complicated, demanding such high-level skills, should ever have been left to a trial-and-error process of learning, is difficult to understand. On few points do we find more general agreement than on the concept that transcription needs the full attention of a well-qualified teacher.

Considerable space has been taken to establish the foregoing point. It is done with the feeling that if the teacher is really aware of the importance of transcription, he will not be so apt to treat it lightly. A student in a methods class once remarked, "Transcription! Why all this fuss? What's there to know about transcription? I dictate, they type it, we check it, and that's it. They go to work anyway before we get half started, so what's the difference?"

Students seldom learn unless they sense a need. (The same goes for teachers.) As stated before, students practice because they *want* to learn; they do not necessarily learn because they practice. Unless the teacher is convinced that he *needs* to know the materials available in transcription, that he *needs* to know some techniques that have proved helpful to others, the material which follows is of little value.

Introduction to Transcription

Transcription needs to be introduced with great care. Every possible block must be taken away so that all that is left in the assignment to puzzle the student is the sheer skill of translating familiar shorthand symbols into equally familiar typewritten words. It often helps to have the teacher compose the first few transcription paragraphs from familiar and interesting incidents that have happened around school. Those teachers using the methods advocated earlier in this chapter on beginning shorthand have by this time a whole collection of easy, student-compiled paragraphs, used at that time for speed building, but which can now be used to introduce transcription. If these are not available, paragraphs built around the coming school dance, play, or football game might serve the purpose. The sentence structure of the paragraphs should be simple; the format, full-length line, double spaced. There should be no words that the student cannot spell. The only punctuation mark should be the terminal period. If possible, the student should type this exercise from print several times so that he can "keep the carriage moving" when typing from his shorthand notes. Even so, on the first few trials there will be the typical "mad" for "made" and "gat" for "gate." This type of error is to be expected. It requires no special attention. It will disappear in a day or so without any corrective drill.

Students should transcribe these exercises several times until they get the feel of writing from shorthand notes. If introduced carefully, students will form the opinion that transcription is going to be easy, that it is fun. Each succeeding exercise should be presented in the same careful manner. Exercises should be increased in length and difficulty only as the students develop power to handle them. Rather than pick materials carelessly and then check all the errors made by the students in their initial attempts to transcribe, the teacher should set the stage so that the student will not make many errors. Thus, with careful guidance the student passes through the introductory phase of transcription and is ready for transcription proper.

It Takes Time to Learn Transcription

The literature of business education indicates that the teachers are competing with one another to teach basic shorthand in less time. This is a worthy objective, but we should not encourage the teacher or the student to cut short the time for transcription. One executive reports the following incident:

I hired a girl who could write shorthand well and who could type, but who had not had a formal course in transcription. I temporarily assigned her to other duties until she could complete a standard course in transcription on company time. I was well repaid for the cost involved. When she came back to the office as a stenographer, the difference in her ability to handle this level of office work was amazing. Gone were the days when she constantly interrupted everyone who would listen to her with "How do you spell this? How do you punctuate that? Do you underscore this title?" etc.

It is easy to tell the difference between an entering employee who has mastered a good transcription text and a person who has just done some transcribing as a part of his shorthand course, using only the basic shorthand text as material.

The number of details and factual, technical, and format information presented in a standard transcription text is enormous. The study of this information should be a part of every secretary's equipment.

Importance of Good Transcription Materials

A thorough job of teaching advanced shorthand and transcription requires the necessary tools, the most important of which is the transcription textbook. A good text will take into consideration all the links in the transcription chain, and most texts will automatically consider the techniques now generally recommended in the literature of business education.

Most writers advocate that the teacher should occasionally compare the student's typing speed from print with his speed when typing from shorthand book plates and from his own shorthand. A student who can type 40 wpm from print might be expected to transcribe about 35 wpm from shorthand plates and perhaps 30 wpm from his own shorthand notes. If there is a wide gap in speed attainments, the teacher should try to find the reason and attempt to correct it.

The student's ability to proofread and transcribe can be strengthened by the use of actual rough-draft samples collected by the teacher and students. Balsley and Wanous [11] list several excellent proofreading exercises. Punctuation exercises, word usage materials, spelling, helpful hints on

---

[11] Irol Whitmore Balsley and S. J. Wanous, *Shorthand Transcription Studies* (4th ed.; Cincinnati: South-Western Publishing Co., 1968), p. 8.

good office procedures, and office-style dictation can be illustrated with the use of proofreading, transcribing, and typing material. One hundred percent accuracy is imperative.

A teacher who does not insist on a good transcription text with which he is thoroughly familiar is seriously handicapping himself and his students. As a result, he may often be doing a lot of work which has already been done for him by someone else.

In addition to a good textbook, a tape recorder and/or a record player with the necessary tapes and recordings is now considered standard transcription and speed-building equipment. (See page 171 for Langemo's "Twenty-Fve Ways to Utilize a Shorthand Laboratory.")

Mailable Copy

A college administrator reports the following: "My secretary has higher standards of quality and excellence than I have. Her standard is absolute perfection. If I call a small error to her attention, one which I think can be corrected easily with a little fixing up, crowding, spacing, or the like, she insists upon doing the letter over." This is unusual. It is frequently the boss who has to put on the pressure for high office standards.

In some offices, the rule is to let the letter go out if the correction does not spoil the appearance of the copy. It saves time and money. This establishes two basic categories in the handling of letters in the school situation: (1) those letters that can be mailed without any correction whatsoever, and (2) those that can be made mailable with a small correction. Many teachers give full credit for all letters in group No. 1, and half credit for those in group No. 2. This system encourages careful proofreading on the part of the student *before* handing the letter in for credit. If the *student* finds the error and makes the correction *before* the "boss" sees it, he gets full credit; if he waits until the teacher points out the error, he receives only half credit. (See page 162 for elements that make for better mailability.)

Transcription Standards

There is no universally accepted standard for mailable transcription copy; in fact, there is no general agreement of what is meant by any given transcription standard. However, there is almost unanimous agreement that mailable copy should be the only ultimate objective. In view of this, the standard given by Leslie should be given thoughtful consideration:

> At the end of four semesters of shorthand and at least two semesters of typewriting, when dictation is given at 80-100 words a minute in a group of letters comprising a total dictation of 800-1,000 words, the learner should transcribe at the rate of 20-25 words a minute with 20 words as the minimum rate acceptable for credit. At least 75 percent of the letters in any five consecutive daily transcription periods should be mailable.[12]

Some of the items to be considered when setting up standards in transcription are:

1. Speed at which the material is dictated, and how it is dictated.
2. How much coaching is permitted before typing begins.
3. Quality of finished product, and how it shall be rated.
4. Are carbon copies required? If so, how many?
5. If based on letters, what is the average length? Are envelopes required?
6. Difficulty of material used for dictation.

(See page 161 for a recommended standard.)

Office-Style Dictation

An attempt at office-style dictation in classrooms where the rudimentary elements of transcription have not yet been mastered results in utter confusion and a waste of time. Simply to throw learning blocks haphazardly in the student's path is of no purpose and only slows the learning process. On the other hand, if ample time has been allotted

---

[12] Louis Leslie, *Methods of Teaching Transcription* (New York: Gregg Division, McGraw-Hill Book Co., Inc., 1949), pp. 51-52.

to transcription, if the class has advanced to the stage where the students are producing mailable copy regularly, if there is a feeling of confidence that comes from a knowledge of inner power, then the teacher should attempt office-style dictation and use it regularly in the classroom.

The teacher should simulate ordinary office conditions whenever possible so that students might be better prepared for dictation on their first jobs. The teacher should provide helpful hints on what to expect in office dictation and how to cope with minor problems that arise when taking dictation. For example, many beginning stenographers are confused by the informal manner in which their employers might dictate or perhaps the fact that dictators do not say, "Now I am going to dictate." It might be well, therefore, as a sample of office-style dictation, to have the students sit near the desk and have the teacher dictate in a calm, quiet tone—the way an executive must dictate if he is going to keep it up for long periods of time. It is as difficult for the executive to produce good material when dictating as it is for the stenographer to record and transcribe it. It requires mental alertness for both to function well as individuals and as a team. (See page 164.)

The Transcription Chain

A station wagon skidded off the road near Clinton, Iowa. The temperature was five below zero. The members of a small group of homeward-bound Christmas relatives shielded their faces from the driving snow. A tow chain was fastened to the front bumper of the stalled car and a huge semi-trailer truck was about to bring the vehicle back on the road. The car moved a few feet, taking a mountain of snow with it; then all eyes shifted their focus to a single link near the middle of the chain. Slowly this link separated at the weld, opened up, widened, and with a clang that rang through the frozen air, the chain broke and the car rolled back down the grade. This chain failed because of one weak link. Had all the other links been ten times as strong, the chain still would have been useless. So it is with transcription. A person's ability to transcribe is only as good as the weakest link in his transcription training.

Pictured below are the six links of the transcription chain.

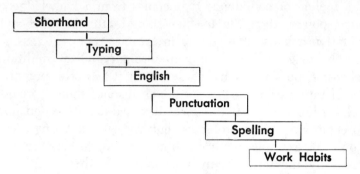

It is suggested that the teacher do everything within her power to keep the entire chain strong. The material given in shorthand and typing should be of help in these areas, as likewise should be many suggestions given in the chapter on office practice. By working in close harmony with the English Department, the teacher can strengthen her efforts in spelling, punctuation, word usage, and English.

Transcription Principles

Man is the sum total of all his experiences. What a person believes to be good transcription teaching procedure is the result of his years in the classroom and of the impact upon his thinking made by his many colleagues who have written on the subject. In listing the following, the authors would like to give credit where it is due, but that is clearly impossible. The ideas presented represent the thinking of many authorities on the subject of transcription.

1. Transcription must be taught vigorously by a teacher who knows how to do it. The know-how is available and can be obtained by attending methods courses, reading the literature of business education, consulting the references at the end of this chapter.

2. Transcription should be introduced as soon as the student has mastered the basic principles of shorthand and can read and write fluently when dealing with easy, familiar material. This introduction in many cases would be at the beginning of the second semester.

3. Whereas the time required for learning the basic shorthand principles can often be shortened without harmful effects, ample time should be allowed for the final and most important phase of the shorthand course—transcription.

4. Since transcription is a very complicated skill, it should be introduced carefully by using well-established introductory techniques. In going ahead to new and more difficult material, students should not be forced beyond their power to operate effectively.

5. Transcription should be taught in a double-period arrangement where one teacher has complete responsibility for the entire training operation.

6. Transcription should be taught in the typing room or in a smaller room where typewriters are available.

7. Slow down when dictating for transcription—make sure that students get it; put on the pressure when striving for higher shorthand speeds.

8. Increase transcription difficulties gradually. Always remain within newly developed power limits. This means careful previewing, particularly in the early stages.

9. Recognize two levels of mailable copy: copy that can be used as is and that which can be *made* mailable with one or two minor corrections. The ability to make such letters usable and still stay within good office quality standards will save valuable rewrite time. It is a skill that needs to be developed.

10. Hold off on office-style dictation until the student has the power to handle it; then choose techniques carefully.

11. Build speed in transcription by using a variety of short speed-building exercises.

12. Use short spurts of dictation to the typewriter to nail down some point in punctuation, English, or spelling.

13. The first few minutes of a class period might well be used to transcribe from shorthand plate exercises in an effort to get the greatest number of perfect lines before the tardy bell rings.

14. When starting to work on mailable copy, make the first letters or exercises so simple that most of the students will be sure to get them right. Let the students experience

the thrill of actually getting a letter ready for the mail early in the transcription course.

15. Maintain high (but efficient) standards of format quality. Don't be too much impressed by rumors that Mr. Businessman doesn't worry about the quality of his letters.

16. Without going overboard on the subject of office-style dictation, gradually introduce actual office customs, short cuts, techniques, and procedures.

17. Develop a working relationship with the English teachers. Try to capitalize on what they are doing that will help your students' transcription.

18. Students should have a dictionary within reach—it is as necessary as the textbook.

19. Spend enough time on troublesome areas for over-learning to take place.

20. Except in the very beginning, mailable copy should be the standard of achievement.

21. As more and more businessmen revise their work while it is still in the shorthand stage, the necessity for the stenographer to read back fluently with expression becomes more and more important.

22. Six mailable letters per hour is a good terminal transcription standard. These letters should be of average difficulty (if there is such a thing), between 125 and 150 words in length, and the material should be dictated between 80 and 100 wpm. One uncorrected carbon copy should be adequate.

23. Good use should be made of the teaching aids available to the transcription teacher, especially dictation tapes, recordings, and films having to do with office techniques and procedures.

24. Everything possible should be done to make the student feel that he has a part in the show, that *belonging* is something that is expected of the office worker. In the office the secretary is always an important member of a team. It's invariably "we" and seldom "they."

25. The position of a stenographer or secretary is a thrilling one. It's exciting to be working where important wheels are set in motion, where big decisions are made. Training for such responsibility should not be cut short. It is worth all the time it takes. Don't rush it.

PROCEDURES AND TECHNIQUES

There are many ways to teach shorthand effectively. Some methods suit one personality; some, another. Condon and Wellman say, "Probably the one best method for all teachers will never be devised. A really enthusiastic shorthand teacher can get good results with any approach or method." [13]

There are many ways in which the principles presented in the first part of the chapter can be applied. In this section we shall illustrate some of these basic principles and, on some occasions, give specific examples of the way or ways in which they can be applied. The reason we present our way rather than pick one from the hundreds that are available in the literature on shorthand teaching is that we have used and refined particular techniques and know from years of experience that they work. These techniques are based on sound psychological foundations; therefore, we do not hesitate to recommend them.

Shorthand Is Easy

"Some time ago, my daughter Alice registered for a course in shorthand at the university," said a lady of our acquaintance. "All week long Alice was in a nervous stew. She *knew* she wasn't going to be able to learn it. Everybody told her that shorthand was difficult. Last night she came home from her first class. She was thrilled. 'Imagine, mother,' said she, 'I wrote 60 words a minute in shorthand. I actually did! It's so easy.'"

Would you like to hear about this first-day class, the one Alice was talking about? We have all the facts; we know the teacher. This experienced teacher tells how he starts a class of beginners:

> I have a few minutes of small talk and chitchat about the weather or the headlines. I tell them what a fascinating subject shorthand is. I tell them about the famous men in history who have used it. I tell them about Leslie's statement that anybody who can learn to write longhand most

---

[13] Arnold Condon and Rowena Wellman, "A Challenge to Some Commonly Accepted Shorthand Teaching Practices," *Business Education Forum*, 9 (October, 1954), p. 9.

certainly can learn to write shorthand. Then with a few illustrations I show how cumbersome longhand is and how simple shorthand is.

"Would you like to see how shorthand is written?" Many nod their heads. That is my cue to put on a show. On this particular evening I used the poem "The Ship of State." I like to write poetry in shorthand. The meter and the rhyme seem to blend in with the rhythm involved in writing the characters. I write as I talk: "Thou, too, sail on O ship of state; sail on O union strong and great. Humanity with all its fears, with all the hopes of future years is hanging breathless on thy fate."

"Before you leave this room tonight," I tell them, "you, too, will be writing like that." Then I erase what I have written and continue, using this paragraph:

Good evening. Here I am, and here you are. I can write shorthand. Mary here (pointing to Mary) said, "I would like to write shorthand. I would like to read shorthand. I would like to read and write shorthand." "See," said Mary, "I can write shorthand. I can read shorthand. My, my, I can read and write shorthand. What fun it is to write shorthand."

After I have written this on the board, I read it to the class, pointing to each word as I read. Next the entire class reads the paragraph in unison. We read it several times. I ask for volunteers to read it. Soon everyone in the class can read it. Then we start to analyze. We spell the word "Mary, M-a-r-y." We learn the letters and learn how they make words. We pick out other words and characters. It becomes a game. Everyone is amazed to find out how much he already knows, just by being able to read the paragraph. I often change this paragraph to tie in with some event that has made the news.

Then we start to write. They have been chafing at the bit to write. Now we are going to give them that thrill. I demonstrate in large letters on the board "good evening," etc. I show them how I make the "g" dig itself into the line. I show that some characters are short and some are long. Soon everyone is writing "good evening" fluently. I insist that they keep up with me as I write on the board. In like manner we work through the entire paragraph. Students help one another with their shorthand penmanship, but we make no effort at refinement at this time—it is the fluency that counts.

We are now ready to take the paragraph from beginning to end. When they get tired, we analyze. Soon they know all the characters in the exercise. By the end of the period most of the members of the class are writing at 60 wpm or better. I have had some beginners who have written up to 100 wpm on the first night, using this very same paragraph.

What have these students learned during this period? They have learned, partly (as all first-time material should be), the following:

Brief forms: can, I, would, and, it, is

Letters: e, a, h, r, d

Special forms: shorthand, fun

The technique of putting sounds and letters together to make words.

The most important thing of all: the fact that shorthand is written fluently and that it is fun. Nothing can stop us now.

Success Is Crucial

The best way to make it possible for every student to achieve some measure of success is to have a classroom organization that is conducive to the "success for all" principle.

There was a time in the history of business education when contests were sweeping the country. Teachers often neglected the rank and file of their students in order to have a few champions shine at a contest. Consequently, a few students experienced a great measure of success; the rest, none at all.

A classroom organization and procedure that makes it possible for almost all to have success must emphasize, among other things, the importance of growth. When progress is pictured on a growth chart, the poor student will often show a greater gain than the one who starts out with a good record. There should be a variety of aspiration levels. Goals should be reasonable, not only for the class as a whole but also for each individual. If an individual reaches the goal set for him, he is successful regardless of what the others are doing. As will be mentioned later, dictation should be of such a nature that every student at sometime or other during the period will get all the dictation and will therefore experience his portion of success.

How to Handle Reading Effectively

Earlier in the chapter we made the statement that a teacher can check the reading of an entire class, regardless of size, in three minutes. The process is simple: The students work in pairs and are designated as "Student A" and "Student B." First A reads to B. B checks the reading in the *Student Transcript* and prompts A when necessary. At the end of exactly one minute, time is called. From the transcript the student determines the speed per minute at which A has been reading. If there were any errors or if promptings were necessary, he deducts five words for each error or prompt and immediately records the net speed on a sheet provided for that purpose. This done, the process is reversed and B reads to A. In not more than three minutes all students in the class have read, and the reading speed of each student has been recorded.

In doing their homework, students are asked to give first priority to reading. Reading homework will therefore have a purpose. The students will try to read as fluently as possible, for they know that a daily check-up is made of their reading.

To the casual observer visiting a reading check-up of this kind, it may seem like sheer bedlam, but it works; and after a few days students accept it as a part of the skill-building pattern and actually look forward to showing what they can do. This type of reading program lends itself to a friendly spirit of competitiveness in the classroom.

In the beginning, as a "success incentive," the students may choose the letters to be used for the next day's reading check-up. Later on, the material for reading may be picked at random from the lesson for the day. A demonstration by an experienced secretary, showing how she and the boss work to improve a letter when it is still in shorthand, often helps to give the students a better appreciation of the importance of reading back fluently from shorthand notes.

How to Provide for Individual Differences

One fall we scheduled our usual course in beginning shorthand. On the first day of class we found that of this group of 20 students, only 12 were absolute beginners. The other eight had completed *Gregg Shorthand, Diamond Jubilee Series,* or the equivalent. The class was therefore divided into "beginners" and "intermediates." The intermediates agreed to use Volume II of *Gregg Dictation, Diamond Jubilee Series.* Since the room was large, the intermediate group was seated around a table in the rear of the room; the beginners, in the front. After a brief introduction, the intermediates were left to themselves to work on their lesson for the next day. Full attention was then given to the beginners, using the first-day procedure outlined on page 143.

The next day and the days that followed the teacher worked back and forth, first with one group and then with the other, making sure that all members of both groups were working at top capacity at all times. In some exercises, like reading, both groups worked together, each at its own level. At other times, while the first group was checking some material just dictated, the teacher worked with the second group. By constantly going back and forth from one group to another in short blocks of time, the show was kept going. We never apologized for the set-up. Each group was constantly challenged by setting goals to be achieved while the teacher was working with the other section.

It takes a little practice to become adept at this sort of thing. When we have a new teacher who is not trained in handling a mixed class, we usually work with her the first day, divide the class for her, and help her get started. Even then it doesn't always work. In one instance we came back to visit a class only to find that the teacher had moved group B to the adjoining room. "You told me to divide my time between the two groups," she said, "so I put one group in this room and one in the other. I spend half an hour with the first group and then go to the second group."

Obviously, she had not caught the spirit of the thing. When we went to the first group to find the teacher, the students said, "We don't have a teacher. She is in the next room." The secret is to keep moving from one group to the other, have *all* students working all the time, insist that the administration furnish the necessary record players, tape recorders, and any other mechanical equipment necessary for the teacher to handle this type of class. Often we have a tape recorder at each section and have the material needed taped in advance.

"The best job I ever did, judging by the progress of my students," said one teacher experienced in this type of thing, "was the year I had *three* groups of about ten each in one large room. I had to give the situation every ounce of energy I had, but we got results." In any multiple-section-class-in-one-room situation, class organization is extremely important.

How to Present New Material in Contextual Form

We think it might be of interest to have a detailed description of an actual class taught by a teacher with considerable experience in handling situations of this kind. Here is a description of his nine o'clock class:

This is Tuesday, December 20. The assignment for today was Lesson 65 in *Gregg Shorthand, Diamond Jubilee,* Second Edition. We have completed the usual work for today having to do with this lesson. The students have done a good job in preparing their assignments. The average score in most of the brackets—reading, vocabulary, brief forms, comparison, and speed—went up today. Everyone is in a good mood. This is the last week before Christmas, and the yuletide spirit is in the air. I have written the new words I want to introduce on the board.

I say to the class in a jovial tone of voice, "What'll we talk about today?" "Let's talk about Christmas," they shout in unison. "All right! Let's get going." The students know by this time that the "dessert" of the class meal is preparing the contextual paragraph containing the brief forms and other key words to be learned in tomorrow's lesson. Many hands go up. All want to say something about Christmas. All have made up a sentence including one or more of the words on the board. I hold their enthusiasm in check until we are pretty well decided what it is that we want to say about Christmas. Then we go to work. As the students dictate, I write on the board in shorthand. When the paragraph is completed, we work it over and improve the English. No matter how poor the grammar, no one ever makes fun of it. We welcome the opportunity to correct the sentence. When the paragraph is polished up, we put in the punctuation marks in color.

This is now their own dictation material. They have a right to be proud of it. It is their speed paragraph for the next day. The paragraph is read several times from the board to make certain that all can read it fluently. Then the students copy it carefully in their notebooks. If time remains, the paragraph is dictated several times to "prime the pump" for the next day.

According to this teacher, the paragraph mentioned above will be a part of the standard work for the day, an item on which the students will be checked for speed. It will be dictated at 40, 60, 80, and 100 wpm. As in the case with reading, a careful day-by-day record is kept of the student's progress.

If the teacher wishes, he can make a wall chart showing the weekly improvement of the class in speed. Some students like to keep their own progress charts in the back of the book, using a special form for that purpose.

How to Provide a Basis for Constant Self-Evaluation

We recommend that students be checked daily on four factors: reading, vocabulary, general quality of their shorthand notes as compared with book shorthand, and the speed at which they can take dictation. The first three minutes are usually devoted to reading. How this may be done has already been explained. A quick spot check on the new vocabulary words or on brief forms, or both, may be taken at the beginning of the lesson. The procedure consists of simply dictating 11 of the words usually given at the beginning of the lesson. Students have had drill on these words the day before as a pump-priming exercise and have reviewed them at home. The first error is not counted. Students who get all words right get the same grade as those who get only ten correct. With that system most of the students usually get a score of 100 percent on vocabulary for the day. Brief forms are chosen at random from those that have been learned at this stage in the course. Such a check-up usually takes about three minutes.

By a show of hands it can be determined how the class has done on vocabulary. If the class scored 90 percent or better, it can be assumed that there is no difficulty with the new vocabulary. The teacher may proceed with the next step which is known as "comparison." In the assignment given the previous day, the teacher indicated a certain letter as the comparison letter. Students then know that this letter will be dictated in class and their notes will be checked with the book shorthand. It is not a speed letter; it is dictated so that everyone can get the take.

After all have completed the dictation, the students pick up their red pencils and check their shorthand with the book shorthand. Minor slips and phrasing are not counted as errors. Again students total their errors. The first five errors are not counted—a technique that helps reduce tension and fear. After the first five errors, it's five points off for each mistake. Students who have done some degree of homework usually get a good score. The class is then asked to make little five-word sentences with the words that caused them trouble. Usually the class scores 80 percent, or better, which is all right. If a student should score low, for example 50 percent, the teacher should work with the student to discover the difficulty.

The final check for the day is for speed in taking dictation. The exercise used is the special paragraph which was developed the previous day. This is again placed on the board. The class chairman for the week usually has it written before the bell rings. Students read in unison and improve the chairman's shorthand where necessary. The teacher may then dictate it slowly—usually 40 wpm. If a student can read it back fluently from his own notes, he is entitled to put down a score of 40 wpm for the day; those who do not get 40, get 20 for trying. The same procedure is followed for the 60 speed, the 80, and the 100. Toward the end of the year some may want to take it at 120. As the students gain power and a definite fluent pattern of writing is established, book material is gradually introduced for dictation.

The papers containing the scores on the four factors are then passed to the class chairman, who, with his assistants, records the results on a master blank provided for that purpose.

The period is now half over. The students have been reading and writing shorthand every minute. They have been learning, and at the same time both they and the teacher have obtained an accurate record of their progress. The remainder of the period is devoted to the assignment for the next class, previewing, priming of the pump, and taking dictation from the material in the day's lesson.

How to Set Up An Effective Daily Classroom Procedure

Class organization and procedure go hand in hand. To keep in operation any given procedure requires a classroom organization that will make such a procedure possible. Every class, including shorthand, should make its contribution to student growth in an understanding of democratic group action and should give the student practice in developing such personality traits as initiative, resourcefulness, poise, and ability to speak before a group—just to mention a few.

The procedures outlined below assume a chairman and a class secretary who automatically take over when the teacher is not there. There may be other assistants if the class is large enough to warrant them. Where possible, a special desk might be set aside for the class chairman to give him prestige. These class officials will be referred to from time to time in the procedure discussions.

It takes a few minutes for the student to adjust himself when he comes to one class after having left another. A preacher was once asked, "What's the most difficult thing about being a preacher?" He answered without hesitation, "Going from one mood to another. Take today for example:

THE SHORTHAND RECTANGLE
(A student-teacher project on procedures)

```
ACTIVITY                                          TIME
    Warm-up.................................... 2 minutes
        Students write memorized material on
        blackboard or in notebooks.  They start
        as soon as they enter the room.

    Check-up on Reading Speed................. 3 minutes
        Students work in pairs; read to each
        other from the day's lesson for one
        minute; record score.

    Daily Brief Form Check-up................. 3 minutes
        Students compose paragraph using the
        brief forms under consideration.  They
        take this material from dictation, check-
        ing key words.

    Word List Check-up........................ 3 minutes
        This is used on days when there are no
        new brief forms.  Same procedure.

    Preview on Today's Dictation.............. 3 minutes
        This is today's lesson, the material
        introduced yesterday.

    Dictation on Today's Lesson...............10 minutes
        Students can read this material flu-
        ently; have had preview and review.
        Good average speed; no undue pressure.

    Presentation of Tomorrow's Lesson......... 4 minutes
        Here the Leslie technique is used--
        spell, spell, spell; also special pre-
        view of tomorrow's speed letter.

    Today's Speed Letter or Paragraph.........10 minutes
        Students have prepared this material
        especially for speed building.  This is
        an intensive drive for maximum speed.

    Dictation for Transcription............... 3 minutes
        In early stages, taken from today's
        lesson; later, on easy new material.

    Transcription............................. 7 minutes
        All students transcribe one short exer-
        cise; good students do additional work.

    Closing Activities........................ 2 minutes
        Time clock rings two minutes before
        regular bell to give students time to
        set room in order.
                                           _____
TOTAL TIME........................... ........50 minutes
```

I was at a boy scout picnic this morning; I had a funeral this afternoon; and tonight I have a wedding." Students who have just come from a lively discussion in a social studies class will find it difficult to get down to business in a skill class without some time to adjust. A few minutes given to routine matters will give the class a chance to settle. The experienced teacher can sense when the class is ready to get down to serious business.

It is a good thing to divide the class time into teaching blocks; then know just what you want to do in each block. For variety, these blocks may be juggled about. Teachers usually expect students to do homework and check to see that this work is done. Therefore, the first part of the period is given over to a quick check-up on reading, vocabulary, comparison of the student's notes with book shorthand, and speed. How this is done has already been discussed. Every minute of this check-up time is also making its contribution to shorthand learning. The results of the check-up are given to the class chairman who, with his assistants, sees to it that the results are recorded. At stated intervals the teacher computes the average to date. It is a good thing to check the papers carefully now and then to make sure that all scores recorded are authentic. These averages come in handy when it is time to make an evaluation at the end of the term. Scores during the last two weeks are, of course, more significant than those made near the beginning. This check-up portion of the lesson is known as Block No. 1.

Block No. 2 consists of the assignment and the "priming of the pump." Here the students are actually started on their homework for the next lesson. The assignment is written on the board, off to the side. The basic items in the assignment are the factors involved in the daily check-up. To get ready for the vocabulary, the words are written on the board; teacher and students go through the quick customary drill—not to learn the words, but just to get familiar with them. Attention is called to the "comparison" paragraph for tomorrow. The main feature of the assignment is the development of the speed paragraph, a technique for presenting brief forms and new words in context. This procedure has already been described in detail under "contextual learning."

The pump well primed, the teacher then goes on with Block No. 3. This is dictation with books open, not for speed, but for practice in taking semi-familiar material. Students already know how to read this material fluently—

demonstrated in the check-up at the beginning of the period. Every portion of class time has been used effectively in reading and writing shorthand.

A classroom-procedure pattern is different from a daily lesson plan. The procedure pattern is the framework into which the daily lesson plan fits and to which it must adjust itself. The classroom-procedure pattern, once carefully worked out, is generally not changed during a term, while the activities within the framework are moved about and changed frequently.

"Operation Rectangle" on page 152 is the result of the working of the entire class on the project. This is how they preferred to spend the period. It may not be perfect in every respect, but it is how they wanted to use their time.

How to Evaluate in Terms of Objectives

Just as the skill-building machinery should be definite, well organized, and accepted by the student, so the evaluation techniques should follow a consistent pattern, should be accepted by the student, and should stress those factors which form the foundation of the course. These techniques should cause as little interruption as possible to the normal progress of learning. It is doubtful if any test or examination given for the purpose of establishing marks, except as it shows the student how he is getting along, actually helps him to learn shorthand, or helps him to increase his speed. What then is a good mid-term or end-of-term evaluation device? The following is a suggestion. It has been developed over the years and has been reviewed by many graduate school classes for its psychological soundness. Each new group should accept it before it is put into operation.

The mid-term and the final evaluation are made up of two parts: the daily averages, with emphasis placed on the near-the-end-of-term scores, and the mid-term and final examinations. All these scores are placed on the student's evaluation sheet, a sample of which is shown on the following page. Part I is simply an average of those factors, which were checked on at the beginning of the period throughout the term. The second part is a formal test on these same factors during the final examination.

As can be seen on the evaluation sheet, the much-discussed word list forms only a small part of the total score. Ten percent of the student's errors are not counted. If the student is too far down in his ability to write words correctly, however, it is a sign of weakness, and it should

Name_____   Date_____

EVALUATION SHEET FOR BEGINNING (FIRST YEAR) SHORTHAND
First Semester

The purpose of this form is to provide a systematic plan and worksheet for determining the student's grade for the semester. The shorthand curriculum is divided into two major parts: 1. Beginning shorthand, two semesters. 2. Advanced shorthand and transcription, two semesters. Beginning shorthand is again divided into two parts: (a) basic shorthand, and (b) speed building and introduction to transcription.

OBJECTIVES FIRST SEMESTER

1. To write shorthand fluently in good form, fine distinction between length of lines and size of circles. Minimum cruising speed* during semester on easy, familiar material, 60 wpm.
2. To be able to read back fluently dictated and text material.
3. By the end of the semester the student should know all of the brief forms and should be able to take dictation fluently on brief form material.
4. Should know vocabulary covered with 85 percent accuracy.
5. Should become progressively more fluent in initiating outlines not specifically given in text but for which principles have been established.
6. The quality of student's shorthand should compare favorably (in principle) with material in text.

GRADE SUMMARY SHEET

(Summary of accumulated daily averages)

Reading: Actual speed per minute _____ x ½   _____

Brief Forms: Actual score in terms of 100 percent   _____

Vocabulary: A 90 percent accurate paper equals score of 100 percent   _____

Quality: 85 percent accuracy on general conformity with text required (After that, 5 points off for each error)   _____

Dictation speed: Material dictated at 60, 80, 100 wpm (Fluent reading back required) Score = speed x 2   _____

          TOTAL SCORE ON DAILY WORK   _____

Reading: Actual speed per minute _____ x ½   _____

Brief Forms: Actual score in terms of 100
    percent   _____

Vocabulary: A 90 percent accurate paper equals
    score of 100 percent   _____

Quality: 85 percent accuracy on general con-
    formity with text required (After that, 5
    points off for each error)   _____

Dictation speed: Material dictated at 60, 80,
    100 wpm (Fluent reading back required)
    Score = speed x 2   _____

      FINAL OR MID-TERM TOTAL   _____

      GRAND TOTAL DAILY AND EXAM   _____

      FINAL GRADE FOR THE TERM   _____

° Since students write 60 wpm beginning with the first class period, it is assumed that they will maintain this basic minimum speed as the material becomes progressively more difficult. After a few weeks, the daily speed takes will range from 60 to 100 wpm.

have something to do with his score. Brief forms are checked in the same way. Here a greater degree of accuracy is expected. The reading score is the speed made on a one-minute reading test—the better of the trials. So that not too much weight is given to reading, the speed is divided by two in order to obtain the reading score for evaluation purposes. Quality of shorthand is also a factor. Here the first 15 percent of errors made are not counted. Two letters are dictated at a moderate speed. The students check the better of the two. With all these advantages in his favor, if a student still makes a low score, one may be sure that he is not doing satisfactory work.

The most significant factor of the evaluation plan is the ability to take dictation and transcribe it. Again, as can be seen from a study of the evaluation sheet, the speed at which the student is able to take dictation is the score, only in this case the score is doubled. A student who can take and transcribe at 80 wpm merits a score in dictation of 160. Since we are talking about beginning shorthand, the material used should be familiar; therefore, the dictation used for the test is taken from the daily speed paragraph. Selections are chosen at random. One is dictated at 40, another at 60, another at 80, and one at 100—and even 120, if there is demand for that speed.

If the class is made up of different ability levels—some who have had previous shorthand, some who have not—a handicap system similar to that in common use in bowling or golf can be used. The students understand this and readily accept it. It does away with the resentment often found among beginners when forced to compete on even terms with those who entered the class with previous training in shorthand.

The importance of objectives mutually established and cooperatively achieved can hardly be denied. What do student-teacher-formulated objectives look like? The following is a copy of the list of objectives agreed upon in a class in second-semester shorthand at an eastern university. It will serve as an illustration. "Be it hereby agreed," said the class, "that by the end of the term we want to reach these goals, and we want to do the things which are listed below:

1. Write shorthand so that we can read it back fluently. Remarks made by graduates now working, quotations from executives, comments heard at a meeting, all put together have convinced us of the need for this skill.

2. Practice reading shorthand outside of class; we think this will help us read back more fluently and will help us with our shorthand.

3. We would like to be able to take dictation on new matter, not *too* difficult, at about 100 words a minute.

4. Those of us who could write some shorthand when we came would like to develop speeds as high as possible, maybe 120 or so.

5. We would like to do a little transcription each day so as to give us a good start for the regular transcription course next fall. It will help us to get jobs. Some of us do not plan to return to school.

6. We are still a little rusty on brief forms. We think we should take up again the brief form paragraphs as we used to do (context brief form matter).

7. We think we did better when you tested us now and then on words, especially since these tests did not affect our grades.

8. We think the speed-building drive should be harder and longer. Sometimes we stop just when we are getting warmed up.

9. Since some of us are planning to become teachers, we should like more experience in writing on the blackboard.

These are the objectives, then, that guided the efforts of teacher and students in this particular class. Whether or not these objectives are valid is for the moment beside the point. The important thing is that in the light of their present understanding, both teacher and class agreed that *this* is what they wanted to accomplish during the coming term. Having established what the class wanted to accomplish, the next step followed quite logically—how should these goals be accomplished?

Since the students are the ones who have to do the work, they should have a share in establishing the procedures by means of which these objectives are to be accomplished—with the help and guidance of the teacher. Usually an objective can be accomplished by one of several different routes. If the class likes the "scenic route" best, it should be taken, even if there is a small detour.

Teacher and students should work together in planning the best way to evaluate learning outcomes in the light of mutually established objectives. How well have we done that which we mutually agreed we wanted to do and have done by mutually developed procedures? Pupil-teacher planning in this area is relatively rare. The first step is to make the transition from the "I" to the "we" attitude. It is not so much a matter of how well did I do as a teacher or how well did the student do, but rather, how effective have *we*, the student-teacher combination, been in realizing our objectives? After much discussion and frequent revisions, the plan on page 159 was agreed upon by class and teacher as the best and fairest method to evaluate the work of the period and to translate such evaluation into the necessary school marks.

A student-teacher grading committee can be quite helpful in preventing misunderstandings in the area of evaluation. Such a committee usually consists of three members; the teacher and two students, usually a boy and a girl. The students are elected by the class. It is the business of

```
          FIVE-PART GRADING PLAN FOR SHORTHAND
            (A teacher-pupil project in evaluation)

 ITEM                                                  SCORE

     Reading
          One-half student's actual reading speed.  If
          student reads 240 words a minute, his score
          will be........................................ 120

     Brief Forms
          Actual percent of key words given in
          context.  If a student misses one out of
          20 words, his score will be.................  95

     Word Lists
          Only 85 percent accuracy required.  If a
          student writes 80 words out of 100 correctly,
          his score will still be......................  95

     Dictation Speed
          The score is double the dictation speed.
          If a student takes dictation at 110, his
          score will be............................... 220

     Transcription
          A USABLE transcript merits 100 points.
          Five points are deducted for each error.  If
          a student makes two errors, his score will be  90

 TOTAL SCORE IN POINTS............................... 620
```

this committee to assign grades on the basis of the pattern
outlined above. Students are urged to bring any complaints
directly to the student members of this committee and then
if necessary to the teacher. There are very few complaints
and still fewer that need the attention of the teacher.

Introductory Techniques for Transcription

Some educators make no special effort to make initial
learning stages easy. "It's good for them; shows their
mettle," is indicative of a philosophy that sees trait-devel-
opment possibilities in having students overcome obstacles.
In skill development a different method should be used.
The initial stages must be as simple as possible so as to
inspire confidence and daring. In typewriting it has been
suggested that all unnecessary elements be omitted the
first day so the students can concentrate on the proper
technique of rapid stroking. In shorthand the size of characters and other small technicalities could well be overlooked in order to obtain fluency. In accounting a simple
but complete cycle is introduced the first day. From this
cycle, other refinements are made.

In transcription, too, the teacher needs to set the stage in such a fashion as to enable full concentration on the isolated transcription factor. Obviously an ordinary letter with a hundred possible difficulties in spelling, word division, choice of words, punctuation, unusual typing combinations, and placement on the page would constitute an ill-chosen exercise with which to begin transcription training.

Much can be done in beginning shorthand and in beginning typewriting to prepare the ground for transcription daily by placing emphasis on anticipated transcription difficulties. Such a preview is the first essential in getting ready for transcription. Other preparatory factors are as follows:

1. Considerable dictation to the machine in typewriting classes during the two weeks prior to the opening of transcription.

2. Typing practice on the vocabulary to be used in the first few letters. The identical letters need not be rehearsed, but the preview should be careful enough to make certain that these words do not constitute typing difficulties.

3. The shorthand exercise to be transcribed should be read orally several times until it can be interpreted with expression indicating the proper punctuation.

4. Arrangement on the page should receive but little attention during the first few days; therefore, straight copy is perhaps the best material.

5. Some teachers have found that transcribing from plates (well-written book shorthand) is helpful as an introduction. The validity of plate typing as an aid to transcription seems to be well documented. Notwithstanding, it is the authors' opinion that this can easily be overdone. Students find it more interesting to type from their own notes. If plates are used, the transition to writing from their own notes should be made as soon as possible. If the best way to learn to take shorthand from dictation is to take shorthand from dictation, then the best way to learn to transcribe your own notes is to transcribe your own notes.

After about two weeks of being thus gradually introduced to the subject, the student will be ready to undertake regular transcription routines and problems. Wanous and Whitmore [14] give an excellent example of the care that specialists in the teaching of transcription give to the manner in which students are first introduced to the subject. According to this outline, beginners are led gradually over the many transcription hurdles so that each step builds a foundation for the next until the student is ready for office-style transcription.

A Suggested Standard

After viewing some of the factors that need to be taken into consideration, the task of attempting to establish a rate of transcription seems hopeless. The following standard is suggested in an effort to provide a beginning from which further refinements can be made.[15]

What shall be the requirements for high school graduation in a four-semester program of shorthand and typewriting, assuming that tests are given near the end of the fourth semester? The following is suggested: six mailable letters an hour, average length—130 words, 600 points. A letter dictated at 100 words a minute is given a credit value of 100 points. Six letters at 100 words would give this required 600 points. A student might do eight or even ten letters but, if only five of the group proved mailable, the total points would still be only 500. A letter dictated at 80 words would equal 80 points. A student would have to transcribe eight letters in order to reach the passing mark. The dictation usually requires about 30 or 40 minutes. The inside address is included in the transcript.

The transcribing time is a full 60 minutes. On completion of the dictation the students go immediately to the typewriters. No carbons or envelopes are required. Mailability is determined according to the letter mailability chart given on page 162. If most of the students miss a certain letter because of the same technical difficulty, it is an indication that such an element should not be included in a letter-mailability test at this stage of development.

---

[14] S. J. Wanous and Irol V. Whitmore, *Effective Transcription Procedures,* Monograph 57 (Cincinnati: South-Western Publishing Co., 1942).

[15] For a more complete treatment of this standard, see Harm Harms' "A Workable Standard for Transcription," *American Business Education,* II (May, 1945), p. 174.

ELEMENTS THAT MAKE FOR MAILABILITY OF LETTERS

I. GENERAL APPEARANCE
  1. Good margins.
  2. Regular type impressions resulting from good rhythm.
  3. Good erasures.
  4. No fingerprints, smudges, or other marks on the paper.
  5. No strikeovers.

II. SPELLING
  A single misspelled word if not corrected will make the finest letter unmailable; therefore, be sure of your spelling.

III. NAMES AND FIGURES
  1. Special attention should be given to the inside address. Persons do not like to have their names misspelled.
  2. Be sure that you are familiar with names used in the body of the letter. You are justified in asking your employer about names with which you are not familiar.
  3. A single error in a figure will make the letter unmailable.

IV. PUNCTUATION
  Although a letter is still mailable when the punctuation does not always live up to the best authority, any punctuation that changes or does not make sufficiently clear the intent of the dictator makes the letter unmailable.

V. ENGLISH
  The violation of any well-established grammatical principle makes your letter unmailable. The fact that the dictator made a slip when dictating the letter does not permit you to repeat the error.

VI. CONTEXT
  Most employers will allow a certain amount of freedom in transcribing dictation. In no event, however, are you justified in changing his meaning.

VII. WORD DIVISION
  Any major violation of good rules for word division will render your letter unmailable.

VIII. CAPITALIZATION
  The more important and generally accepted rules in regard to capitalization must be observed.

NOTE: It should be kept in mind that many of the errors mentioned above can be corrected easily. If such corrections are made, the letter is often mailable and does not have to be rewritten.

Standard style and factual knowledge elements such as are now included in most typing texts and for which printed tests are available are not to be considered as unusual elements.

The illustration on page 164 is an actual example of one student's progress in transcription, as shown by results of a series of letters-per-hour tests. The dotted line indicates the total number of letters transcribed during the sixty-minute period, the solid line shows the number that were mailable. The figures at the extreme top of the page indicate the speed of dictation. There are two minimum standards—6 mailable letters an hour for material dictated at 100 words a minute, and 8 mailable letters for 80-words-a-minute dictation. This gives recognition to the principle that more errors may be expected as the rate of dictation increases; it encourages students to try for higher levels. In this particular instance Mariwyn first attempted dictation at 100 words a minute. Although she transcribed 8 letters, not a one was mailable. She then changed her technique both in transcription and in dictation. She took the test at 80 words a minute and slowed her typing speed so that she transcribed only 7 letters, of which 2 were mailable. On the third trial she decreased her transcription rate still further, with the result that she had 4 letters mailable. This gave her confidence to try the 100 again; however, she dropped to 2 mailable letters. The next week she took the test once more at 80, transcribed 7 letters, and had 5 mailable. The following week she transcribed a total of 8 letters with 7 mailable. Her next trial was at 100; and although she dropped slightly, she still managed to transcribe 7 letters with 6 mailable; thus attaining the minimum standard of 600 points. On the final test she transcribed 10 letters, dictated at 100 words a minute, with 9 mailable—a very fine record.

The effectiveness of the above standard cannot be judged until a large number of schools have experimented with it. A former president of the Administrative Management Society states: "I believe that businessmen in general will be satisfied if they can depend upon it that the girls you send them on the beginning vocational level can turn out an average of six acceptable letters an hour. Such a fact automatically tells us that these applicants can spell, punctuate, and type without too many errors. After office workers are associated with the firm for five or six months, their efficiency will naturally improve."

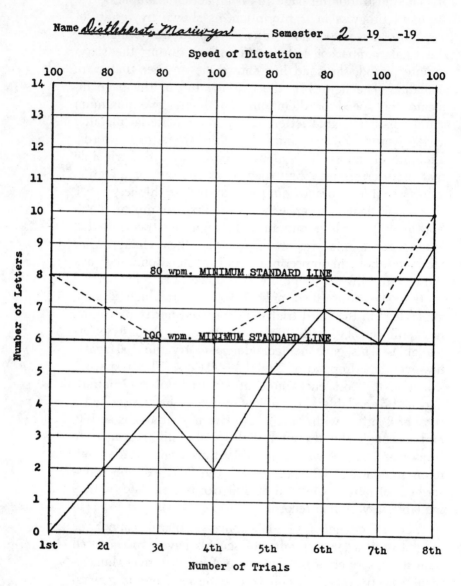

LETTERS-PER-HOUR TRANSCRIPTION RATING CHART

Name Distlehorst, Mariwyn   Semester 2 19___-19___

Speed of Dictation

Office Style Dictation

More and more executives are doing their revisions while the material they have dictated is still in the shorthand stage. This type of efficient teamwork might well be used in all but the most complicated dictation, such as contracts, reports, and involved statistical letters. It is necessary for the stenographer to read back the dictation fluently and with proper expression so that the dictator can actually hear the punctuation that the stenographer plans to use. It means, too, that her notes should not be crowded on the page; she must make allowance for editing. Experience will soon tell her how far she needs to go in making provision for this type of dictation.

It takes a great deal of practice for students to develop this "fix-it-up-while-it-is-in-the-shorthand-stage" skill. As a beginning, the teacher might want to go back now and then and change a word or so. Later, a complete sentence can be slightly reworded, or a paragraph which is in the present tense can be changed so that it will be in the past, etc. At first it is agonizingly slow for students to catch on. After several months the teacher can make a slip, correct, and go right on without hesitation.

Whenever possible the teacher should include in each day's transcription dictation one letter that is actually going to be put in the mail. Students often ask, "Is this for real?" If the teacher says "It sure is," they get nervous and excited. The fact that it is the "real McCoy" seems to do something to them until they get used to it. But when the best letter is selected by popular vote, with the first carbon placed in the department file and the second, with proper recognition, in the student's file, there is a sense of satisfaction of having done something of actual value, of having entered for a brief moment into the lifestream of business.

It is most aggravating to have a secretary who never becomes a part of the job, who won't know tomorrow what happens today, who forgets everything that occurs (except coffee break and paycheck) as fast as it happens—just as though she were some detached entity, hired to go through certain motions until saved by the bell at the end of the day.

Transcription students need to take a series of letters having to do with a certain situation in which they are expected to know and remember what is going on. The alert students will quickly catch small mistakes in dates, figures, names, and the like, because they are familiar with the situation; others will need some time to get into the groove. One teacher set up a small office in the classroom in an effort to develop this *belongingness*.

In the average office there are usually a good many directives that go along with the day's dictation. The ability to follow directions is a skill that can be developed. Drill in following directions is good office-style dictation. Many employment tests include check-ups on the candidate's ability to follow directions. One member of the National Secretaries Association keeps a red pencil handy to make memos when her boss gives directions. "Before I start to transcribe," she says, "I take care of the 'red letter' items first." This, or something similar, is a good technique to include in office-style dictation.

The foregoing examples are perhaps enough to give a general idea of what should be stressed in office-style dictation.

A Navy consultant who gives in-service training courses in letter writing, where the classes are made up of supervisory personnel who have recently been promoted and are now expected to dictate, quotes one of his students: "They gave me a private office and a secretary. I have never had a secretary before. I have to dictate letters. I am scared to death. What shall I do?" In such cases, this consultant acts as the secretary and has the class dictate to him while he writes their letters on the board in shorthand. Their first attempts usually leave much to be desired, but after going over the material as a class, they usually wind up with something suitable for mailing. It takes almost as long to train a good dictator as it does a stenographer. This fact might console the young stenographer who is just setting out to earn her spurs.

RESEARCH AND OPINIONS OF EXPERTS

In this last major section of the chapter, the authors would like to undergird the principles stated earlier with pertinent research or opinions of experts working in the area of shorthand.

Students Should Write Rapidly, Fluently, From the Beginning

We have already stated that it is possible for a class to write 60 wpm or better at the beginning of the course, in fact, at the end of the first class period. It should be stated again, however, that no matter what the procedure or device, the student should, at all times, function well within his power to handle the situation. Dr. Pullis' 1970 research report indicates that the writing approach, word lists, and insistence on a modest degree of accuracy, may have a fair degree of validity after all. (For a full report on this, see page 174.)

The Human Organism Needs Success to Develop Normally

Presidio, a magazine published by the Iowa State Prison, quotes *School and Society,* September 27, 1958, in the article, "Were the Starkweather Murders Necessary?" Starkweather was the young man from Lincoln, Nebraska, who committed a long string of murders before he was finally apprehended and later executed. There was much discussion as to the why of it. This article concludes with:

> Any school that succeeds in making a child feel he really belongs as a respected member of his group reduces the number who grow up to become criminals. Good schools provide learning experiences in which all children achieve a degree of success. Not only does success help to make good citizens, it helps to do the job we need to do in the classroom.

A Good Reading Program Is Essential to Skill Development

Concerning the importance of reading, Rowe has this to say:

> The reading of shorthand plates is the best avenue to familiarity with correct, well-proportioned outlines. Most plate writers emphasize proportion and fluency in outline construction. The more shorthand reading the student experiences, the better outlines he will write—in terms not only of proportion and fluency, but of accuracy as well.[16]

Tonne, Popham, and Freeman give some standards as to the speeds we can expect our classes to attain in reading:

---

[16] John L. Rowe, "The Art of Previewing," Part Two of "The Four Arts of Shorthand Teaching," *Business Education World,* XL (December, 1959), p. 25.

The teacher can grade her timed readings on the class average, or say that near the end of the first semester students should be reading around 100 wpm and near the end of the second semester around 200. Or she may wish to use the suggested timings for reading plates given in the 1955 Functional Manuals.[17]

The importance of fluent reading of shorthand notes is also stressed by Pullis. (See page 174.)

Students Should Compare Their Notes With the Plates

By constantly looking at the Great Stone Face, Earnest, himself, became the man of renown for which the village had been waiting. In shorthand, we have advocated that students make it a practice to compare their notes with well-written models. Tonne, Popham, and Freeman say:

> The teacher who thinks that there is no paper checking will find that the quality of shorthand that his students write will rapidly deteriorate unless he has some standards to which he holds them. He should not try to regulate the size of notes written, but he should check to see that straight lines are straight, that curved lines are curved, and that circles are correctly turned.[18]

The philosophy of having students write "any old way, just so they can read it" has gained considerable acceptance. Findings of the Pullis study, cited on page 174, refute this position.

A Well-Organized, Psychologically Sound Classroom Procedure Is Imperative

The shorthand program outlined by Brown and Frerichs is too long to be presented here, but it has in it many desirable features. Concerning having a good framework within which to operate, they suggest that a teacher might do well to study thoroughly several good, well-balanced shorthand teaching programs, evaluate each, then

---

[17] Herbert Tonne, Estelle Popham, and M. Herbert Freeman, *Methods of Teaching Business Subjects* (3rd ed.; New York: Gregg Division, McGraw-Hill Book Co., Inc., 1965), p. 154.
[18] *Ibid.*, p. 174.

pick the one that best fits his needs, or, if he desires, take the usable parts from each and build a program of his own.[19]

Tonne, Popham, and Freeman give definite plans for both the first and second semester. One plan, for example, lists the following as a good use of class time during the second semester:

> 5—Oral reading from homework notes. 30-35—Dictation of homework assignment, using the "pyramiding" technique. 2—Chalkboard preview of new-matter, 80-word "take" from previewed dictation. 5—Dictation of "take" at 80 words. 2—Preview of new matter, 5-minute 60 wpm take. 5—Dictation of "take" at 60 words.[20]

The psychologist Lawther also advocates "sound mechanics" and the "way to do it."

> The attainment of a high level of skill necessitates the adoption of a form that employs sound mechanics and which is adapted to the structural and functional characteristics of the individual. Form is the "way to do it," the design of performance, the work method. For the individual, it answers his major question after he has a purpose, namely, how to achieve the purpose most effectively.[21]

That's the teacher's job, to show the student how to do it, how he can use his time most effectively. The student most often "gets" this form by imitation; therefore, the teacher should make it easy for the student to imitate.

Make Assignments Within the Lesson's Framework

In good teaching, gone are the days when only a lick and a promise were given to the assignment in the final moments of the class. Clark and Starr suggest the following:

> What, then, are the marks of a good assignment? The following list will suggest some criteria for evaluating an assignment:

---

[19] Frances A. Brown and Alberta J. Frerichs, "A Successful University Shorthand Program," *Business Education Forum*, 14 (October, 1959), pp. 7-10.

[20] Tonne, Popham, and Freeman, *op. cit.*, p. 173.

[21] Charles Skinner (ed.), "Learning Motor Skills," *Educational Psychology* (4th ed.; Englewood Cliffs, New Jersey: Prentice-Hall, Inc., 1959), p. 505.

1. Is it worthwhile?

2. Does it seem worthwhile to the pupil? In other words, does it capitalize on pupil interest or create pupil interest?

3. Is it clear?

4. Is it definite?

5. Does it provide for the differences in pupils—that is, their different aptitudes, abilities, and interests?

6. Is it reasonable as far as length and difficulty are concerned?

7. Does it show the pupil how to go about it? Does it suggest methods and materials which may be used profitably?

8. Does it provide the pupil with the background necessary for completing the assignment satisfactorily, for example vocabulary? [22]

Spelling Aloud Is a Must in Beginning Shorthand

As mentioned on page 129, we do not have at our fingertips a valid study proving the importance of spelling aloud in beginning classes, but most authorities seem to be in favor of it. Strony is one of the many who advocate this technique. In her lesson plan which she presents in this article, she devotes four minutes of the period to the presentation of new material. She insists that this be spelled:

> This spelling lays the groundwork for the new material that will be dictated at some future date—the importance of spelling several times was explained so simply by a young man who was rather slow. He said to the teacher, "You know, it is a good thing we are spelling those things three times because the first time I don't know what's being said; the second, I hear it; and the third time, I say it." [23]

Himstreet agrees with Strony on spelling:

> Spell, spell, spell. These words could be written a thousand more times, as they have been before, without losing their value and meaning for beginning shorthand instruction.

---

[22] Leonard H. Clark and Irving S. Starr, *Secondary School Training Methods* (New York: The Macmillan Co., 1959), p. 76.

[23] Madeline S. Strony, "Streamlining Shorthand Instructions," *Business Education Forum*, 9 (October, 1954), p. 13.

Word previews and the introduction of new shorthand principles gain effectiveness when the outlines are spelled according to the sounds involved. Like the use of flash cards in brief form learning, spelling aloud ties the shorthand characters and the sound together. Do not forget that the end result of shorthand instruction is the development of the ability to record the spoken word according to sound! A silent shorthand class is simply too far removed from the end product to be effective.[24]

Transcription Must Be Taught

There is almost universal agreement among teachers on the concept of *teaching* transcription. This subject, involving the integration of English, shorthand, and typing skills, is too complicated to be left to a hit-or-miss process of learning. Merrill, for example, states:

> . . . It is imperative that the teacher *teach* transcription. Transcription is a skill that crowns and unifies the other basic skills of shorthand and typing. While typing is a useful art in itself, shorthand is of practically no value without efficient transcription skill.[25]

Liles and Gratz are equally definite:

> Transcription must be taught; it is not a class to be merely supervised by a teacher who does nothing but correct papers. Therefore, a shorthand class and its corresponding transcription class must be taught by the same teacher.
>
> Also, many administrators are not aware that the effectiveness of teaching transcription is seriously impaired when, for example, a shorthand class is scheduled in the morning and its corresponding transcription class in the afternoon.[26]

Shorthand Laboratories

Langemo contributed the following material on the use of a shorthand laboratory:

1. Warm-up dictation exercises which correlate with the textbook lessons can be provided.

---

[24] Himstreet, *op. cit.*, p. 16.
[25] Frances E. Merrill, "Let's *Teach* Transcription," *The Journal of Business Education*, XXXIV (October, 1958), p. 16.
[26] Parker Liles and Jerre Gratz, "Theory and Practice," *The Journal of Business Education*, XXX (May, 1955), p. 366.

2. New-matter dictation ranging from 60-250 words a minute can be presented, utilizing a variety of skill-building plans.

3. When students first begin to write shorthand from dictation, the lab can be utilized so that the teacher can check individual students as they write—for correct outlines, good writing habits, proper page-turning techniques, and writing rates.

4. Letters from textbook lessons can be dictated on tapes at various speeds, thus making it possible to provide for all speed ranges at one time during portions of a shorthand class.

5. Letters from textbook lessons can be placed on tape and used for homework in place of copying plates or self-dictating.

6. Special speed-building exercises may be prepared at varying speeds for students at different levels of ability and for students with special weaknesses in any area of shorthand.

7. Speed tests for purposes of evaluation may be placed on the lab.

8. Letters, instructions, and "alertness exercises" may be available for students in transcription classes.

9. Tapes with specialized terminology—business, technical, medical, educational, and congressional—can be provided.

10. Taped lessons can be provided for sessions when the shorthand teacher cannot be in attendance.

11. Tapes of "office-style" dictation with dictation from several different individuals can be made available.

12. A tape reviewing basic "tips for transcription," fundamental rules of punctuation, and other techniques and procedures common to business offices can be made available.

13. Spelling tests on commonly misspelled words followed by the proper spellings of the words can be provided for self-spelling study and self-checking of progress.

14. Transfer students or those who have been away from the use of shorthand for a period of time can be encouraged to use the dictation lab to regain their skills.

15. Business education teachers can use the lab to maintain and further develop their own skills.

16. The lab might, as a public relations medium, be made available to school, campus, or area secretaries for use in furthering their skills.

17. Brief form tapes, correlated with brief form charts in textbooks, may be provided so that the brief forms may be practiced from dictation.

18. Lectures in all areas (bookkeeping, accounting, business communications, data processing, methods courses, records management, office management) may be taped any time that a student or students are to be absent from class. These tapes can then be made available at a later time in the shorthand laboratory.

19. Instructions for difficult problems, case studies, computer programs, and other highly specific student assignments can be recorded and made available in the lab.

20. Information about coming special events and announcements of importance to secretarial students can be taped and made available. This material can also be used as an additional source of new-matter dictation.

21. Student-made tapes can be provided as a source of dictation from several different individuals and as a device for training prospective teachers and businessmen in the art of dictation.

22. Tapes correlated with lessons in typewriting textbooks can be made available to provide additional or remedial typewriting practice.

23. "Begin" and "stop" instructions for varying lengths of time—12 seconds, 15 seconds, 30 seconds, 1 minute, 3 minutes, and 5 minutes—can be dictated on tape and available for student use in practice timed-writings and other timed drills.

24. Music tapes may be available for students to use for brief periods of relaxation.

25. Provide for typewriting composition practice through such activities as:
    a. Questions requiring a one-answer response.
    b. Questions requiring sentence answers.
    c. Questions, such as the necessity of making a comparison, requiring a paragraph answer.

    d. Titles for short compositions.

    e. Opening lines and the first paragraph of a letter, but requiring remaining parts of the letter to be composed by the students.[27]

SUMMARY

A 1970 research study on shorthand by Joe M. Pullis produced a number of findings confirming the tenets brought forth in this book. It has been maintained from the beginning, for example, that writing can be introduced early, that word lists are not obsolete, that accuracy of shorthand notes, to a certain extent, is important, and that the ability to read back fluently from shorthand is still a desirable factor in transcription.

The following are excerpts from the Pullis research:

From the findings of this study, there seemed to be strong indication that success in shorthand as measured by achievement in shorthand dictation was significantly related to one's ability to construct accurate shorthand outlines.

1. There was a significant positive relationship (r—.8326) between the student's ability to write accurate shorthand outlines and his achievement in shorthand dictation.

2. There was a significant positive relationship (r—.9305) between the ability of the student to write accurate shorthand outlines and his ability to transcribe the outlines.

3. There was a significant positive relationship (r—.8056) between the ability of the student to transcribe isolated shorthand outlines and his achievement in shorthand dictation.

4. Competency in transcription increased with competency in shorthand accuracy.[28]

It was found that the students' ability to write accurate shorthand outlines was apparently established by the first six months of shorthand instruction and appreciable increases

---

[27] Mark Langemo, "Twenty-Five Ways to Utilize a Shorthand Laboratory" (From a manuscript contributed January, 1970, Wisconsin State University, Eau Claire, Wisconsin).

[28] Joe M. Pullis, *Methods of Teaching Shorthand: A Research Analysis* (Washington: U.S. Department of Health, Education, and Welfare, Office of Education, 1970), pp. 2-3.

in shorthand accuracy did not occur during the latter months of the course.[29]

Shorthand systems which reduce the memory load may benefit students of lower intelligence while handicapping students of higher intelligence.[30]

Though shorthand transcription ability is significantly related to achievement in shorthand dictation, it is the student's ability to construct accurate shorthand outlines which enables him to transcribe the outlines which he has written.[31]

If being highly proficient in knowledge of shorthand theory does not benefit the student, then this knowledge need not be tested; however, based upon the high positive correlation between the student's ability to write accurate shorthand outlines and his achievement in shorthand dictation, it would seem that shorthand word-list tests would prove beneficial for the students. It may be that word-list tests would motivate the students in their study of shorthand theory and would assist the teacher in identifying learning difficulties of the shorthand students.[32]

SELECTED BIBLIOGRAPHY

Anderson, Ruth I. "Shorthand and Transcription." *Informal Research by the Classroom Business Teacher*, Vol. 18 of the *American Business Education Yearbook*. Somerville, N.J.: The American Business Association, 1961, pp. 125-138.

Balsley, Irol Whitmore. *Current Transcription Practices in Business Firms*, Monograph 86. Cincinnati: South-Western Publishing Co., 1954.

_____, and S. J. Wanous. *Shorthand Transcription Studies*, 4th ed. Cincinnati: South-Western Publishing Co., 1968.

Brown, Frances A., and Alberta J. Frerichs. "A Successful University Shorthand Program." *Business Education Forum*, 14 (October, 1959), pp. 7-10.

Clark, Leonard H., and Irving S. Starr. *Secondary School Training Methods*. New York: The Macmillan Co., 1959.

---

[29] *Ibid.*, p. 5.
[30] *Ibid.*, p. 7.
[31] *Ibid.*, p. 39.
[32] *Ibid.*, p. 40.

Condon, Arnold. "How Can Shorthand Be Introduced Most Effectively?" *Business Education Forum,* 19 (October, 1964), pp. 10 and 22.

_____, et al. *The Selection and Use of Multiple-Channel Equipment in the Teaching of Shorthand,* Monograph 121. Cincinnati: South-Western Publishing Co., 1969.

_____, and Rowena Wellman. "A Challenge to Some Commonly Accepted Shorthand Teaching Practices." *Business Education Forum,* 9 (October, 1954), pp. 9-11.

Douglas, Lloyd V., James T. Blanford, and Ruth I. Anderson. *Teaching Business Subjects,* 2nd ed. Englewood Cliffs, N.J.: Prentice-Hall, Inc., 1965.

Dry, Nellie Ellison. "Simplified and Diamond Jubilee Memory Load." *The Delta Pi Epsilon Journal,* XI (August, 1969), pp. 9-16.

Eyster, Elvin S. "Prognosis of Scholastic Success in Stenography." *National Business Education Quarterly,* 7 (December, 1938), pp. 31-34.

Gibson, E. Dana. "Automation and Business Education." *Business Education Forum,* 14 (January, 1960), pp. 11-13.

Gleason, Bernard. "Team Teaching in Shorthand." *The Balance Sheet,* LI (January, 1970), pp. 196-199.

Harms, Harm. "A Workable Standard for Transcription." *American Business Education,* II (May, 1945), p. 174.

Himstreet, William C. "Shorthand Can Be Taught in Less Time." *Business Education Forum,* 9 (October, 1954), pp. 15-17.

Howard, Doris. "The Stenographic Program: Individualize Early Dictation." *Business Education Forum,* 25 (March, 1971), pp. 21-22.

Jester, Donald D. *The Shorthand Transcription Process and Its Teaching Implications,* Monograph 108. Cincinnati: South-Western Publishing Co., 1963.

Lamb, Marion M. *Your First Year of Teaching Shorthand and Transcription,* 2nd ed. Cincinnati: South-Western Publishing Co., 1961.

Langemo, Mark. "Twenty-Five Ways to Utilize a Shorthand Laboratory." Unpublished manuscript, Wisconsin State University, 1970.

Lemaster, A. J. "Notehand in Today's Curriculum." *Business Education World,* L (January-February, 1970), pp. 20-23.

Leslie, Louis A. *Methods of Teaching Transcription.* New York: Gregg Division, McGraw-Hill Book Co., Inc., 1949.

Liles, Parker, and Jerre Gratz. "Theory and Practice." *The Journal of Business Education,* XXX (May, 1955), pp. 365-368.

Lloyd, Alan C. "Practice in Pretranscription Typing." *Business Education World,* XXIX (December, 1948), pp. 226-229.

Merrill, Frances E. "Let's *Teach* Transcription." *The Journal of Business Education,* XXXIV (October, 1958), pp. 16-19.

National Business Education Association. *The Emerging Content and Structure of Business Education.* Eighth Yearbook of the NBEA. Washington, D.C.: National Business Education Association, 1970.

Oliverio, Mary Ellen. "Selected Aids for Shorthand and Transcription." *Business Education Forum,* 12 (January, 1958), pp. 29 and 31.

Prince, Delma Jo. "Use Word Frequency Lists for Accurate Transcription." *The Balance Sheet,* L (September, 1968), pp. 18-20.

Pullis, Joe M. "A New Standard Work in Shorthand?" *The Journal of Business Education,* XLVI (January, 1971), pp. 144-145.

_____. "Implications of Research for Shorthand Pedagogy." *Business Education Forum,* 25 (February, 1971), pp. 23-25.

_____. *Methods of Teaching Shorthand: A Research Analysis.* Washington, D.C.: U.S. Department of Health, Education, and Welfare, Office of Education, 1970.

Reynolds, Helen, and Margaret H. Ely. "Transcription—Early or Late." *Business Education Forum,* 8 (October, 1953), pp. 14-16.

Rowe, John L. "The Art of Previewing," Part Two of "The Four Arts of Shorthand Teaching." *Business Education World,* XL (December, 1959), pp. 25-28.

Russon, Allien R. *Methods of Teaching Shorthand,* Monograph 119. Cincinnati: South-Western Publishing Co., 1968.

Sharpe, Hollie W. "A Few Essentials for Teaching Shorthand and Transcription Successfully." *Business Education Forum,* 11 (October, 1956), pp. 17-18.

Skinner, Charles (ed.). "Learning Motor Skills." *Educational Psychology,* 4th ed. Englewood Cliffs, N.J.: Prentice-Hall, Inc., 1959.

Sloan, Rita. "Why the 95 Percent Accuracy Measure in Shorthand Skill Development?" *The Balance Sheet,* L (January, 1969), pp. 207-209.

Strony, Madeline S. "Streamlining Shorthand Instructions." *Business Education Forum,* 9 (October, 1954), pp. 12-14.

Tonne, Herbert A., Estelle L. Popham, and M. Herbert Freeman. *Methods of Teaching Business Subjects,* 3rd ed. New York: Gregg Division, McGraw-Hill Book Co., 1965.

_____. "The Present and Future of Shorthand." *Business Education Forum,* 15 (October, 1960), pp. 11-13.

Visual Aids for Business and Economic Education, Monograph 92. Cincinnati: South-Western Publishing Co., 1969.

Wanous, S. J. "Let's Break the 'Egghead' Stranglehold on Business Education." *The Balance Sheet,* XLII (November, 1960), pp. 104-110.

_____, and Irol V. Whitmore. *Effective Transcription Procedures,* Monograph 57. Cincinnati: South-Western Publishing Co., 1942.

Zoubek, Charles. "Different Shorthand Teaching Practices for Different Shorthand Objectives." *Business Education Forum,* 17 (October, 1962), pp. 7-10.

_____. "Shorthand on the Way Out, Hardly!" *Business Education World,* XLI (November, 1960), p. 3.

Chapter 5

OFFICE PRACTICE

FUNDAMENTAL PRINCIPLES OF TEACHING OFFICE PRACTICE

A study of what high schools are offering in office practice indicates three basic areas: (1) secretarial office practice, (2) clerical office practice, and (3) business machines. In some instances a double period is provided for office practice, which makes possible a greater flexibility in arranging learning experience. Stenographic skills, clerical skills, and office procedure knowledges can be integrated into a meaningful whole through this method of scheduling.

Regardless of the particular emphasis, this course is a capstone vocational business course, one in which job competencies should be developed and refined for employment after graduation. Since office-level work in shorthand and transcription has already been discussed, the bulk of this chapter will be devoted to the clerical and related job performance aspects and methods of planning and organization specially applicable to this unique area of education for business.

The direction in which schools must aim in the preparation of office workers of the 1970's is pointed out by Pearen:

> If we are to prepare our students for the offices of the '70s, we must look at some of the changes that have taken place or are taking place and gear our program to take these changes into account.

The photocopier has made the copy-typist obsolete because it can produce materials quicker, more accurately, and at far less cost than a copy-typist. This, plus all the other aids which automate routine tasks, will free the office worker for more creative thinking and increased responsibility. This indicates that we should spend much less time having our senior students copy directly from the textbook. What is needed is a person who can think at the typewriter rather than one who simply copies what has been placed beside him. Therefore, once the proper styles of letters have been learned, the assignment might be to answer the textbook letter rather than to make a copy of it. If in earlier typing courses composition at the typewriter is started, a point will be reached where it is natural to compose a reply to a letter at the typewriter. The student might begin with a rough draft, but eventually the letter should be typed directly as the finished copy.

No future office worker will be ready for the job without some training in the methods of processing data. I do not mean that the office practice teacher should go as far as to train programmers, but that every student should know something of the development of manual and electronic data processing systems and how these systems can assist the office worker in his job. He should welcome automation because it will make his position more interesting and challenging by eliminating much of the routine from his job.

For too long, we have stressed "how" to do something without stressing enough "why" it is done in a particular manner. Our students will be of more value if they know not only how to type an invoice but the reasons why so many copies are required, where they all go, and how each copy increases the efficiency of the business. If our graduates are to feel that they are an important part of the office team, they must know how their position affects the overall operation of the business. To show how businesses are organized for maximum efficiency, flow charts can be effectively used.[1]

The office practice course is the connecting link between school and business by means of which the student is initiated into business practices and procedures. The more

[1] F. N. Pearen, "Office Practice for the '70's," *The Balance Sheet*, LII (February, 1971), p. 202.

effective this initiation process, the more like actual business the schoolroom becomes; the more fundamental knowledges of business practices and procedures the student absorbs, the better will be the course in office practice.

This, then, is the task of the office practice instructor. For the new teacher, or one who has not taught the course, there is the need to develop know-how for this fast-paced course. In the pages that follow, a number of fundamental principles of teaching office practice are outlined, all based on sound psychology of learning. These basic considerations are necessary to the successful attainment of the general aims of the office practice course.

Advance Planning—the Nucleus of Successful Teaching

Being "ready" for the office practice course implies that the teacher has given careful consideration to several aspects of good planning: (1) course objectives, (2) routines and procedures, and (3) physical facilities.

Objectives. The present needs of business together with what we can reasonably expect them to be in the near future determine in a large measure the objectives of the office practice course. Today's graduates are finding employment in a variety of job situations—generally in one of two major classes: specialized office routines of the large office, or general office duties of the small-business office. Desired outcomes should be planned on the following rationale:

Employees are often selected in terms of measurements of their competency in specific office or store tasks, and they are evaluated in large measure by their success in undertaking these tasks. It is important, therefore, that the school base the learning experiences and goals in job courses upon the work that will be done in the office or store, rather than upon standard learning materials which may be out-of-date or based upon the teachability of the learning material and not necessarily its job use. Random questioning of businessmen and graduates, and general studies undertaken elsewhere may be better than nothing, but they are poor substitutes for job analyses.[2]

Routines and Procedures. The office practice teacher must be ready the first day of classes to plunge headlong into a three-ring circus of varied activities. Selection of material may prove to be a problem because there is so much of it. The preplanning covers a wide area of possible ideas. When actually meeting the class for the first time, however, certain cuts may have to be made or new items added. The application of routines to the selected content material to produce the desired outcomes is then dependent upon the approach that is most useful: the rotation plan, the battery plan, the integrated plan, or the cooperative plan. The selection of the approach will be determined somewhat by the job to be done, the number of students enrolled, the physical equipment and space available, and the philosophy of the teacher.

Physical Facilities. Physical facilities is the key to planning an office practice course. Planning for the first session of such a class is a unique experience. One teacher comments as follows: "I didn't get to bed until 2 a.m. As soon as registration was over, I went to see how many I had enrolled in the class. 'An even thirty,' they told me. I knew I would have to fit these students into the facilities available and team them up in such a fashion as to make the maximum use of each machine and to give every student the optimum practical, 'I-can-use-this-on-the-job' type of experience. This involved setting up a rotation schedule with actual names—a schedule that would have to go into effect the minute the bell rang in the morning and keep going until the end of the term. Every step had to be planned in advance. We had 'rotation within rotation,' a battery system for filing, and a set-up where we made an attempt at integration. Everyone who has had experience with this type of thing will agree with me, I am sure, that this is no job for a novice. It's a difficult piece of engineering. I was

---

[2] *Guidelines in Business Education—1969* (Albany: The State University of New York, 1969), p. 19.

glad for one thing—I had a large room all my own, to use as I pleased. This gave me the necessary elbow room so imperative for maximum efficiency in office practice."

Students Learn by Doing

The "learning by doing" concept is well documented in the literature of education. It applies with double force to office practice. An office practice course must include a great deal of activity. What was stated earlier in connection with teaching typewriting and shorthand can be underscored in office practice instruction. That is, when the pupils leave the class the first day, there should be an air of general enthusiasm about them. This air of "get-up-and-go" is not generated by the teacher lecturing on the "history of the computer," worthy as the subject may be. Most students who enter the office practice room for the first time come with a feeling of eager expectation. Let's not kill this spirit by an extended lecture. *This is a class for doing.*

Not Every Student Will Have the Same Homework

Teaching office practice is different from the teaching of other courses and requires unique techniques. This is particularly true in relation to assignments. Nowhere in the hurly-burly rush through the teaching day is the need for preparation to handle the variety of student materials so great as it is in office practice. The business teacher who exclaims, "With all these different papers coming in, how can I keep up with my grading?" is in a tight spot; but he doesn't *have* to be. Assignments designed to meet the varying needs and levels of skill of from fifteen to thirty or more pupils can be handily developed. This assumes (1) a frame of mind to accept the condition, and (2) readiness through systematic routine.

The important fact is that there *must* be considerable variance of assignments because of the very nature of the course itself. Individual differences have to be met. There may be times when some students have no out-of-class assignments because of the nature of their immediate task, such as running stencils or spirit duplicator masters. At other times, as in the study of general office theory or filing, considerable headway can be made through homework.

There is a degree of recognition of this need to meet individual needs in the office practice course, as described by Copeland:

> A major problem confronting today's teachers is planning a program that will benefit each individual student, rather than a program that is geared to the average or typical student. This is especially true in the business and office vocational program—especially in the office machines unit. Ideally, the business and office vocational program should be built to fit each individual student. If this goal is met, the rotation plan that is normally used for the various machines taught in the course of such a program is no longer appropriate. Students do not aspire to the same goals in life. Even for those students who do possess the same vocational aspirations, all of them do not possess the same abilities. Each student needs a plan tailored to his specific abilities and vocational intentions.
>
> Rather than making the program fit the individuals, we as teachers tend to make the individuals fit the program. However, with a little planning on the part of the teacher, it is not too difficult to build a rotation plan to fit the needs of individual students.[3]

Know the Machines

It has been said that a good teacher is one who shows the pupil how to do something and then lets the pupil do it. This system was recognized long before the day of the modern "progressive" education. A demonstration of an office machine is worth a thousand words of explanation. Some words *do* need to be used in carrying out the demonstration, but these words are underscored by the visual impact of the concrete illustration. The effectiveness of the learning situation is enhanced through the student's ability to see the "whole" of the operation rather than to struggle

---

[3] Amanda Copeland, "Individualize Your Rotation Plan," *The Balance Sheet*, LII (March, 1971), p. 247.

through a series of isolated steps, never quite being able to tie them together.

Students Learn Best By Doing REAL Jobs

Nowhere in the business curriculum is the need to produce a vocational atmosphere so imperative as in office practice. This is not generally an exploratory course; it is fashioned as a "finishing" course. One teacher has called it the "frosting on the cake" in reference to the business curriculum.

By the time students start a course in office practice, they have developed a variety of basic skills. Now is the time to crystallize them for production competency. There are many kinds of work, real work, readily available for excellent laboratory experiences: assistants for the school office; a service bureau for the school for typing and duplicating materials; cooperative assistants to teachers in which dictation and other skills can be sharpened under the direction of nonbusiness classroom conditions; cooperative experiences under the direction of businessmen in the community, or a well-organized standard cooperative program.

Learning In An Office Atmosphere

The work in the office practice "laboratory" is a simulation of the real thing. Duties that are performed will not be of the same type as those in smooth, "in-concert" typewriting classes. For example, office employees are quite often given handwritten copy with which to work. Practice of this sort, especially if the handwriting is not particularly good, is typical of the office situation and will provide excellent experiences for the students. The authors have used this technique and know what to expect the first time: a siege of questions, such as "What's this word?" "What does he mean in this sentence?" and "Shall I follow this style the way it's given in the rough draft?" All of these questions are reasonable. However, it behooves the office practice teacher to let students get this kind of practice in school rather than get caught "cold" on the job.

One relatively standard procedure to help create an office atmosphere is to develop a "model" office setup. Certain students can act in the roles of office managers, assistants, clerks, and receptionists. Each student who in turn serves his post as a group director tends to gain a sense of appreciation (and sympathy) for the employer or manager in his task of keeping office routines moving. Especially is this valuable in bringing home the implications of absenteeism—how absence and tardiness cut down the efficiency of the whole operation.

The office practice course also can introduce the student to the slogan of "first things first" that prevails in the office. Newcomers to office employment are quite frequently frustrated by the necessity of putting aside a half-completed job in order to complete a "rush-rush" job. Frustrating? Yes! True to life? Yes! With the experience approach, office practice students can enjoy the feel and spirit of the real office and thus develop a higher level of job intelligence and job sense.

Practice Is Essential

"Practice makes perfect" if the learning experiences used are psychologically sound. Because there is such a wide range of activities in the office practice class, from filing to the building of personality, development of a sound pattern of drill is essential. Psychologically sound techniques involve the following factors:

1. It is important that the skill be practiced correctly the first time it is attempted by the learner. The first practice determines to a large extent the manner in which the work will be performed in succeeding attempts.

2. The sooner the pupil can practice the skill after he has seen it demonstrated, the easier it will be for him to perform it correctly.

3. The more often the practice of skill is repeated by the learner, the more fixed the habit will become.

4. The first impression which the learner receives of the skill is the most lasting. This means that the teacher's first demonstration of the skill must be clear and accurate.

5. The learner must know why he is doing a specific drill and at the same time have a short-range objective for that drill.

Because of the tendency to move away from double-period classes in skill development, some arrangement must be made to provide access to the office practice room in periods when it is not being used for regular classes. Individual differences in the class will necessitate additional drill sessions for a number of pupils.

The "Why" of Instruction

"Here is your instruction book and there is your machine. Go to it." This is a common direction from the harried office practice teacher to a student just beginning a new unit of work. With a number of varied activities going on, it is easy to fall into the trap of forgetting the fundamental psychological fact that pupils learn best when they can get a glimpse into the "inner sanctum" of understanding what it is all about. Learning is more meaningful and more economical if it can be closely linked with its application. This only emphasizes the fact that the student learns more rapidly an activity for which he sees the need. When the size of the unit is not too large, it may be advisable to practice the whole while keeping in mind various parts that need special attention. Determining the proper whole is one of the arts of teaching. For example, Jack may see mimeograph operation as a whole, while Pete may have to have his "bite" of the entire process limited to feeding the paper through the machine. And understanding the whole implies that there is both the recognition of requisite skills and the recognition of techniques essential to job-getting and job-holding and necessary in the job market of the 1970's.

Continuous Evaluation of Students

Office practice work must be evaluated in terms of acceptability under the standards of business employment. To say that work can be graded under degrees of acceptability, such as "A," "B," "C," or "D" work, is not being realistic. Most of us grew up with a rating system of some sort, but one of the hardest "facts of office life" we found is that in business there is only one real system: acceptable work or unacceptable work. To make the office practice course meaningful, the teacher should consider these aspects of evaluation:

1. Evaluation of skills should be as nearly like real office standards and methods as possible. One procedure suggested by a number of prominent authorities is to invite businessmen in occasionally to evaluate work being completed. In many instances, Civil Service Commission tests can be used for practice.

2. Evaluate at the completion of a specific unit. This means that students will be taking tests on machines or on other aspects of their work continually throughout the term.

Ideally, no grades would be given as such in the course. Since there is no justification for the acquisition of knowledge for its own sake in this area of learning, the only purpose of the instruction is to develop real business application of skills. Yet the school administration, and also the pupils, to meet their psychological needs, require a measurement of achievement in order to show progress.

Whether this evaluation process is fair and accurate will depend upon the extent to which the teacher is familiar with evaluation techniques and procedures. The final judgment should reflect more than the acquiring of business facts. It should also be a reflection of the pupil's probable readiness to take his place as a competent person in a business office. The more valid the evaluation, the more difficult it is to make.

TEACHING OFFICE PRACTICE

The preceding part of this chapter has been set up in the form of principles—abbreviated guides for teachers of office practice. Perhaps these principles can be one means of encouraging teachers to teach better than *they* were taught.

This part of the chapter is directed toward the same goal—specific analyses which we hope will be of assistance in office practice. It is hoped that this material will aid the teacher to plan, present, demonstrate, individualize, use sensory aids, evaluate, and develop an understanding of the various teaching procedures. Providing job-simulated work experience may help the student to make a realistic bridge from the classroom to the office.

Many beginning teachers have expressed the desire to have at hand a "list" of procedures which they might use as guidelines in the teaching of office practice. The procedures that follow have been selected *because they work.* They do not represent everything that has been written about office practice methods.

Planning the Teaching of Office Practice

Office practice is the connecting link between school and business. It is by means of this link that the student is initiated into business practices and procedures. The more effective the teacher makes this initiation process, the more knowledge of business office policies the student absorbs, the better will be the course in office practice.

A course in office practice may be organized under various plans: the rotation plan, the battery plan, the simulated office plan, the cooperative plan, or some combination of all of these. The two most significant of these are the rotation plan and the battery plan.

Rotation Plan. The students may work individually or in small groups. Under this plan the student operates a certain machine for a given length of time and then shifts to another. The group plan and the individual plan are feasible, depending on the number of machines and equipment available. Before the course is completed, each student will have had some time at every machine or work station. The time schedule should be arranged so that those who show special aptitude at any machine may be given additional practice in its operation. Under the rotation plan students are not necessarily expected to acquire occupational competency in the operation of these machines. If occupational competency is the objective, an intensive course using the battery plan is more desirable. For example, some

ROTATION SCHEDULE A

One-Semester Course

Group Letter	Student Number	90 Class Periods--One Semester / 80 Laboratory Periods					Reserve Periods
		16	16	16	16	16	10
A	1 2 3 4	Stencil Duplicator / Fluid Duplicator (1,2); Fluid Duplicator / Stencil Duplicator (3,4)	Ten-Key Printing Calculator	Transcribing	Bookkeeping / Card Punch (1,2); Card Punch / Bookkeeping (3,4)	Electronic Calculator	May be interspersed throughout the semester for organization, group discussions, field trips, interruptions, and machine demonstrations.
B	1 2 3 4	Electronic Calculator	Stencil Duplicator / Fluid Duplicator (1,2); Fluid Duplicator / Stencil Duplicator (3,4)	Ten-Key Printing Calculator	Transcribing	Bookkeeping / Card Punch (1,2); Card Punch / Bookkeeping (3,4)	
C	1 2 3 4	Bookkeeping / Card Punch (1,2); Card Punch / Bookkeeping (3,4)	Electronic Calculator	Stencil Duplicator / Fluid Duplicator (1,2); Fluid Duplicator / Stencil Duplicator (3,4)	Ten-Key Printing Calculator	Transcribing	
D	1 2 3 4	Transcribing	Bookkeeping / Card Punch (1,2); Card Punch / Bookkeeping (3,4)	Electronic Calculator	Stencil Duplicator / Fluid Duplicator (1,2); Fluid Duplicator / Stencil Duplicator (3,4)	Ten-Key Printing Calculator	
E	1 2 3 4	Ten-Key Printing Calculator	Transcribing	Bookkeeping / Card Punch (1,2); Card Punch / Bookkeeping (3,4)	Electronic Calculator	Stencil Duplicator / Fluid Duplicator (1,2); Fluid Duplicator / Stencil Duplicator (3,4)	

ROTATION SCHEDULE B

One-Year Course

Group Letter	Student Number	36 Weeks--One Year / Weeks					
		1-6	7-12	13-18	19-24	25-30	31-36
A	1 2 3 4 5	Typing Problems	Typing Problems	Filing Jobs	Dictation and Transcription	Duplicating Machines	Adding and Calculating Machines
B	1 2 3 4 5	Typing Problems	Filing Jobs	Dictation and Transcription	Duplicating Machines	Adding and Calculating Machines	Typing Problems
C	1 2 3 4 5	Filing Jobs	Dictation and Transcription	Duplicating Machines	Adding and Calculating Machines	Typing Problems	Typing Problems
D	1 2 3 4 5	Dictation and Transcription	Duplicating Machines	Adding and Calculating Machines	Typing Problems	Typing Problems	Filing Jobs
E	1 2 3 4 5	Duplicating Machines	Adding and Calculating Machines	Typing Problems	Typing Problems	Filing Jobs	Dictation and Transcription
F	1 2 3 4 5	Adding and Calculating Machines	Typing Problems	Typing Problems	Filing Jobs	Dictation and Transcription	Duplicating Machines

high schools have an entire room of bookkeeping machines, and instruction is given much as in a course in typing.

In getting ready to handle a class by the rotation plan, the teacher first takes an inventory of machines and equipment available or that will be purchased for the department.

---

[4] James R. Meehan, Mary Ellen Oliverio, and William R. Pasewark, *Secretarial Office Procedures Manual* (8th ed.; Cincinnati: South-Western Publishing Co., 1972), pp. 8-9.

The next step is to ascertain the number of students in the class. The machines are then arranged in groups, and students are assigned to these machines. For administration of the plan, a rotation schedule is made. This is a *control sheet* for the handling of the class. It assures each student a chance to work on all machines at some time during the term. The rotation plans on page 190 are samples of such guides.

BATTERY AND OFFICE PRACTICE
ROTATION CHART

1st 6 weeks	2nd 6 weeks	3rd 6 weeks
FILING Group A	FILING Group B	FILING Group C

The filing group is taught as a class (battery).
Each student has a set of filing practice materials.

DUPLICATING Group B	DUPLICATING Group C	DUPLICATING Group A

Each student must do a standard list of jobs;
additional work warrants extra merit points.

MACHINES Group C	MACHINES Group A	MACHINES Group B

See chart below for rotation of
students within the machine group.

STUDENTS IN
Group A
1. Meyer
2. Harris
3. Jones
4. Pitzenbarger
5. Dean
6. Massey

Group B
1. Little
2. Barber
3. Kohler
4. Snyder
5. Douglass
6. Henderson

Group C
1. James
2. Donovan
3. Smith
4. Lytell
5. Mason
6. Anderson

ROTATION SCHEDULE FOR
MACHINE GROUP

	Students 1, 2, and 3			Students 4, 5, and 6		
	3 weeks			3 weeks		
	1st wk.	2nd wk.	3rd wk.	4th wk.	5th wk.	6th wk.
Ten-key adding machines						
Rotary calculator......	4	6	5	1	3	2
Electronic calculator..	5	4	6	2	1	3
Billing machine........	6	5	4	3	2	1

EQUIPMENT

Filing practice materials
1 mimeograph and supplies
3 ten-key adding machines
1 rotary calculator
1 electronic calculator
1 billing machine

Battery Plan. In the battery plan, all students work on the same subject matter at the same time. The rotation sheet on page 191 includes a battery element in the teaching of filing. The key to the battery plan is equipment. There must be enough units—for example, electronic calculators—to enable a group to be taught as a class. For many schools with limited facilities, this constitutes a handicap. Therefore, some use a plan which is a combination of rotation and battery. Teaching under the battery plan lends itself to filing units, arithmetic review, and clerical typing.

Simulated Office Plan. The simulated office plan endeavors to duplicate an actual office setup. Usually a model office is arranged with appropriate duties for each member of the class. Students learn as they see the flow of business papers in simulated business situations. In some instances it requires quite a stretch of the imagination to feel the "office atmosphere," while in others the staging is quite complete with telephones, individual departments, special work areas, and so on. Simulation is described in detail in Chapter 10.

Cooperative Plan. Use of the cooperative plan generally means that students are doing actual office work in a real job setting. This approach to learning involves a carefully devised plan which features actual application and immediate reinforcement of basic skills, knowledges, and attitudes being learned in a regular school setting. For the student, depending on the arrangement of the plan, this may mean working afternoons, attending school in the mornings, or some variation of this arrangement. On-the-job application of business skills is coordinated by a regularly assigned supervisor from the business education department in the school.

An integral element of the cooperative plan, to distinguish it from work experience as such, is the planning for an educational objective for the student. Detailed discussion of planning, organizing, and utilizing a cooperative plan in business education follows in Chapter 9.

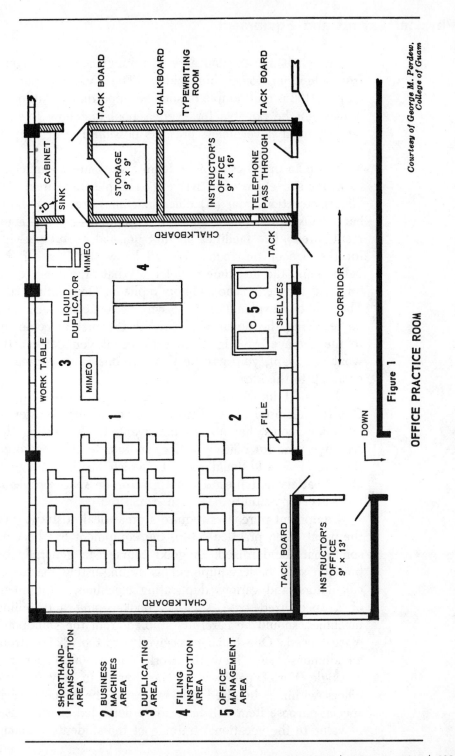

OFFICE PRACTICE ROOM

Figure 1

1 SHORTHAND-TRANSCRIPTION AREA
2 BUSINESS MACHINES AREA
3 DUPLICATING AREA
4 FILING INSTRUCTION AREA
5 OFFICE MANAGEMENT AREA

Courtesy of George M. Perdew, College of Guam

Physical Layout and Equipment

The challenge to plan a room arrangement and layout from blueprint comes but seldom. The one-room pattern on page 193 is an example of such an opportunity. Although it may not be possible for every school to follow this arrangement, it nevertheless presents possibilities for adaptation.

The plan provides for five definite work areas—sufficient room for a beehive of activity: (1) duplicating area; (2) filing instruction area; (3) office machines area; (4) short-hand-transcription area; and (5) reception and "management" area. The facilities are not unusual except perhaps for the size of the room. We all know the story of the bellhop and the first-time traveler. "What's the average tip for that service?" The bellhop replied, "One dollar, sir." The bellhop's explanation as to why he looked so surprised on receiving the dollar was, "You're the first to come up to the average." So in office practice, if you get exactly what you want, you may be the only one in your area to come up to the ideal.

The most important thing to try for is enough space. One teacher used to excellent advantage a small cluster of adjoining rooms that no one else wanted. By shifting the schedule time for office practice, another teacher acquired the use of an additional room to which he then assigned all his battery activities. Do not give up on space problems until every possibility has been exhausted.

Equipment purchases require a great deal of study. For the usual office practice setup, the equipment has become somewhat standardized. A good course can generally be built on such basic equipment as adding-listing machines, calculators, and various duplicating machines. Equipment of a specialized type, such as bookkeeping and billing machines, should be carefully studied from the standpoint of real need. One teacher received a gift of $2,000 from an alumnus. She "blew the works" on a Vari-Typer—not a single Vari-Typer was to be found in any of the offices within a hundred-mile radius of the school. Each special-purpose item will have to be defended on the basis of value to the vocational training of the students. Among the most important considerations are: (1) the community in which students are to find employment, (2) the length of time required to learn how to use the machine, and (3) the resources (budgetary allowances) made available to the department of business education.

Student Participation

Office practice is a "doing" situation and should be treated as such. Students participate in planning and enter actively into the class routine. The office practice course may become involved and frustrating for the teacher unless full use is made of the potential leadership that can be developed in the students. Studies in psychology show that students are motivated when they have a part in setting up goals and routines. That is, if students have a definite part in initiating an activity through their own planning, they become extremely interested in seeing it through to completion.

In the office practice class, there are some routines that are performed daily, such as checking over the machines, seeing that supplies are available, checking attendance, checking in assignments, checking out machines manuals. All of this could occupy more time than a teacher ought to spend. Developing routines in which students have a part in planning has two values: (1) it develops initiative, and (2) the cooperative planning and work routines contribute to the necessary on-the-job traits, including the ability to work with others.

There are numerous activities in which the students can do more than "just listen." Among the most valuable projects that the office practice teacher can initiate is the production of "real" materials: a form for the school office, direct-mail sales letter projects, materials needed for charity fund drives, and so forth.

The atmosphere created is no longer one of "Is this good enough for a grade?" but one of "Will it meet the standards of the main office?" The matter of economy of time is also made more realistic. They know that *this* job has to be completed today.

The school office will appreciate the help of the office practice class members in preparation of routine jobs.

OFFICE PRACTICE I
(Acquaintanceship Level)

Job Instruction Sheet No. M (A & C)-2

(Ten-Key Adding-Listing Machine)

ADDING AND SUBTRACTING ON THE TEN-KEY ADDING AND LISTING MACHINE

Pupil's name_____   Evaluation_____

Period_____Date started_____   Date finished_____

Approved_____   :
                (Instructor)   (Person for whom work was done)

EQUIPMENT: Ten-key adding and listing machine, desk, chair.

MATERIALS: Textbook or manual, pencil, answer sheet.

DIRECTIONS:

Adding larger amounts or amounts with a varying number of digits
(4.54, 54.76, .89) on the ten-key adding and listing machine is done in
the same way as the simple addition performed in Job Instruction Sheet
No. 1. However, in adding long columns of items the operator sometimes
desires to know the total of items listed up to a certain point without
clearing the machine. In this case he takes a sub-total. In your textbook or manual on p._____ find out how to take a sub-total on your machine and how the sub-total is indicated.

Locate on your machine the minus (-) key or subtract lever. These
parts will be used in subtraction problems. Review these terms minuend
(top number); subtrahend (number to be subtracted); remainder (answer).

Steps	Key Points
1 Position machine and materials correctly. Assume good posture.	1 Machine should be at right and at a slight angle; materials in writing position.
2 Adjust tape and clear machine.	2 Clear symbol must precede each new problem.

3 To add: 6.83
          45.52
           .37
               (sub-total)
          7.51
          6.02
        123.10
               (total)
Add the first 3 items into machine. Take a sub-total. (Refer to your manual or textbook for directions on your machine.) Sub-total should be 52.72 S.
	3 For fingering method, refer to Job Instruction Sheet No. 1.

4 Continue to list remaining items in the usual manner. Take a total. Total should be 189.35.	4 Symbols following the sub-total and total amounts should differ.
5 On p._____ of your textbook or manual do_____ addition problems. Record both sub-total and total on your answer sheet indicating by an S the sub-total amount. (Example: 52.72 S)c 189.35)	5 Indicating on the tape, in pen-cil, the number of the problem will aid you in recording the answer.

6	To subtract 869 (minuend)
	     -371 (subtrahend)
	      498 (remainder)
	
	Clear the machine. Add in the minuend in the usual manner.		

7	Depress the keys for the subtra-hend (371). In your textbook or manual p. _____ find out how the subtracting operation is completed.		
8	Take a total in the usual way.		
9	On p. _____ of your manual or text-book do _____ subtraction problems. Record your answers.	9	Clear machine before each new problem. Number problems on tape.
10	Subtraction is also used when an item is listed in error. For ex-ample: 417 is listed for 471. To correct this: Add 417 into your machine. Subtract the same amount (417). Add the correct amount into machine (471). Take a total. The correct amount, 471, will appear.	10	An amount may be cancelled by a subtraction of the same a-mount. Use this method when an error in listing occurs in your adding of a column.
11	Do all addition and subtraction problems again. Time yourself. Compare your tapes. Compare items where answers disagree and re-check incorrect problems on the machine.	11	You should be able to do all problems in Step 11 in _____ minutes. Use checkmark to indicate correct answers. Use X to indicate an incorrect answer.

QUESTIONS:

   1 On your machine how is the sub-total amount indicated? the total amount?
   2 Why does one take a sub-total?
   3 On your machine how is subtraction done?

NOTE:

   Attach your answer paper and folded tapes to this Job Instruction Sheet and submit to instructor as directed.

Self-direction is made possible for students through various means, including the Job Instruction Sheets,[5] illus-trated on pages 196-197.

Office Practice Assignments

Success in any course depends in part on the ability of the teacher to develop meaningful assignments, to check

---

[5] *Job Instruction Sheets—Machines* (*Adding and Calculating*), *Office Practice* (Albany, New York: The State University of New York, Bureau of Business and Distributive Education), pp. 49-50.

those assignments, and to make the results available to the students. Worthwhile jobs, successfully completed, are a strong motivational force that should not be overlooked.

Assignments in office practice work are varied. One of the most productive ways of handling these materials is to use the "folder" system. Students place samples of their mimeograph and other duplicated work in one section of the folder, sheets on which answers to adding and calculating machine problems have been recorded in another, and miscellaneous reports and materials in another. Students then file the folder in a file cabinet provided for special use of the class. Assignments, or jobs, are checked off on a control sheet fastened in the folder. These folders are inspected frequently by the teacher with a notation of "Audited." Student assistants can perform a valuable service in making sure that the class members file materials properly.

Uniform sheets on which answers to computing machine problems are recorded by students simplify the work of checking accuracy of performance. These sheets may be duplicated and are particularly useful if the business department owns the problem manuals and does not permit answers to be entered in the books themselves. The uniformity of these sheets does away with the problem of trying to check accuracy of solutions turned in on a variety of kinds of paper. Illustrated on page 199 is a sample of a sheet that can be adapted to use with most machine problem manuals.

Demonstration of Office Practice Machines

Demonstration is one of the most effective teaching methods available to the office practice teacher. It clarifies the purpose of drills, it shows correct motions, and it serves to motivate the student, assuming, of course, that *the teacher herself is proficient.* The tempo, or speed, of the demonstration depends on the class situation. At times speed is not essential; for example, the demonstration of the bookkeeping-posting machine. At other times the pace should be increased to high-level touch performance, as in the use of the 10-key adding-listing machine.

UNIFORM ANSWER SHEET

NAME *Ellen Lou Campbell*
MACHINE *10-Key Underwood*
JOB NUMBER *#1*
DATE *April 10, 19—*

P. 11	P. 15	P. 17
1. 1210	54. 340.31	70. 27.93
2. 1239	55. 315.36	71. 33.62
3. 1567	56. 345.14	72. 27.30
4. 1520	57. 577.47	73. 31.95
5. 1522	58. 421.54	74. 34.57
6. 8983	59. 419.75	75. 34.30
7. 14023		76. 22.18
8. 17103		
9. 11277		
10. 13473		

A distinguishing feature of demonstration in the office practice classroom, as opposed to the typewriting class, is that the demonstration will be completely individualized or used for very small groups. In instances of whole-class demonstrations, good use can be made of equipment salesmen for demonstrating their products.

Demonstration teaching is most effective when students see the procedure and hear the explanation. Today, with a variety of visual aids available, especially films, the teacher's effort can be reinforced by such films and by filmstrips showing important factors in the machine and its use. In addition, the overhead projector, with its "big screen" and ease of preparation of transparencies, can play an important role in visualization. Diagrams and drawings can be transparentized and flashed on a screen 6 x 6 feet or larger and are helpful when reviewing certain processes for the whole class.

In recent years single-concept films and film loops with recorded tapes to accompany the illustrations have begun to play a larger part in the demonstration of techniques. The single-concept film permits breaking of instruction into single ideas or operations. Students can view these films repeatedly, until they understand the concept being presented.

One recent film loop is the result of a U.S. Office of Education project.[6] The film loop, "How To Transcribe," illustrates how a stenographer should be able to utilize correct transcription procedures.

Work Experience as a Supplement to Class Work

Earlier in this chapter emphasis was placed on the fact that office practice ought to bridge the gap between business and the classroom. Assigning the student to actual work experience in offices while he is going to school is one important factor in bridging the gap successfully.

Work experience in education is frequently referred to as cooperative education. When compared with other phases of business education, the cooperative idea is relatively new. In 1919 the Federal Board for Vocational Education recommended cooperative part-time instruction in connection with business courses in public high schools. Logically then, when office practice was introduced into the curriculum—its chief purpose being to furnish a link between school and business—various methods of cooperative endeavor were organized, frequently in connection with office practice courses but often as a department or school program.

Many of the articles that appear in the literature of business education describe cooperative office practice plans which are phases of work experience and not a part of a comprehensive cooperative office practice plan. In general, these experiences amount to doing work in the school office, taking over the switchboard to relieve the regular operator, taking dictation, grading papers for instructors, and occasionally helping out on a special job in a downtown office. These plans are frequently loosely organized and function

---

[6] Patsy B. McMurtrie and Eleanor Skimin for the Department of Health, Education, and Welfare, Office of Education, *Development and Evaluation of a One-Semester Stenography Course*, OE-5-10-362-2-32 (BR 5-8277) (San Francisco: San Francisco State College, 1966).

as opportunities for work occur. Such practices might well be labeled "work experience" but could hardly be considered on a level with the carefully worked out cooperative part-time education programs. Chapter 10 provides a full treatment of the simulated office laboratory, block-time, and in-school laboratory arrangements.

Development of Intangibles

Some time ago a comment was made concerning the attributes of personality which is as current today as it was at that time:

> Charm is an attribute of personality which cannot be turned on or off as we desire. It is that part of one's self which radiates graciousness and all the finest qualities of living. It is the quality the bearer exemplifies when he becomes interested in *you* as a person, an individual, a human being. Charm is hardly that big smile and handshake you give the boss when you are trying to pull yourself out of the mire by the bootstraps. It is most likely that inner glow you feel after having done a good deed, which very likely will be known only to the recipient, yourself, and your God.[7]

More persons obtain positions and promotions because of personality and personal factors than for any other reason. More people lose their jobs because they lack these traits than for almost all other reasons combined. Many personnel managers are so concerned about personality that they prefer the interview method as their basic tool of selection, using other testing techniques only incidentally. It stands to reason, therefore, that teachers should be seriously concerned with personal factor development not only in business education but also in all areas of education. The office practice course provides the opportunity to give special attention to personality.

Of the many traits that may be listed as desirable, the following includes those requisite for business success and efficiency:

---

[7] J. Russell Coffey, "Charm," *The Physical Educator*, 20 (May, 1959), p. 47.

Desire to Succeed	Proper Speech
Proper Attitudes	Admitting Mistakes
Following Instructions	Keeping Confidences
Good Posture	Pleasing Voice
Avoiding Gossiping	Avoiding Arguments
Neat and Clean Clothes	Day's Work for a Day's Pay
Body Cleanliness	Doing Important Things First
Good Grooming	Good Social Etiquette
Proper Dress	Good Health
Friendly Disposition	Interest in School Activities
Tact	Courtesy
Confidence	Determination
Poise	Perseverance
Ambition	Promptness
Initiative	Good Manners
Knowledge	Honesty
Judgment	Loyalty
Dependability	Accuracy
Integrity	Sincerity
Adaptability	Patience [8]
Self Control	

Student Evaluation

Evaluation in any business course, whether office practice or any of the basic business subjects, should be in accordance with the program objectives. Evaluation should ascertain whether or to what extent the objectives have been realized and what changes or improvements are necessary. Evaluation should be based on the actual needs of the students in terms of actual employment requirements in the potential area in which the youth will work.

We are not always sure of what business does want; however, it is not realistic to go our own way disregarding what the employer feels is a reasonable standard. An attempt to bring general order into this dilemma is illustrated by the plan below:[9]

STUDENT EVALUATION

Office procedures courses have a variety of activities that must be evaluated; a well-planned grading system

---

[8] J. Frank Dame and Albert R. Brinkman, *Guidance in Business Education* (3rd ed.; Cincinnati: South-Western Publishing Co., 1961), p. 201.

[9] Meehan, Oliverio, and Pasewark, *op. cit.,* p. 9.

should, therefore, be developed. There are two important criteria for an office procedures grading system:

1. Flexibility of the grading system to accommodate a variety of class activities.
2. Realism of the grading system based on actual business offices.

Flexibility of the Grading System

1. The teacher may wish to use numerical grades because, in comparison with alphabetic grades, they can be easily divided, added, and otherwise calculated.
2. Determine a grade for each unit in the course so students know their level of achievement for each unit.
3. If some units deserve more value, the teacher can "weight" those units by doubling or even tripling those scores.

Realism of Grading System

Since the office procedures course is planned to prepare students for beginning jobs, the grading plan should incorporate, as much as possible, the same standards by which students will be evaluated in an office. For example:

1. Transcribing machines. Most business offices have three standards for transcribed letters.

   a. Excellent—the letter is perfect or almost perfect and the employer proudly signs it.
   b. Good—the letter is mailable; it has a slightly noticeable erasure but not serious enough to retype the letter.
   c. Unmailable—the letter has a serious error and would not be mailed in a business office; for example, a misspelled word.

In grading the teacher may also wish to consider the time needed by the student to accomplish a task. A stenographer who could produce only one mailable letter in an hour is not a productive stenographer.

Obviously different offices and even different employers in the same office have different standards for transcribed letters. This fact of office life should be discussed with students.

2. Duplicating machines. The finished product should receive a grade based on the teacher's evaluation of how

the work would be judged by an actual office employer. So the student has a guide of how his work is to be evaluated, he can read the DUPLICATING EVALUATION form before he starts the job and complete the form after the job is done.

Name _____

Student No. _____ Job No. _____

Group No. _____ Date _____

DUPLICATING EVALUATION

Did you proofread this job while it was still in the typewriter?

Yes _____ No _____

	Good	Fair	Poor
Planning	_____	_____	_____
Placement	_____	_____	_____
Clean type	_____	_____	_____
Stroking	_____	_____	_____
Corrections	_____	_____	_____
Quality of duplication	_____	_____	_____

How can this job be improved?

---

3. Adding and calculating machines. When evaluating student performance on adding and calculating machines, the teacher might use a form similar to the following:

TEN-KEY ADDING LISTING MACHINE

Name _____

Period _____ Date _____

Time Completed _____

Time Started _____

Time Required _____

No. of Problems _____

No. of Errors _____

Rating _____

Granting that the primary aim of office practice is vocational preparation, then the big job for teachers is to work with students to prepare them to meet employment standards. But it is not that simple. Except for speed in shorthand and typing, there appears to be little agreement among businessmen on tangible standards. In the periphery skills there seems to be much that is vague.

IMPERATIVES FOR PERSONS SEEKING INITIAL OFFICE POSITIONS [10]

A beginning office employee should have:	RATING SCALE			
	Excellent	Good	Average	Poor
1 A general over-all familiarity with office layout				
Customs				
Regulations				
Basic procedures				
2 Desirable business attitudes such as				
A desire to please				
Ability to accept criticism graciously				
A desire to do a fair day's work				
3 Ability to read with comprehension				
Simple directives				
Written directions when clearly stated				
Routine written communications ...				
4 Ability to follow oral instructions				
When clearly stated				
When given over the telephone ...				
5 Ability and desire to use democratic procedures				
In everyday living				
In getting along with others				
In "fitting in" the office				
6 Acquired desirable habits of				
Neatness and good grooming				
Willingness to contribute his share or more				
Making the office a desirable place to work				
7 Reasonable degree of skill in fundamentals				
Simple arithmetic				
Legible handwriting				
Spelling				
Punctuation				
8 A real understanding of the value of accuracy				
9 Ability to type from 40 to 50 wpm with an acceptable degree of accuracy				
10 Knowledge of most frequently used business forms and experience and skill in filling them in				
By hand				
Using the typewriter				
11 Stenographic skills, if interested in a stenographic position, at these levels				
Take dictation at about 80 wpm ..				
Read back fluently when called upon				
Transcribe from five to six usable letters of average length in an hour				
12 Filing knowledges and skills as follows				
Ability to alphabetize				
Fundamentals of filing procedure ..				
Knowledge of common filing systems				

---

[10] Contributed by Harm Harms, based on the original checksheet devised for the Columbus, Ohio, AMS Chapter.

One of the most authoritative statements of a group of businessmen concerning a basis for evaluating the "finished" office practice student is that of the Columbus, Ohio, chapter of AMS (Administrative Management Society) shown on page 205.

The control and criteria sheets which follow represent successfully used techniques for providing students with a means of continuous self-evaluation throughout the course:

CONTROL SHEET

Name _____

		Instructor's Evaluation
Stencil Duplicator (Gestetner)	( ) Stencil 1 ( ) Stencil 2 ( ) Stencil 3	A - Excellent B - Good C - Fair D - Would not pass office standards
Stencil Duplicator (A. B. Dick)	( ) Stencil 1 ( ) Stencil 2	A - Excellent B - Good C - Fair D - Would not pass office standards
Spirit Duplicator (Ditto)	( ) Master 1 ( ) Master 2	A - Excellent B - Good C - Fair D - Would not pass office standards
Rotary Calculator (Friden)	( ) Job 1 ( ) Job 2 ( ) Job 3 ( ) Job 4 ( ) Review Test	Job Answer Check Review Test ( ) 100% ( ) 100% ( ) 90% ( ) 90% ( ) 80% ( ) 80% ( ) 70% ( ) 70%
10-Key Adding Machine (Remington)	( ) Job 1 ( ) Job 2 ( ) Job 3 ( ) Job 4 ( ) Review Test	( ) 100% ( ) 100% ( ) 90% ( ) 90% ( ) 80% ( ) 80% ( ) 70% ( ) 70%
10-Key Adding Machine (Underwood)	( ) Job 1 ( ) Job 2 ( ) Job 3 ( ) Job 4 ( ) Review Test	( ) 100% ( ) 100% ( ) 90% ( ) 90% ( ) 80% ( ) 80% ( ) 70% ( ) 70%
Electronic Calculator (Sharp)	( ) Job 1 ( ) Job 2 ( ) Job 3 ( ) Job 4 ( ) Review Test	( ) 100% ( ) 100% ( ) 90% ( ) 90% ( ) 80% ( ) 80% ( ) 70% ( ) 70%
Full-Bank Adding Machine (Allen)	( ) Job 1 ( ) Job 2 ( ) Job 3 ( ) Job 4 ( ) Review Test	( ) 100% ( ) 100% ( ) 90% ( ) 90% ( ) 80% ( ) 80% ( ) 70% ( ) 70%
Full-Bank Adding Machine (National)	( ) Job 1 ( ) Job 2 ( ) Job 3 ( ) Job 4 ( ) Review Test	( ) 100% ( ) 100% ( ) 90% ( ) 90% ( ) 80% ( ) 80% ( ) 70% ( ) 70%
Voice-Writing Machine (Stenorette)	( ) Letter 1 ( ) Letter 2 ( ) Letter 3 ( ) Letter 4	Evaluation Note:
Electric Typewriter (IBM)	( ) Lesson 1 ( ) Lesson 2 ( ) Lesson 3 ( ) Lesson 4 ( ) Plain Copy Test	Evaluation Note
Bookkeeping Machine (National)	( ) Accounts Receivable ( ) Bank Statements	A - Excellent B - Good C - Fair D - Would not pass office standards
Office Pool	( ) Job _____ ( ) Job _____ ( ) Job _____	Evaluation Note:

CONTROL SHEET

Name_____

		Instructor's Evaluation
Rotary Calculator (Monroe)	( ) Job 1 ( ) Job 2 ( ) Job 3 ( ) Job 4 ( ) Job 5 ( ) Job 6 ( ) Extra Jobs	A - Excellent B - Good C - Fair D - Would not pass office standards
	( ) Skill Test	A B C D F
Rotary Calculator (Marchant)	( ) Job 1 ( ) Job 2 ( ) Job 3 ( ) Job 4 ( ) Job 5 ( ) Job 6 ( ) Extra Jobs	A - Excellent B - Good C - Fair D - Would not pass office standards
	( ) Skill Test	A B C D F
Electronic Calculator (Friden)	( ) Job 1 ( ) Job 2 ( ) Job 3 ( ) Job 4 ( ) Job 5 ( ) Job 6 ( ) Extra Jobs	A - Excellent B - Good C - Fair D - Would not pass office standards
	( ) Skill Test	A B C D F
10-Key Adding Machine	( ) Job 1 ( ) Job 2 ( ) Job 3 ( ) Job 4 ( ) Job 5 ( ) Job 6 ( ) Extra Jobs	A - Excellent B - Good C - Fair D - Would not pass office standards
	( ) Skill Test	A B C D F
Full-Keyboard Adding Machine	( ) Job 1 ( ) Job 2 ( ) Job 3 ( ) Job 4 ( ) Job 5 ( ) Job 6 ( ) Extra Jobs	A - Excellent B - Good C - Fair D - Would not pass office standards
	( ) Skill Test	A B C D F
Posting Machine	( ) Accounts Receivable ( ) Extra Work	A - Excellent B - Good C - Fair D - Would not pass office standards

FINAL COURSE EVALUATION:

1. Job Evaluation . . . . A B C D F
2. Skill Test Average . . . . A B C D F
3. Instructor's Evaluation of
    Techniques and Procedures . . . A B C D F
4. Mid-Term and Final Examination
    Average . . . . A B C D F

FINAL COURSE GRADE

_____

Criteria for Evaluating Class Work

Definition of Marks

A—*Superior*: Work of a quality that places it far above in comparison with its kind in all respects.

B—*Good*: Work that rates commendation as being better than the minimum expected.

C—*Satisfactory*: Work of a quality that meets basic requirements established.

D—*Poor*: Work that does not meet minimum requirements.

F—*Unsatisfactory*: Work that is not acceptable.

Assignment of a Mark

The assignment of a mark for a particular area of assigned work will be based on a consideration of the following elements:

1. *Quality*: Work that shows a careful and comprehensive study of the subject involved.

2. *Quantity*: Effort exerted to meet minimum requirements, or more than is necessary for a passing grade.

3. *Presentation*: Work presented in a pleasing format, on time, and with errors corrected. Work that is presented in such a manner that it reflects care and concern on the part of the student.

Deadlines for Assignments

Dates set for various assignments must be observed.

RESEARCH AND OPINIONS OF EXPERTS

In the pages that follow, certain proven concepts are presented by well-known teachers in business education, particularly those who have spent a great deal of time in the area of office practice. Consistent with the pattern already established, comments, ideas, and outlines that appear to be of most immediate value to the beginning teacher in office practice are presented.

Dividends of Planning

Instruction in relevant concepts is crucial in the classroom. In a recent seminar in business teacher education, an attempt, based on the NOBELS Project,[11] was made to consider what should be taught in school to develop needed competencies. Using the verb list developed by NOBELS

---

[11] The NOBELS (New Office and Business Education Learning System) Project developed a systematic approach of assessing and modifying learning programs in which the purpose was preparation for office jobs.

to indicate the various tasks that office workers performed, the seminar participants developed a list of learnings (steps) to be taught in school. Part of this list follows:

Verb	*School Learning*
Add:	information from one source to another accurately.
Answer:	telephone efficiently, including answering technique, recording information, and speaking clearly and concisely.
	people applying rule of business etiquette.
Arrange:	travel and hotel accommodations.
	carbon packs and other papers according to specific method.
	materials and data according to an organized plan.
Attach:	staples with proper use of equipment.
	office data without obstruction of needed information.
	enclosure to letters and envelopes to letters.
Call:	others on the telephone.
Check:	different types of check endorsements.
Compute:	numbers mentally (add).
	two amounts mentally (subtract).
	cash.
	using 10-key adding machine.
	using calculator.
	using rotary calculator.
	using adding machine and calculator.
	gross pay
	net pay for employees.
	applicable tax.
	figures for extensions.
	percentages.
Correct:	errors on stencil.
	errors on spirit master.
	omitted information on a key-punched card.
	punched card.
	keypunched card.
	keypunch document sheet.
Deliver:	materials to personnel and departments accurately (learn locations, personnel and departments).

Destroy: appropriate items.

Determine: name, functions of departments, and names of officers in those departments.

techniques of correction; identification of errors.

uses of particular stationery.

correct classification for materials to be filed.

aspects of credit worthiness of customers.

type style for reporting; how to set typewriter.

Direct: a group, giving directions.[12]

Good planning involves maximum utilization of space, facilities, and equipment. The following equipment is used by Copeland in a rotation plan for a class of 24 students:[13]

Type Machine	No. of Machines
Ten-Key Adding Machines	2
Printing Calculators	2
Key Punch Simulators	2
Full Keyboard Adders	2
Executive Typewriter	1
Key-Driven Calculator	1
Rotary Calculators	2
Transcribing/Dictating	4
Electric Typewriters	9
Spirit Duplicator	1
Stencil Duplicator	1
Wet Copy Machine	1
Dry Copy Machine	1

The State University of New York syllabus for teaching office practice in grades 11 and 12 offers excellent suggested charts for possibilities in developing a rotation plan:

Several charts are given which illustrate different types of class organization based upon the rotation plan. The time basis used is 180 days. Using 180 days as the time basis for office practice permits additional time that can be used for preliminary class organization, pretesting, special holidays, unexpected disruptions, field trips for the entire class and the

---

[12] "The Determination of School Learnings Needed by Initial Office Workers: A Pilot Study, Part II," *Journal of Business Education,* 46 (February, 1971), p. 203.

[13] Copeland, *op. cit.,* p. 247.

like. The charts are based upon the following time schedules for the six basic units.[14]

Suggested number of periods to be devoted to different training levels

Basic units	Title	Acquaintance-ship level	Practical use level	Vocational competency level
I	Typewriting	30	75	255
II	Machine transcription	15	60	180
III	Duplicating	15	60	180
IV	Machines (adding and calculating)	30	75	255
V	Filing	30	75	120
VI	Office practice and procedures	15	60	180
	Total time for six basic units	135 periods		

Charts showing different rotation plans for single-period courses (180 periods)

PLAN 1

NOTE: Each block represents 15 periods.

Pupils	First semester						Second semester					
5	I	I	II	III	IV	IV	V	V	VI			
5	IV	IV	I	I	II	III	VI	V	V			
5	V	V	III	II	I	I	IV	IV	VI			
5	I	I	IV	IV	III	II	VI		V	V		

This chart indicates a rotation plan for four groups of five pupils each, based on minimum equipment requirements. Each block represents 15 periods. Numbers in the blocks represent six basic units. Forty-five periods are available for training beyond the acquaintanceship level.

PLAN 2

Pupils	First semester						Second semester					
4	I	I	V	V	III	II	VI		IV	IV		
4	VI	I	I	III	IV	IV	V	V	II			
4	IV	IV	I	I	V	V	III	II	VI			
4	II	III	VI	I	I		IV	IV	V	V		
4	V	V	IV	IV	I	I	II	III	VI			

---

[14] *Syllabus and Teaching Suggestions for a Course in Office Practice, Grades 11 and 12* (Albany, New York: The State University of New York, 1958), pp. 25-30.

Plan 2 on page 211 is prepared for five groups of four pupils each. All other conditions are the same as in Plan 1.

Charts showing possible rotation plans for single-period courses (180 periods)

PLAN 3

NOTE: Each block represents 15 periods.

Pupils	First semester							Second semester			
4	I	I	V	V	II	III	VI		IV	IV	
4	I	I	V	V	III	II	IV	IV	VI		
4	V	V	I	I	IV	IV	II	III	VI		
4	IV	IV	I	I	V	V	III	VI	II		
4	V	V	IV	IV	I	I	VI	II	III		

This chart covers the same conditions as in Plan 2. The units are arranged differently.

PLAN 4

Pupils	First semester							Second semester			
5	I	I	IV	IV	II	V	V	III	VI		
5	I	I	V	V	IV	IV	III	II	VI		
5	I	I	II	V	V	III	IV	IV	VI		
5	I	I	III	II	V	V	VI		IV	IV	

This chart indicates a battery plan for the typewriting unit (where a typewriting room is free) and a rotation plan for all other units. Provision is made for four groups of five pupils each. Forty-five periods are available for training beyond the acquaintanceship level.

NOTE: Blank blocks indicate free time, not specifically designated for any particular unit under the 180-day period. The time is not necessarily available as a block of time that falls near the end of the school year, but will be used up during the term for examinations, school holidays, field trips, and the like, or may be used for instruction beyond the acquaintanceship level in the various units.

Planning for office practice should ultimately recognize the need for inclusion of data processing concepts, such as those outlined by Dr. Irene Place:

OBJECTIVES OF DATA PROCESSING IN OFFICE PRACTICE

All good lesson plans begin with a statement of objectives. Since a lesson plan for the first exercise in key-punching a card is given further along in this article, the following list of objectives serves as a framework for that lesson and identifies other aspects of data processing that can be taught in an office practice course:

1. To *acquaint* students with some elementary yet fundamental phases of automatic data processing.
   a) Punched cards design and purpose
   b) Key-punch equipment

2. To give students *initial* skills and vocabulary in automatic data processing.
   a) How to design a card
   b) Key-punch operations
   c) How to wire a *simple* board

3. To acquaint students with the evolution of electronic data processing.
   a) What computers can and cannot do in business data processing (Use very simple examples.)
   b) What is required to prepare computers to do their work
   c) What programming is
   d) Levels of computer equipment (Keep it basic and realistic.)

4. To give students information about job opportunities in automatic data processing.
   a) Initial job opportunities with key-punch equipment
   b) Initial job opportunities with electronic data processing equipment
   c) Sources of advanced training

5. To give students information about the status of the data processing function within an organization (government as well as private).
   a) The "tab" room
   b) The computer center
   c) Responsibility: line and staff functions

d) Research and new data processing horizons such as operations research and the new applications of statistics and mathematics to management decision-making.[15]

Vocational Standards for Grading and Evaluation

Although in certain courses we have dual objectives—vocational and personal use—the consensus of business educators is that office practice ought to be treated as a vocational course, designed to prepare the student to meet the requirements of his first job. The chief characteristic of the classroom work should be purposeful activity in skill building, discussion of factors that will enable students to become acquainted with the essential facts of office employment, and the development of attitudes conducive to successful job performance.

Up-to-date research on evaluation of business students points out that student self-evaluation of his achievement is significant:

> A great deal of attention currently is being given to student self-evaluation and to cooperative teacher-student appraisal. Perhaps business education is ahead of most other areas of education in this respect. In order to acquire job competence, it is of utmost importance that the student be able to evaluate his own product and his own behavior.[16]

Standards are difficult to determine, and this is particularly true in the multi-faceted office practice course. A sample of realistic standards in relatively subjective terms is illustrated on page 215 by the performance review guide used in business.

Levels of performance, or what the office employee *really* is expected to produce, have been classified and described by Lambert:

---

[15] Irene Place, "Data Processing and Office Practice," *Business Education Now and in the 1970's* 25th Yearbook of the Business Education Association of Metropolitan New York (New York: New York University Bookstore, 1964), p. 110.

[16] Mathilde Hardaway, *Testing and Evaluation in Business Education* (Cincinnati: South-Western Publishing Co., 1966), p. 11.

Performance Review Guide

Name ——————————————

Job Classification ——————————— Department ————————

MAJOR ITEMS TO CONSIDER	COMMENTS AND EXAMPLES
QUALITY OF WORK: Is the volume of work he turns out about average? Is it either definitely more or less than you would normally expect on this job? Is he occasionally slow or late with his work? Is he unusually fast and prompt?	
QUALITY OF WORK: Does he follow instructions? Is his work slipshod or thorough? Does he make too many mistakes? Is he neater or more accurate than most employees? Does he make decisions that reflect careless thinking, or is his thinking unusually sound?	
ABILITY TO GET ALONG WITH OTHERS: Is he occasionally involved in little disputes and personality clashes? Is he an unusually good team worker? Is he generally cheerful, sociable, and easy to get along with? Is he sometimes short on cooperativeness?	
INDUSTRY— APPLICATION TO WORK: Is he often late or absent? Does he go to work promptly? Does he need urging to do the job? Does he require close supervision? Does he seem to make a real effort to do the work? Is he unusually conscientious? Or is he a time-waster?	
INITIATIVE: Does he seem too content with things as they are? Does he reach out for more work or more responsibility? Or does he carefully avoid duties that are not strictly his? Is he interested in improving the way things are done? Is he practicing self-development? Does he resist changes in procedures, etc., or help make them work?	
RELATIONSHIP WITH SUPERVISOR: How does he react to constructive criticism? What is his attitude toward instructions and suggestions? Does he ask for help when needed? What difficulties arise in supervising him?	
MISCELLANEOUS QUALITIES: Comment on any other points that you want to cover with this employee.	

The classification of office work by levels might be broken down into two or many more levels depending upon the nature of the work under consideration. For purposes of this discussion five different levels are presented, but this is not meant to imply that there are five and only five levels.

The first level of job performance in office work might be called the *appreciation* level. At this level the worker must have the vocabulary necessary for understanding the nature of the work being performed around him. He must have the vocabulary necessary for writing letters, answering questions in using the telephone, and talking with others in the office. The student or worker is familiar with "petty cash," but he uses the term in his vocabulary and does not administer the petty cash fund. The worker understands what petty cash is when the term is used by his peers.

The second level of job performance might be called the *operation* level. At this level the worker must typewrite, sort, file, or complete other routine tasks that involve petty cash. The worker might copy someone else's work, or he might complete on a purely routine basis a voucher for reimbursement by the petty cash fund. He does not make the decision on whether the petty cash fund is to be used for that particular type of payment or reimbursement. In summary, the worker typewrites, files, or completes some other routine task.

The third level of job performance is the *interpretation* level. At this level the worker has a complete understanding of the task being performed. He understands the system in his work to the extent that he can explain the system to others in the office. He has the understanding necessary for interpreting the nature of petty cash and explaining how it works, and as a sequel to the operation level he may continue to work with petty cash in a relatively routine way.

The fourth level might be called the *judgment level*, the level at which the worker tends to make decisions. The student or worker makes decisions as to the appropriateness of using the petty cash fund. He decides whether an expenditure is to be handled by petty cash or more appropriately handled by a purchase order and other operating funds of the business. The criterion for this level is that the worker makes the decisions.

The fifth and highest level is called the *construction level*. It is at this level that the worker may play some role in determining company policy. He creates or designs the system for the accomplishment of a given task. Continuing to use petty cash as an example, the worker may create a new system for accomplishing the petty cash task or he may reorganize or refine an existing system.

An interested teacher of an office practice course may develop the "level-kind" matrix by organizing column headings labeled as *appreciation level, operation level, interpretation level,* and so on. In the stub (or heading for the rows, as opposed to the columns) the teacher may indicate the kinds of office practice experiences that are necessary or desirable for employment in a specific cluster. It can be seen readily that each task or kind of experience is amenable to being classified by the performance level scheme. An example follows:

The voicescription experience can extend from simple acquaintanceship with the machines, the input mechanism, and the recording medium to the point where the prospective machine stenographer may be dictating responses to problem letters that have been put before him.

1. The *appreciation level* merely exposes the student to a machine transcription device; he knows the purpose of the machine and the process, but he is not an operator of the machine.

2. At the *operation level* the student becomes skilled as a relatively routine machine transcriber of mailable communication.

3. At the *interpretation level* the student becomes sufficiently experienced with the machine transcription process so that he can explain the procedure to others who are unfamiliar with it.

4. At the *judgment level* the prospective clerk-stenographer is skilled to the extent that he makes decisions related to the communication process. He may edit copy or may supervise the work of other machine transcription operators. He may make decisions about format and on the acceptability of final copy that is produced.

5. At the *construction level* the student creates or designs a new system or alters the existing system for handling the machine transcription process. His actions approximate management-level actions, though this statement is not intended to imply that the student is capable of making management decisions on broad corporate policy. However, he is sufficiently informed and skilled to the extent that he

could decide which machine process best meets the needs of this particular office.[17]

Once the teacher is able to determine what can be accepted as realistic business standards, the task becomes one of fitting these proficiency goals to the particular teaching situation. The teacher of office practice should understand that complete, valid, and reliable standards to be used are difficult to find and it may be necessary to develop one's own standards in a given situation, keeping in mind the characteristics of the business community in which the students will generally function.

SUMMARY

Office practice is a necessary part of the preparation of young men and women for office occupations. It is an important part of the business education curriculum. Studies show that more and more attention is being given by businessmen to proficient use of an array of skills and knowledges not always completely developed in a class in shorthand, typewriting, or accounting. These skills and knowledges are the content of the office practice course.

There is no magic formula for teaching these important concepts. What is needed is the teacher who can richly supplement the vocational skill training by setting up conditions through which students learn to make decisions, carry responsibility, become self-reliant and adaptable, practice leadership and cooperation, and develop their personalities. These tools of success in business employment are sometimes complex and require realistic practice conditions.

SELECTED BIBLIOGRAPHY

Business Education Forum. Monthly selected issues.

Coffey, J. Russell. "Charm." *The Physical Educator*, 20 (May, 1959), p. 47.

---

[17] John D. Lambert, "Standards and Evaluation," *The Office Practice Program in Business Education*, 43rd Volume of the Eastern Business Teachers Association Yearbook (New York: Eastern Business Teachers Association, 1970), pp. 178-79, 182.

Copeland, Amanda. "Individualize Your Rotation Plan." *The Balance Sheet,* LII (March, 1971), pp. 247-249.

Dame, J. Frank, and Albert R. Brinkman. *Guidance in Business Education,* 3rd ed. Cincinnati: South-Western Publishing Co., 1961.

"The Determination of School Learnings Needed by Initial Office Workers: A Pilot Study, Part II." *Journal of Business Education,* 46 (February, 1971), pp. 203-5.

Emerging Content and Structure of Business Education, Eighth Yearbook of the NBEA. Washington: National Business Education Association, 1970.

Green, Helen H. "Today's Communications in Clerical Practice." *Business Education Forum,* 25 (February, 1971), pp. 14-16.

Guidelines in Business Education—1969. Albany, New York: The State University of New York, 1969.

Hardaway, Mathilde. *Testing and Evaluation in Business Education,* 3rd ed. Cincinnati: South-Western Publishing Co., 1966.

Job Instruction Sheets—Machines (Adding and Calculating), Office Practice. Albany, New York: The State University of New York, 1956.

McMurtrie, Patsy B., and Eleanor Skimin for the Department of Health, Education, and Welfare, Office of Education. *Development and Evaluation of a One-Semester Stenography Course,* OE-5-10-362-2-32 (BR 5-8277) San Francisco: San Francisco State College, 1966.

Meehan, James R., Mary Ellen Oliverio, and William R. Pasewark. *Secretarial Office Procedures Manual,* 8th ed. Cincinnati: South-Western Publishing Co., 1972.

"Office Education." *Changing Methods of Teaching Business Subjects,* Tenth Yearbook of the National Business Education Association. Washington: National Business Education Association, 1972.

Office Practice Program in Business Education, Forty-Third Yearbook of the EBTA. New York: Eastern Business Teachers Association, 1969.

Pearen, F. N. "Office Practice for the '70's." *The Balance Sheet,* LII (February, 1971), pp. 202-203, and 225.

Place, Irene. "Data Processing and Office Practice." *Business Education Now and in the 1970's,* Twenty-Fifth Yearbook of the Business Education Association of Metropolitan New York. New York: New York University Bookstore, 1964.

Syllabus and Teaching Suggestions for a Course in Office Practice, Grades 11 and 12. Albany, New York: The State University of New York, 1958.

Tonne, Herbert A., and Louis C. Nanassy. *Principles of Business Education,* 4th ed. New York: Gregg Division, McGraw-Hill Book Co., Inc., 1970.

Tonne, Herbert A., Estelle L. Popham, and M. Herbert Freeman. *Methods of Teaching Business Subjects,* 3rd ed. New York: Gregg Division, McGraw-Hill Book Co., Inc., 1965.

Wilsing, Weston C. *Is Business Education in the Public High Schools Meeting the Needs and Desires of Businessmen?,* Monograph 99. Cincinnati: South-Western Publishing Co., 1960.

Chapter 6

ACCOUNTING

LEARNING CONCEPTS APPLIED TO ACCOUNTING

It would be difficult in the limited space available to attempt to describe accounting as it exists in business today. Certainly it is characterized by standardized forms, many of them loose-leaf so that they can be adapted readily to the bookkeeping and computing machines that now form an integral part of many accounting processes. Another characteristic is the extent to which division of labor is being used. Seldom in any large office does an accounting clerk have an opportunity to work with the entire accounting cycle, and fortunate is the office worker who is able to see through the interrelated mechanisms and devices that go to make up the entire picture. A number of persons work with sales tickets; some type invoices for use on duplicating machines; others write checks on bookkeeping machines; a department head visits all machines at a specified hour and obtains balances for the controlling account sheet (card); special clerks watch the data processing equipment compile summaries and statements, stock controls, and inventories. This list could be extended almost indefinitely. Such is the picture of accounting in a large modern office.

In the small office, clerks perform clerical routines, depending upon the nature of the business and the equipment available, while accountants balance the books and make tax reports and statements. In some cities portable accounting offices go from store to store during the evening hours and do the necessary accounting in a very short time through the use of standardized forms and machinery designed for the job. In the small shop and on the farm a simple multi-column combination cash book and journal is frequently adequate to meet the owner's needs.

This emphasis on record keeping is indicative of a trend in American society. For the schools this means an increased attention to accounting instruction. Conditions in business impose a responsibility on business education—particularly on instruction in accounting—for the best possible kind of program, a program that is realistically planned and that employs teaching and supervisory services of the highest order.

In the classroom and in other organized or informal learning situations, the teacher seeks to influence the behavior of the pupils. The *direction* in which he seeks to influence their behavior depends on what the teacher accepts as the goals of education. The *effectiveness* with which he influences behavior depends on the methods he selects. Not all teachers will choose the same methods when working with youth in the schools. Teachers use many different methods of instruction. In the selection of a method, the teacher has made a choice. He has rejected certain ways of teaching skills and knowledges and has accepted others; he has made decisions with respect to organizing the class for learning and with respect to organizing subject matter. This is a challenging task. Whether there are ten students or forty students, they all need intensive attention and direction as *individuals*. Some choices of method we make are on-the-spot decisions, such as, "Shall I include the section on payroll taxes this term, or include it as a part of the work of next term?" Some are long-range decisions which involve a great deal of thought.

Methods, to a large extent, determine the effectiveness of the teacher. It is assumed that the teacher is enthusiastic about his own method. The important thing is to be consistent. It is our purpose to provide some assistance in making intelligent decisions concerning the selection of methods. Certain time-tested principles of teaching accounting will be presented. Other parts of this chapter contain specific research by leaders in accounting instruction.

Accounting Must Be Taught

"A little knowledge is a dangerous thing: Drink deep or taste not the Pierian Spring." So wrote the poet Alexander Pope. The principle is apropos when applied to the teaching of accounting. How often do we leave students with just enough knowledge to get them into really deep water! At times a teacher finds that his students have completed a work sheet in an apparently masterful fashion, yet a "quickie quiz" on *understanding* shows complete ignorance of the application of the principle. A standard procedure in accounting classes when introducing the work sheet can be as follows: As soon as it is completed and presented by students, ask the question "So what?" Everyone in the class will know what to expect: specific questions on the meaningful use of the work sheet as an accounting tool. The discussion continues until everyone thoroughly understands. Learning bits and pieces of a process leads to *mis*understanding rather than understanding.

Demonstration in Accounting

The development of visual and audio-visual education material has been based on a cliche, but one that is nevertheless valid: A picture is worth a thousand words. Students learn from what they see. For the accounting teacher, showing and demonstrating are necessary parts of the instruction. If students can't learn from concrete illustrations, how can we possibly expect them to learn from abstract presentations? Nowhere in the business curriculum does the use of visual aids have such possibilities, and nowhere else is it as necessary as in accounting.

Included in the teacher's planning should be materials and procedures for maximum use of visual and audio-visual aids. The more skill a teacher can develop in handling them, the better his teaching will be. Demonstration devices are not the easy way out, but the average accounting teacher can be quite successful if a few basic principles are observed. Refer to Chapters 7 and 10 for some good methods and sources of materials for demonstration.

Help Accounting Students To See the "Whole"

Accounting teachers should at various times check to see if the pupils in the class can visualize the entire process they have been studying. Results of such an evaluation are sometimes enough to throw the teacher into the "Slough of Despond" described by Bunyan in *Pilgrim's Progress*. After all, says the teacher, the students have been doing *something* all this time! Papers have been submitted, theory tests given, practice sets completed—all these seem to indicate that pupils know what is going on. However, given an examination of a type that covers the "complete cycle" relationships, the result may be dismal.

Gestalt psychology has influenced much modern teaching. The "whole" approach is perhaps the missing link between the mechanical learning and real understanding. One way to help students visualize the accounting cycle is the "Complete-Cycle" approach described in detail on page 234. In using the complete-cycle, the standard accounting cycle is developed quickly—the whole of it during one class session—as simply as possible the first time through; that is, without adjusting entries and with only simple journals and ledgers. Each time the student works through the basic problem again, he adds basic information. On some trips around the cycle, the student adds merchandise adjustments; on other trips, he adds returns of merchandise, and so on. An important part of this approach for "whole" understanding, is to construct the problem so that everything needed is on a single sheet of paper. The student not only goes through the steps of the accounting cycle, but he also can literally see it develop in a unified, purposeful whole.

Idea Assignments Are the Most Challenging

Experience in teaching accounting has indicated that most pupils are eager to do their assignments, at least at the outset of the course. The teacher must work to maintain enthusiasm throughout the course.

The crux of the assignment problem lies not in the work itself, but in the degree of understanding by both the teacher and pupil of the true goal to be served by solving problems. Unless a pupil knows *what* he is doing and *why* he is doing the assignments, the only outcome for the majority of students is a painstaking filling out of work sheets and other accounting papers with an attitude of "what's the use, anyway." Even if the sheets come back beautifully written out, subsequent tests often cast doubt on the value of such homework.

Whatever the circumstance, proper mind-set is important. An accounting teacher who is prone to divide the textbook into "so many pages a day" will find that while the reading has been done, *it is already forgotten.* If, in planning for the next period, attention is given to making the assignment important for the pupils, they will leave the class fairly itching to get into the problem. Teachers need to set the stage so that students will be in a proper frame of mind to energize the newly kindled interest. Instead of simply assigning Problem No. 14, for example, the teacher should take time to comment on some phase of the exercise. A simple introduction is enough, such as "I'm going to ask you to work the next problem outside the class. Poor Mr. Miller! He worked so hard and yet didn't make a profit." This followed by a story about a certain lumber dealer, much like Mr. Miller, who undersold everybody in the community. To his friends he was known as a go-getter; to the home office, as the dealer with the lowest net profit in the state. His margin was too small. His gross profit wasn't large enough to take care of his legitimate expenses no matter how he pared them down. Before the class leaves the room, they are irresistibly impelled to do something about Mr. Miller.

The Accounting Teacher Is a Teacher of Arithmetic

In every accounting class there will be a number of students who are not able to do the necessary arithmetic computations. Where this skill is deficient, it is the accounting teacher's job to do something about it. How he does it will depend on circumstances. Some authors have included drill problems in texts or supplementary materials. Others prefer to wait until a student experiences the need for arithmetic when attempting to do a problem. We have ample evidence that genuine learning takes place only when students are motivated to learn. Effective learning of the needed arithmetic skills can be developed through meaningful relationships developed by the accounting teacher, with an avoidance of rules, formulas, or memorization of processes.

Student confidence is the key to successful application of arithmetic fundamentals. The teacher who covers accounting material rapidly will, in this age of accountability, inevitably find that some students are unable to complete course requirements because they do not grasp arithmetic fundamentals. To move too slowly has the result of boring many of the able students in the class. An assessment must be made of student capabilities. The writers of the Accounting Career Objective section of *Business Education for the Seventies* stress this point in describing objectives, content, and instructional methods for business mathematics:

> Selected topics in financial mathematics are chosen to provide students with an insight into understanding business transactions. . . If the accounting student has not had the course, it is advisable to administer a diagnostic competency examination in business mathematics at the beginning of the accounting course.[1]

Select One Approach and Teach It Well

A great deal of confusion sometimes comes about in accounting because a teacher introduces a "pet" teaching approach that conflicts with accepted practice. Students

[1] Ruth B. Woolschlager (ed.), *Business Education for the Seventies* (Springfield, Illinois: Office of the Superintendent of Public Instruction, 1972), p. 148.

may find it difficult to follow through in the textbook. One should avoid introducing too many alternative explanations of a process—building too many "grooves" at the same time. We all want our students to develop maneuverability in record keeping and accounting; but in our eagerness we may move in too many directions at once, all to the confusion and frustration of our students.

It is crucial that teachers realize that many students have no ready source for their questions once a class is dismissed for the day and, therefore, must be guided toward an acceptable approach and learn it well. There is ample time for additional patterns to be learned during the course.

Teach Simple Transactions Without Involved Vocabulary

Just as anyone who learned to write longhand can also learn to write shorthand, so anyone who can do average work in the usual school subjects can also learn accounting. If students fail to learn, the chances are that the fault lies with the teacher. Perhaps his students are not comprehending the "accounting lingo." Thus, the leader seems to be setting up a barrier to learning.

We *do* have an obligation to teach the language of accounting. Fundamentally, double-entry accounting is built on the Paciolian foundation of *debitori* and *creditori*. It is necessary to understand how this principle functions. Some teachers have found their greatest success, at least for students at a certain level, in having the class memorize "left side for debit; right side for credit." However, rote learning is not lasting and certainly is not explanatory. The words "debit" and "credit" themselves are a source of confusion to many students. Winnett, for example, points out common misconceptions placed on the words "debit" and "credit" and shows where this can lead in immature or illogical reasoning:

You will have to use all of the intelligence, knowledge, and ingenuity at your command to search for ways to relate daily experiences of students to the work of the bookkeeping class. "Credit" in the mind of students represents something good. Therefore, since "debit" is opposite to "credit," "debit" must be bad. But, the mind of the student reasons, additions to cash are said to be "debits," and that of course is good. How confusing this vocabulary is to students.[2]

By approaching this fundamental principle from a student point of view, omitting technical terms for the time being, the teacher will give his pupils an opportunity to develop *what* is being taught in their thinking in relation to *how* and *why* with a minimum of memorization of terms or rules. Boynton points out that "debit and credit are reasoned actions for the students and not procedures based on a memorized set of "blind rules." [3]

The Need for Neat Handwriting

In this machine age the value of handwriting is underestimated by most of us. In spite of all our elaborate electronic developments, in the majority of cases it is still necessary to convert thoughts into symbols in order to communicate. For this, handwriting remains our principal tool. How important it can be to accounting and record keeping is indicated by this case-history statement of a national handwriting consulting service:

In many large department stores a Charga-Plate system is used. This insures legible names and addresses provided, of course, that the Charga-Plate is undamaged and that carbons are carefully placed between the order sheets. This, however, does not provide for the legible writing or lettering of items of merchandise and the numbers indicating the cost of same. Many costly errors are due to illegible number information. It is estimated that the average cost in time alone to correct a single error is one dollar. Large stores may have from 50 to 100,000 transactions a year that find their way into the adjustment department. Legible handwriting is,

---

[2] William L. Winnett, "Debits and Credits at the Blackboard," *National Business Education Quarterly*, 27 (Winter, 1958), p. 29.
[3] Lewis D. Boynton, *Methods of Teaching Bookkeeping-Accounting* (2nd ed.; Cincinnati: South-Western Publishing Co., 1970), p. 397.

therefore, one of the very important items in error control in a department store.[4]

The age of computer technology has proven beyond doubt that errors introduced into the complex machine are derived from handwritten records. Neatness in handwriting is essential. If the accounting teacher can foster this habit in his classes, the general overall standing of the pupil will improve. We, as teachers, can encourage or discourage neatness in students' handwriting. A hastily scrawled T account with hardly legible entries on the chalkboard is not an encouragement to the students to be neat in their own work.

Evaluation is a Means to an End, Not an End in Itself

The good teacher is one who so organizes his work that the process of evaluation is continuous.

All problems that are assigned should be checked, but this does not mean that the teacher must necessarily spend hours doing the work himself. Valuable learning results come about when students correct their own problems. One explanation given on the spot, in context with the subject, is more valuable than a dozen "red marks" the next day.

There must be a significant purpose behind the testing that is done in the accounting class. In general, tests serve two functions: (1) the test serves as a basis for remedial instructional work, and (2) the test furnishes information on which to partially determine a grade. Whether the teacher uses printed tests furnished by the publisher of the textbook or other agencies or makes his own, certain considerations of good testing procedure must be kept in mind:

1. Tests given must be related to the teaching being done.

---

[4] William L. Rinehart, "The Case for Handwriting," *American Business Education*, XV (March, 1959), p. 162.

2. Testing may hinder the progress of education just as easily as it may help.

3. A test may be objective in terms of scoring, but leave certain personal factors, such as attitudes, unchecked.

Evaluation serves as the method to detect the quality or lack of quality of instruction. If there are an overwhelming number of low grades, it may be an indication that the teacher needs to review his teaching materials and methods.

PROCEDURES AND TECHNIQUES

The first part of this chapter has been devoted to a description of sound principles of learning applied to the teaching of accounting. Many of these call for discrimination and good judgment on the part of the teacher, and the method used will depend largely on the circumstances of a given situation. The pages that follow contain a number of practical ideas applicable to these principles. These suggestions have to do with areas that teachers find most troublesome, for example, the efficient use of practice sets. Many teachers, in small communities, do not have access to libraries of reference materials. Perhaps some of the methods outlined here will make it possible for them to teach first-year accounting with some measure of accomplishment.

Organizing to Teach for Understanding

Being properly prepared for the first day's class gives poise to the teacher and confidence to the student. Confidence in one's self is a necessary element in successful teaching and learning. The beginning teacher will do well to use written outline forms of the type that follow to plot the scope and sequence of the course, both from an overall point of view and for day-to-day activities.

Good planning means that every minute of the class period is used to the best possible advantage. Every class period should be based on an established lesson plan, the detail of which will depend on the background and experience of the teacher. In a good lesson plan one usually finds the following:

Review: (Elements of recording transactions in the cash receipts journal, for example.)

Assignment Check: (Through the use of the chalkboard, charts or overhead projector, a "quickie" review or a self-audit of the previous day's assignment.)

Presentation (New Material): (Take the students through the new elements of the day's material.)

Discussion (or Drill): (Question and discussion of the new concepts, followed by a short practice period.)

Summary: (A drawing together of the new concepts presented.)

Assignment: (A brief but thorough review of the instructions and special materials to be used in the assignment.)

Good Demonstration Inspires Confidence

Seeing, understanding, and participating are three important factors in demonstration. The T account, for example, must be seen to be understood. One student thought the teacher had been talking about a "key" account before he *saw* it on the board. Work sheet and payroll problems can best be presented through demonstration. Students can fill in the forms without supervision, but directed instruction is more productive.

How can we get these materials on the board when there is so little time available between classes? For a number of years the writers used a canvas sheet, painted on one side with chalkboard paint. This made an excellent "chalkboard" surface. The work sheet, or any problem involving a great deal of writing, was filled out on the canvas sheet before class. Then the "board" was hung on hooks provided for it on the regular chalkboard. A lot of work? Certainly! But the satisfaction that is gained when students are thus able to grasp an entire process in a minimum of time is well worth the extra effort. A variety of visual aids of all kinds are now available.

The overhead projector provides valuable assistance in demonstrating difficult concepts. Whole problems can be filled in either before class or along with the class in good form with a minimum of last-minute physical arrangements. While the teacher is writing on the transparent slide, he is facing the class and can answer questions or explain points without losing the attention of the class.

Some suggestions have been made which will enable teachers to be most effective in the use of the overhead projector:

1. Keep presentations simple.
2. Do not present too much information at one time. Break up complex subjects into digestible units and add the units sequentially through the use of transparent overlays.
3. Keep the students' attention on the point being discussed. Use sliding or hinged masks to disclose information progressively, so the students cannot read ahead.
4. All letters on transparencies should be large enough to be read by students in the last row. Material copied directly from books, magazines, and the like should be large enough to be read by all students.
5. Color should be used to emphasize and differentiate. Excessive use of color can detract from the point the instructor is trying to make. Several types of transparent colors are available: felt-tip pens, acetate inks, films, and tapes.
6. A small pointer or pencil should be used to call attention to important segments of the transparency.
7. The transparency should be placed on the stage of the projector *before* turning on the lamp.
8. The lamp should be turned off before removing the projectual. It should not be turned on again until another projectual is in place. A bright, blank screen is distracting. The switch should be used to transfer the students' attention from the instructor to the screen and then back to the instructor.
9. The projector should be kept low and the screen high for maximum visibility.

10. The top of the screen should be tilted forward to correct "keystoning" of the image.[5]

For professional-looking transparencies it takes only a supply of inexpensive 10″ by 10″ cellophane, Vu-Graph carbon paper, and a regular or Ampli-type typewriter. Professional, permanent-type transparencies can be easily made with direct image transparency sheets and an office copying machine.

On these finished transparencies as much material can be filled in as the teacher desires and the significant points left blank for classroom completion. For extended problems that cannot be completed in one period, such as some work sheet or payroll problems, the transparencies can simply be put aside for the next day's work—no more "do not erase" notes for the teacher to fret about.

The best demonstration device universally available to the accounting teacher is the chalkboard. The teacher should use every possible opportunity to practice and develop his skill in the use of the chalkboard.

One need not be an artist to do good work on the chalkboard. A little practice on a uniform lettering or writing style will do the job for the accounting instructor. In general, we try to teach too much too quickly in a demonstration, and often the writing becomes hard to read. The teacher should be prepared to illustrate good style in accounting forms, rather than talk about them. Because most rooms are used by a number of other instructors, the accounting teacher should have his own basic equipment. This consists of good quality chalk, in various colors for emphasizing points in discussion, and a good straight-edge instrument. Experienced teachers like to use a ruler such as that illustrated and described by Musselman and Hanna:

I. Use an extra-wide yardstick. A T-square from which the end-piece has been removed makes an excellent stick.

[5] American Accounting Association, *A Guide to Accounting Instruction: Concepts and Practices* (2nd ed.; Cincinnati: South-Western Publishing Co., 1968), pp. 99-100.

2. Attach a hand grip to the stick. This permits you to hold the stick firmly in place with one hand and rule with the other. A window-sash lift makes a convenient grip. It can be fastened to a small block, which in turn may be fastened to the stick.

3. Place the hand grip on one side of the stick so that it can be held without interfering with the ruling along the other side.[6]

If the chalkboard is not in immediate demand by other teachers, semi-permanent forms for ledgers, journals, and other books of record can be lined on the board by first wetting the board and then drawing the lines on the wet surface. These lines will last for at least two weeks of fairly heavy use and can be easily removed for new material by washing the board; or they can be renewed by wetting and relining. Perhaps the accounting teacher should carefully examine the room schedule before drawing these long-lasting forms on the board. One non-accounting teacher remarked not long ago when attempting to erase the board for his English class, "That fellow has put some kind of arithmetic problems on the board so that I can't erase them. What *sort* of chalk does he use anyway?" Chalkboard space is a critical factor.

Finding time to get the materials on the board is also a problem. It is in this respect that a student assistant, or "chairman," can be of great value to the teacher in helping him organize class materials. A part of the effectiveness of the demonstration is lost if the teacher has to spend an inordinate amount of class time getting ready.

The Complete-Cycle Approach

As an approach to accounting, the complete-cycle method means that (first-day stage-setting procedures excepted) the teacher faces the class with the challenge of presenting the entire story of accounting in one sitting:

---

[6] Vernon A. Musselman and J. Marshal Hanna, *Teaching Bookkeeping and Accounting* (New York: Gregg Division, McGraw-Hill Book Co., Inc., 1960), p. 84.

journalizing, posting, pencil footing, trial balance, balance sheet, the check with the original capital to find the profit for the period, the income statement, and again, the net income check. The complete-cycle method is also an excellent review device which can be used to good advantage before introducing the practice set. Complete-cycle problems may be used as remedial exercises for students who are confused and who fail to see the significance of the various steps in the cycle.

No attempt is made to introduce the cycle on the first class day. There are too many adjustments that need to be made before teacher and pupil can work together effectively. However, much can be accomplished during the first meeting of the class that will help to make the first day of the cycle more successful. The story of Mrs. Miller (proprietor in the problems) and how she came to go into business can be told. Foundations established in general business courses can be enlarged. A few basic terms such as assets, liabilities, and net worth can be clarified.

One of the important factors of complete-cycle problems is to have the entire exercise on one page—all writing to be done directly on this page. The technique is simple. The sheets are passed out to the students, and the teacher and students work the exercise together in class. Explanations as to "why" are held to a minimum. Experience in the use of this method with high school classes has shown that not every member of the class will understand the process. This is to be expected. A duplicate sheet is given each student at the end of the period when homework is the rule. With the sheet worked in class as a guide, the students again do Problem No. 1. The next day the entire class repeats the exercise; the good students help those who have not yet grasped all phases of the problem.

During the first few days of the course and in the week following, if desired, a new complete-cycle problem is given each day. Problem 2 would introduce the old inventory and sales on account; Problem 3, purchases and sales returns; Problem 4, the special journals. The illustrations of Problems 1-4 on pages 237-240 show how the statement of the problem and the necessary forms—general ledger, accounts, trial balance, income statement, and the balance sheet—are provided on a single page.

In the use of the complete-cycle method, the cycle is developed quickly—during the space of one class period—and usually without adjusting entries or other complicating features. Each time the student works through the cycle he adds to his basic understanding of the activities required in double-entry accounting.

After the complete-cycle problems have given the student a mental toe-hold on the subject of accounting, the regular text can be used to complete the job, or the students can proceed to the regular practice set work. As in any Gestaltist picture, the details can now be filled in. However, instead of listing a few more assets here and some more sales returns there, as is so often the case, the growth will now be from within—an internal integration and development of a student. The student sees the steps that are necessary in order that the final objective—profit or loss for the owner—may be ascertained and recorded properly. It should be kept in mind, however, that tasks of the accountant do not always include a complete cycle.

The following factors apply to the accounting cycle:

1. Sometimes the accountant does only part of a complete cycle.

2. At times the accountant will move into an activity not directly cyclical, such as checking the accounts receivable ledger against the controlling account. After completing this check, he will return to the basic cycle of activities.

3. The basic cycle activities can be performed at any time rather than just at the end of a fiscal period.

Complete-Cycle Teaching Suggestions. The following precautions should be observed in presenting and working with students on complete-cycle exercises:

1. Omit explanations under journal entries.

2. Omit posting references; use check mark in journal, none in ledger.

COMPLETE-CYCLE PROBLEM No. 1

Mrs. Miller has received permission to place her ice box in a corner of the ice cream store in which she is working as a cashier. She plans to sell flowers as a little business of her own. She is to pay $5 a month rent. She begins business Sept. 1 by bringing the ice box, value $300, and by investing cash, $50. She continues to transact business as follows: Sept. 2, purchases flowers wholesale, $15; Sept. 3, sold flowers for cash, $7; Sept. 4, sold large bouquet for cash, $10; Sept. 5, miscellaneous small sales, $5; Sept. 6, purchases flowers wholesale, $25; Sept. 7, sold flowers, $12; Sept. 8, cash sales for today, $6; Sept. 9, paid expenses: wages, $3; rent, $5; Sept. 10, Mrs. Miller is eager to know whether she has made a profit, so she counts all roses on hand and finds she has a total wholesale value of $19. This is known as the new inventory, or the inventory of Sept. 10.

GENERAL JOURNAL

CASH

OLD INVENTORY

NEW INVENTORY

EQUIPMENT

RENT

MILLER, CAPITAL

WAGES

PURCHASES

PROFIT AND LOSS

SALES

TRIAL BALANCE

BALANCE SHEET

Assets		Liab. & Prop.	

INCOME STATEMENT

Sales . . . . $
    Purchases . . . . . . $
    Less Sept. 10 Inv. . . $
    Cost of Goods Sold . . . . . $
Gross Profit . . . . $

Expenses

Rent . . . . $
Wages . . . . $ $____
    NET INCOME $____

COMPLETE-CYCLE PROBLEM NO. 2

Mrs. Miller decides to continue her part-time business operation. Her assets on September 11 are: Cash, $42; Equipment (Ice Box), $300; Inventory of flowers, $19. On September 12 she has cash sales, $8; Sept. 13, purchases on account, Ames Floral Co., $15; Sept. 14, large order to Capital Univ. on account, $20; Sept. 15, cash sales, $5; Sept. 16, paid for an ad in local paper, $6; Sept. 17, miscellaneous cash sales, $18; Sept. 18, purchased on account, Ames Floral Co., $30; Sept. 19, cash sales, $12; Sept. 20, sold on account to Capital Univ., $15; paid wages, $3. The remaining inventory of flowers on September 21 is $21.

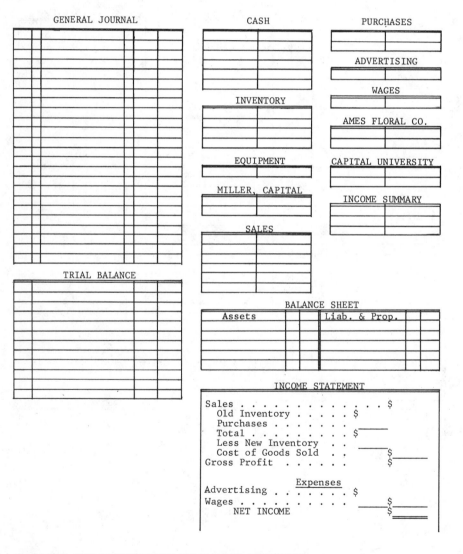

COMPLETE-CYCLE PROBLEM NO. 3

Mrs. Miller continues business with the following assets: Cash, $76; Accounts Receivable (Capital Univ.), $35; Inventory, $21; Equipment, $300; Accounts Payable (Ames Floral Co.), $45. On September 22 she received cash on account from Capital Univ., $20; Sept. 23, paid Ames Floral Co on account, $15; Sept. 24, sold to Harmony Haven Dormitory on account, $18; Sept. 25, purchased flowers from Ames Floral Co. on account, $25; Sept. 26, Harmony Haven returned some flowers saying they were not as ordered. Mrs. Miller allowed them $3 credit. Mrs. Miller returns these same flowers to the Ames Floral Co. They allow her $2 credit. Sept. 27, cash sales, $30; Sept. 28, paid wages, $3; repairs to ice box, $4. Inventory on Sept. 30 is $22.

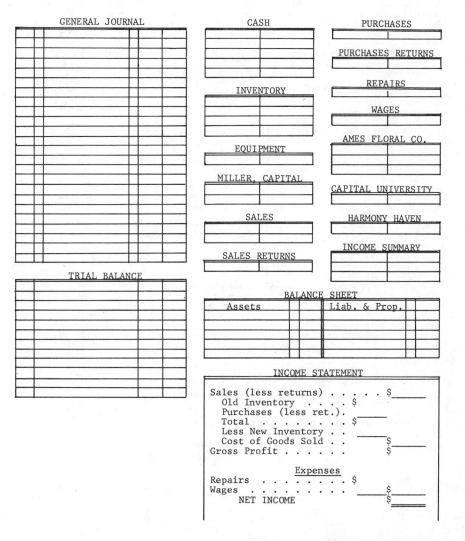

GENERAL JOURNAL

CASH

PURCHASES

PURCHASES RETURNS

INVENTORY

REPAIRS

WAGES

EQUIPMENT

AMES FLORAL CO.

MILLER, CAPITAL

CAPITAL UNIVERSITY

SALES

HARMONY HAVEN

SALES RETURNS

INCOME SUMMARY

TRIAL BALANCE

BALANCE SHEET

Assets		Liab. & Prop.	

INCOME STATEMENT

Sales (less returns) . . . . . $_____
  Old Inventory . . . . $
  Purchases (less ret.). _____
  Total . . . . $
  Less New Inventory . . _____
  Cost of Goods Sold . . $_____
Gross Profit . . . . . . $

Expenses

Repairs . . . . $
Wages . . . . _____ $_____
    NET INCOME $_____

COMPLETE-CYCLE PROBLEM No. 4 (SPECIAL JOURNALS)

On Oct. 1 Mrs. Miller decides to change to special journals. The ledger of last month will be continued. Accounts given below show totals. Oct. 2, purchases from Ames Co., $10; sold to Capital University, $5; to Harmony Haven, $8; Oct. 3, purchased from the Best Co., $15; cash sales, $12; received cash from Capital University, $15; from Harmony Haven, $10; Oct. 4, cash sales, $20; sold to Harmony Haven, $11; purchased from Ames Co., $15; from Best Co., $10; Oct. 5, paid wages, $3; rent, $5; cash sales, $15; paid Ames Co., $33; paid Best Co., $15. Goods on hand, $25.

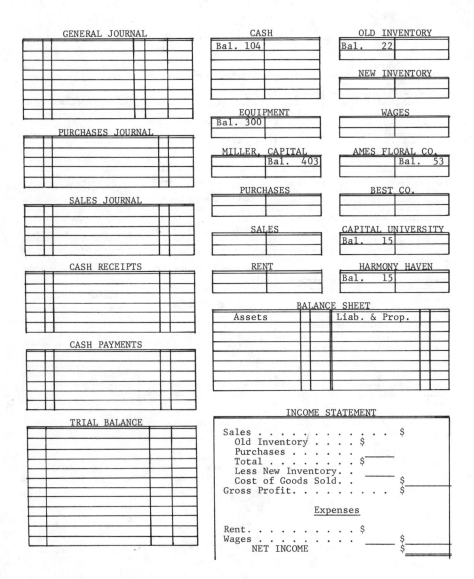

3. Give students mimeographed form with all the necessary rulings for the complete cycle.

4. Type in the account headings—the words "assets" and "liabilities" in the balance sheet, and the income statement terms.

5. Omit all references to supply inventories and like items that need adjusting.

6. Do not require books to be closed in the first day's presentation. This can be done at the end of the week.

7. Use extremely simple figures and in round numbers—no cents.

8. Give sales totals to save time and to eliminate chances of error in figuring amounts.

9. Avoid any discussion having to do with the why of things. "We are planning to take that point up in detail in a day or two," will generally rest the matter.

10. Do not introduce new elements until this basic cycle problem is mastered.

11. Use simple and meaningful language.

12. Do not feel that it is necessary to mention the words "debit" and "credit" on the first day. Later these terms can be introduced in such a manner as to leave the correct meaning—simply a matter of left and right rather than some other meanings that the student may have associated with these terms before coming to class.

Advantages of Complete-Cycle Approach. Advantages accruing to the accounting teacher through the use of the complete-cycle approach may be summarized as:

1. The student has a complete cycle before him at all times, on a single sheet of paper.

2. No blank spaces are left in the cycle to be filled in later as the student studies additional steps. Neither does he receive a description of all the steps and then have to wait several weeks to find out what the steps actually mean.

3. As special journals and ledgers are introduced, they are considered as refinements of the basic cycle.

4. This method can be used in the development of understanding of accounting principles regardless of the textbook being used. In addition, it does not displace well-accepted principles of accounting; it simply acts as a method to help the students to "see the light" without weeks of agony and frustration.

A service business may be used instead of the mercantile business outlined in the sample problems. The merchandising situation involves a more complete picture and has a little more "meat" for complete understanding of the various activities in the cycle.

Complete-Cycle Check-Up Test. After the first three problems of the complete-cycle series have been presented and all students have demonstrated that they can do them fluently, it might be well to have a quick check-up to see what the students have learned thus far. The Spielman exercise (page 243) might serve for such a test. To do this problem, either standard complete-cycle forms or ordinary journal and ledger paper may be used. The usual experience is that students "sail" through this problem in record time and without any difficulty. Complete-cycle Problem No. 4, page 240, may be presented at any time; however, most teachers prefer to wait and use it as an introduction to special journals when this work is taken up in the text.

The One-Month Complete-Cycle Review. By this time the student is thoroughly familiar with what it takes to do a complete-cycle problem. He has done three, each one involving ten days of business. He has also done the Spielman problem as a check-up exercise. Problems No. 1, No. 2, and No. 3 may now be worked as a unit. For this exercise the teacher may design a new complete-cycle form similar to the ones with which the student is familiar—on legal-size paper—to allow room for a month's transactions. The teacher may, of course, use standard journal and ledger paper. The use of legal-size paper enables the student to see the whole of accounting on one sheet. Attention

Mildred Spielman has just received $1,000 from her uncle in Europe. She has, therefore, decided to open up a hat shop on Drexel Avenue. The first thing Mildred does to start the wheels turning is to deposit her $1,000 in the Ohio National Bank. She arranges with the Drexel Beauty Shop for one-half of the shop at a rental of $25 a month. Since today is March 1, she will pay her rent.

March 2   Mildred buys 5 red hats from the New York Hat Company on account, at $1 each.

               Buys 10 blue hats from the Philadelphia Hat Company at $2 each.

March 4   Hires Miss Ellen Locsos to work in the store during noon hours and sometimes after school. (Pay to be determined later.)

March 6   Buys some furniture and other equipment for $100 cash.

March 7   Sells one of the red hats for $2 each.

March 8   Sells to Miss Wright, on account, one blue hat at $5.

March 9   Buys from the Chicago Hat Company 5 green hats at $5 each.

March 10   Sells to Miss Rutherford one green hat at $10, on account.

March 11   Mildred is called out of town on business for a week. When returning on March 18, she finds that Miss Locsos has sold the following merchandise for cash:

               2 red hats at $2 each
               5 blue hats at $5 each
               1 green hat at $10

               Pays Miss Locsos $5 for her services up to that time.

               Remaining Inventory, $25.

Required:

    1. Mildred wants to know whether or not she has made any profit and how much, so she is asking you to make journal entries for all transactions and to list them on the day on which they occur.

    2. Post these to ledger accounts.

    3. After posting to the ledger, make a trial balance, a balance sheet, and an income statement.

should be called to the fact that the income for the month now equals the sum of the profits obtained on the three ten-day problems.

Idea Assignments as Meaningful Learning Experiences

Most accounting teachers agree that reinforcement of teaching is essential to the total learning experience. But what a task to get students to greet "homework" with attitudes that ensure learning! The practice set, for example, can be a "filling-in" assignment, or it can be cast in a structure which puts the student on his own and causes him to want to succeed because he has a special role to play.

A workable practice set procedure, even for the beginning accounting teacher, is a method sometimes called the *accounting office* system. Although this is only one of several relatively standard methods, this approach stimulates interest and helps in two specific ways. It helps: (1) the extremely fast student who completes the set in a very short time, and (2) the extremely slow student who never gets quite finished. The *accounting office* approach provides for both types of students:

> The following plan has been used successfully: When the class is ready to begin the first practice set, it is divided into work groups of three or four students to each group. The work groups are so divided that bright and rapid workers are teamed with an average student and a slow student. The team works as a group on one practice set. One member of the team keeps the cashbook, another member keeps the general journal and the sales and purchases journal, and another member keeps the ledger. The members of the team rotate every ten or twenty transactions so that each student gets the experience of keeping the other books. The teams are given a set time in which the transactions are to be completed. When the end of the fiscal period is reached, they work together in taking a trial balance, with each member of the team making a trial balance. They again work together in making the adjusting entries, in making the income statement, and in making the balance sheet. Each student prepares a copy for himself. The closing entries are completed by the group and are posted, and a final trial balance is taken. Before proceeding to the transactions for the next fiscal period, this team takes another practice set and again goes through the recording of the transactions in exactly the same manner. If student "A" began with the cashbook the first time through, he would begin with the journals, and the other members of the team would rotate in like manner. Each team keeps an accurate record of the number of minutes necessary to make all the transactions, and during the second time through the set they are required to do the work in one half the time required for the first time through. They again

take a trial balance to insure the accuracy of the work and go through the other phases of the end of the fiscal period. When this set is completed, the team of three students again goes through the same practice set attempting again to cut the time in half. When the set has been completed the third time, the students proceed with the next fiscal period in the same manner.

Experience has shown that three students, working cooperatively as they would in an office, can go through three practice sets and complete the work of the fiscal periods in the time usually required for the average student to go through the set once. The great advantage of the team method of work on the practice set is that it actually gives the student *practice* and *repetition* under timed pressure to the extent that he attains a vocational skill for which business will be willing to pay.[7]

Evaluation Is More Than Testing

In Chapter 2, reference was made to the necessity of helping the student receive a daily answer to his question "How am I doing?" Every accounting teacher faces the problem of evaluation. Since the classroom teacher must in most cases assign a final grade to the pupil, it behooves him to do so only after he has carefully considered how this grade, together with how it was determined, fits into the framework of the course objectives. Whether or not this grade is accurate will depend upon the extent to which the teacher has used the various evaluation techniques and procedures which are available to him.

The final grade is often based on too narrow a foundation—printed test scores plus a few quizzes. The accounting teacher need not limit himself to this narrow concept; there are other choices available, some of which lend themselves to a good overall analysis of student progress and effort. It seems reasonable that the following criteria could well be applied in most cases:

1. Written problem assignments.
2. Participation in classroom discussion.

---

[7] Authors' Note: Credit should be given to Dr. Hamden L. Forkner for the origin of this idea, although it has been used in many similar forms throughout the years.

3. Regularly announced tests and quizzes.

4. Practice set work.

5. Attitudes displayed in the classroom, including attendance and punctuality.

6. Mid-term and final examinations.

Written Problem Assignments. A major problem for most beginning teachers is how to score and grade the volume of papers. The "quick-review check" system is of significance. A mark is placed on the papers by the teacher in a quick check of the problems in the folder: +1 (for high quality excellence), O.K. (for work that has most of the elements necessary for clarity), and −1 (for those papers that fall short of useful application of principles). This marking system, used together with the self-check by the students, helps the students keep themselves informed as to their progress in problem work.

Practice Set Work. The analysis of the practice set is described below illustrating the "audit" sheet and "quick review" test. For grade purposes, a numerical weight is given to each element on the audit sheet, the total score representing 100. A useful approach is to assign an audit score to each part of the usual two-part practice set and to the "quickie" test. The two audit scores will then

---

PRACTICE SET TEST

James Wholesale Shoes

Directions: Write the proper answer in the space provided at the left.

1. _____ What was the proper amount of cash received during the month?

2. _____ What is the net increase in capital for the month?

3. _____ How much cash was paid out during October on accounts payable?

4. _____ What is the amount of James' long-term liabilities at the end of the month?

5. _____ How much were the cash purchases during the month?

PRACTICE SET AUDIT SHEET

NAME _____   SCORE _____

ITEM	EXPLANATION
APPEARANCE	
Failure to use ruler in ruling or correcting	
"Written-over" numerals	
Different colors of ink used	
General neat appearance of books	
FORM	
Omission of dates	
Accounts incorrectly ruled	
Journal footings omitted	
Column totals incorrectly forwarded	
Ledger footings omitted	
Ledger folio numbers omitted or incorrect	
Omission of key letters on working papers	
Incomplete explanation of ledger corrections	
Failure to record and post adjusting and closing entries	
ACCURACY	
Incorrect journal column totals	
Incorrect after-closing ledger balances	
INCOME STATEMENT	
Net Sales	
Cost of Goods Sold	
Gross Profit	
Selling Expenses	
General Expenses	
Net Operating Income	
Other Additions or Subtractions	
Net Income	
BALANCE SHEET	
Asset Items	
Liability Items	
Equity Items	
MISCELLANEOUS	
Incomplete Schedules	

REMARKS

have a weight factor of ⅔ of the total score and the test score, ⅓.

Regularly Announced Tests. Testing can be either problem-point or based on objective-type tests, such as true-false, multiple-choice, and completion, or even essay. The best approach seems to combine problem testing with objective-type theory tests. The philosophy of the teacher concerning the evaluation approach will determine whether he is more interested in problem application or in verbal definition and classification. Students should be given the chance to demonstrate their abilities to analyze as well as perform problem routines. A two-part test with one part devoted to "theory" and one part containing a problem that can be completed within the time limits of the period seems to work best. It is assumed, of course, that the teacher will check with the publisher of his textbook to make certain that he has the testing materials that are designed to accompany the text.

Other Elements. This title indicates that there are other considerations beside numerical scores that should be considered—the intangible yet insignificant factors businessmen rate highly: neatness, accuracy, cooperation with fellow workers, ability to cope with unusual situations, and the whole perplexing array of "nonmeasurable" attributes that make for job success.

Lack of space does not permit a full treatment of the formalities of testing, including the standard mathematical procedures. However, two sources of information for the beginning teacher in terms of this problem are imperative:

American Accounting Association, *A Guide to Accounting Instruction: Concepts & Practices*, 2nd ed., Cincinnati: South-Western Publishing Co., 1968.

Mathilde Hardaway, *Testing and Evaluation in Business Education*, 3rd ed., Cincinnati: South-Western Publishing Co., 1966.

In summarizing the evaluative criteria, each of the most objective elements might well be weighted as follows:

Written problem assignments — ¼
Tests and quizzes   — ¼
Practice set   — ⅛
Other elements   — ⅛
Final and mid-term exams   — ¼

The weights applied will depend on the importance of the element to the objectives of the course. The important thing is that the teacher give consideration to a *number* of factors in determining the final grade for the course.

RESEARCH AND OPINIONS OF OTHERS

A vast array of books and magazine articles on teaching accounting are available to the beginning and in-service teacher. The majority of these are useful, if utilized in an intelligent way and adapted to particular situations. For the inexperienced teachers of accounting this great volume of "advice" may tend to be confusing because of its very size. Therefore, in this chapter the authors have tried to select a set of workable principles of teaching accounting, some specific methods, and a sampling of the research and opinions of others knowledgeable in the field.

Several specific areas of concern to researchers and experts in the field follow in this section. These areas are not specifically keyed to the principles in the first part of the chapter, but are included to provide the reader with information concerning major trends of thought.

Organization and Planning

A carefully detailed illustration of the daily lesson plan is illustrated by Boynton [8], part of which is presented on pages 249-253.

SAMPLE DAILY LESSON PLAN NO. 2

1. Title:	Locating common errors that sometimes appear in a trial balance.

[8] Boynton, *op. cit.*, pp. 130-133.

2. Aim:	To bring students to an understanding of a systematic approach for locating errors that sometimes appear in a trial balance.
3. Materials Needed:	On the board diagram of city streets, two-color chalk, eraser, stenciled problems, duplicated homework material. An overhead projector with appropriate materials could be used instead of a chalkboard.
4. Preparation:	Tell story of brother parking his car and not remembering on which street he left it.
	Trace hit-and-miss route taken to find it.
	"What would have been a better way to find his car?"
	Have student trace suggestion on the board.
	"What is the advantage of this suggestion over the hit-and-miss method my brother and I used?"
	"This is what I want to do for you today—save you time and effort on homework."
	Cite typical story of students who claim they spend a half hour doing a problem and another half hour finding an error.
	"How many in class have had a similar experience?"
	Tell class that you are now going to show them how to save time and energy on homework when an error is disclosed in the trial balance.
5. Presentation: (Salient points	Pass out problem sheets. Tell class to add each column in trial balance

to be covered)   #1 once only—insert totals—and turn paper face down.

When all or most class members have finished, call for hands as to number in class who did not find columns in balance.

"If I had not stopped you, what would you have done when you saw that the columns were not in balance?" Ans. Re-add the columns. *"All right —do this."*

Actually this first problem is in balance, yet some students in a large class will not arrive at a balance the first time they add the columns.

Place on the board the heading and Step 1:

STEPS FOR LOCATING SOME COMMON ERRORS DISCLOSED BY TRIAL BALANCE

Step 1. Re-add to check accuracy of addition.

Tell class to add each column in trial balance #2 once only—insert totals— and turn paper face down.

"How many did not get a balance in #2?"
"What is your first step for locating errors?"

Have class re-add to check accuracy of addition.

"What are some of the errors that may have occurred?"

List on the board:

1. Entered amount on wrong side of trial balance.

2. May have copied amount incorrectly.

3. Amount of balance in ledger may have been computed incorrectly.

4. An amount posted to ledger may have been incorrect.

5. May have made error in original journal entry.

Place on the board:

Step 2. Find difference of totals in trial balance and divide by two.

This may help disclose an amount on trial balance that has been entered in the wrong column.

"Why do we divide by two?"

Tell class to add each column in trial balance #3 once only—insert totals—and turn paper face down.
Have class members repeat rules #1 and #2.
Refer to common trial balance errors already listed on the board.

Place on the board:

Step 3. Find difference of the totals in trial balance and divide by 9.

(a) Explain transposition of numbers.

If time remaining in class period seems sufficient, use trial balance #4 for teaching sliding numbers.

(b) Explain sliding numbers.

"What errors on a trial balance will these steps fail to disclose?"

Stress point that these steps give opportunity for a quick systematic approach for finding many errors. Refer to original story about trying to find auto.

6. Application:

There was a constant application of learning as this lesson was being presented. After each step for locating an error had been taught, the students were required to apply their learning of that step by performing it each subsequent time a trial balance failed to balance. Further application is called for in the homework assignment.

7. Summary:

"Now let us see what we have learned."

Ask questions similar to the following:

1. What is the first step you would take if a trial balance didn't balance when you added it?
2. If it still doesn't balance, what is the second step?
3. If you still haven't found your error, what is the third step?
4. What would you do next?
5. What step have we previously learned to follow so as to eliminate a certain type of error before we even start to total the trial balance?
6. Do these suggestions cover the finding of all errors on a trial balance?

(Note: This summary could be handled in a 2-3 minute written quiz.)

8. Homework:

Assign the completion of several trial balances containing errors similar to those covered in this lesson.

9. Teacher's Remarks:

Data Processing and Accounting Instruction

Planning, to be in tune with the times, must certainly include provisions for data processing concepts. Hanson describes an integrated approach to the teaching of data processing and accounting, presenting the following outline of topics to be included:

I. Introduction
   A. Meaning of Data Processing
   B. Types of Data Processing Systems
      1. Manual
      2. Mechanical
      3. Punched Card
      4. Electronic
   C. Historical Background and Development of Automated Data Processing
   D. Employment Opportunities

II. Bookkeeping/Accounting and Automation
   A. Changes in Processing Procedures
   B. Responsibilities of the Bookkeeper or Accountant

III. Introduction to Electronic Data Processing
   A. Primary Elements of Electronic Computers
      1. Input Unit
      2. Central Processing Unit
      3. Output Unit
      4. Secondary Stage

IV. Input and Output: Media and Devices
   A. Punch Card
      1. Description of Standard Card
      2. Card Design and Layout Techniques
         a. Data Base Concept
      3. Recording of Numeric and Alphabetic Information
   B. The Card Punch Machine
      1. Basic Components
      2. Basic Functions

Although writing for development with office practice courses, one could well consider the objectives cited by Place on page 213 as being consistent with the modern-day demands on accounting instruction.[10]

Leonard Robertson sets forth visual presentation of accounting concepts through the use of a symbolic flow chart, a visual presentation plan consistent with modern computer age: [11]

---

[9] Robert D. Hanson, "An Integrated Approach to Teaching Data Processing and Bookkeeping/Accounting," *Business Education Forum*, 25 (March, 1971), p. 25.

[10] Irene Place, "Data Processing and Office Practice," *Business Education Now and in the 1970's*, 25th Yearbook of the Business Education Association of Metropolitan New York (New York: New York University Bookstore, 1964), p. 110.

[11] From "Symbolic Flowcharting as a Teaching Device," by Leonard Robertson, in *Practical Tips for Teaching High School Accounting*, reprinted from *Business Teacher*, p. 23, copyright 1967, 1968, 1969. Reproduced with permission of McGraw-Hill, Inc.

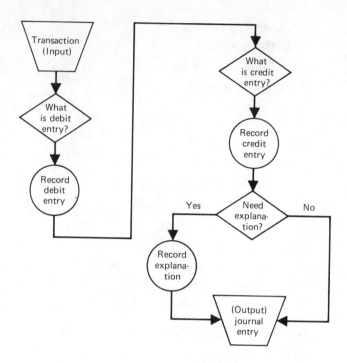

SUMMARY

It has been said that almost any plan of teaching accounting can bring satisfactory results if used by an energetic, alert teacher who observes the fundamental principles of learning. In the preceding pages some suggestions have been offered to serve as guidelines to help make the teaching successful, regardless of the particular textbook or plan used.

Planning is a significant part of teaching success. Perhaps we don't do enough of it. The planning should fit the objectives of the school, the teacher, and the student. Time should be taken to perfect a classroom organizational pattern that will make it easy for the teacher to hold his job, save the teacher and student time, and provide for the differences found in these students.

SELECTED BIBLIOGRAPHY

American Accounting Association. *A Guide to Accounting Instruction: Concepts & Practices,* 2nd ed. Cincinnati: South-Western Publishing Co., 1968.

Boynton, Lewis D. *Methods of Teaching Bookkeeping-Accounting*, 2nd ed. Cincinnati: South-Western Publishing Co., 1970.

Business Education Forum. December issues, bookkeeping.

"Curricular Implications of Automated Data Processing for Educational Institutions." *Delta Pi Epsilon.* U.S.O.E. Contract No. OE-6-85-030. Boulder, Colorado: University of Colorado, September, 1968.

Developing Vocational Competency in Bookkeeping and Accounting, 40th Yearbook of the Eastern Business Teachers Association. New York: New York University Bookstore, 1967.

Emerging Content and Structure of Business Education, Eighth Yearbook of the National Business Education Association. Washington, D.C.: National Business Education Association, 1970.

Hanson, Robert D. "An Integrated Approach to Teaching Data Processing and Bookkeeping/Accounting." *Business Education Forum*, 25 (March, 1971), pp. 24-26.

Hardaway, Mathilde. *Testing and Evaluation in Business Education*, 3rd ed. Cincinnati: South-Western Publishing Co., 1966.

Musselman, Vernon A., and J. Marshall Hanna. *Teaching Bookkeeping and Accounting.* New York: Gregg Division, McGraw-Hill Book Co., Inc., 1960.

Place, Irene. "Data Processing and Office Practice." *Business Education Now and in the 1970's*, 25th Yearbook of the Business Education Association of Metropolitan New York. New York: New York University Bookstore, 1964.

Rinehart, William L. "The Case for Handwriting." *American Business Education*, XV (March, 1959), p. 162.

Robertson, Leonard. "Symbolic Flowcharting as a Teaching Device." *Practical Tips for Teaching High School Accounting.* New York: Gregg Division, McGraw-Hill Book Co., Inc., 1969.

State University of New York. *Syllabus, Bookkeeping 1 and Bookeeping 2.* Albany, New York: State University of New York, 1964.

Tonne, Herbert A., and Louis C. Nanassy. *Principles of Business Education,* 4th ed. New York: Gregg Division, McGraw-Hill Book Co., Inc., 1970.

Winnett, William L. "Debits and Credits at the Blackboard." *National Business Education Quarterly,* 27 (Winter, 1958), pp. 24-31.

Woolschlager, Ruth B. (ed.). *Business Education for the Seventies.* Springfield, Illinois: Office of the Superintendent of Public Instruction, Vocational and Technical Education Division, 1972.

Chapter 7

TEACHING THE BASIC BUSINESS SUBJECTS

THE EVOLUTION OF A BASIC BUSINESS TEACHER

The area of basic business is one that has as a major aim the development of general understanding and knowledge necessary for successful business employment and everyday living:

> All vocational business programs should be built on a solid foundation of basic business education. Students who are preparing for work in marketing or distribution and those preparing for office work have an equal need to understand the business system in which they will be employed. The understandings these two groups need are identical. It makes no sense to say that the business system should be understood from the office worker's point of view or from the sales worker's point of view. Fundamental understandings about the business system are also needed by the factory worker, the farmer, the business manager, the professional person, the construction worker, and every other wage earner one can name. It is especially important, however, that such education be required for all students whose stated purpose is to prepare for careers in business. Otherwise business educators show that they have little understanding of their total obligation.[1]

---

[1] J. Curtis Hall, "Better Basic Business for the Secondary School," *Business Education Forum*, 24 (May, 1970), p. 7.

This area is without question one of the most challenging in which a business teacher can work.

There is frequently an understandable feeling of insecurity on the part of the teacher who was "pushed" into teaching the basic business courses. At almost every gathering of business teachers a lack of confidence in "how to teach" these subjects is revealed; knowledge of subject matter is seldom a problem. Even some of the leaders in the business education area feel that business teachers have oversold the specialized skill phases of education for business at the expense of the nonspecialized area of general or basic business education. The rationalization that the skill areas are all-important has in many instances led to the "general and unfortunate idea that any teacher can take over a basic business class—'You know, anyone can go in there, talk about common business information, and keep the students too busy for mischief.'" [2]

It is incumbent on the business teacher, whatever his special preference in subject matter, to develop teaching techniques that will enable him to do a high-level job of teaching and to create conditions under which students will learn. Kincaid refers to this development of the art of teaching as a "teaching plus"—"that something extra that enables the teacher to practice his art with more satisfaction to himself and with more enduring values in the lives of his students." [3] Harms also refers to this "extra" in the illustration of the following diagram: [4]

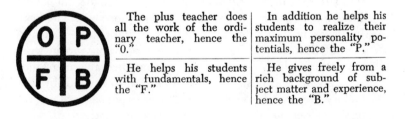

	The plus teacher does all the work of the ordinary teacher, hence the "O."	In addition he helps his students to realize their maximum personality potentials, hence the "P."
	He helps his students with fundamentals, hence the "F."	He gives freely from a rich background of subject matter and experience, hence the "B."

Porter points out the importance of the well-informed teacher in the business education program when he says:

[2] M. Herbert Freeman, *Basic Business Education for Everyday Living*, Monograph 74 (Cincinnati: South-Western Publishing Co., 1951), p. 27.

[3] James K. Kincaid, "Teaching Pluses," *American Business Education*, XII (December, 1955), p. 107.

[4] Harm Harms, "The Plus Factor in Teaching," *American Business Education*, XII (March, 1956), p. 183.

Probably in no phase of education have more rapid strides forward been taken in recent years than in business education. Instructional materials have been greatly improved, audio-visual aids have been developed, and the equipment utilized in instruction has been modernized. Fine new physical facilities are being provided today in new school buildings or in buildings which have been renovated and remodeled. Yet, surrounded by new facilities, excellent equipment and the best of instructional materials, the teacher remains the key factor in any program of education for business.[5]

If the "plus" teacher will search diligently, he can uncover ways and means to generate life in basic business courses such as economic geography, business law, consumer economics, general business, and others. How this may come about is illustrated by the following incident.

Several experienced business educators were discussing the question "What makes a good basic business teacher?" The majority of those present began their classroom careers by teaching the skill subjects of shorthand, typewriting, and accounting. Each one told how under pressure he first agreed to teach something in the basic business area. Most of them were of the opinion that they now preferred basic business. One member of the group drove home the fact that the techniques required for teaching typewriting, for example, are entirely different from those needed in the basic business subjects. "In fact," said he, "it is difficult to imagine anything more unlike. What is good in the skills—time clocks, speed pressures, repetition, production—has very little place in the teaching of basic business subjects. That is why many teachers fail in their first attempt. They usually try to adapt their skill-teaching methods to general business, when what they need is an entirely different approach."

It is like trying to learn a foreign language. As long as one is still translating from English to French, he hasn't arrived as a French student. It is only when one begins to *think* in French that he finds himself making progress in the language. So it is with the teaching of the basic business

---

[5] Gerald A. Porter, "Evaluating the Competency of a Business Teacher," *The National Business Education Quarterly*, 24 (Summer, 1956), p. 16.

subjects. One has to think in terms of basic business techniques—not in the techniques used for shorthand, typewriting, or accounting.

The "metamorphosis" of a basic business teacher is not easy. Therefore, in this chapter is presented a series of guiding principles, together with techniques and concrete suggestions, for teaching basic business subjects.

The Metamorphosis

What are the first signs of an awakening interest in the basic business area? They differ with the individual. In some cases the teacher is "warned" that next year he will teach one or more classes in the basic business area. This teacher then goes to summer school and takes a graduate-level course in the methods of teaching basic business subjects. He will read and write as much as possible in the special subject area that has been assigned to him. He will make use of the opportunity to build up a strong resource unit in each of the subjects in his fall schedule. Thus he will become a basic business teacher. For others, the induction process may have to be more gradual.

"In my own case," said a former skills teacher, "I think the first step in developing enthusiasm for basic business came when I realized one day that it was fun not to do all of the talking—that I could capitalize on student discussion. I realized that directing discussion requires a great deal of skill and that there is satisfaction in the results. I resolved to find out more about this technique."

The chart on page 263, based on an idea of the late H. G. Enterline, shows the steps by which a skills teacher may progress when endeavoring to increase his professional usefulness through development of competence in the basic business area.

The Influence of Physical Factors

What are the essential physical factors that make possible a setting in which discussion can thrive?

1. **Room Size.** The room should be just large enough. The group should not feel crowded, hemmed in; neither

STEP No. 1 —	Teacher does most of the talking. Students "recite." Learning the textbook is the goal. Much rote memory work, much drill. Teacher resents being "stuck with this class"; is looking forward to next term and a change in the schedule.
STEP No. 2 —	Teacher introduces workbook. Students do all the exercises, whether they are apropos or not. Teacher makes some use of material at the end of the chapter—if answers are in the teacher's manual or key.
STEP No. 3 —	Teacher brings in some supplementary material, makes bulletin board display and ties it in with the lesson for the day. Is proud of his display. Shows a film—no discussion, no follow-up. Students, nevertheless, have brief interchange of ideas. Teacher does not interrupt discussion to "bring class back to order."
STEP No. 4 —	A student spontaneously makes a report on something interesting that he has read. Students talk about it. Teacher begins to see value in the process. Teacher checks library for interesting things in connection with the next chapter. Encourages outside reading. Outlines definite reading program. Enthusiasm is growing. He no longer says, "I got stuck with this course."
STEP No. 5 —	Teacher has been reading in methods of basic business subjects. Makes careful plans for each unit. Talks unit over with some of the better students. The unit is broken down into suitable study sections. Committees are appointed. Students are encouraged to bring in their own material, make their own bulletin board displays, handle their own classroom organization.
STEP No. 6 —	Teacher helps class select or slant problem to tie in with something of general school interest. Plans all class sessions carefully. Attempts to use good group discussion techniques. Is rapidly gaining power in this type of work. Is familiar with techniques listed in this chapter and makes frequent use of them.
STEP No. 7 —	Student associates what he is doing with real-life situations. Self-evaluation techniques have been established. Students are more and more handling their own affairs by democratic and scientific methods learned in class. They use these concepts to interpret and analyze other life situations. Teacher is happy in work.

should it occupy but a corner of a room that is much too large.

2. **Room Furniture.** It is not by accident that we speak of King Arthur's Round Table or that we see the members

of the President's Cabinet seated around an oval table—that's the way they do their best work. The furniture in a basic business classroom, or a classroom that is occasionally used for basic business classes, should be movable. Tables should not be too heavy to be arranged in a large rectangle or in small groups as circumstances demand. Comfortable but sturdy lightweight chairs are a part of the setting. A tour of elementary school classrooms indicates that their furniture is usually much better adapted to intimate discussion than that found in many high schools and colleges.

3. **Freedom from Noise.** Many put freedom from noise high on the list as a necessity for a good discussion group. Not all persons have perfect hearing. Even those who have no difficulty with average conversation have trouble when the hearing organism has to sift out or disregard many distracting noises. Some people become nervous and irritable in the presence of conflicting sounds. It is for this reason that discussion leaders stress freedom from noise.

In skill classes, just the opposite is often true. In shorthand, for example, Leslie wants his responses LOUD. In typewriting, however, although noise is also part of the situation, talking is not.

4. **Freedom from Other Distractions.** The intercommunications system has been a great boon to the central office, but it has wreaked havoc with many a class. In some schools, the faculty has taken the initiative to establish policies which keep class interruptions to a minimum. The managers of theaters and concert halls feel that freedom from distraction is so important that doors are often locked after the performance begins, and latecomers are admitted only at certain intervals. Teachers might strive with the same diligence to eliminate objectionable factors of distraction.

5. **Last-Minute Preparations.** If at all possible, the discussion leader should personally check to see that everything is in order. One small detail can often mar the effectiveness of a meeting. At an audio-visual aids conference, the light

bulb in a major piece of equipment burned out during the first five minutes of the demonstration, and no replacement was immediately available. In another case, the chalkboard had been delivered, but there was no chalk. On still another occasion, there were charts to be hung, but no provision had been made for hanging them. At a speech conference, the screen was so far away from the speaker that it was difficult for him to get any unity into the discussion. The constant shifting of their eyes from screen to speaker became very annoying to the participants.

We all, of course, can remember many conferences where every detail was arranged beforehand. It is only when something is missing or when equipment does not function that we become aware of the significance of careful planning and preparation.

Organization and Planning

It is safe to say that when discussion-type basic business classes fail, even though the physical conditions are satisfactory, the reason generally lies in poor organization and planning. Most professional golfers run over in their minds before the tournament the entire rounds they are about to play. They map out strategy for each hole in relation to the competition they will have to face. A good discussion leader or a basic business teacher will plan his lesson well in advance. He may select one or more of the devices mentioned in this chapter in order to achieve his objective, or he may plan various steps within the discussion itself.

He may want to take another look at the problem for discussion. Is it one in which the entire group is interested? Have those present had actual experience with it? Is it so stated that the average person will immediately catch its meaning and significance? Is there a solution to the problem? Can it be solved by discussion?

If the discussion leader arrives at a satisfactory answer to the above questions, he might look to see if it is possible to get the necessary facts for arriving at a solution. How are these facts going to be obtained? How are they going to be validated? What technique is he going to use to determine which facts are related to the problem?

If in his planning the leader has scored a hit on both a significant question and the method of arriving at a solution, then he must consider the next and most important aspect of all, the evaluation and formulation of a workable conclusion. The leader needs to have a definite plan as to how he is going to proceed at this stage of the discussion. How can he help the group to evaluate what has been done? How can he help them formulate in effective, straightforward English a statement of the decisions of the group? What technique is he going to use to check on the workability of these conclusions? To what extent will these conclusions have the support of the group concerned? Are these solutions in line with basic established company policy? If not, what should be done to change either the conclusions or the company policy so that they will harmonize?

The Honorable Peyton Smith, a famous discussion leader in New England, once made the statement that it is often far easier to plan and give a major address than it is to prepare and lead an important discussion. A study of the points mentioned above does not make it difficult to accept such an assertion.

Some teachers like to have a complete set of officers for each class: president, secretary, etc. This is good if it contributes to the smooth operation of the group. If, however, there is danger of becoming bogged down in a parliamentary procedure, the less of such organization, the better. A good person to have in the class is an observer. Technically a disinterested person who sits on the sidelines, he gives his opinion of the functioning of the class as a discussion group. Since it would be difficult to find someone outside the class, a student is usually selected. The position is rotated so that all members will have at least one such opportunity during the term. Reports from observers are often most interesting and to the point. They frequently go something like this: "Joe's question got us off the track. Took us a long time to get back." "Everybody seemed to have an opinion; no one produced any facts." "No material from the reading list was presented."

Class Participation

Many of the well-known techniques listed in this chapter and discussed later are particularly useful in getting full class participation: the group project, the field trip, the film, the debate, and so on; but it is not always easy to get full participation in a straight discussion class.

The direct question is often advocated as a technique to "draw into" the discussion those who are not taking part. As we shall see when we discuss questioning, that technique is being frowned upon today by those who have made an intensive study of the art of questioning. The danger of using the direct question technique to get someone to take part in the discussion was brought out recently in a faculty meeting. The professor—let's call him Jones—was the only member present representing his department. The chairman turned to him and said, "Dr. Jones, what do *you* think about it?" Dr. Jones seemed startled at the question. Later he protested such questioning procedure, saying that he had been embarrassed. Thus, we may need to look for other methods to get full group participation.

There are many ways in which this can be done. The problem itself should, of course, be of vital interest to the entire group; the physical setup should be conducive to full participation, etc. One of the most effective participation-getting devices that has recently come to our attention is one observed when visiting a class taught by Dr. Cameron W. Meredith at Northwestern University. Dr. Meredith told us that some of his students were talking too much, while others were not talking at all. He said he was going to do something about it—and this he did. His technique was a simple one. He invited us to come in and see how it worked. He gave a spirit duplicator master to one of his student helpers. On this master was the seating arrangement of the class. The teacher asked his helper to make lines indicating the flow of the conversation during the entire period. If the teacher spoke to a person in seat No. 6, a line was drawn from the teacher's desk on the chart to No. 6. If Nos. 6 and 10 interchanged ideas, lines were made to indicate that fact.

CLASS PARTICIPATION CHART

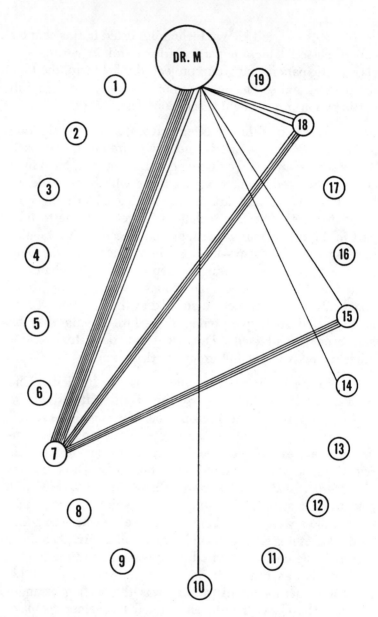

When the class was over, Dr. Meredith duplicated enough copies for the class. The illustration shown above shows the result of that day's discussion. It points out plainly that most of the activity had involved the teacher and No. 7, No. 18, and No. 15. Fourteen members of the class had not made a single contribution during the course of the period.

The next day Dr. Meredith distributed copies of the chart. The results were startling. Those who had not taken part in the discussion up to this time got into the act, and those who had done all the talking the day before subdued their eagerness.

Questioning

The dislike of direct questions is not limited to college professors. In a class of graduate students at the University of Maine, a shy young lady asked the teacher after the first class session, "Will you do me a very great favor? Don't call on me. I'll read all the references on the list. I'll write a term paper. I'll do anything. Just don't call on me. It makes me freeze up inside, and I get all nervous."

The next day the instructor announced to the class, "I want you to hand in a slip of paper with your name and one word on it—'yes' or 'no.' If during the entire term you do not want me to call on you in class, that is, if you don't want me to ask you a single question, write 'no' on the slip of paper. If you don't mind being asked questions in class, write 'yes.' I shall be careful not to ask you anything that will embarrass you. I shall never ask a factual question. I shall always seek your opinion on the matter we are discussing. If with that assurance you want to be questioned, say 'yes.'"

Of the 42 students in the class, how many do you think said "yes"? When the teacher gathered up the slips, he got quite a shock. There were only *three* papers with "yes"! "All right," the teacher said, "you're paying the tuition. You have my word, I shall not ask any member of this class a single direct question during this entire term. If you want to get into the discussion, you will have to volunteer."

This instructor reports that this was then one of the best discussion classes he ever had. There was complete relaxation and freedom from fear. The experience caused a complete about-face in his style of teaching. He discontinued the use of the direct question altogether, even as a device for getting nonparticipating members to join in the discussion.

Of course, the adoption of such a rule makes it harder on the teacher. One can no longer use the old-fashioned question for which there is a single, definite answer—the yes-or-no-type, the dead-end interrogative. What is needed is the chain-reaction question, but it is not always easy to construct.

Among the more pleasant memories in connection with the senior author's graduate work is a class with Dr. Boyd Bode, an artist in the use of the chain-reaction question. The writer thought it must be wonderful to have such a gift—to be able, during the course of a discussion, to find just the right way to phrase a question so the discussion would gain momentum.

One night Dr. Bode invited five class members to dinner at his home. As the group left to go to the campus for class with him, Dr. Bode gathered up five sheets of paper and added a few more words to the pages he had already written. The material consisted solely of questions. Dr. Bode explained, "I always like to have plenty of ammunition." Here was a man whose ability was much envied loaded with five pages of handwritten questions for his class—one single class! Many student teachers (and some others) think they have done well if they read over before class the suggested questions given by an author at the end of a chapter!

Emotional Factors

Astronomers tell us that if we look beyond our universe of sun, moon, and stars, we shall find other universes something like ours. In a basic business class, each individual represents a universe in which there are no limitations of time and space—the body may be in class, but the mind is apt to be with the men walking on the moon, or back in the preceding class where things didn't go well. Just as we need a transitional sentence so that the reader may go smoothly from paragraph to paragraph, so there needs to be a transition from class to class, from activity to activity.

If the students in a certain class are all pepped up about a school event, it may be good to have them get it out of their systems by a brief discussion about it; then by some clever device, make the transition to the subject of the day.

In one form or another, to a greater or lesser degree, all students come to our classes with mental involvements that are difficult to synchronize with what we as teachers are attempting to do. There are times when the majority of the members of the class are excited about something. Students-may be unhappy about a surprise test given during the preceding period. The class could be allowed to talk for a few minutes about whether there should be tests of this kind and about testing in general. From that, the teacher could go to some evaluation problems in his own class and then to the topic of the day. The transition will work, and a fine class discussion will result because everything is again calm, all emotions under control.

If there has been a recent emotional "blow-up" in class, this is a good time to discuss what psychologists have to say about controlling one's feelings. A basic business class where the discussion is apt to become pretty heated at times is a good place to practice this type of mental adjustment. Every victory won here will help to condition the person for the office job after graduation. Exhibitions of temperament and gross deviations from the norm are not tolerated in office employment. A survey of the chief causes for dismissal will bear out that fact.

The teacher of a discussion class should be quick to discover an emotional situation before it builds up. He should do something about it before the explosion takes place. The teacher might interrupt with a "We probably need more information about this particular phase; in the meantime, why don't we see what we can do about Mike's suggestion?"

The treatment of mental illness requires more hospital space than physical ailments; and since health heads the list of educational objectives, it is the duty of all teachers—particularly those in basic business—to devote some time, as occasion gives the opportunity, to do something about mental health.[6]

Fire Power

During wartime, the circumstance of the well-known phrase "too little, too late" is a factor in losing some military encounters. A class discussion, likewise, will be weak and uninteresting if there is no real fire power in the group. When his father was in his nineties, the senior author really enjoyed visiting with him. His dad's perspective of almost a century was fascinating. One day when he asked, "Dad, why don't you go down to the post office any more to talk with your cronies?" the reply was, "There hasn't been a new idea in that group in the last six months."

A class that has to rely on the individual experiences of its members will soon run dry. They need reinforcement. They need to supplement their "fire power." This power is acquired through reading. It is the basic business teacher's responsibility to carefully select the reading material and make it readily available. Here, as was mentioned in the skills, the teacher needs to prime the pump by introducing the class to the material. It helps to actually show them the books, pamphlets, and magazines from which the readings are taken. It helps to ask for volunteers to report on certain specialized readings.

In our basic business classes, we have frequent requests from discussion leaders wanting to know something about the fire power in the group. Out of these requests grew the "reading control sheet." (See page 273.) In the reading control sheet, each student reports briefly what he has read on the subject and adds a few comments about the readings. These sheets serve two purposes. (1) They encourage wider reading. (Reading usually doubles or triples after the introduction of these sheets.) (2) It gives the discussion leader an idea of the kind and amount of idea-ammunition in the class.

---

[6] See "Predicting Teacher Behavior" by Hazel Mosely, *Texas Outlook* (January, 1970), for an interesting summary on how future teachers are likely to act when on the job.

```
READING CONTROL SHEET
```

```
NAME_____     TOPIC_____
                                      (In support of which
                                      this reading has been
COURSE_____         done.)

        The purpose of this sheet is to give the discussion
        leader some idea of the fire power of the group.  In
        the spaces below, please give the references you have
        read recently which you think have a bearing on the
        above topic.  Please add a few remarks of your own
        in connection with each title.
```

AUTHOR	TITLE	PUBLICATION

REMARKS:

AUTHOR	TITLE	PUBLICATION

REMARKS:

Duties of the Discussion Leader

How much should the teacher or discussion leader talk? How can he know when he is talking too much or too little? How much of himself should he give? That, of course, depends upon circumstances. In the usual course evaluation at the end of the term, if the majority of the students say, "You had so much to offer but gave us so little; we can hear these students prattle any day," then perhaps you did not talk enough. If they say, "We had some important people in the class; they had a wealth of experience, but we did not get to hear from them," then the chances are you talked too much. If the ratio is about 50-50, that is,

50 percent say you talked too much and the other 50 percent maintain that you should have talked more, then the chances are that your balance was about right. It is probably safe to say that the teacher who gives freely of himself—not only of that which lies in the narrow confines of the immediate subject matter but also of such other things as his philosophy of life, his aesthetic experiences, sports and recreational interests, opinion on world events—will provide great take-home values of intellectual and lasting quality.

Lest we give the idea that the ideal discussion leader has little to do, here is a review of the qualities of leadership and responsibilities of a discussion leader as given by Dr. Halbert Gulley:

Qualities of Leadership

1. Knowledge of group process
2. Knowledge of the problem
3. Ability to think quickly
4. Respect for others
5. Social sensitivity
6. Language and speech skills
7. Ability to listen
8. Ability to be impartial
9. Persistence, firmness, sense of humor

Responsibilities of a Discussion Leader

1. Planning: analyzing needs, planning the agenda, selecting participants, identifying and wording the question, drawing up a pattern-outline, distributing resource materials, calling a prediscussion meeting, making physical arrangements, publicizing

2. Introducing: introducing the participants, introducing the problem

3. Guiding: guiding the group as it moves from problem to outcome, recognizing tangents and irrelevancies, rebounding, clarifying and restating, asking the right questions, offering transitional summaries

4. Regulating: exercising a minimum of control over the group, striving for balanced interaction

5. Summarizing: at end of discussion summarizing what has been said, stating the outcome agreed upon, and giving participants an opportunity to confirm or reject his statement.[7]

Making the Generalization— Coming to a Conclusion

Not long ago the writers were invited to visit an Armed Forces class in management. After the meeting, the teacher was very enthusiastic. "That was a fine discussion we had today, don't you think? We really got them stirred up, eh?" Before we could answer, one of the supervisors from the group came up and confirmed the teacher's opinion: "We had a wonderful time today, Dr. Dixon. Brother! Did Harry show that guy up!"

Fortunately, no one pressed us for a comment, for our verdict would have been that the session was a complete failure. The problem under consideration had to do with a recent ruling. The group was trying to decide what to do about it. True, there had been much discussion—some of it pretty heated—but there was no attempt to get all the facts on the table in an orderly fashion; no effort made to cut off the fruitless arguing in order to leave time to look at the facts that were available; no effort made to seek a possible solution, even though tentative; no effort made to try a dry run with a tentative solution; and, finally, there was no effort made to arrive at a workable solution. In our opinion the meeting was a complete failure.

Just as a salesman's efforts will, for the most part, be in vain unless he gets the signature on the dotted line, so the loudest and most vigorous discussion is not much more than idle talk unless the teacher or discussion leader succeeds in getting something on the dotted line—some conclusion or workable solution which will add to the smooth operation of the organization.

---

[7] Halbert E. Gulley, *Discussion, Conference, and Group Process* (New York: Holt, Rinehart and Winston, Inc., 1963), pp. 243-265. The development of the list of qualities of leadership and responsibilities is available in full in this reference.

Efficient learning is based upon insight. The outcome of a well-directed discussion brought to a significant conclusion should be greater insight into that particular problem, the frame of reference in which the problem is found, and other problems of a similar nature. Problem solving is not the result of reinforcement of correct responses by success over many trials unless reinforcement and success are both thought of in terms of greater insight.

A skillful arbitrator has found the following diagrams helpful in leading a group from a deadlock to a working agreement:

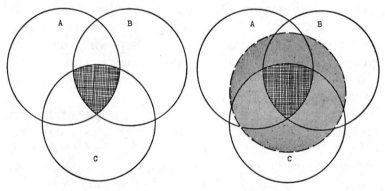

Groups A, B, and C in deadlock   A, B, and C in a working agreement

The three circles represent three groups with conflicting interests. They are in a peacemaking session, hoping to reach an agreement. The small black area in the middle represents the few points on which they all agree. It seems impossible ever to reach a solution acceptable to all.

Patiently, the discussion leader seeks for areas of compromise where only two disagree. He succeeds in getting a concession here and a little less opposition there until he has reached an area of agreement large enough for the company to operate effectively. The initial stage of the discussion is pictured at the left; the final solution at the right.

The area of agreement, even though not at all what each one originally had in mind, represents an arrangement where dignity has been maintained, and the profit margin is still such that the work can continue successfully. The slogan is: Keep your eye on the spot in the center, the area of agreement.

The Follow-Up and Feed-Back

Just as a letter that is actually to be put in the mail adds zest to a transcription class, so will decisions that lead to action stimulate a discussion group. No one likes to engage in make-believe activities when the real McCoy is available.

Likewise, teachers can challenge students to benefit the school and business community by having them solve relevant problems in the classroom. One teacher coming back from a meeting of office executives where irregularities in observing coffee breaks were discussed took the matter up in one of his classes. It served as a springboard for a general consideration of office etiquette. To condition themselves for the coffee break, which was soon to become a part of their daily experience, this group introduced its own coffee break and formulated rules to govern its control.

Business classes can tie their solutions of economics problems, for example, to the national scene and check them with decisions made by Congress. The "so what?" of the modern generation needs to be answered. In a basic business class this can be done by using problems that are meaningful, by encouraging feed-back, and by following up the solutions.

Evaluation

Those who speak about evaluation in connection with the basic business subjects usually talk about two things: (1) the evaluation of the teacher or discussion leader, and (2) the evaluation of the class in terms of the objectives set for the course. Let us consider the evaluation of the teacher first.

1. **Evaluation of Teacher Effort.** Teachers, like students, must know how they are doing in order to be happy in their work. The self-rating chart on page 278 might serve as a beginning for teachers, discussion leaders, and committee chairmen.

CHECKLIST OF PERFORMANCE OF DISCUSSION LEADERS

The Discussion Leader	Excellent	Fair	Unsatisfactory
1. State problem clearly			
2. Stimulated free discussion			
3. Made good use of blackboard			
4. Made use of cases to bring out facts			
5. Used good questions to stimulate discussion			
6. Knew where he was going and held discussion to the point			
7. Refrained from answering questions but referred them to group			
8. Maintained an easy, helpful manner			
9. Made advance preparation for conference			
10. Summarized conference discussion			
Other comments:			

A basic business teacher should ask himself the following questions; then he should decide upon the philosophy under which he wishes to operate: [8]

To what degree am I, a basic business teacher, democratic in my classroom procedures? As we work toward a more desirable style of leadership, it is the *direction* which is *significant progress* rather than the style of leadership at any one time. An efficient, cooperative, and happy climate is the result of hard work:

[8] Based on a lecture by Dr. Cameron Meredith, Northwestern University.

Leader-Centered	Group-Centered
Members are permitted freedom and rights, but they flow from the leaders.	Members have freedom and rights in their own hands. Permission of leader is not required. Leadership often rotates.
Leader takes responsibility for good discussion and adequate summary. Takes responsibility for not fulfilling his role.	Discussion is a group responsibility. Leader reluctant to keep things going and to summarize. Often assumes role as a member.
Leader presents several alternate goals, activities, etc., and lets group select.	Leader gets group's suggestions for goals, activities, etc., and then the group selects.
Time allocation and way in which group proceeds is in hands of leader. He may delegate.	Time allocation and way in which group proceeds is gradually relinquished. Group becomes independent of leader as *leader*.
Leader takes responsibility for group troubles. Leader may ask for suggestions, but usually gives suggestions and allows group to choose.	Leader tries to get group to diagnose group troubles by getting group suggestions first. It is made primarily a group responsibility.
Leader uses methods of evaluation, but does not discuss them unless asked.	Techniques of evaluation and group evaluation is a topic of discussion.
Leader assumes role of resource person concerning matters of information. He controls selection, order, and presentation level of content. He may delegate, but control remains in his hands.	Leader gradually relinquishes control of content. Members decide what is to be discussed, order, and presentation level. He exploits group for information rather than promptly giving his own.
Leader is the source of support, rewards, and punishments.	Group is source of support, rewards, and punishments (not malicious punishment).
Leader makes no particular attempt to aid identification or perception of interdependence among members.	Leader tries to develop identification and perception of interdependence among members.
Leader will phrase situations more often in terms of "I" and "you."	Leader will phrase situations in terms of "we."

A summer school class at the University of Maine, under the co-chairmanship of Clara Swan and Mildred Bradford of Husson College constructed a basic business teacher evaluation chart as its project for the term. The following instrument, with some modifications by the authors is the result of their study:

BASIC BUSINESS TEACHER EVALUATION CHART

(10 points is a perfect score for each part; 100 points for perfect score on all parts.)

THE TEACHER .... ( )

Does he seem to know his subject? Is his speech such that it can be heard in the rear of the room? Poise? Appearance? Sincerity? Does he like to teach? Eye contact? General adequacy?

THE STUDENT .... ( )

Is the student an important part of the picture? Is the class interested in what is being done? Do the students seem to *want* to learn? Are there factors which seem to disturb the growing interest of the class?

OBJECTIVES .... ( )

Are they clearly stated? Illustrated on blackboard or otherwise? Is an effort being made to have students underwrite them? Are they worthwhile? Needed? Attainable? Needed now?

ATMOSPHERE .... ( )

Has a mood or mind-set been created for the lesson? Is the general atmosphere of the classroom conducive to efficient learning? Light? Ventilation? Noise? Size? Movable furniture?

EFFICIENCY .... ( )

Has the lesson been well planned? Is the teacher getting the most out of the period? Is the tempo too slow? Too fast? Is there evidence of marking time? Materials at hand well organized? Getting things done?

INTERACTION AND PARTICIPATION .... ( )

Is there active participation on part of *all* members of the class? Are individual differences being met? Is the teacher making use of one or more of the basic business teaching techniques?

MOTIVATION .... ( )

Are the simple psychological rules for good motivation being observed? Knowledge of progress? Is problem meaningful? Need solution? Student level? Praise? Success? Are devices pertinent? Aspiration set at attainable levels?

VISUAL AIDS AND WORKING MATERIALS .... ( )

Is efficient use being made of the chalkboards? Of the bulletin boards? Other forms of visual aids? Does he have at hand the routine materials? Reference books? Other texts? Methods books?

MEANINGS .... ( )

Are the students actually getting something out of the lesson? Does it mean something to them, really? Can they use this particular knowledge in business? In later school work? Is the student now a different person?

EVALUATION .... ( )

Is some effort made to check up before the end of the period to see what has been accomplished? Do students take an active part in the evaluation? Is it realistic? Does it serve as a learning device?

The following factors cannot be rated at every individual lesson—they pertain generally to the unit. Use judgment and answer as occasion warrants.

Classroom organization————— Committee activity————— Use of community resources————— Use of the library————— Is source unit available————— Use of the library————— Is democracy in action ————— Contribution to health ————— Better living—————

2. **Evaluation of Student Effort.** The ability to properly evaluate student effort is a power that one develops with experience. As the teacher gains confidence in handling basic business subjects, as objectives become more meaningful, he will also acquire insight into how one should evaluate outcomes in terms of course objectives. This growth in the power to evaluate usually develops along the following pattern. Beginning teachers frequently use only Stage No. 1.

Stage No. 1: Term grade is based mostly on the final examination, with some value given to the mid-term examination, if there is one. In order to make a high score, the student must learn and remember a great many facts. Company-published, textbook-correlated, printed tests are frequently the only method used in ranking students. The teacher, of course, does everything. Objectives of the course are generally not clearly stated, and the final examination often has little in common with these objectives.

Stage No. 2: Stage No. 2 is similar to No. 1, except that an effort is made to enlarge the base used to determine the final grade. Projects like term papers, reports, and class tests are considered in the final score. Teacher uses "homemade" tests to supplement printed tests. Teacher still assumes full responsibility and does all the work.

Stage No. 3: After the term is underway, and the class is functioning nicely as an efficient body of learners, teacher and students review the objectives of the term. They then discuss techniques whereby they can best evaluate themselves; they seek to find how the actual outcomes at the end of the term compare with the anticipated outcomes established in the beginning. Teacher and students work together to determine mark for the term. A "grading committee" representing the students often works with the teacher.

Stage No. 4: Students grade themselves. Teacher remains in the background as group leader, helps in establishing valid criteria.

3. **The Evaluation Control Sheet.** The specific method of evaluation used in any class will, of course, depend upon

the subject and the objectives set for the course. Regardless of the system used, the base should be a broad one—broader than that encompassed by a printed textbook test.

In the preceding chapters, when discussing the skill subjects, the authors presented various "evaluation control sheets." In the basic business subjects, we likewise recommend the use of a control sheet. The control sheet serves much the same purpose as the worksheet in accounting: it enables the teacher to get on one sheet all facts that should be taken into consideration in order to arrive at a valid mark for the term. These factors can be weighted to correspond with the importance that has been placed on the various units or discussion areas covered during the semester. The authors have used the following control sheet, modified as needed for any given class, with good success:

EVALUATION CONTROL SHEET
(For Basic Business Subjects)

TEACHER'S ESTIMATE (100 points) . . . . . . _____
REPORTS, TERM PAPERS, ETC. (100 points) . . _____
MID-TERM EXAMINATION (100 points) . . . . . _____
MAJOR TERM PROJECT (100 points) . . . . . . _____
FINAL EXAMINATION (100 points) . . . . . . _____
TOTAL SCORE . . . . _____

It is suggested that the teacher make an evaluation blank for each student and that he begin to make entries on this sheet early in the term. The official roll book will, of course, be kept as usual, but from time to time the teacher might wish to make notations on the student control sheet. For example, on the first item, "Teacher's Estimate," he might want to enter in pencil a beginning score of 75 points. Then at each time during the term when a student goes up in the teacher's estimation because of some unusual contribution, the teacher might want to raise the score; or, if because of absenteeism, tardiness, or lack of cooperation the teacher's rating of a student goes down, the teacher might wish to lower the score. If nothing significant happens one way or the other, it might be an indication that the final score of "Teacher's Estimate" should be not more than the original 75 points. The other blanks can be filled in as tests are given or as term papers and reports are turned in.

At the end of the term, when all facts are in and all items have been entered, the teacher totals the control sheet. A perfect score would be 500 points. This, divided by five, puts the score sheet on a percentage basis—a perfect score of 100 percent. To arrive at the usual "A," "B," or "C," marks, the following scale might be adopted: 90 to 100 percent equals "A"; 80 to 89, "B"; 70 to 79, "C"; 60 to 69, "D," and below 60, an "F." The teacher may wish to grade the class on the curve of normal distribution or on a combination of the fixed scores and the curve.

At various times parents may protest a mark made by a son or daughter. If the teacher has something on the order of a control sheet to show the protesting parent, the teacher can usually establish that the mark awarded was fair and reasonable. When the teacher has only a single mark in his grade book to justify the student's grade for the term, explanations are difficult.

An Experiment in Self-Evaluation

An experiment in student self-evaluation was conducted by one of the authors at a university a few years ago. The students were told that they would be allowed to grade themselves for the term. It soon became evident that in order to grade themselves they would need criteria on which to base their judgments. Two days were spent developing these criteria. On the basis of its findings, the class developed a scale. The instructor acted only as the discussion leader, with the students organizing the standards for letter grades. The class listed the following factors as necessary for a grade of "A":

1. *Opinion of the class.* It must be the spontaneous judgment of the class that this person deserves an "A."

2. *Teacher judgment.* The teacher, without doing any figuring or averaging of any kind, should have this student pegged as an "A"-calibre student.

3. *Outside reading.* An "A" student on his own initiative goes far beyond the line of duty in his reading.

4. *Contribution to the class.* An "A" student is the one who always brings something new and interesting to class. He soon becomes known for his fine contributions. He is thus an outstanding and valuable member of the group. Even the teacher often learns something from what this student has read or observed.

5. *Logical organization of knowledge and experiences.* The "A" student is the one who welcomes the opportunity to bring to the group in organized and well-written form the outcomes of the term as he sees them. The entire class benefits from the fine presentation of his term paper or report.

6. *Leadership.* The "A" student eagerly assumes leadership responsibilities. It is the "A" student who volunteers to be chairman of class committees. It is through these committees that the term problem is broken down into its component parts, each committee working intensively in its own particular area. The results of all are then put together for the total outcome of the entire term.

After these criteria had been established, scales were also worked out for "B" and "C" grades. A few of the factors that characterize the "C" are as follows: student should be there every day; he must do the minimum reading; he must participate in committee work when asked to do so; he must make contributions to class discussion if and when inclined to help; he must be familiar with the basic understandings and knowledges that form a part of the outcome of the course. Space does not permit a full outline of the "B" characteristics, but they lie somewhere between the "A" and the "C."

While the class was working on the criteria, some of the author's colleagues thought he was in for trouble. "They'll all want 'A's.'" However, when a poll was taken in the class, only three out of a group of 36 wanted an "A."

Here, then, was a class with the basic fear removed— the fear of not passing the course or of being embarrassed by a low grade.

TECHNIQUES AND PROCEDURES

We have discussed, thus far, general principles underlying group dynamics as a whole, principles that apply to almost any specific technique the teacher may want to use. The principles listed in this chapter lose some of their effectiveness unless they are applied in connection with specific basic business instruments or teaching procedures. The following is a list of 21 techniques that teachers in the basic business subjects have found useful. These devices will be described in some detail, with additional elaboration and specific applications in Chapters 8, 9, and 10.

1. The straight lecture
2. The lecture—augmented with chalkboard illustrations
3. Question-answer method
4. Problem-solving
5. The demonstration
6. Guest speakers—community resource persons
7. The panel discussion
8. The case problem method
9. Brainstorming
10. The buzz group
11. Role-playing—dramatic skits
12. The class report
13. Scrapbooks—notebooks
14. Instructional films
15. The project—individual and group
16. Field trips—educational tours
17. Gaming and simulation
18. Bulletin boards—display boards
19. The tape recorder
20. Television—using the overhead projector
21. Miscellaneous techniques—debate, term papers, "analytical approach"

The concept calling for the use of a variety of different classroom procedures seems to be well documented. Musselman, for example, attempts to point out the possibilities available for this "interest-getting" element:

We know that students learn best when they are interested. How, then, do we interest them in a new topic in general business? There are many handles that fit this tool—variety, visual aids, demonstrations, dramatizations, pupil participation, utilization of community resources. Aids for introducing new unit topics include:

1. Films or filmstrips.
2. Bulletin board exhibits or the flannel board.
3. Dramatic skits.
4. Newspaper accounts of some happening in the local community.
5. Student or teacher demonstrations.
6. Well-illustrated supplementary materials.
7. Oral reports that were assigned a few days earlier.
8. A case history of one of your own experiences or one you have observed.
9. A visiting speaker from the local community.
10. A pretest—include in it unusual and interest-stimulating items.
11. An overview of the unit.[9]

It is not difficult to determine from the foregoing list that teachers should recognize the importance of variety in their methods. The following partial list from Schorling and Batchelder also shows the range of possible devices "if one wishes to avoid the very bad habit of restricting his work to a few procedures": [10]

1. A pupil makes an oral report.
2. A committee demonstrates.
3. A film is presented with comments.
4. A talk illustrated with slides is given.
5. The teacher reports on common errors found in test papers.
6. Pupils and teacher discuss a basic question.
7. A teacher lectures.
8. Pupils engage in a debate.

---

[9] Vernon A. Musselman, "Helping General Business Students to See, Hear, and Think," *The National Business Education Quarterly*, 27 (Winter, 1958), p. 34.

[10] Raleigh Schorling and Howard T. Batchelder, *Student Teaching in Secondary Schools* (3rd ed.; New York: McGraw-Hill Book Co., Inc., 1956), p. 175.

9. A dramatization is presented.

10. A class engages in a rapid oral review.

11. A pupil demonstrates.

12. A teacher demonstrates.

13. The class discusses supplementary reference material.

14. The class considers the written report of a class excursion.

15. Pupils discuss an assignment and anticipate difficulties and plan reports of source materials.[11]

Crank points out an attribute of a "plus" teacher:

> The level of understanding will depend greatly on how thoroughly the teacher explores the possible insights, relationships, conclusions, and generalizations. One of the most common mistakes made by teachers is failure to "nail down" the understanding. This "nailing down" procedure probably is best accomplished by asking students to verbalize the understanding. Students need help in seeing relationships and drawing conclusions.[12]

A teacher will either "teach as he was taught to teach," or "teach as he was taught." Because teaching the basic business subjects poses a challenge of greater proportions than the skill subjects for many beginning teachers, the patterns that follow will be of some help in selection of the method to be used under given circumstances.

The Straight Lecture

The straight lecture, in some areas of education and at some levels, is still the most frequently used method of instruction. The weaknesses of the lecture method, particularly in high school classes, have been pointed out forcefully on many occasions. One might draw the conclusion that it does not have a place in the classroom. This is far from true. The lecture method seems to be the best method when the following conditions are present:

---

[11] *Ibid.*, pp. 175-6. (The entire list of 35 excellent procedures is given in the cited work.)

[12] Floyd L. Crank, "Improved Methodology in Basic Business Education," *Business Education Forum*, 14 (March, 1960), p. 7.

1. When a nationally known authority possesses a large body of information and experiences not shared by his listeners, and when these listeners are eager to have this information.

2. When the subject matter dealt with is factual in nature and there is very little opportunity for differences of opinion or for problem-solving.

3. When time is limited—speaker will be available only for a day or so.

4. When the straight lecture is later reinforced by other techniques. A recent observation of lectures given to classes of two hundred or more showed the following pattern: no questions were permitted during the first hour; there was no discussion. During the following period, the class broke up into sections of fifteen students where the points presented during the lecture were taken up in detail and discussed. (The decisions were later reported to the assembly as a whole by a single person representing his particular group.)

The lecture as a teaching method is more generally associated with college and university teaching than at the level of the secondary school. This is consistent with what is known about the learning abilities of young people and adults and of abstraction compared with concrete or sensory experiences. The lecture, when used at all, should be supplemented by demonstration, discussion, and practice. Brooks and Pierson feel this is true even at the university level:

> It is extremely doubtful that students in a survey lecture course are going to have much opportunity to apply newly acquired knowledge to problem solving. There would be no time for discussion in class, a fact which leaves the students with the task of memorizing meaningless data. They learn least from having an instructor prescribe a solution without giving them any opportunity to question or criticize; most from their own efforts to deal with a situation. They should be participants rather than members of an audience.[13]

[13] Wayne A. Brooks and A. P. Pierson, "Case Vs. Lecture Method for the First Course in Business Law," *Collegiate News and Views*, 13 (May, 1960), p. 29.

It has been said that too much of secondary school business education consists of a maximum of lecture and a minimum of discussion, demonstration, and student participation. This condition is changing rapidly as more and more high school teachers are availing themselves of the newer techniques and procedures presented in basic business methods courses.

In deference to its time-honored place in teaching methods, the lecture, when used effectively, requires a great deal of preparation and a well-refined manner of presentation. The occasional use of the illustrated lecture procedure brings verbal description within the learning limits of the students. It provides an opportunity to talk with students, to exchange questions and answers with them, to explain and to demonstrate for them.

The Lecture—With Chalkboard Illustrations

Probably the most common variation of the straight lecture is one in which the chalkboard is used to clarify abstract concepts. A teacher of world history provided the authors with an excellent method of procedure. His lectures were very formal. They were packed with content. The vocabulary—names and places—in these courses were totally unfamiliar to the students. These names would have had very little meaning had he not used two sets of chalkboards and a set of maps to augment his lectures. He made elaborate preparations for each lecture. He brought in two portable chalkboards so that he could outline his material before class and be sure it would not be disturbed. In the front of the room was his array of maps—including blowups of small areas to give details. To the right was a portable chalkboard on which he had hand lettered all the names and places in the order in which he planned to take them up in class. To the left was his outline for the entire lecture. He would first go over this outline quickly with his class, showing them what he was going to cover during the period. On his desk were numerous reference books from which he would occasionally read interesting anecdotes having to do with kings, rulers, generals, and statesmen that were to pass in review. What a contrast between these classes and those in which an instructor "drones" through an hour's lecture using nothing more than his lecture notes!

Question-Answer Method

Use of the question-answer method is as common in business education as it is in other areas. It is frequently used as an oral quiz technique, and it can be effectively used to stimulate discussion by posturing controversial questions.

Question-answer procedure may be used to advantage in uncovering student attitudes, needs, interests, and problems; in probing for understanding; and in guiding discussion. The wise selection and timely use of questions, and the observation of good questioning techniques, may revitalize student interest in the basic business subject under study. Login gives the following review of the questioning technique, a matter of concern because of the frequent use of the method:

1. Before you call upon a particular student, are your questions:
   a. Directed to the entire class?
   b. Digested by the class?
   c. Directed to the pupils in irregular order?
   d. Directed to the pupil who is inattentive?
   e. Distributed among all pupils?
   f. Of difficulty directed to brighter pupils? Of factual recall directed to slower pupils?
   g. Varied in tone and phrasing to avoid a monotonous manner?
   h. Returned to the pupil who failed to answer a similar question?

2. Do you avoid the following form of questions?
   a. Multiple
   b. Ambiguous
   c. Tugging
   d. Echo
   e. Categorical
   f. Concert or chorus
   g. Leading

h. Guessing

i. Pumping

j. Repeat [14]

The greatest value of direct questioning lies in the amount of forethought that has been given to the possible questions that can be used to fully develop an idea or concept under discussion.

Problem-Solving

"I didn't come to this class to memorize a lot of stuff. I came here to THINK!" a student once told his teacher. Taking the standard liberal arts program has long been assumed to be synonymous with learning how to think. Yet, in senior-level classes liberal arts majors and business majors have often been indistinguishable.

Students at all levels and in all courses must be taught *how* to think, regardless of their programs. Just as a musician must know the notes or a dancer the steps before he can work on the art of expression, so the person who wants to think must first KNOW (memorize, if necessary) what he is going to think about. He must be able to state this in clear, meaningful terms, backed up by examples and down-to-earth illustrations before he can go in with the higher levels of organization, sublimation, developing alternatives, setting up criteria to be used in making selections, and making the final decision for the course of action he is ready to recommend.

The initial task of the teacher and the students is the determination of what constitutes problem-solving. The following is a standard listing of the steps:

1. Definition of the problem.

2. Analysis of the problem.

3. Division of labor for different class members.

4. Procurement of source materials.

5. Finding, analyzing, and interpreting the information needed.

---

[14] Abraham Login, "Questioning," *A Handbook for Teachers of Business Education*, Twenty-Second Yearbook of the Commercial Education Association of the City of New York and Vicinity, 1958, pp. 23-24.

6. Determination of a conclusion.
7. Consideration of other solutions.

Lebeda gives an excellent illustration of this method in a basic concept found in a number of basic business courses—"Putting Money to Work." In brief, her approach to the problem follows this pattern:

1. Broad areas are subdivided into kinds of stocks, advantages and disadvantages of ownership of stock, who invests in stocks, how to read a financial page, how to know a good stock, and many others.
2. The next task is to determine where and how to find the necessary information. For this purpose, the class may be divided into committees, or individual class members may work by themselves. Some of the information will be in the textbook, and students can learn to use the book as a source of information rather than as a means of reading and studying a certain number of assigned pages each day.
3. The teacher should also have available materials from educational bureaus and institutes, business magazines, and financial sections from local newspapers. Students may contribute some materials from their homes. Films may furnish information, and either the teacher or a committee of students may invite a local businessman to speak on some phase of investments.
4. After the students have gathered information about their particular questions or problems, analysis through class discussion can be made.[15]

Demonstration

Whether provided by the teacher, by resource persons, or by the students themselves, the demonstration provides visual experience which quite frequently transcends verbal explanation. Most demonstrations in the business subjects do not require extensive equipment or laboratory techniques and are well within the capacity of any teacher. This fact makes possible the use of the demonstration in almost any

[15] Agnes Lebeda, "Problem Solving in Basic Business," *Business Education Forum*, 12 (February, 1958), p. 29.

classroom. It is less time consuming than some individual procedures, and it emphasizes essential points which might otherwise be minimized.

While demonstrations are most used in the skill areas of business education, they are of particular importance in the verbalized basic business areas. Boduch points out the following example of the use of student demonstration in consumer education:

> To reinforce understanding, the students are asked to devise diagrammed illustrations of the monetary control procedures on posterboards or transparencies. These are similar to flow charts prepared by computer programmers as graphic representations of logical steps in solving a problem. Transparencies are now available in 8½" x 11" size sheets. The student draws his illustrations on the transparencies which have carbon backing. The carbon tracing adheres to the transparency and the student thus does not need a transparency-making machine. The student is then required to explain each of his illustrations to the class. Classmates may challenge the accuracy of the explanations and earn points for themselves and at the same time take points away from the student explaining his illustrations. This activity forces the student to organize his thinking about the use of monetary controls under conditions of inflation or deflation.[16]

Heimerl makes this comment on the use of the demonstration:

> Demonstrations are valuable in consumer education: burn tests on cloths and fabrics; weight tests; what questions to ask a salesclerk; how to analyze advertisements—these and other demonstrations do more than teach how; they also teach the importance of understanding, of knowledge, of wariness and confidence, and so on, and these are the fundamentals of consumer training.[17]

---

[16] Ted J. Boduch, "Teaching Economic Concepts in Secondary Schools . . . in Consumer Economics," *Two Decades of Partnership in Economic Education* (Washington: National Business Education Association and Joint Council of Economic Education, 1969), p. 35.

[17] Ramon P. Heimerl, "Ten Basic Social-Study Techniques Applicable to a Consumer Class," *Business Education World*, XXXIV (June, 1954), p. 17.

Musselman advocates the use of pupil-demonstration to drive home points in the basic business courses:

> Have you tried initiating your class study of Shipping Services by having a pupil demonstrate the correct way to wrap a package in contrast to an incorrect method? It's a good way to hold attention. One way to launch a unit on Communication would be to have a committee of students demonstrate the various ways of sending a message—semaphore, blinker light, flags, Morse code, telephone, telegraph, etc.[18]

It is important that complete and detailed preparations be made for the demonstration. The most important pre-demonstration considerations are:

1. Be aware of the specific purpose of the demonstration before presenting it.

2. Be sure to know the demonstration procedure through rehearsal before class.

3. Have all materials and equipment.

4. Examine the room situation beforehand to make sure that everyone can see.

5. Make use of the "whole" method so that even if parts are presented, they can be tied in with the whole activity or process.

6. Try to anticipate the steps which are most difficult for students to grasp and be prepared to clarify these points.

7. Arrange to have all but the most pertinent questions asked after the demonstration is completed.

8. Direct the pupils' observation and attention by words and gesture—avoid talking too much.

Guest Speakers—Community Resource Persons

The use of guest speakers in the basic business classes brings to the classroom the varied skills and experiences of many persons who, by virtue of specialized training or

---

[18] Vernon A. Musselman, "20 Ways to Launch a General Business Unit," *Business Education World*, XXXV (December, 1954), p. 28.

experience, have a contribution to make to business education. These persons can discuss matters of immediate concern to the young people in the classroom. They can provide information, give demonstrations, use unique illustrations to stimulate interest, and provide motivation in ways not generally used by the teacher. The supply of these persons is usually greater than the demand for their services.

Careful planning for the use of speakers is essential. Just any time won't do. The hour chosen should be the period of greatest student interest in a particular business problem. The visitor should be advised as to the grade level of the group and their interest in and knowledge of the problem. The speaker should be told what will be expected of him. He should be informed as to the exact class meeting time and be asked whether or not he will be available to answer questions or grant personal and group interviews after the talk. The invitation to appear may be issued by the teacher or it may be a committee project of the class.

The teacher needs to recognize that it is possible to overdo the number of visits in a given semester or year; that quality rather than quantity is desired; that the purpose is to enrich the general business education experiences of the class members. The business program will profit most from the use of guest speakers when instruction is developed around the needs, problems, and interests of the class rather than around arbitrarily fixed business textbook content.

In order to ascertain class reaction to the use of guest speakers, a device of some sort is needed. Lewis suggests the questionnaire that follows on page 296,[19] with the hope of reconciling the possible negative reactions from the class members:

1. How will the students react to an outsider?
2. What adult would care to spend part of his busy day addressing high school students in addition to the time he must give to preparing his remarks?
3. Can the businessman adapt the material for his talk to the understanding of the secondary school freshman?
4. Are not we who have had years of training better qualified to present the same material to our students without

---

[19] Harry Lewis, "Do We Want Guest Speakers?" *Business Education World,* XXXV (December, 1954), p. 10.

STUDENT QUESTIONNAIRE

Through the following questions, we are trying to determine your reaction to the lesson you had on Social Security last Thursday. Your answers will be of great value to us in planning this unit's work for future classes.

Place a checkmark in the space provided before the answer that most closely approximates your attitude.

1. You found the film to be:
   _____ Very interesting
   _____ Interesting
   _____ Dull

2. You feel that the speakers from the Social Security Agency were:
   _____ Very interesting
   _____ Interesting
   _____ Dull

3. You think the speakers dealt with you as:
   _____ Adults
   _____ Children

4. You believe that this lesson:
   _____ Should be given as the first lesson on Social Security
   _____ Should be given as the last lesson on Social Security
   _____ Should not be given at all

5. You found that the program:
   _____ Cleared your mind and answered all questions
   _____ Didn't answer all questions completely
   _____ Wasn't of any help
   _____ Raised new questions that need answers

6. It would be of greater value if this talk were given to you as seniors rather than as part of the Business Arithmetic course:
   _____ Yes
   _____ No

7. You would advise that this lesson be given to Business Arithmetic classes in the future:
   _____ Yes
   _____ No

If there is anything further you would care to add, we should greatly appreciate it. Please use the reverse side of this paper for these comments.

exerting ourselves to arrange for what may be unwilling guests? [20]

Just as the field trip has excellent value when thoughtfully planned and executed, visits of speakers and resource persons from the community require careful thought. There should be a pattern of mechanics by which to ensure that all value possible will be derived from the visit. Callan presents an excellent checklist that should cover most of these contingencies:

[20] *Ibid.*, p. 9.

1. Have all factors concerning the location for use of the resource person been considered?

2. Have the students been prepared for the speaker or demonstrator?

3. Do the students know who the resource person is, the company he represents, and what they might expect to learn from him?

4. Has the class formulated questions to ask the resource person? Have these questions been forwarded to the resource person?

5. Do the students understand the importance of courteous conduct and attention?

6. Has the resource person been given complete information concerning the group to be addressed?

7. Has a time limit for the resource person been set? Is he aware of the time limit?

8. Has the resource person been told the important points that the teacher wants stressed?

9. Has a follow-up plan been given consideration so that the students will be able to relate the resource person to the classroom work? [21]

The follow-up has been singled out as a point of primary significance by Giffin and is referred to as "recognition" of the visitor:

> In the interest of good public relations it is wise to give the visitor the recognition he deserves for the time and effort he has given the class. This may be done by the class in the following ways:
>
> 1. Send the speaker a "thank you" letter after his appearance.
> 2. If the speaker is an employee, send his employer a letter of appreciation.
> 3. Write a news article about the speaker for publication in the community newspaper and the school news.
> 4. Prepare an account of the visit for a regularly scheduled news broadcast if you have a local radio station. [22]

---

[21] John Henry Callan, *Community Resources Handbook in Business Education*, Monograph 87 (Cincinnati: South-Western Publishing Co., 1954), pp. 16-17.

[22] James F. Giffin, "A Community Resource: The Guest Speaker," *Business Education Forum*, 10 (January, 1956), p. 9.

The guest speaker method is not the easy way out; the teacher must accept the facts of using the method. *It takes time and involves problems.* Gaston comments on the use of the method:

> The problems faced by many teachers in securing guest speakers result because they are too ambitious. If they teach in or near a state capitol, they want to invite learned judges and legislators to their classes. There is prestige in having the "director of this" or the "supervisor of that" address your class. All too often, however, their efforts end in failure and frustration.
>
> Any community houses within its geographical limits a wealth of available speakers for the business law class. Most businessmen and professional people are more than willing to be of assistance. The goodwill they create for themselves cannot be purchased with money, and they know this. The teacher should take advantage of the situation.
>
> The automobile or appliance dealer would probably be quite willing to speak to a class on the topic of warranties and product liability. The likelihood is that they have had firsthand experience in this area. A large store manager might be the one to discuss truth in packaging, fair trade, or weights and measures. Realtors should be available to handle discussions on leases and the transfer of real property. All these people are little more than a phone call away.[23]

Panel Discussion

The panel discussion is another way of using class participation to get a job done, a concept taught. The panel serves to enhance the regular course material by permitting students to "get into the act." Alcorn, Kinder, and Schunert describe the basic structure and utilization of a panel:

> Panels and symposiums may be used in either large or small classes, or in groups smaller than those considered to be class size. The purpose is to provide an opportunity for a few well-prepared students to discuss pertinent topics. In the panel discussion, four to eight students are selected for

---

[23] Neil Gaston, "Business Law," *Changing Methods of Teaching Business Subjects,* Tenth Yearbook of the National Business Education Association (Washington: National Business Education Association, 1972), p. 32.

the discussion. There is usually a free exchange of ideas among the members of the panel. The presentations are considered impromptu, but the participants are well informed, and should be students with divergent points of view.

A good panel technique places large responsibility on a chairman, who may be selected by the teacher, the class, or the panel members. He acts much as a good chairman of any discussion meeting. He states the topic for consideration, introduces the panel members, and makes a statement or two concerning the topic. It is his responsibility to bring all the members of the panel into action, yet to control the discussion so that the time is not monopolized by a few. Another duty of the chairman is to recognize contributions from the floor. Finally, he summarizes the talks, closes the discussion, and dismisses the panel.[24]

In order to avoid the disintegration of the panel into a dull series of short speeches, the teacher must play an active part in the organization and procedure; he cannot sit back and let the students "take over." Purposes of the method must be made clear, mechanics developed, and plans made for appraisal.

Wright, in the use of the panel discussion in a salesmanship class, gives these procedural steps:

Assuming a class size of thirty students . . . six groups of five members each are designated as separate panels. Dates for their joint effort are set, with care being exercised to separate the time of panel appearance and sales demonstrations of each student. Discussion topics are then assigned to each panel by the instructor, largely as a matter of expediency to get work started. There is no other reason why each panel could not arrive at its own subject for discussion.

Each panel is instructed to meet and elect a chairman whose responsibility it is to divide the research to be done. When panel day arrives, the chairman acts as moderator. The panel is seated at a table in front of the class. Each member is allotted time for short opening remarks, the

---

[24] Marvin D. Alcorn, James S. Kinder, and Jim R. Schunert, *Better Teaching in Secondary Schools* (New York: Holt, Rinehart and Winston, Inc., 1970), pp. 164-165.

chairman summarizes, and discussion follows. The last quarter of the hour should be reserved for questions from the class.[25]

Values of the panel discussion as a method for a change of pace for the basic business class are outlined briefly by Wright:

1. The panel is currently fashionable in business as a means of communication. . . . Thus, the student is receiving training in a technique he may be called upon to use in his business career.
2. Every opportunity a person has to express his ideas before a group is an enriching experience.
3. An opportunity to do research on a given problem is provided.
4. A challenge to think out some problem to its logical conclusion is likewise presented.
5. A greater fund of knowledge is possible, as each panel in a sense becomes the teacher for the entire class.
6. Members of the class obtain a "close-knit" feeling.[26]

Case Problem Method and the Incident Process

As a further variation of the use of group dynamics in basic business teaching, the business teacher might want to experiment with the case problem method—a teaching technique whereby an actual "case" or incident, or circumstance, is used as a basis for class discussion and problem-solving. The case method is not widely used in high school teaching, but it has become quite popular with industrial relations and management groups. The Incident Process, developed by Pigors and Pigors [27] and produced by the Bureau of National Affairs, Inc., is a technique using the case problem, or "incident," as an approach. The problems are taken from actual cases on file in Washington, D. C., under Labor Arbitration Reports—Dispute Settlements. Generally, it is a union-company dispute which has gone to arbitration. The student

[25] John S. Wright, "A New Idea for the Salesmanship Course," *Collegiate News and Views*, 11 (October, 1957), pp. 7-8.
[26] *Ibid.*, p. 8.
[27] Paul Pigors and Faith Pigors, *The Incident Process* (Washington, D. C.: Bureau of National Affairs, Inc., 1957).

leader has all the facts, but he gives them out only as answers to questions by the students. The class is given the "incident" in a few words; and to get all the facts, questions must be asked to establish the real reason for the grievance. The incident is a short sketch of something that actually happened. The facts are brought out by group interview of the leader, who has all the information.

After learning all the facts of the grievance, each member of the class renders his decision as if he were the arbitrator of the case. Naturally, the decisions will be different. Usually about one half of the class decides that management is right and the other half favors the employee. Each side then is asked to back up its decisions by reasons. Finally, then, the decision of the arbitrator, who had the actual case, is read to the class. Before leaving this case, the group discusses how this grievance might have been avoided by proper management procedure.[28]

Teachers who have used the case method are enthusiastic about it. All the elements of problem-solving are there. The values of the case method become clear once the teacher begins to plan: recognition of a central problem, determination of possible solutions, selection of a solution most appropriate under the given circumstances, and relation of theory to the case elements. Satlow stresses a policy of *gradualism* in the use of the case method:

> The attack on cases assumes three phases: In the *first phase*, pupils are trained to: (a) select from the facts stated in the problem those that are salient and organize them in their proper time sequence, (b) determine the point in dispute, and (c) settle the argument by ascribing a reason. . . . In the *second phase*, pupils are required to give their answers in terms of legal principles followed by one-word decisions. . . . Upon developing facility in isolating legal principles, the work advances to the *third phase*, in which pupils are introduced to a three-column tabular arrangement which calls for the headings: Principle of Law, Discussion or Application, and Decision. Once this form has been introduced, it is required on all homework, board-work, and tests.

---

[28] The description of the Incident Process was contributed by Mr. Ruben Dumler, Division of Business Administration, St. John's College, Winfield, Kansas, 1970.

Principle	Discussion	Decision
1. A contract in reasonable restraint of trade is legal.	Cook's promise not to open a grocery store in the entire state was unreasonable.	Yes. He may open a store three blocks away.
2. A contract for personal service terminates when the party who is to perform the service dies.	The painting of a portrait calls for personal services.	No. Mrs. Smith will not be required to sit for the portrait.
3. A promise to pay another person's debt must be in writing.	Clark's promise was an oral one.	No. Brown will not be able to collect.[29]

Brainstorming

Present-day problems require boldness and imagination on the part of the instructor. A method certain to draw out ideas from the otherwise "quiet" student is known as brainstorming. Dumler gives a comprehensive explanation of the technique and its application:

Brainstorming is a conference technique which has been used with a great deal of success by banks, schools, churches, the military services, civic organizations, and even political parties. New ideas are difficult to get, but this approach sometimes shakes them loose from the most unexpected sources. Generally, here are some of the basic rules for a successful brainstorming session:

1. No criticism or evaluation is permitted during the session. Everyone should pop out with *any* idea related to the problem which comes to his mind. No negative ideas are allowed.

2. The wilder the idea, the better it is; some of the "silly" solutions hit pay dirt.

3. Quantity—the greater the number of ideas, the more likely you are to get acceptable ones.

4. Ideas beget ideas. A suggestion of one person may stimulate the thinking of others.

---

[29] I. David Satlow, "Handling Cases in the Law Class," *Business Education Forum*, 11 (November, 1956), p. 28.

5. *All* ideas should be recorded.
6. A time limit is set for each session; when the time is up, the meeting is over.
7. Later on, the ideas are put into categories and a regular conference is called for evaluation.

In the classroom, problems from the textbook or from every-day life situations can be treated by the brainstorming method. Situations of current importance to everyone offer the best possibilities for the use of the method.[30]

The Buzz Group

The buzz group is a discussion technique wherein a problem is placed before the class or assembly as a whole. The topic is briefly explored. At conventions this is frequently done by means of a keynote address. The problem is then broken down into a series of logical subtopics. The class, or group, is divided into small groups. Each section is assigned a subtopic. The small groups organize themselves for action, discuss their assignment briefly and vigorously, then report back to the assembly or class. A statement covering the total solution is then formulated.

The buzz group technique can be applied successfully to basic business classes, particularly those influenced by the day's headlines, such as economics and consumer education. One of the best available treatments of the buzz group is given by Grambs, Carr, and Fitch:

> Short-term, or buzz, groups, which are typically used to attack specific jobs, are limited in scope. The tasks can usually be completed in a short period of time—from 5 to 20 minutes. Good preplanning enhances the probability of success of buzz groups, with all the accompanying bonus of improved morale.
>
> *Deciding on the problem for the groups to discuss.* The task of the buzz group must be clearly defined in the mind of the teacher and fully recognized by the groups. Typically, buzz groups are useful for getting a quick reaction to a controversial issue, for planning the next steps in a unit, for

---

[30] This material was contributed by Mr. Ruben Dumler, Division of Business Administration, St. John's College, Winfield, Kansas, 1970.

assessing the relative importance of proposed topics of study, and for setting up rules or regulations for class activities or materials.

Choosing the strategic moment to initiate the buzz group. A buzz group may serve to organize a discussion and extend the involvement of the class. For example, a group might be engaged in a heated discussion about athletic policies. It would soon be discovered that not everyone could express his opinion. At this time the teacher could set up buzz groups so that all students could speak their minds on the topic. Such a buzz-group session would occur, then, midway through a discussion period. Buzz groups may also be used to warm up a class for general discussion. Still others may be used to bring together and organize ideas expressed at the end of a discussion or study period.

Determining how the buzz groups will be chosen. The several ways of choosing buzz groups are important enough to require a separate discussion. For the moment, let us say that the method of choosing will be based on which kind of group composition will "jell" fastest and still suit the purpose. The buzz group will usually number about five persons, though any number from three to six can "buzz" effectively. A group that is too small has too few resources to call upon; a group that is too large lets some members take a silent role or become disruptive when not involved.

Setting the time limits. Time is the most effective discipline for keeping lively adolescents focused on the problem to be solved. The time allowed should be as short as possible while still allowing members to explore the topic. *It is always better to allow too little time than too much.*

It does take experience to determine how long adolescents can talk about something productively before the discussion degenerates into horseplay. If the teacher underestimates the time, he can let the students know that, since the task has not yet been accomplished, they can have another 3 or 4 minutes to finish. Or, if some groups finish sooner than expected, he can call time on them all. The students will not be watching the clock if the problem is both real and absorbing.

Establishing group organization. Only a chairman and a recorder or reporter are needed for organizing each group. But how will they be chosen? Sometimes the teacher can select them ahead of time on the basis of known qualities of leadership or knowledge of the field. Sometimes the tasks can be used to bring in students who do not usually participate. It is often good policy to use very arbitrary means: "The person whose name is nearest the top of the alphabet will be chairman; the person whose name is nearest the bottom of the alphabet will be recorder." If the group members are strangers to one another, such a procedure means that they have to introduce themselves by name. And it makes retreat from the assigned role difficult.

Giving the group its leadership rather than allowing the group to choose its own is useful particularly if the class is unfamiliar with group work. Later, the roles will be assumed rather naturally. But at the beginning, structuring the group helps get work under way quickly. In long-term groups the selection of leadership is vital; in short-term groups it is less important.

Arranging for group reports. Usually the appointed reporter will tell the rest of the class what was decided in his group. These decisions may be listed on the board; they may be the basis for further discussion by the whole class; or the reporters may be asked to form a group to summarize all the findings. If the reports are brief and to the point, it is ordinarily useful for each group to hear and see its own report presented to the total class. Then a certain pride of ownership encourages the youngsters to want to engage in this kind of activity again. The involvement of each person in "his" group's report is assured as each reporter tells what the group accomplished.[31]

Role-Playing

Dramatization may take many forms. The natural tendency of youth to imitate and to mimic suggests the use of dramatic activity for certain basic business courses. Price, Hopkins, and Duff describe the broad scope of utilization of role-playing in the classroom, regardless of subject area:

In role-playing, hypothetical but representative circumstances involving interpersonal relationships are established, and participants take roles in which they act and react spontaneously. Role-playing has been defined as a method

[31] Jean D. Grambs, John C. Carr, and Robert M. Fitch, *Modern Methods in Secondary Education* (3rd ed.; New York: Holt, Rinehart and Winston, Inc., 1970), pp. 191-192.

of human interaction that involves realistic behavior in an imaginary situation. People act as though what they are doing is "for real" in a make-believe kind of situation. Role-playing may serve any of the following teaching purposes in the general business classroom:

1. To present alternative courses of action
2. To develop better understanding of problems
3. To develop better understanding of other peoples' points of view
4. To prepare for meeting future situations
5. To increase spontaneity and encourage creative interaction
6. To give students practice in what they have learned
7. To illustrate principles from the course content
8. To maintain and/or arouse student interest
9. To stimulate discussion
10. To develop more effective problem-solving ability
11. To develop desirable attitudes

Role-playing is a method of providing the individual student an opportunity for active participation in the subject matter being studied. Students are able to live critical incidents, to explore what happened in them, and to consider what might have happened if different choices had been made in the effort to resolve the problem or situation involved. Such practice allows students to learn from mistakes under conditions that protect them from any actual penalty.

Two examples of role-playing situations that may be used to help develop concepts and understandings follow:

1. The students organize into a community of self-sufficient households, each producing its own goods and services. What happens to income?
2. A teen-age boy wants to buy an automobile. He needs to get his parents' agreement, obtain credit for part of the amount, and purchase insurance.[32]

Role-playing differs from the planned play or drama in that emphasis is on individual performance and on the role itself. The classroom teacher who becomes skilled in the

_____

[32] Ray G. Price, Charles R. Hopkins, and Thomas B. Duff, "Basic Business," *Changing Methods of Teaching Business Subjects,* Tenth Yearbook of the National Business Education Association (Washington: National Business Education Association, 1972), pp. 5-6.

basic techniques enjoys a unique opportunity to help pupils explore their own problems. Since role-playing is unrehearsed, it is necessarily free from the restrictions and complications of the apprehensions developed in the course of extensive preparation and rehearsal. McKillop reviews the aims of the use of role-playing for a salesmanship class and illustrates an actual plan for such a class:

> The objectives of such a program (in a class in beginning selling) are three in number: (1) to create tools to aid the teacher in successfully applying theory studied in the classroom, (2) to obtain some measure of the individual's actual ability and progress in the sales situation, (3) to create an atmosphere as close to reality (on-the-job) as possible.

> Let us examine the plan in action. For the first three or four days the instructor created a series of artificial salesman-customer situations. The class acted as audience and critics. Then two students were assigned specific parts as in regular role playing. The person who was to play the salesperson was given specific merchandise information, which he could write down or memorize before he was sent out of the room. The salesperson having left the room, the "customer" was then instructed in the part he was to play. Since the customer's objection was the crux of the problem in almost every case, it was very important that he understand his part thoroughly. In that way he could play his part to the hilt. Before the "customer" left, the audience suggested various solutions to the problem and voted on the best solution. The stage had thus been set.

> The two players entered and carried out their parts in the drama. As they were carrying on the dialogue, the instructor picked out specific points and jotted them down. When the sales presentation had been concluded, the instructor called these points to the attention of the salesperson and the customer.[33]

Role-playing is only one dramatic technique. Standard written and rehearsed skits are another form. When students are brought into the development and writing of the script itself, even greater values accrue to the learners. For example, the wide range of activities needed to prepare a

[33] John McKillop, "Role Playing in Sales Classes," *Business Education Forum,* 7 (May, 1953), p. 39.

skit involve the varying capacities of many students, as Claypool indicates:

> Before the skit is actually written, the committee chairman requires a written report listing the law principle involved, the subject matter of the case, and other ramifications. With the approval of the teacher, the teams work to construct the court case. Students use the business department library, the school library, and outside authorities in assembling their case. During the development of the case, an excellent opportunity is provided for a trip to a court of law and an interview with a local attorney, justice of the peace, or another legal official. The trial briefs, when completed, are submitted to the instructor for approval. At this point, the class is reorganized into committees consisting of six or seven members. These committees are the approval committees. They read the submitted manuscripts, check rules of law, and make a list of suggested changes and corrections. The approval committee is returned to members of the committee who wrote the skit; then they revise and revamp their skit. Approximately forty copies of the case brief are reproduced; one is given to each member of the class; and several are kept for our files. Each year the law class prepares approximately ten skits which are given in class. A vote is usually taken to determine the best skit.[34]

In the utilization of this method, the business teacher is cautioned, of course, that the place to develop dramatic techniques and to emphasize dramatic experience is the drama club or drama classes. Although the values of dramatic activity as a creative experience or of self-expression are recognized, these values remain secondary to those of instruction in basic business knowledge and concepts.

Class Report

The current events flavor of class reports on topics of immediate relationship to course subject matter need not restrict the subject fields in which this method is used. It emphasizes the art of reading and reporting, oral and written. For the purpose of giving the reader insight into the

---

[34] Donald G. Claypool, "Teamwork, Originality, and Understanding through Skits in the Business Law Class," *The Balance Sheet,* XLII (January, 1961), p. 211.

actual use of this procedure, the following statement by Davis is given below:

My favorite technique in teaching the nonskill subjects in business requires that students do a certain amount of outside reading in national publications such as *U. S. News & World Report, Time, Newsweek,* and *Business Week.* It is especially effective in teaching economics and related subjects. This technique can be used particularly well in the latter part of the semester or school term to perk up the group and let them get an idea of the practical application of the subject being studied.

On Mondays—this could be any day of the week for that matter—I ask the students to be prepared to discuss some article concerning economics that they have read during the past week in one of the current magazines or newspapers. At the beginning of the class, I quickly ascertain the topics included in the students' reports. Generally, subjects that are especially timely, such as gross national product, gold movement to and from the United States, government expenditures, are included in this list. After discussing with the group the scope of their articles and their application, one student is chosen to give his report.

I use two methods in promoting class discussion on the basis of this student's report. Sometimes the student completes his report and the class determines how economic theory applies to this situation, but very often I ask that the student let us discuss an issue right at the time it is contained in the report. For instance, if a student should give a report on the deterioration of the stock of gold in the United States, this could start a discussion on "What difference does this make since no one can transfer his money into gold anyway?" or "Why should European nations be interested in our gold supply?" and so on. As can be seen, just one statement taken from one of these reports can stimulate student thinking in many different areas of economics or related subjects.[35]

Gaston presents a varying treatment of the value of class reporting in the basic business subjects:

Oral reports should not be assigned. The student giving an oral report should feel so strongly about the subject of

---

[35] This material was contributed by Dr. A. Reed Davis, Dean, West Virginia Institute of Technology, Montgomery, West Virginia, 1971.

his report that he willingly seeks out all available information to be had. Often, the students and subjects can be identified during class discussion. For example, the student who refuses to accept the decision of an actual case might be disposed to studying the text of that case at a law library or a friendly attorney's office. By giving an oral report on his findings, the student will share the rationale of the decision with his classmates—a rationale that is often lost in the single-paragraph solution of the textbook key.

Anytime a student comes to a teacher with information he has found supporting or disputing that which was taught, he should be encouraged to report his finding to the group. Oral reports need not be formally structured; they should be made to take advantage of the time and issue.[36]

Earlier in this chapter a procedure whereby the discussion leader can ascertain quickly the extent of reading done by the members of the group was presented. Bahr also has developed an evaluation form, shown on page 311, for reviewing the reading of the class.[37]

Scrapbooks—Notebooks

The scrapbook, in the minds of some teachers, enjoys the dubious distinction of a busywork assignment. As in the case of many other classroom methods, this device has lesser or greater value in direct proportion to the awareness of the teacher as to its possibilities for enriching the learning experiences of students and to its effectiveness in weaving this pupil activity into the total program.

In basic business courses, the keeping of scrapbooks by pupils brings into use a number of fundamental skills—collection, classification, reading, selection, and so on. Heimerl lists the following uses for the scrapbook in a major basic business subject:

The consumer student can make analytical collections of advertisements, of labels, of kinds of fabrics and weaves, experiment reports, news clippings appropriate to a specific topic, such as the cost of living.

---

[36] Gaston, op. cit., p. 29.
[37] This report form has been provided by courtesy of Gladys Bahr, DePaul University, Chicago, Illinois.

ECONOMIC READING REPORT

By .... Date ....

INFORMATION

Name of Book, Magazine, or Pamphlet ....

....

Author or Authors .... Publisher .... Yr. ......

Topic in Economics to which reference applies ....

....

Number of pages read ....

FACTS

Brief Outline (this may be a summary in outline form, chapter
   headings, a paragraph on its content, etc.)

OPINIONS

Suitable for ... Freshmen-Sophomores, ... Junior-Senior, ... Adults

Interesting? Yes ... No ...

Compared to our text, Harder to understand ... Easier ...

Compared to Reader's Digest, As interesting ... Not as interesting ...

Evaluate the reading (give your own opinion)

Or he can make a notebook on any of a score of important topics such as: a buyer's guide for a particular product,
the kinds of insurance, their purposes and costs, clippings
about legal cases involving consumer interests, a diary
of consumer experiences, an annotated personal budget
history.[38]

As a product of committee activity, the scrapbook or
notebook may extend the area covered by a unit of study,
thereby enriching the total unit experience of the whole
class. Rainey describes the use of the notebook technique for
a class in economic geography:

> The teacher can have the class prepare an economic-
> geographic history of the county (or area) in which the
> school is located, complete with maps, illustrations, statis-
> tical tables, and so on. The completed history can then
> be mimeographed and bound. . . . Several periods should be
> spent in conditioning the students for the project before
> assignments are given. Time spent in developing student

---

[38] Heimerl, *loc. cit*

interest and motivation will not be wasted. Once the students are motivated, the class can be divided into groups or committees and special assignments and procedural instructions given.[39]

The availability of duplicating equipment is a material aid to the scrapbook-notebook project device. Bahr points out the use of the duplicating machine in making supplementary materials available to the students:

> The duplicating machine may be used as a vital tool in a nonskill business subject. Its product serves as a learning guide to suit the needs of a basic business class as to its interests and abilities.
>
> In an investment unit, the class may need to study the *Wall Street Journal*. A worksheet which alerts the pupils to valuable features of this financial paper can be prepared.
>
> The pupils may need to know facts about basic business in their particular town, state, and the nation. It is well to reproduce the small loan law of the state, the revolving credit terms of a local department store, or comparative business indicators.[40]

Weather the scrapbook is of an individual student nature, or the product of a committee, its development lends interest and motivation to the basic business class. An individual student scrapbook project of particular interest to most basic business students is described by Arensman and Maxwell:

1. Direct students to design their own letterhead. Give them their choice of designing letterheads for (a) companies with which their fathers are affiliated, (b) companies for which students now work, (c) companies for which the students someday intend to work, (d) companies which the students know by national reputation, or (e) imaginary companies.

2. Have students bring in (for a scrapbook) and study letterheads from firms (particularly local) that reflect the

---

[39] Bill G. Rainey, "Economic Geography A'la Mode," *Business Education Forum,* 14 (May, 1960), p. 28.
[40] This material was contributed to the authors by Gladys Bahr, DePaul University, Chicago, Illinois.

nature of the firm and the impression to be created by letterhead content and layout.[41]

Instructional Films

An instructional film carefully selected, well-timed, and skillfully presented is a profitable aid to instruction in nearly all classes. A film may be used to introduce the lesson, project, demonstration, or unit activity in order to stimulate interest and establish a common ground of readiness. When used to introduce a topic area, it can serve as a medium to illustrate the "whole," as, for example, in the study of banking and its related activities. Having once been shown, the film may be rerun as a terminal activity to refresh the memory and to clarify understanding. Timing is important! It is better not to use the film at all than to attempt to "patch it in" at an inappropriate time.

Previewing the film selected from catalog description is essential. It enables the teacher to ascertain specific details so that he can correlate the film content with the lesson, the text, supplementary reading materials, or other materials being used. Previewing shows the teacher how, when, and where it is best to use the film. Some films have decided advantage as introductory materials, such as *Productivity—the Key to Plenty*, which can be used to introduce the beginning course in economic principles, while others increase informational content or are best used for review. Previewing helps students to identify new words and concepts.

Much highly desirable class activity may result from the effective presentation of a good film. Class discussion and panel discussions may be more fruitful after the film viewing; optional reading or independent study may be stimulated by it; it may suggest new projects; or it may, and frequently does, evoke questions from the class which suggest the need for additional information or for review of certain areas.

The following suggestions by Dale for instructional film use are pertinent:

---

[41] Ray W. Arensman and Gerald W. Maxwell, "Twelve Motivational Vitamins for Business Correspondence Classes," *Collegiate News and Views,* 13 (December, 1959), pp. 5-6.

* Know the best films available in your field.
* Know film catalogs and other film sources.
* Observe effective classroom uses of films.
* Familiarize yourself with film guides.
* Learn how to make proper physical arrangements in the classroom.
* Learn how to operate a projector.
* Specify the learning problem.
* Preview and use lesson plan.
* Organize a class discussion before the showing.
* Carry out discussion and follow-through activities.
* Evaluate the film for later use.[42]

Most classroom showings are conducted under conditions which provide enough light for students to take some notes. For this purpose, a film discussion sheet can be duplicated and distributed before the showing. This instrument can serve both as a means for evaluating the film and for "reminders" in later class discussion. An illustration of such a sheet is given on the following page.

The film follow-up is a critical factor in obtaining full value from the time spent. Giffin lists several points of primary consideration on the follow-up:

1. Discuss the film after it is run. Rerun it if necessary to make certain things clear.

2. Draw conclusions from the story in the film.

3. Relate the story of the film to the lesson and move naturally back into the lesson or unit under consideration, or into the assignment for the following day.

4. Use the experience of the film in subsequent discussions for illustrative purposes.

5. Prepare and use questions based on the film. They should become part of the test used for the unit.[43]

Filmstrips—Slides—Transparencies

Although it may be expected that enthusiasm is greater for certain teaching aids than for others, the use of the

---

[42] Edgar Dale, *Audiovisual Methods in Teaching* (3rd ed.; New York: The Dryden Press, Inc., 1969), pp. 409-412.
[43] James F. Giffin, "To Teach Economic Literacy—Show Them!" *Business Education World*, XL (February, 1960), p. 37.

```
┌─────────────────────────────────────────────────────┐
│           FILM REVIEW AND DISCUSSION SHEET            │
│                                                       │
│  Course: _____   │
│  Student's Name _____     │
├─────────────────────────────────────────────────────┤
│                                                       │
│  NAME OF FILM:                                        │
│                                                       │
│  SPECIFIC POINTS SHOWN RELATED TO CLASS STUDY:        │
│                                                       │
│                                                       │
│                                                       │
│                                                       │
│  QUESTIONS ON FILM RELATED TO COURSE:                 │
│                                                       │
│                                                       │
│                                                       │
│  OTHER STUDY AREAS COVERED BY THE FILM:               │
│                                                       │
│                                                       │
│                                                       │
│                                                       │
│  REMARKS:                                             │
│                                                       │
└─────────────────────────────────────────────────────┘
```

motion picture to the complete exclusion of slides, filmstrips, and other projectible materials ignores many devices that are extremely adaptable to basic business subjects. The value of any one of these devices is determined by the teacher's method and by the instructional content. The teacher needs to be familiar with slides and other projectible materials in order to use them effectively in his classroom.

In terms of still projection, there is probably no single machine as useful to the teacher in the basic business subjects as the overhead projector. The overhead projector, in contrast to the opaque projector, can be used in a fully lighted room. The overhead projector can be used without the necessity of a darkened room and without an expensive screen. Materials for this medium of projection can be tailor-made to fit the particular situation in the teaching plan. With the use of a ball-point pen, opaque carbon paper, cellophane, and a typewriter, readily usable materials can be prepared on the spot or in the teacher's office. For involved, intricate materials direct image transparency film in several colors is available which can be processed in only a few seconds with an office copier.

Instead of trying to place intricate drawings on the board between classes, these transparencies can be prepared in connection with the planning for the course. Artistic inability plagues many teachers with the result that last-minute reliance on the chalkboard reveals efforts of doubtful clarity to the students. Types of materials that can be quickly copied for projection are illustrated on page 317.

After getting himself "all tangled up" during a lecture in which he was using a dozen or more transparencies, one teacher devised a technique which he has been using ever since. Instead of the standard 8 x 10 transparency, he now prepares his lectures on 6 ft. 10 in. wide strips of heavy, clear plastic, bought in bulk and then cut to size. In such a roll, space can be allowed for special ready-made inserts or overlays that the teacher might want to include in the lecture. A teacher can give an entire lecture, using one roll, and the cost is about one-fourth that usually paid for transparencies.

In studying student reaction to the overhead projector, the authors have found the following:

1. Color adds interest. It is difficult to overdo the use of color in connection with the overhead projector.
2. Motion is important as an interest-getting and interest-holding device. The teacher should leave space so he can make "live" fill-ins during the class period. Underscoring a certain word or concept in red while he is talking helps.
3. Occasional intermittent use of the chalkboard helps also.
4. Flipping back at the end of the period to certain high-spots on the transparency is good. Even better is a student review put on the screen.
5. Using student material increases interest. In letter writing as many as 25 letters can be reviewed during one period, if all work is required on transparencies.

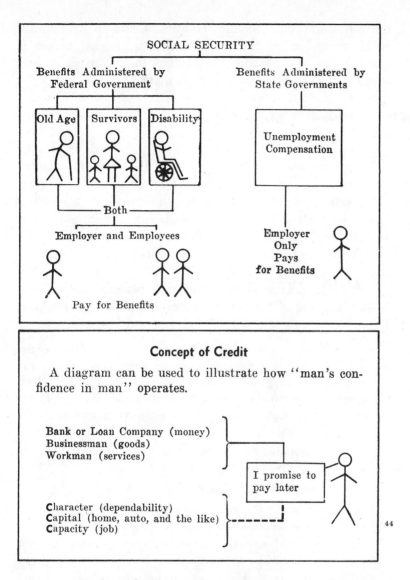

SOCIAL SECURITY

Benefits Administered by
Federal Government

Benefits Administered by
State Governments

Old Age Survivors Disability

Unemployment
Compensation

Both

Employer and Employees

Employer
Only
Pays
for Benefits

Pay for Benefits

Concept of Credit

A diagram can be used to illustrate how "man's confidence in man" operates.

Bank or Loan Company (money)
Businessman (goods)
Workman (services)

I promise to
pay later

Character (dependability)
Capital (home, auto, and the like)
Capacity (job)

44

Each student's creation is thus seen on the screen; each student sees it polished into usable condition by his fellow students.[45]

Filmstrips play an important part, too, because they may be used under conditions of less than total darkness and do

[44] Ted J. Boduch, "Developing Concepts in Basic Business," *Business Education Forum*, 14 (March, 1960), p. 15.

[45] The 3-M Company supplies transparencies for student use put into pads something like typing paper. All each student needs is a sheet from this pad and a carbon set and he is in business.

not require special viewing facilities. Close-up lens equipment, available on the modern 35mm. camera, makes it possible for most teachers to produce their own slides and filmstrips, tailored to fit the immediate situation.

The Project—Individual and Group

The project is frequently used in, and is appropriate to, the basic business subjects.[46] Based on the concept of learning by doing, this is generally recognized as a good classroom procedure. It is implied that pupils *do something* about an existing problem in their business surroundings to the point of bringing about a change in the situation or the development of ideas consistent with the needs of the problem.

There is no lack of possibilities for project development in the teaching of the basic business subjects. For business letter writing, for example, Arensman and Maxwell say:

> Business correspondence is more meaningful when the situations handled through business letters are real to the students. If they write letters about business affairs which seem abstract to them, their motivation may be "We-gotta-do-it-for-a-grade" rather than "I-can-really-see-the-worthwhileness-of-this."

How about using some local school and community situations as the basis for assigned writings? For instance:

1. Appeal for attendance at pep session.
2. Appeal to faculty for support of athletic programs.
3. Clever invitations to school social activities.
4. Series of appeals for social agencies such as Red Cross, cancer drives, etc.
5. Letter requesting creation or improvement of city parks.
6. Letter turning down selected appeals and requests listed above.
7. Letter explaining why certain "uncomfortable" campus regulations (parking, no running in the halls, etc.) must be enforced.[47]

---

[46] This subject is treated extensively in the later chapters. Only a few references, showing the application of this concept to basic business are given at this time.

[47] Arensman and Maxwell, *loc. cit.*

For organization of a small business Witherill suggests:

> The success of a project depends on careful counseling with each student before, and following, his particular project. In order to make the project as realistic as possible, actual available locations must be found; rental rates (or building costs) obtained; license applications must be obtained and filled out; tax and insurance rates should be obtained and figured; inventory lists prepared complete with costs and suppliers' names and addresses; organization charts must be made; diagrams made of plant or store layout; advertising programs planned. In short, everything should be done except actually spending money.[48]

For a project in consumer education, Gladys Bahr describes the following:

Taste Testing

Taste testing lesson is valuable and fun.

Purpose:	To prove that similar products do not vary as much as their ads proclaim. For example, brands of cola drinks do not vary in taste.
Needed:	Committee of student arrangers. Its task:
	To obtain brands of cola drinks, pour into unidentifiable containers, each numbered. Scarves for blindfolding. Paper cups.
Testing:	Begins with students, probably only five or so. Each taste tester drinks a sample of each cola drink; his vote for a certain number is recorded on the chalkboard.
	Containers are identified at the end of the taste test.
Conclusion:	Hypothesis is true, because confusion exists as to identifying brand names.

Taste test can be used with potato chips and other products that really are not very distinguishable as to taste. With college students, cigarettes, beer, coffee tests have been very effective.

(Note: Be sure to treat the entire class.) [49]

---

[48] Robert D. Witherill, "Course Projects Add Realism in Small Business Management," *Collegiate News and Views,* 13 (May, 1960), p. 7.

[49] Gladys Bahr, "A to Z Teaching Activities for Consumer Education" (unpublished manuscript, 1971).

The committee technique can be employed in the use of this method. Not only does the pupil do something for himself and further his own development, but he can also become a member of group activity. Maedke points out the value of the committee as an adjunct to the project method:

> All learners must realize the importance of working together as members of a group. This is especially important in business management activities because each business organization produces in direct ratio to the combined efforts of its employees working toward the same goal. If the business principles and management instructor can motivate each learner to contribute properly to a small group, the committee can be an effective teaching tool. The instructor should plan carefully a number of alternative group assignments from which each learner can choose one in accordance with his interests. Committee membership should be kept small in order that each learner has sufficient responsibility. Then, too, shy learners are more willing to take part in the committee's work. In order that committees may achieve the results and benefits which should accrue from that type of assignment, the projects should be broad enough in scope to encompass the major portion of the unit being studied. The committee assignment thus brings together, in a way different from the individual project, otherwise unrelated factual information into a "doing" activity.[50]

Evaluation of the project as a teaching device in the basic business area is especially essential because it involves varied activities which are carried out over an extended period of time. Witherill presents a justification for the time spent in the use of this procedure:

1. The project stimulates and motivates student interest in the course.
2. Since the business is usually selected by the student, the project provides insight into costs and management problems of a business he may eventually face.
3. Projects tend to point out the validity (or invalidity) of principles taught through classroom lecture.[51]

---

[50] Wilmer O. Maedke, "Business Principles and Management," *Changing Methods of Teaching Business Subjects*, Tenth Yearbook of the National Business Education Association (Washington: National Business Education Association, 1972), pp. 46-47.
[51] Witherill, *loc. cit.*

The project method, despite the opportunity that it provides for learning by doing, is time consuming. It should not be the sole method of instruction when time allocations are sharply limited. In every instance, it should be supported by related reading, by discussion and demonstration, and by the use of well-selected visual aids.

Field Trips

Educators have granted certain values to the field trip, such as: to enable students to see concrete illustrations of classroom theory; to reinforce understandings developed from reading and discussion; to see, smell, and touch or hear the objects or processes previously described; to enter into conversation with the people who are actively engaged in business; to ask questions that might not arise in the classroom.

Some exponents of the field trip hold that there must be a "solid" preparation for the trip and the things observed should be carefully outlined and described by the teacher in advance. The students should not be concerned with the novelty of the situation; rather they should observe what is considered as relevant by the teacher. As opposed to this, there are those who say that the value in a trip is to be placed upon the exploratory element, where only the general objective is known, not the details, which the pupils discover for themselves. Whether the educational values to be derived are general or specific will be determined by the purpose of the trip.

Before field trips can be expected to yield benefits to the class beyond "a day off," careful consideration of certain guidepoints must be made:

1. *Purpose of the trip.* "Is this trip necessary?" This question is a common quip in the hectic days of military service. It is *apropos* to the school class excursion or tour. Is the educational experience gained worth the trouble involved? Students will have to miss other classes; they will require special transportation; legal responsibility will have to be assumed or assigned; parents may have to

be notified; advance and follow-up contacts need to be made. Is it worth it?

2. *Preparation for the trip.* If one believes in pre-trip preparation, the following elements are helpful for getting "in the mood": annual reports of the firm to be visited, descriptive public relations materials about the company, 2 x 2 slides taken by the teacher or an assistant and shown to the class, products made by the company, photographs of the activities of the company.

In addition, advance preparations must be made with officials of the company. This can be done as a class project by letters, phone calls, or personal visits to the people to be visited. Many companies are well prepared for this type of activity as a part of their public relations program. They will have to know the principal objectives of the group, the age or grade level, and other similar details.

School officials will need to approve the trip, and parents must be aware that the pupils will not be in class attendance on the particular time involved. This usually makes necessary an official consent slip signed by the parents concerned and filed in the school administrative office.

3. *Appraisal of the trip.* As soon as possible after the completion of the tour, classes should appraise the results so that the maximum educational value can be derived from the trip. Committee appointments can be used for reports on certain phases of the activities observed. In addition, certain groups can be responsible for a follow-up letter to the firm, expressing thanks to the officials, guides, and others involved. At times, officials of the company are interested enough in seeing the results of the trip that they will consent to visit the classroom for a follow-up discussion. The instructional values of a visit to a company or plant do not terminate with the trip itself. To merely drop the subject or to ignore a follow-up is to leave questions unanswered and opinions unexpressed.

Callan developed a list that can serve well as a basis for a summary checkup device to ascertain the completeness of the trip planning:

1. Will the planned field trip contribute to the students' understanding and appreciation of the problems being studied?

2. Is the planned field trip of sufficient value to warrant the expenditure of time and effort?

3. Has the class assisted in the planning and arranging for the trip?

4. Is the purpose of the trip clearly understood by the members of the class?

5. Have the students been sufficiently prepared to take the trip?

6. Have arrangements been made with the business for the trip at a specific time?

7. Is the trip itinerary carefully planned and flexible?

8. Has the study guide been prepared and used by the class in planning for the trip?

9. Have provisions been made for possible "stragglers"?

10. Have signed consent slips been obtained for each student and filed in the office of the school principal?

11. Have plans been made for an evaluation of the trip? [52]

Gaming and Simulation

Gaming, originally set up as a management training device, has grown to such proportions that the hardware of it is handled by big corporations. The rapid growth of the stocks of these companies attests to the popularity of gaming. One can now purchase the materials so that he can "play" at being a coach, a top-flight industrialist, or, perhaps, a stockbroker. The use of gaming and simulation in basic business classes is practically unlimited. Terry tells us how this device works:

> Actually, this [gaming] is a type of simulation. . . . Advocates of gaming state that it is helpful when the problem is concerned fundamentally with the actions of competitors. . . .
>
> One approach in using "business games" is to begin with each decision maker in an identical position as shown by a balance sheet revealing the current condition of his enterprise. Auxiliary economic information to supply a needed background is provided. Decisions are made which affect the balance sheet, and periodically subsequent decisions are determined, keeping in mind [sic] the results derived from the previous decision and also the effect of the decisions of competitors. . . .

---

[52] John Henry Callan, *op. cit.*, p. 14.

"Playing the game" provides the manager [and the student] with practice, insight, and improvement in managerial actions. And he decides his courses of action from typical situations that he experiences in his everyday managerial activity.[53]

Bulletin Boards—Display Boards

So-called "bulletin" boards—tackboards—are found in most schools and classrooms. If these display boards are used only for memos from the administration, the use of a valuable teaching aid is lost.

The bulletin board may be considered an all-purpose board or medium to be used to the fullest possible advantage for many purposes within the school. When designed for entire school use, it serves as a display board for notices of a general nature. In the basic business classroom, however, it can be used as a unit-development plan board, for display of materials collected, and in connection with class activities. Pictures, maps and charts, graphs, clippings, and three-dimensional materials may be tacked or placed on it. Solid objects may be hung from it to give the illusion of depth. Pupil committees may be assigned the responsibility for providing these displays and for maintaining the board.

Emphasis should, of course, be placed on the *quality* of material for display rather than the *quantity*. A single piece arranged in an especially attractive way may bring greater rewards in conveying a message or concept than greater quantities and variety of material that require considerable time in reading for understanding. *The board that is of especial importance is one that conveys a single idea at a glance, much the same way as our modern billboard.*

The bulletin board is an excellent technique through which the basic business subjects can be enriched.

Even the "first-day jitters" of students can be ameliorated through the use of the bulletin board. Witherow explains the application of this technique:

Since students usually do not have textbooks the first day, the bulletin board display can be used as a springboard

---

[53] George R. Terry, *Principles of Management* (5th ed.; Homewood, Ill.: Richard D. Irwin, Inc., 1968), pp. 125-126.

for a short introduction. Then have the class write two or three paragraphs on how business serves them.[54]

Sources for free and inexpensive materials are numerous. There is no shortage of excellent material for display. In some instances special display boards, such as those described by Lynott, add flexibility to the use of this device:

> The three boards I have are made of beaver board, 33 inches wide by 47 inches long. For all three the cost was less than four dollars. Each board was bound with masking tape for a smooth, neat finish. A wooden easel supports each board, or they can be placed against a blackboard. Portable boards are a valuable aid if you lecture away from your classroom.[55]

The criteria sheet on page 326 is used as a guide to bulletin board quality.

Tape Recorder

One of the modern-day devices of considerable importance in its motivational impact in the basic business courses is the tape recorder. This teaching aid has been emerging for a number of years, getting its first great impetus in business education in 1953, with Leslie's *Tape Recording in Business Education*,[56] and moving ahead rapidly with the establishment of more and more tape collections in libraries in the various states.

Now, with innovations in the manufacture of tape recorders so that high fidelity and precision in recording are made possible under ordinary room conditions, the tape recorder has come into its own. Taped recordings of such programs as "60 Minutes," "Meet the Press," and "Firing Line" are excellent class material. Economics and general business classes respond immediately with the use of this medium of teaching. Current examples of the use of this

---

[54] Mary Witherow, "Using Visual Displays in Basic Business to See, to Know, to Remember," *Business Education Forum*, 15 (October, 1960), p. 31.

[55] Mary Louise Lynott, "Teaching Aids for Business Letter Writing Courses," *Collegiate News and Views*, 8 (October, 1954), p. 15.

[56] Louis A. Leslie, *Tape Recording in Business Education* (St. Paul, Minnesota: Minnesota Mining and Manufacturing Company, 1953).

BULLETIN BOARD CHECKSHEET

Item	Excel-lent	Good	Fair	Poor
Subject Contains one thought or idea, if possible; organized to emphasize this main thought.				
Caption Entices the viewer to investigate further what is being presented; wording is simple and is directed toward the viewer; made up of a few well-chosen words and tied in well with the arrangement.				
Materials Used Illustrations, photographs, drawings, cartoons, and actual objects used to illustrate the idea; textured materials, colored materials used for mounting three-dimensional devices, etc., to attract attention.				
Arrangement Arranged in a manner which is attractive and interesting—effective horizontal, vertical, and/or diagonal space division; good balance, simplicity, and neatness.				
Lettering Large and simple enough to be read from any distance in the classroom; lettered in upper and lower case; high contrast between letters and their background; appropriate spacing between words and letters.				
Comments				

teaching aid in the basic business classes are described by Boduch:

> The cassette recorder is one of the more recent technological developments that enable the teacher and students to bring new life to consumer education learning. In the past, a heavy tape recorder had to be carried to and from

the school in order to obtain any interviews for class use. This discouraged the use of this equipment. Teachers were also reluctant to entrust such expensive equipment to the students for fear of damage. Today, many students have their own compact recorders and do not hesitate to use them to solicit expert opinions on current consumer problems.[57]

Malahan gives more specific examples of today's use of the recorder in this area of business education:

In sales classes the tape recorder can be used in connection with a term project. If this project is the development of a sales presentation, for example, the final presentation can be more effective and have more meaning when it is taped.

Law classes usually make use of the case method of learning. As good as this method is, it becomes even more effective with the tape recorder. Dramatizing the cases, taping them, and then playing them back to the class helps the students. They hear the case twice, seem to listen more closely to the points involved, and tend to discuss the case more fully.

Freshman classes in general business, too, provide many opportunities for the use of the recorder. Oral reports that are to be taped are done more conscientiously, and the class will be more attentive to them. More reports will be made on a voluntary basis when students know they will be recorded.[58]

With the coming of the portable recorders and the cassettes, a whole new field of tape recorder usefulness has opened up.

Television

Television, with its added visual element, appears to be enjoying more rapid and more general acceptance as an educational tool than did radio at a comparable stage of development. It appears to hold even greater promise than did radio despite the fact that it takes more time and is more expensive. This newcomer on the educational scene

---

[57] Boduch, op. cit., p. 14.
[58] Andrew J. Malahan, "Tapes are Tops," Business Education World, XXXIX (May, 1959), p. 27.

holds a strong potential for enriching the content and method in both the skill and basic business courses. Some of the critical problems in secondary education, and in business education in particular, may be resolved through the use of television.

Since television production costs are high, to the point of being prohibitive for many school systems, it is probable that dependence upon commercial stations will continue for years to come.

Current experiments show that a variety of values accrue for business education. Brophy cites this point of view:

> The impact of viewing one's self on video tape for the first time is so great that it may overshadow the instructional values in the eyes of the student. However, after two years of teaching salesmanship by TV at Sacramento State College the novelty aspect has worn off and the following observations are in order:
>
> 1. Students learn more when TV is used in teaching salesmanship. Scores in a standardized test verify this.
>
> 2. Students spend more time and effort in preparing demonstration sales and present them better when the TV medium is used.
>
> 3. Class time is used to a better advantage. The best sales presentations are played back and rated by the students. Time-wasting, ill-prepared demonstrations do not usurp valuable class time.
>
> 4. Students compare their own ratings of their performance with those of the teacher and fellow students thus mixing objectivity with subjectivity.[59]

Earlier experiments with this medium of instruction indicate a preference for the lecture method through the medium of television, as compared with the regular classroom lecture:

> In the spring semester of 1954 . . . for the first time, accounting lectures were given on television (in Houston). . . . The favorable points emphasized by students were:

---

[59] John W. Brophy, "Supplement DE Instruction with Television Video Tape," *Business Education Forum*, 26 (November, 1971), p. 49.

1. Students were not distracted by classroom noises.
2. The difficulty of "back seat" students not being able to see the instructor's work was eliminated.
3. Students experienced the psychological reaction that the instructor was talking to the individual watching him, which gave a greater intimacy to the lecture than could be accomplished in the classroom.[60]

The following suggestions are proposed for the teacher faced with the necessity for planning and preparing television programs for school and classroom business education subject matter:

1. Care must be taken that the program content fits the needs and interests of the viewing group.

2. When at all possible, pupil participation in the program should be anticipated and used.

3. Teaching competence and technical excellence in production should be assured.

4. Specific teacher planning and preparation are of primary importance to the success of the medium.

5. The program should fit into the framework of the unit activity, or be integrated rather than "patched in" or superimposed on the unit.

6. As with the use of other methods and devices, television is only one of many teaching aids. It should not be used when other methods are more effective.

American Samoa has received world-wide attention because of its program of television education. In one particular instance, a modern station with six channels, a staff of technicians, and a corps of specially trained television teachers handle the job. The teachers plan their lessons much as one would plan a dramatic production, sometimes working alone, sometimes in teams. Anything they need in the way of display is furnished to specifications by the Art Department. Each schoolroom has a television set and a classroom teacher who introduces the program, handles the

[60] I. E. McNeill, "Teaching Elementary Accounting on Open Broadcast Television," *Collegiate News and Views*, 10 (March, 1957), p. 2.

discipline during the showing, and conducts the follow-up. Classes in hygiene, first aid, and health were particularly good, one teacher observed. Where there is only one section of a subject (office machines, for example) on the entire island, however, one may wonder if the matter could be handled better by the teacher in the classroom who makes her own demonstrations and handles problems on the spot. Television may be a valuable teaching tool that should not be overlooked; but the classroom teacher is still the key factor in the education process.

Miscellaneous Techniques

1. **Debate.** Development of the oral facility in the language arts is a part of the task of the business teacher. In the basic business subjects, this facet becomes a significant part of the planning. Students of business *must* be able to communicate effectively orally, both in their occupational lives and as members of their community. Material for debate in the basic business subjects is plentiful.

Debate offers an excellent opportunity to develop points of view and to arouse thinking on facts and concepts that do not often lend themselves to "book" answers. Teams representing sides on such diverse points of view as "What difference does our gold supply make on the value of U. S. money?" arouse interest in certain subject content that might otherwise play second fiddle to a new rock record.

Most students are familiar with basic debate techniques. A discussion using this method can be planned and organized on the spur of the moment.

2. **Term Papers.** A time-honored reporting device, the term paper, is still in evidence as a teaching device, particularly in those business subjects in which reading of resource materials is an important part of the course. Happily, the term paper, as a paper, is being rapidly supplanted by the more valuable term project or class report. In the latter methods, students are encouraged, and ultimately expected, to produce material that shows a command of the written word.

Expression of oneself through written communication is essential for all who plan to work in business occupations. Hildreth points out the importance of good written communication and gives suggestions on sound classroom practice for the business teacher:

Clear, effective writing contributes to effective citizenship through facilitating communication from one person to another. Good English expression is an essential for anyone who is going into a vocation or profession that demands a high level of skill in writing, e.g., secretarial work, newspaper reporting, teaching, advertising, and so on. . . . One recommendation (to help students organize their ideas in written form) is to eliminate formal theme writing. There are too many occasions in a live school program that require real writing to necessitate spending time on stereotyped compositions. In place of formal theme writing, there can be practice in everyday letter writing, written reports on reading done for class projects, or work on a project that calls for considerable writing, such as getting out an edition of the class paper. Another suggestion is not to demand formal book reviews; but those students who enjoy writing reports of interesting books they have read should be given every encouragement to do so.[61]

3. **The "Analytical Approach."** This method of helping students gain a realistic point of view as opposed to giving "right" answers to students in our business classes, is described by Leith:

Another of our serious problems is that our students have been taught by us to get the "right answer." They assume that there is such an answer to all problems. We "take off" for a strikeover and give full credit for a perfect copy; we use multiple-choice items on our examinations with only one correct answer; we debit cash and we credit sales when a cash sale is made. It is understandable, then, that our students want to know the right answers to business and economic problems. We are obligated, therefore, to help our students understand that in many areas of life there are no definitive right answers; there are only alternative

---

[61] Gertrude Hildreth, "Remedial Learning in Written Expression," *The Fundamental Processes in Business Education,* American Business Education Yearbook, Volume XII (New York: New York University Bookstore, 1955), p. 144.

courses of action. This is particularly true in the area of business and economics. A major purpose of the analytical approach in advanced basic business, then, is to help the student see that there are alternative courses of action—that he must seek out these alternatives, evaluate them, and then take that course of action which seems best in the light of the evidence he is able to obtain.[62]

INNOVATIONS THAT FORESHADOW EVENTS TO COME

This decade will produce some fantastic developments to supplement routine classroom procedures. There is, for example, an ungraded, one-room elementary school just west of Houston, Texas, where some four hundred students are getting an education on a level not dreamed of until now. An enormous resource area cuts a strip across the middle of the room, where the students use tape recorders, cartridge films in individual booths, microfilms, etc., on their own and in a manner heretofore associated with graduate students.

New high schools are providing facilities that are fully in line with this push button space age. One such high school, in Platteville, Wisconsin, is described as follows by Ronald Sime, curriculum coordinator there:

The Platteville High School, occupied for the first time in September, 1968, was designed with an eye to the future. The instructional materials center is the hub of the building as well as the program.

In addition to the traditional library, the center features a section of "dry" carrels for individual study and a mezzanine equipped with dial access carrels with forty-eight programs available at any one time and tape decks in carrels for individual programs. The center is staffed with a full-time librarian and assistant, and a full-time audio-visual coordinator and secretary. The foreign language lab and study rooms complete this area.

The entire school is built in clusters in a general "cross" design. The humanities cluster features a stepped-floor, large-group instruction room in the center, complete with

---

[62] Harold Leith, "An Advanced Course in Basic Business," *Business Education Forum*, 15 (March, 1961), p. 9.

rear screen projection and complement of appropriate A-V equipment. Around this large group room are several "seminar" rooms for small group use, large rooms for groupings of 20-30, and work and storage rooms for staff use. Similar facilities are available for math and science, business, industrial-vocational, physical education, and other facets of the curriculum.[63]

SUMMARY

Good teachers of the basic business subjects, as the reader has seen from the references given, have been rather successful in making their teaching effective. Their close alliance with the development of the motor skills and repetitive practice classes has not kept them from seeing value in providing a way of learning which enables the pupils to experience activity with all the senses.

One point of caution is evident in all that we have tried to present in this section of the book: excessive talking by the teacher, without reinforcement by other materials, robs the pupils of time and opportunity for more valuable experiences. Pupils either do not like the "talking" business courses or they become apathetic and let the discussion "bounce off" so that the teacher is conducting a one-man show. Sensory aids and group dynamics are challenging, realistic supplements to verbalized course material.

We hope that the techniques described will induce the new and inexperienced basic business teacher to utilize and refine methods of his own to fit his immediate classroom situation.

SELECTED BIBLIOGRAPHY

Alcorn, Marvin D., James S. Kinder, and Jim R. Schunert. *Better Teaching in Secondary Schools*. New York: Holt, Rinehart and Winston, Inc., 1970.

Arensman, Ray W., and Gerald W. Maxwell. "Twelve Motivational Vitamins for Business Correspondence Classes." *Collegiate News and Views*, 13 (December, 1959), pp. 5-8.

---

[63] From a manuscript by Ronald Sime, Platteville High School, Platteville, Wisconsin, February, 1970.

Audio Aids for Business Education. Mountain View, Calif.: Educational Products, Co., 1970.

Bahr, Gladys. "A to Z Teaching Activities for Consumer Education." Unpublished manuscript, 1971.

Boduch, Ted J. "Developing Concepts in Basic Business." *Business Education Forum,* 14 (March, 1960), pp. 14-17.

——————. "Teaching Economic Concepts in Secondary Schools . . . in Consumer Economics." *Two Decades of Partnership in Economic Education.* Washington: National Business Education Association and Joint Council of Economic Education, 1969.

Brooks, Wayne A., and A. P. Pierson. "Case Vs. Lecture Methods for the First Course in Business Law." *Collegiate News and Views,* 13 (May, 1960), pp. 29-30.

Brophy, John W. "Supplement DE Instruction with Television Video Tape." *Business Education Forum,* 26 (November, 1971), p. 49.

Business Education Forum. Washington: The National Business Education Association, March, 1970.

Callan, John Henry. *Community Resources Handbook in Business Education,* Monograph 87. Cincinnati: South-Western Publishing Co., 1954.

Claypool, Donald G. "Teamwork, Originality, and Understanding Through Skits in the Business Law Class." *The Balance Sheet,* XLII (January, 1961), pp. 211 and 238.

Crank, Floyd L. "Improved Methodology in Basic Business Education." *Business Education Forum,* 14 (March, 1960), p. 7.

Dale, Edgar. *Audiovisual Methods in Teaching,* 3rd ed. New York: The Dryden Press, Inc., 1969.

Daughtrey, A. S. *Methods of Basic Business and Economic Education.* Cincinnati: South-Western Publishing Co., 1965.

Douglas, Lloyd V., James T. Blanford, and Ruth I. Anderson. *Teaching Business Subjects,* 2nd ed. Englewood Cliffs, N.J.: Prentice-Hall, Inc., 1965.

Faidley, Ray A. "Equal Emphasis for General Business Subjects." *The Journal of Business Education,* XLVI (March, 1971), pp. 246-247.

Freeman, M. Herbert. *Basic Business Education for Everyday Living,* Monograph 74. Cincinnati: South-Western Publishing Co., 1951.

Gaston, Neil. "Business Law." *Changing Methods of Teaching Business Subjects,* Tenth Yearbook of the National Business Education Association. Washington: National Business Education Association, 1972, pp. 24-38.

Giffin, James F. "A Community Resource: The Guest Speaker." *Business Education Forum,* 10 (January, 1956), pp. 7-9.

Grambs, Jean D., John C. Carr, and Robert M. Fitch. *Modern Methods in Secondary Education,* 3rd ed. New York: Holt, Rinehart and Winston, Inc., 1970.

Gulley, Halbert E. *Discussion, Conference, and Group Process.* New York: Holt, Rinehart and Winston, Inc., 1963.

Hall, J. Curtis. "Better Basic Business for the Secondary School." *Business Education Forum,* 24 (May, 1970), p. 7.

Harms, Harm. "The Plus Factor in Teaching." *American Business Education,* XII (March, 1956), pp. 182-185 and 199.

Heimerl, Ramon P. "Ten Basic Social-Study Techniques Applicable to a Consumer Class." *Business Education World,* XXXIV (June, 1954), pp. 16-17.

Hildreth, Gertrude. "Remedial Learning in Written Expression." *The Fundamental Processes in Business Education,* American Business Education Yearbook, Volume XII. New York: New York University Bookstore, 1955, p. 144.

Kincaid, James K. "Teaching Pluses." *American Business Education,* XII (December, 1955), pp. 107-109 and 113-114.

Lebeda, Agnes. "Problem Solving in Basic Business." *Business Education Forum,* 12 (February, 1958), p. 29.

Leith, Harold. "An Advanced Course in Basic Business." *Business Education Forum,* 15 (March, 1961), pp. 9-12.

Leslie, Louis A. *Tape Recording in Business Education.* St. Paul, Minnesota: Minnesota Mining and Manufacturing Co., 1953.

Lewis, Harry. "Do We Want Guest Speakers?" *Business Education World,* XXXV (December, 1954), pp. 9-10.

Login, Abraham. "Questioning." *A Handbook for Teachers of Business Education,* Twenty-Second Yearbook of the Commercial Education Association of the City of New York and Vicinity. New York: Commercial Education Association of the City of New York and Vicinity, 1958, pp. 23-24.

Lynott, Mary Louis. "Teaching Aids for Business Letter Writing Courses." *Collegiate News and Views,* 8 (October, 1954), p. 15.

Maedke, Wilmer O. "Business Principles and Management." *Changing Methods of Teaching Business Subjects,* Tenth Yearbook of the National Business Education Association. Washington: National Business Education Association, 1972, pp. 39-53.

Malahan, Andrew J. "Tapes Are Tops." *Business Education World,* XXXIX (May, 1959), p. 15.

McGill, E. C. "How to Make Basic Business Alive." *Business Education Forum,* 11 (March, 1957), pp. 11-12.

McKillop, John. "Role Playing in Sales Classes." *Business Education Forum,* 7 (May, 1953), pp. 39-40.

McNeill, I. E. "Teaching Elementary Accounting on Open Broadcast Television." *Collegiate News and Views,* 10 (March, 1957), pp. 1-3.

Mosely, Hazel. "Predicting Teacher Behavior." *Texas Outlook* (January, 1970).

Musselman, Vernon A. "Helping General Business Students to See, Hear, and Think." *The National Business Education Quarterly,* 27 (Winter, 1958), pp. 32-37.

——————. "20 Ways to Launch a General Business Unit." *Business Education World,* XXXV (December, 1954), p. 28.

Pigors, Paul, and Faith Pigors. *The Incident Process.* Washington: Bureau of National Affairs, Inc., 1957.

Porter, Gerald A. "Evaluating the Competency of a Business Teacher." *The National Business Education Quarterly,* 24 (Summer, 1956), pp. 16-19.

Price, Ray G., Charles R. Hopkins, and Thomas B. Duff. "Basic Business." *Changing Methods of Teaching Business Subjects,* Tenth Yearbook of the National Business Education Association. Washington: National Business Education Association, 1972, pp. 1-10.

Price, Ray G. (ed). *Improved Methods of Teaching the Business Subjects,* Monograph 63. Cincinnati: South-Western Publishing Co., 1945.

Rainey, Bill G. "Economic Geography A'la Mode." *Business Education Forum,* 14 (May, 1960), p. 28.

Satlow, I. David. "Handling Cases in the Law Class." *Business Education Forum,* 11 (November, 1956), pp. 28 and 32.

Schorling, Raleigh, and Howard T. Batchelder. *Student Teaching in Secondary Schools,* 3rd ed. New York: McGraw-Hill Book Co., Inc., 1956.

Shell, Walter. "Twelve Ways to Improve Your Classroom Teaching." *The Journal of Business Education,* XLVI (January, 1971), pp. 155-156.

Sime, Ronald. Manuscript presented at Platteville High School, Platteville, Wisconsin, February, 1970.

Terry, George R. *Principles of Management,* 5th ed. Homewood, Ill.: Richard D. Irwin, Inc., 1968.

Tinsley, David G., and John P. Ora. "Catch the Child Being Good." *Today's Education* (January, 1970), pp. 24-25.

Tobin, A. "Art of Persuasion." *Marketing Insights* (January 12, 1970), pp. 8-10.

Tonne, Herbert A., Estelle L. Popham, and M. Herbert Freeman. *Methods of Teaching Business Subjects,* 3rd ed. New York: Gregg Division, McGraw-Hill Book Co., Inc., 1965.

Tonne, Herbert A., and Louis C. Nanassy. *Principles of Business Education,* 4th ed. New York: Gregg Division, McGraw-Hill Book Co., Inc., 1970.

Visual Aids for Business and Economic Education, Monograph 92. Cincinnati: South-Western Publishing Co., 1969.

Witherill, Robert D. "Course Projects Add Realism in Small Business Management." *Collegiate News and Views,* 13 (May, 1960), pp. 7-10.

Witherow, Mary. "Using Visual Displays in Basic Business to See, to Know, to Remember." *Business Education Forum,* 15 (October, 1960), p. 31.

Wright, John S. "A New Idea for the Salesmanship Course." *Collegiate News and Views,* 11 (October, 1957), pp. 7-8.

Chapter 8

DISTRIBUTIVE EDUCATION

PRINCIPLES AND CONCEPTS

Distributive education has received increased recognition in recent years because of the importance of marketing and distribution to the economic growth of our nation. Distribution, along with production and consumption, is one of the nation's three leading economic activities. Our system of mass production is based on an efficient system of mass distribution. If distribution fails to achieve its maximum efficiency, our nation will fall short of reaching its full economic potential.

Employment in the distributive occupations, now at an all-time high, will increase faster than in most other occupations. Moreover, the advancement of technology and the growth of incomes will increase this figure, with fewer workers needed to produce goods and services and more needed to distribute them. The demand for persons trained in distribution is therefore strong, and is expected to gather momentum in coming years.

Preparation for jobs in marketing was once gained through practical experience alone. Today, as a result of the complexity of operating procedures in distribution and marketing, specialized preparation is required. To serve this need, vocational education programs in distribution were designed.

Distributive Education:
A Program of Instruction

Distributive education is a program of instruction in distribution and marketing. Distribution, often used synonymously with marketing, relates to those activities that direct the flow of goods and services, including their appropriate utilization, from producer to consumer. These activities include such marketing functions as sales promotion, buying, operations, market research, and management.

The distributive education instructional programs have been developed to serve the educational needs of individuals within the framework of their distributive careers, whether they are preparing themselves for entry, upgrading themselves in their specialization, or involving themselves in management decision-making activities. The U.S. Office of Education has identified the following areas of occupational instruction in the field of marketing and distribution:

> Advertising services; apparel and accessories; automotive; finance and credit; floristry; food distribution; food service; general merchandise; hardware and building materials; farm and garden supplies and equipment; home furnishings; hotel and lodging; industrial marketing; insurance; international trade; personal services; petroleum; real estate; recreation and tourism; transportation; retail trade (other); and wholesale trade (other).[1]

In addition, distribution and marketing has come to be recognized as a function found in a variety of occupations, such as agriculture, trade and industry, home economics, health, and the service industries.

The major purpose of distributive education is to prepare people for employment in distribution. Lucy Crawford, in a federally funded national study, identified the following basic beliefs for distributive education:

> That preparation for gainful employment and for advancement in a distributive occupation is the primary goal of the distributive education program.

---

[1] U.S. Department of Health, Education, and Welfare, Office of Education, and the U.S. Department of Labor, Manpower Administration, *Vocational Education and Occupations*, OE 800061 (Washington: U.S. Government Printing Office, 1969).

That the distributive education program should foster an awareness of the civic, social, and moral responsibilities of business to society.

That the distributive education program should engender an understanding and appreciation of the American private enterprise system as a cornerstone of the American Democracy.

That the distributive education program should encourage and promote the use of ethical standards in business and industry.

That the distributive education program should stimulate the student's interest in his chosen distributive occupational field by providing an understanding of the opportunities it offers him to be a contributing member of society.

That the distributive education program should prepare distributive personnel to analyze consumer demand and to satisfy the needs and wants of consumers intelligently, efficiently, and pleasantly.

That the distributive education program should provide training that results in increased efficiency in distribution and marketing.

That the distributive education program should contribute to the improvement of the techniques in distribution and marketing.

That the distributive education program should be sensitive to changes in distributive and marketing practices and procedures as they are affected by societal, economic, technical, and educational developments, and adapt to such changes.

That the distributive education program should advance the objectives of the total educational program.

That the distributive education program should strive to develop among employers, employees, and consumers a wider appreciation of the value of specifically trained personnel in distribution.[2]

Distributive education instruction is offered for high school students, post-secondary students, and adults. The instruction may be *preparatory* or *supplemental* in nature. Preparatory instruction is for both youth and adults who desire preparation for entering employment in distribution. Supplemental instruction is intended for adults already

[2] Lucy C. Crawford, *A Competency Pattern Approach to Curriculum Construction in Distributive Teacher Education,* OE-6-85-044 (Blacksburg: Virginia Polytechnic Institute, 1967).

employed in distributive occupations who desire further training to update their present competencies or advance to positions of increased responsibility.

High School Programs. Preparatory instruction in high schools is organized and operated under either the cooperative plan or project plan. (See Figures 8-1 and 8-2.) In both plans each student has a career objective in the field of distribution. Learning experiences are planned and conducted to help the student progress toward this occupational goal. Cooperative plan programs combine vocational instruction in the classroom with regularly scheduled supervised experience and on-the-job training related to each student's occupational goal. The term "cooperative" reflects a working relationship between school and business which provides each student with learning experiences that increase his employability.

Project plan programs combine classroom instruction with supervised and coordinated laboratory activities related to each student's occupational goal. Learning experiences are provided through a series of projects correlated with school and business which may include some opportunities for employment. The primary objective of project plan programs is to ready the student for employment upon completion of the program.

Both plans seek to achieve the same learning outcomes—preparing youth for selected careers in marketing and distribution. It is only in their method of combining classroom instruction with laboratory experiences that they differ. A cooperative plan student gains experience in an actual on-the-job situation; the project plan student is involved in a series of projects or activities that enable him to apply and practice the principles and theory learned in the classroom.

The teacher-coordinator has the responsibility for directing all of the instructional activities of the program, which include planning, teaching, supervising, and coordinating learning experiences. In both programs a training plan is developed and maintained for each student to assure that the student will progress toward the levels of competencies required for his occupational goal.

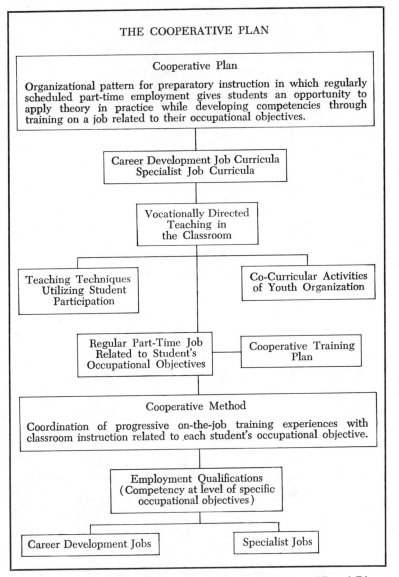

THE COOPERATIVE PLAN

Cooperative Plan

Organizational pattern for preparatory instruction in which regularly scheduled part-time employment gives students an opportunity to apply theory in practice while developing competencies through training on a job related to their occupational objectives.

Career Development Job Curricula
Specialist Job Curricula

Vocationally Directed Teaching in the Classroom

Teaching Techniques Utilizing Student Participation

Co-Curricular Activities of Youth Organization

Regular Part-Time Job Related to Student's Occupational Objectives

Cooperative Training Plan

Cooperative Method

Coordination of progressive on-the-job training experiences with classroom instruction related to each student's occupational objective.

Employment Qualifications (Competency at level of specific occupational objectives)

Career Development Jobs

Specialist Jobs

Adapted from: U.S. Department of Health, Education, and Welfare, Office of Education, *Distributive Education in the High School* (Washington: U.S. Government Printing Office, 1969), p. 48.

FIGURE 8-1

Post-Secondary Programs. In recent years distributive education has received increased emphasis in post-secondary institutions. These institutions include junior colleges, area vocational-technical schools, and technical programs in colleges and universities.

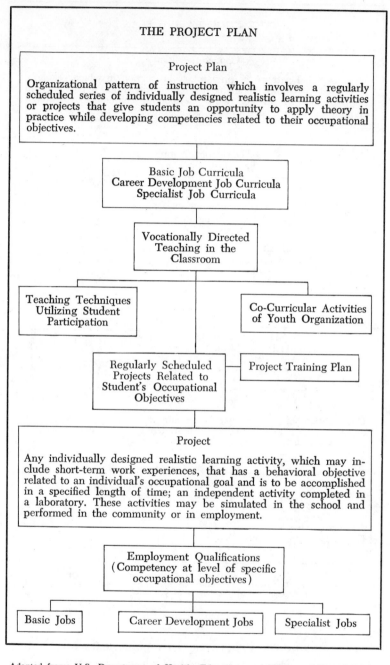

THE PROJECT PLAN

Project Plan

Organizational pattern of instruction which involves a regularly scheduled series of individually designed realistic learning activities or projects that give students an opportunity to apply theory in practice while developing competencies related to their occupational objectives.

Basic Job Curricula
Career Development Job Curricula
Specialist Job Curricula

Vocationally Directed Teaching in the Classroom

Teaching Techniques Utilizing Student Participation

Co-Curricular Activities of Youth Organization

Regularly Scheduled Projects Related to Student's Occupational Objectives

Project Training Plan

Project

Any individually designed realistic learning activity, which may include short-term work experiences, that has a behavioral objective related to an individual's occupational goal and is to be accomplished in a specified length of time; an independent activity completed in a laboratory. These activities may be simulated in the school and performed in the community or in employment.

Employment Qualifications (Competency at level of specific occupational objectives)

Basic Jobs

Career Development Jobs

Specialist Jobs

Adapted from: U.S. Department of Health, Education, and Welfare, Office of Education, *Distributive Education in the High School* (Washington: U.S. Government Printing Office, 1969), p. 49.

FIGURE 8-2

The character of a curriculum, coupled with the age and interest of students, has permitted great flexibility in providing different patterns of employment and laboratory experiences. The post-secondary program has been particularly well suited for training in specialized areas of distribution, such as a particular commodity or service field. Programs have been established which prepare students for middle management or specialist responsibilities in such fields as petroleum distribution, supermarkets, general merchandising, real estate, and the hotel and restaurant industry.

Adult Programs. In terms of the number of people served, the largest segment of the total distributive education program is for adults preparing to enter a distributive occupation, for those interested in gaining greater job proficiency, and for those who seek new and specialized skills to qualify for advancement and promotion.

Three types of adult distributive education programs have been identified to serve the following groups: employees, supervisors, and managers. Employee classes vary in complexity according to their major purpose: to prepare people for employment in distribution, to increase the effectiveness of workers already employed, or to prepare for advancement opportunities. Supervisory classes are intended for persons with responsibility for supervising the work of others. Examples of classes for supervisors include: Methods of Job Instruction, Human Relations, Techniques of Supervision, and advanced courses in a marketing field, such as buying, merchandise control, or personnel management. Management classes are oriented to the needs of managers and owners. Instruction in various aspects of marketing, economics, management, and operations problems is designed to serve those with decision-making responsibilities.

Classes can be *general* in nature, applying to many types of distributive businesses; or they may be *specialized* according to some particular product or service area, such as real estate, restaurant operation, advertising, or export trade.

Adult classes are usually organized in cooperation with advisory groups of businessmen. Classes vary in length, depending on the type of course or program offered, and are held at the convenience of the participants, either during the day or in the evening.

The Discipline of Distribution

The content in distributive education focuses upon the major purpose of the program—preparation for or advancement in the field of distribution and marketing. This content is categorized into five competency areas:

The *marketing competency* relates to the functions of marketing common to all distributive occupations, including selling, sales promotion, buying, operations, marketing research, and management.

The *technology competency* refers to the knowledge and skill concerning a product or service. A knowledge of this technology becomes the focal point upon which other knowledges and skills are applied.

The *social competency* is concerned with a set of personal characteristics necessary for success in distribution. Personal appearance, traits, attitudes, and human relations all contribute to social competency vitally important in this people-oriented occupation.

The basic *skill competency* refers to the application of mathematics and communications in an employment situation. Accuracy in computations and facility in communications are basic in every distributive job.

The *economic competency* reinforces and puts into perspective the other competency areas and includes an understanding of governmental regulations, the role of profits, consumer demands, and channels of distribution.

These five competency areas form the essential content of the distributive education curriculum. These areas represent, at different levels of complexity, the standards for employment in distribution.

Role of DECA in the Distributive Education Program

DECA (Distributive Education Clubs of America) is the vocational youth organization for distributive education. Chapter activities are designed to supplement and complement the total instructional program, and serve to enhance the employability of the students.

DECA is regarded as an integral part of the instructional program, because it provides opportunities for students to demonstrate and refine competencies required in distributive occupations. Opportunities for leadership development are provided in the student-centered environment. DECA supports an awards program which gives recognition to student achievement in various areas of study. DECA's greatest contribution, perhaps, is motivating youth to learn how to perform as leaders and how to cooperate as members of a team. Youth group activities help to interpret the distributive education program to businessmen, faculty, parents, and other students.

The broad purposes of DECA are symbolized by the four points of the diamond which form the DECA emblem:

Vocational Understanding

Civic Consciousness

Social Intelligence

Leadership Development

FIGURE 8-3

Advantages of Distributive Education

The program benefits the distributive education student:

1. By helping him develop a marketable skill which leads to successful employment immediately upon graduation.
2. By providing an occupational orientation to the business world and the American economic system through a combination of classroom instruction and directed experiences.
3. By making him aware of his own potential for success.
4. By providing greater opportunities for advancement and job satisfaction.

5. By showing him the importance of additional education and training to develop full potential.

The program benefits employees:

1. By increasing job satisfaction.
2. By preparing them for better job opportunities and advancement.
3. By improving customer relations.
4. By increasing the opportunity for financial gain.

The program benefits the employer and the owner of business:

1. By providing instruction in the operational phases of his business.
2. By reducing turnover of personnel.
3. By providing better trained personnel.
4. By decreasing training costs.
5. By assisting him to better serve the public and to operate more profitably.

The program benefits the consumer:

1. By increasing efficiency in distribution and marketing.
2. By providing well-trained personnel who help customers buy more wisely.
3. By providing improved marketing services which result in greater customer satisfaction.

It immediately becomes apparent, therefore, that several large groups of citizens have a direct interest, and a still larger group an indirect interest, in distributive education. These groups are composed of all those persons who produce for distribution, all those who engage in distribution, and all those who benefit from distribution.

Constructing the Curricula

Many distributive education programs are doomed to failure before they begin because too little effort has been expended in constructing the curricula. The time, effort, and energy expended in the planning of any vocational education curricula is always a sound investment. The following five-step curriculum construction process has yielded excellent results when used to design new curricula or to revise an existing instructional program.

Determination of Occupations in Area. The first step in constructing the curriculum is the determination of the distributive occupations which are found within the area. This step can best be achieved by determining the jobs actually found in the area; the necessity for and amount of training required; the number and type of persons presently employed; the turnover, the approximate number of new employees needed in a given period of time, and employment conditions; and the extent to which advancement is dependent upon training for various levels of jobs.

In most cases, the acquisition of this information will require a survey of the employment area served by the school. Frequently, occupational surveys are conducted with the assistance of either steering or advisory committees. The U.S. Office of Education publication *Vocational Education and Occupations* is an excellent source document for identifying jobs according to various types of instructional programs. Due to limitations on time and financial resources, most curriculum studies are based on a sample of businesses. Data from studies made by various local, state, and national governmental agencies, such as the U.S. Bureau of the Census, should also be used to verify local data and provide a comprehensive employment picture.

Determination of Occupations for Training. Based on the findings of the first step, a determination of the occupations for which training is to be provided must be made. School administrators, teachers, steering or advisory committee members, and other individuals must make a number of very important decisions and recommendations. The following factors must be carefully weighed before final decisions can be made:

1. The climate in which the program will be offered.
2. Ability of school to support the proposed program in terms of equipment, teaching personnel, and related services.

3. The number of jobs that can be filled each year and the number of students who will enroll in the program.

4. Employment trends in the occupations for which training is planned.

5. The estimated cost of the new or revised program in terms of facilities, equipment, and salaries.

Determination of Content. The determination of the instructional content of the program is based on well-known, but slightly used, techniques of task and job analysis. In curriculum revision programs, task and job analysis data should also be supported by follow-up studies of former students employed in the occupations being studied.

The instructional content of a distributive education program is identified with the knowledge, understanding, and skills needed for employment in the field of distribution. The following five major competency areas form the

---

OUTLINE OF AREAS OF INSTRUCTION IN PREPARATORY CURRICULA

A. MARKETING

1. Selling
2. Sales Promotion
3. Buying
4. Operations
5. Market Research
6. Management

B. PRODUCT OR SERVICE TECHNOLOGY

1. Product Knowledge and Techniques
2. Service Knowledge and Techniques

C. SOCIAL SKILLS

1. Business and Social Skills
2. Ethics
3. Human Relations
4. Supervisory Skills and Leadership

D. BASIC SKILLS

1. Application of Mathematics
2. Application of Communications

E. DISTRIBUTION IN THE ECONOMY

1. Channels of Distribution
2. Job Opportunities in Distribution
3. Distribution in a Free Enterprise System

Source: U.S. Department of Health, Education, and Welfare, Office of Education, *Distributive Education in the High School* (Washington: U.S. Government Printing Office, 1969), p. 18.

FIGURE 8-4

content of distributive education curricula: marketing, product or service technology, social skills, basic skills, and distribution in the economy.[3] (See Figure 8-4.)

Careful planning must be done so that the competencies are developed in relation to one another. The integration of the competencies is essential if students are to be employable upon the completion of the instructional program. The U.S. Office of Education publication *Distributive Education in the High School* clearly describes and illustrates the interrelationship of the competency areas in distributive education instructional programs:

> Competencies are always developed in relation to one another. Marketing with its distributive functions of selling, sales promotion, buying, operations, market research, and management is the discipline of distribution. Marketing is the nucleus of the curriculum around which the other areas of instruction are grouped.
>
> The product or service is the focal point in the performance of the distributive functions, such as selling. The technology of a distributive occupation would be studied in relation to each of these marketing functions.
>
> Social skills are related to marketing and product or service technology in that proficiency in personal attributes, attitudes, and standards of service facilitates the performance of the distributive functions. It enables the worker to use his product or service knowledge and techniques effectively.
>
> Basic skills relate to marketing, product or service technology, and social skills in that one engaged in distribution must make constant application of the basic skills of communications and mathematics. These skills are essential in performing the distributive functions, in using product or service knowledge and techniques, and in applying the social skills.
>
> Distribution in the economy relates to marketing, product or service technology, and social and basic skills because economic understandings stimulate decision making and motivation for distributive personnel. To achieve economic objectives, the worker should be motivated to improve his social and basic skills. These skills, together with economic

[3] U.S. Department of Health, Education, and Welfare, Office of Education, *Distributive Education in the High School*, OE 82019 (Washington: U.S. Government Printing Office, 1969), p. 18.

understandings, help him to carry out the distributive functions included in the marketing area of instruction and to apply product or service knowledge and techniques.

Because of these interrelationships, any one unit of instruction in a curriculum necessarily is concerned with the development of competencies other than those of its area of concentration. A unit on selling, for example, inevitably is involved with product or service knowledge and techniques; with ethics and human relations as social skills; with the basic skills of effective speech and the mathematics of selling cost; with economic understandings related to disposable income and the role of selling in the marketing process; and with all other functions in the marketing area of instruction.[4]

Figure 8-5 illustrates the interrelationship of the areas of instruction. Marketing, the discipline, as the nucleus of

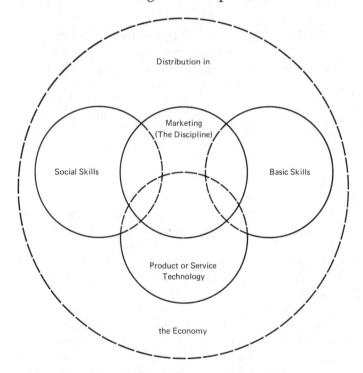

Source: U.S. Department of Health, Education, and Welfare, Office of Education, *Distributive Education in the High School* (Washington: U.S. Government Printing Office, 1969), p. 22.

FIGURE 8-5

[4] *Ibid.*, pp. 19-23.

the curriculum is completely encircled with a solid line. Dotted lines represent integration of instructional areas in a curriculum. This integration is realistic in terms of relating instruction to the interdependent competencies needed in distributive employment.

Organization of Subject Matter. The organization of the subject matter and determination of teaching strategy can clearly be seen in the U.S. Office of Education diagram showing curriculum and instruction interrelationships.

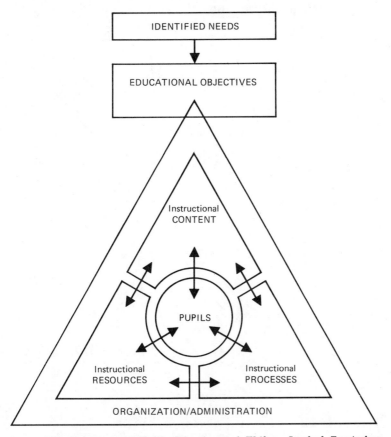

Source: U.S. Department of Health, Education, and Welfare, *Standard Terminology for Instruction in Local and State School Systems,* Third Draft (Washington: U.S. Government Printing Office, May, 1967).

FIGURE 8-6

Identified student and community needs provide the essential input for designing distributive education curricula.

The identification of specific student needs is a continual process. However, student needs must be recognized and the instructional program adjusted to serve these needs. The challenge of individualizing instruction in distributive education has never been greater than it is today. Instructional content, resources, and processes must be organized and administered effectively to serve students' occupational needs.

The distributive education teacher or teacher-coordinator who tries to serve the diverse needs of all of his students finds himself in the situation shown in Figure 8-7.

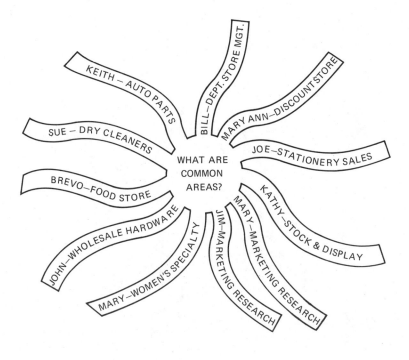

FIGURE 8-7

He can use one of two strategies in attempting to prepare his students for careers in distribution and marketing. He may ignore the needs of individual students and teach the class as a group. However, teachers who mastered the techniques of individualizing instruction are using the following system.

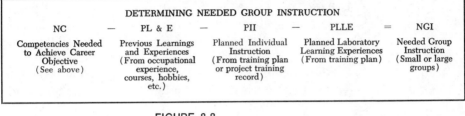

DETERMINING COMPETENCIES NEEDED FOR CAREER OBJECTIVE						
E & TS	+ AC	+ T & PA	+ CE & I	+ SE & I	=	NC
Employers and/or Training Sponsor	Advisory Committee	Trade and Professional Associations	Teacher-Coordinator Experience and Investigation	Student Experience and Investigation		Needed Competencies

DETERMINING NEEDED GROUP INSTRUCTION				
NC	— PL & E	— PII	— PLLE	= NGI
Competencies Needed to Achieve Career Objective (See above)	Previous Learnings and Experiences (From occupational experience, courses, hobbies, etc.)	Planned Individual Instruction (From training plan or project training record)	Planned Laboratory Learning Experiences (From training plan)	Needed Group Instruction (Small or large groups)

FIGURE 8-8

By using this system, the teacher-coordinator at least knows how to plan instruction. But the problem still hasn't been totally solved. The teacher-coordinator must now design the instructional program.

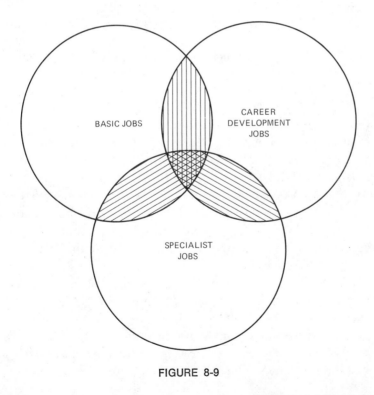

FIGURE 8-9

To assist in the implementation of distributive education programs, many educators are designing curricula to better serve groups of students who vary in ability, motivation, and job maturity. The following three levels of curricula can assist in the homogenous grouping of marketing students:

1. Basic Job Curricula—Instructional programs which prepare students for elementary or basic distributive occupations involving minimal employment, responsibility, and which emphasize fundamental techniques in sales and sales-supporting services, simple marketing concepts, social competencies, and basic skills in computations and communications.
2. Career Development Job Curricula—Instructional programs which prepare students for career-type positions involving competencies and responsibilities necessary for self-direction, and emphasize the functions of marketing, merchandising, and management within the discipline of distribution.
3. Specialist Job Curricula—Instructional programs which prepare students for distributive specializations in functions, product areas, or service fields involving leadership competencies and management responsibilities in relation to personnel, finance, merchandise, or service.

Even though a majority of the specialized curricula are housed in post-secondary institutions, an increasing number of secondary schools are designing specialized programs in such areas as advertising, petroleum marketing, food distribution, food service, hotel and lodging, and personal services. Area vocational centers and vocational schools are also developing programs in skills such as display. Many of these programs have been designed to better prepare students who will be entering employment at the basic job level in a metropolitan area.

The potential for offering a wide variety of instructional programs in high schools is almost unlimited. Earlier in this chapter the 21 U.S. Office of Education instructional programs in distribution and marketing were listed. Multiply these 21 programs by the three levels of curricula in high school distributive education (basic, career development, and specialist), plus additional skill center type programs for a total of over 70 programs. Multiply 70 by the duration of the instructional program (less than one semester, one semester, one year, two years, three years, etc.) and it is entirely possible to have over 500 different high school instructional programs in distributive education in a community. The potential for developing interdisciplinary programs in other vocational areas would add additional programs.

Before any instructional program can be implemented, a number of key decisions must be made. Questions such as those listed below must be carefully thought through.

1. How much time will be devoted to achieving program objectives?
2. What courses will make up the program?
3. What will be the grade level placement of the courses?
4. How will the program be scheduled?
5. How will staff members be selected and assigned?
6. Which existing courses need revision?
7. What new courses must be added?
8. How will guidance and exploratory experiences be provided?
9. How are students to be selected?
10. How much credit or recognition for satisfactory completion of instruction will be given?
11. What type of occupational experience laboratory programs will the students participate in—project or cooperative?
12. Who will administer the program?

The following list of recommended guidelines has been used by school personnel in planning and evaluating distributive education programs:

1. Services of occupationally aware guidance and teaching personnel are utilized in advising students concerning career choices and planning.
2. Each student has a realistic career objective of which his present instructional program is an integral part.

3. The student-learners are selected by the staff on the basis of need, interest, and ability to profit from the instruction.

4. The classroom instructional phase of the program is preceded by a program of well-planned courses which are designed to assist in the occupational preparation of the student.

5. The vocationally-oriented classroom phase of the program is taught by the staff.

6. Enrollment in the class is determined by availability of adequate classroom facilities and staff time to provide individualized instruction.

7. The instructional program is confirmed or changed by periodic analysis of the occupations for which the program is designed.

8. An advisory committee, including representatives of both the school and the business community, advises and assists in planning, developing, and implementing the program.

9. The instructional facilities in which the classroom instruction is given provide an opportunity to simulate the facilities of businesses in the world of work.

10. An adequate budget is provided to update the classroom facilities and instructional materials.

11. The local chapter of the Distributive Education Clubs of America is effectively developed and recognized as a co-curricular phase of the total distributive education instructional program.

12. Students receive credit toward graduation for both the classroom and laboratory (cooperative or project) instructional phases of the program.

13. The staff has sufficient technical course preparation, plus a well-rounded current business experience background, to enable them to realistically teach the discipline of distribution.

14. The staff has derived from their professionalized distributive education courses the diverse abilities required for the effective implementation of the program.

15. Individual student training records (including a training plan) have been carefully developed by the staff in consultation with the student and businessmen.

16. A minimum of one-half hour per week per student is provided for by the staff to effectively correlate the

classroom instruction with the laboratory (cooperative or project) instruction.

17. Home visitations and/or parental conferences are an integral part of the job of the staff to assist them in the total development of each student-learner.

18. Follow-up studies are conducted regularly and the results of studies are utilized to improve the program.

19. The staff members are provided with extended contracts to enable them to develop community resources, conduct follow-up studies, make home visitations, develop training plans, up-date program records, develop adult education programs, and other program development activities.

Making the Program Work. If the program has been properly designed, the following principles for the development of curriculum will have been achieved:

1. The curriculum is identified with student-learners' occupational objectives.

2. The curriculum is planned so that the proportion of time devoted to the various areas of instruction is related to the competencies required for the particular job level—basic, career development, or specialist.

3. The curriculum is consistent with the type of school in which it is located—comprehensive, area vocational, or technical.

4. The curriculum is adapted to the particular instructional plan that assures vocationally directed learning experiences (cooperative or project) for those enrolled.

5. The curriculum is planned in relation to the sequence of job preparation activities available to students in the school, community, area, and state so that students may participate in advanced training.

Once the program has been properly sold, instructional materials secured and designed, and the program operating, the plan for evaluation should be implemented. Students, advisory committee members, teachers, and guidance and administrative staff members should be involved in the program evaluation. Changes in the program can most efficiently be made if a continuous follow-up plan is designed.

TEACHING TECHNIQUES
AND PROCEDURES

The teacher of distributive subjects must be proficient in using all the teaching techniques and procedures used by skill and nonskill teachers, adult education instructors, and training directors in business and industry. The distributive education teacher must truly be a director of learning. He spends a great majority of his total teaching time designing learning activities to prepare students for employment in the field of marketing and distribution. Successful distributive teachers are those instructors who have succeeded in individualizing instruction.

Selecting the most appropriate teaching technique or procedure for literally millions of learning situations is the challenge facing the distributive education teacher. Teaching requires a quick-thinking, imaginative response to a kaleidescopic array of problems and needs. Unfortunately, no two situations are the same and few magic formulas exist to guide the teacher.

The three lists below illustrate the instructional function of the teacher, when viewed as an information system involving activities which require continuous decision-making:

INPUT	PROCESSING	OUTPUT
Observing	Selecting	Motivating
Listening	Planning	Managing
Reading	Evaluating	Leading
Diagnosing		Directing
		Coordinating
		Providing
		Telling

The INPUT activities of a distributive subjects teacher are particularly crucial because of the need to individualize instruction. Techniques for utilizing training plans as a diagnostic tool are presented in Chapter 9. The distributive subjects teacher who is a teacher-coordinator of a cooperative plan or project plan program will find the concepts presented in Chapters 9 and 10 appropriate.

The basic PROCESSING activities of distributive subjects teachers are presented in Chapter 2. The PROCESSING activities which are useful for teacher-coordinators of cooperative plan or project plan programs are presented in Chapters 7, 9, 10, and 11.

The OUTPUT activities that are applicable for all teachers of secondary school distributive subjects are presented in this chapter and those which are primarily applicable to cooperative or project plan teacher-coordinators are presented in Chapters 7, 9, 10, and 11.

Basic Concepts and Generalizations

The beginning teacher should not expect to master the teaching strategy of a professional teacher from the start. The process of learning to teach may be compared to the process of learning to play golf. If the beginning golfer tries to concentrate on all the principles of the correct swing of the club as he gets up to the first tee, he would probably find himself doing everything wrong. It is far better to pick out a few of the most important techniques to learn first, concentrate on them, and practice them until they have been mastered. Then the golfer can work on more sophisticated techniques. So it is with the beginning teacher in selecting and implementing his teaching techniques and procedures.

The time and effort devoted to the study of the learning process will pay rich dividends. A teacher who believes in something and is willing to test his assumptions and beliefs is well along the path to becoming a professional educator. One university teacher-educator begins his methods class by asking his students the following questions: "What is your philosophy of education?" and "Why do you think you should be a teacher?" Having to provide responses to such questions is a real shock to the prospective teachers, who have devoted their time to studying about teaching without really thinking about why they are in the field. Increasingly, school administrators are asking similar questions in an effort to secure dedicated professional staff members. School administrators are well aware of the fact that they cannot direct every program in the school and, therefore, must count on staff members to do so. They must rely upon teachers who have thoroughly thought through their own beliefs and know what they have to offer in terms of professional expertise.

The first week of teaching can be a traumatic experience for the teacher who waits until a few weeks before school starts to carefully plan his teaching strategy. Serious thinking and tryout time must be devoted to secure answers to the following:

1. What will be my strategy during the first week of school?
2. How much will I expect from my students?
3. How will I earn the respect of my students?
4. What will I do to prevent discipline problems?
5. How will I handle discipline problems?
6. What type of relationship do I wish to establish with members of the school and business community?
7. What type and degree of commitment am I willing to make to my profession?
8. What kind of teacher do I want to be?
9. What type of "climate" do I want in my classroom?
10. What are my priority goals for my first year of teaching?

Hopefully, through a well-planned student teaching or internship experience program, a majority of the answers to these and similar questions will become clear. However, the aspiring teacher in training must be alert and observant during these experiences or he will not gain the insight necessary to begin his professional teaching career.

A Good Teacher

Possibly the simplest way to describe a good teacher is to say, in the following order, that he is *firm, fair,* and *friendly.*

Unfortunately, a rather significant percentage of beginning teachers have forgotten what it was like when they were in high school. They forget about the teacher who resigned at the end of the first semester because he couldn't control his class. They can't remember the teacher that they thought was such a "great guy," but yet the class members really gave him a "rough time." Why? Probably because little was learned in these classes, and the fun that was had at the expense of the teacher didn't leave a lasting impression.

The teachers who are remembered are individuals respected by the students. They are strong individuals students can identify with because students know they can trust them. Every school has a number of such teachers. How can such a model teacher be described? Certainly age, sex, dress, and other physical descriptions are not adequate.

An experienced and successful distributive education teacher describes a good teacher as one who:

1. Knows how to assemble his knowledge into a course of study and then to organize it into units and lessons.

2. Has an expert knowledge of his field of work.

3. Is constantly seeking new and better methods and techniques of teaching, and learning how to use these new tools where they will do the most good.

4. Is interested in helping others to learn. Is enthusiastic about his job of teaching. Takes an interest in his students, their needs, desires, comforts, and welfare.

5. Is cooperative in working with fellow teachers, administrators, and other professional and non-teaching staff members.

6. Takes his routine teaching duties seriously, such as preparing reports, taking attendance, and class record-keeping.

7. Provides for active participation of all members in the work of the class.

8. Individualizes instruction to serve the needs of all the students.

9. Is always open-minded; welcomes suggestions for improvement; has an earnest desire to grow professionally.

10. Has complete control over his group at all times. Teaches only to complete attention. Anticipates trouble

and prevents its outbreak. Handles occasional trouble, when it occurs, tactfully and effectively.[5]

Teaching Distributive Subjects

Probably the simplest way to describe teaching is to quote a rather common expression in the field of education: Teaching is lighting a lamp, not filling a bucket. This is a hard lesson for beginning teachers to learn. The typical aspiring teacher has just gone through almost four years of college training. Lecturing is the teaching method most used in a typical college classroom. A majority of beginning teachers will attempt to use it, "teaching as they were taught." As a result, most high school students will literally "turn him off." How long will it take these teachers to recover from the damage done and recall that in their professional training they learned how to use a variety of teaching methods? The answer depends greatly upon a number of factors, such as how long has the poor practice been going on, the school system, the type of students, the amount and quality of supervision provided, and the overall competence of the individual teacher.

The distributive subjects teacher who is willing to adopt the following philosophy is probably well on his way to becoming a master teacher, "If the student hasn't learned, the teacher hasn't taught." The challenge of teaching isn't just to determine what is to be taught, but how to teach it, under what conditions, and to determine what the student has learned.

Experienced distributive subjects teachers who have been most successful have basically adopted the following four-step procedure for teaching: prepare the learner, present the material to be learned, have the learner apply what he has learned, and follow up to assess learning and determine need for reteaching. Different terms may be used to describe the steps, but it is important that all of the purposes listed in Figure 8-10 are achieved.

[5] *How to Teach Business Subjects,* Business Education Publication No. 108 (Sacramento: California State Department of Education, 1963), p. 6.

FOUR STEP PROCEDURE FOR TEACHING		
STEPS	PURPOSES	SOME SUGGESTED PROCEDURES FOR IMPLEMENTATION
1. Prepare learner (Preparation, introduction, preview, or other appropriate heading)	1. Get learner ready to receive instruction. 2. Awaken interest so learner will know what he is to learn. 3. Stimulate learner so he wants to learn and believes it is worthwhile to expend the needed effort. 4. Insure that learner understands what is expected of him.	1. Determine what learner already knows. 2. Clearly identify the realistic expected performance goals for the learner. 3. Relate what the learner is to learn to what he knows and to his past experiences. 4. Illustrate importance of what the learner must learn through use of cases, exhibits, curiosity type questions, and similar interest-arousing techniques. 5. Ask questions to make sure learner understands his goals.
2. Presentation (New material, content, or other descriptive heading)	1. Present new ideas, information, facts, skills, procedures essential for developing learner knowledge, understanding, skills, and attitudes. 2. Tell, show, and demonstrate to learner how to use newly presented material. 3. Help learner build new knowledge, understanding, skills, and attitudes out of old ones.	1. Use the most effective teaching strategy. 2. Carefully select teaching methods appropriate for the learner. 3. Use appropriate teaching media, such as overhead projector, single concept films, or television. 4. Relate key points to learner experiences.
3. Application (Application by class members, practice, assimilation, or other appropriate heading)	1. Give learner an opportunity to apply knowledge, understanding, skills, or attitudes to a similar or identical situation. 2. Give learner an opportunity to apply knowledge, understanding, skills, or attitudes to a different situation.	1. Learner performs with teacher assisting as necessary. 2. Learner asks questions. 3. Learner answers questions, solves case problems, applies newly developed competency in different situations.
4. Follow-up (Testing, checkup, review, or other descriptive heading)	1. See if learner has achieved expected level of performance. 2. See if teaching was successful. 3. Determine need for reteaching. 4. Motivate learner.	1. Re-examine expected performance goals of learner. 2. Determine and select most appropriate evaluative instruments for measuring learner performance. 3. Evaluate and reteach to achieve realistic expected learner performance level. 4. Stimulate learner to use what he has learned. 5. Provide opportunity for learner to apply new competencies.

FIGURE 8-10

This procedure for teaching can be most effectively implemented if the teacher is willing to utilize as many of the student-centered techniques listed in the right hand column of Figure 8-11 as possible. Many beginning teachers are discouraged because they don't achieve the desired results the first time they attempt a technique. They should keep experimenting; experience has shown that teachers

---

TEACHING TECHNIQUES

Teacher-Centered Techniques	*Student-Centered Techniques*
Subject matter taught is not closely related to the students' real needs and interests.	Classroom material is related to real life situations.
Learning activities are controlled by the teacher, or other adults, with little or no opportunity to let the students participate.	Pupils participate in the purposing and the planning. They prepare lists of "things to do" and "things to find out."
The students themselves receive little or no experience in assuming responsibilities or in making choices.	Student committees have specific responsibilities. Each pupil makes some contribution to every learning situation.
All students are given the same contacts with the same material; little provision is made for individual differences.	Activities are broken up into tasks that are small enough and simple enough that even the slow-learner can see his progress.
Too much dependence upon textbooks— only the verbally skillful students can succeed.	Whenever possible, concrete things the students can see, feel, and handle are used.
Learning activities are usually centered in the past in the "accumulated" culture; little reference to the present or future.	Problem situations and meaningful, interesting activities constitute the chief body of work to be done.
Too heavy a reliance upon formal methods, assignments, distinct lesson types, printed materials as chief sources; learning experiences few and formal.	Visual aids, field trips, speakers, panels, dramatizations, and demonstrations are used frequently. The students preview films, prepare bulletin board exhibits, and make the arrangements for speakers and field trips.
Assignments are made by chapters and pages; recitations are based on questions at the end of the chapter.	Students' aims are stated in terms of definite tasks to be done. These tasks must be desirable, specific, immediate, and attainable.
The student's ability to answer questions correctly—either orally or in writing—form the chief evidence of a good preparation.	Part or all of the class period is used for independent study. The teacher assists students as they solve a problem or work on a project.
Outcomes are fixed, and known in advance, required uniformly of all learners, centered around the acquisition of facts and mastery of subject matter.	Students measure their own progress. Ability to work with other pupils and willingness to accept responsibility are considered important.

FIGURE 8-11

who use student-centered techniques are much more effective than those who use teacher-centered techniques.

Methods of Teaching Distributive Subjects

Distributive teacher-educators frequently provide their methods students with a sheet of paper listing many of the potential materials and methods for use by distributive subjects teachers and coordinators.

No attempt will be made to discuss all of the materials and methods in this chapter. Methods and techniques which are most commonly used as an integral part of either the cooperative plan or project plan program will be presented in Chapters 9 and 10. Additional methods are presented in Chapter 7. The techniques for implementation, uses, advantages, and disadvantages for each of the following methods are presented: question-and-answer, lecture, group discussion, panel or round-table discussion, buzz sessions, brainstorming, role-playing, case or incident problem, and the conference method. It is important to keep in mind that in most cases a combination of methods is used and not a single method.

Question-and-Answer. The question-and-answer method too frequently does little to stimulate thinking. However, if carefully phrased questions are properly administered, the method can be used to stimulate group discussion and identify student interests, weaknesses, and difficulties. Effective questioning techniques provide the basis for implementing a majority of the group methods used in teaching distributive subjects. Distributive subjects teachers who are skillful in asking questions are able to quickly turn what might be a routine question-and-answer session into a dynamic learning activity.

The question-and-answer method can easily become a technique for the poorly prepared teacher to use, a "teacher-tell" and "student-tell" procedure with the teacher raising a question and asking for students to respond. If the techniques of good questioning are not followed, the question-and-answer session can become a very boring and non-productive learning experience for the students. Hopefully, the teacher will secure responses from two or more students

MATERIALS AND METHODS FOR USE BY
DISTRIBUTIVE SUBJECTS TEACHERS

Partial List of Learning Activities Desirable for Use in D.E. Classes:

A. Teaching methods and materials in which the teacher may be or often is the main participant:

1. Chalkboard techniques
2. Use of commercial materials
3. Use of community resources
4. Demonstration by the teacher
5. Lecture
6. Visual aids: charts, graphs, films, filmstrips, etc.
7. Unit method of teaching (experience unit)
8. Pupil-teacher planning
9. Textbooks
10. Evaluation

B. Group discussion methods needed in D.E. classes:

1. Group discussion
2. Committee work
3. Debates
4. Conference leading
5. Panel
6. Oral reports
7. Role-playing
8. Symposium
9. Dialogue
10. Parliamentary rules
11. Buzz sessions
12. Round-table discussions
13. Team role-playing
14. Progressive buzz session
15. "66" sessions

C. Group learning methods (other than purely discussion):

1. Case problems
2. Youth group work (DECA)
3. Contests (DECA)
4. Demonstrations
5. Displays and exhibits
6. Experiments
7. Field trips
8. Model business activities
9. Style shows
10. Surveys
11. Skits
12. Evaluation
13. Guest speakers
14. Questionnaires
15. Business simulation
16. Multi-media system
17. Television
18. Learning response systems
19. Electrowriter
20. Learning by inquiry
21. Incident problems
22. Games

D. Individual learning methods:

1. Individual counsel
2. Supervised study
3. Field interviews
4. Job analysis
5. Manuals and notebooks
6. Merchandise studies
7. Ratings of many types
8. Field observations
9. Reference reading
10. Research
11. Shopping reports
12. Job study guide
13. Occupational experiences
14. Window displays
15. Programmed instruction
16. Evaluation
17. Single concept films
18. Sound-filmstrips
19. Computer assisted instruction
20. Projects of various types
21. Audio-tutorial systems
22. Student learning carrels
23. Television
24. Laboratory and experimentation
25. Learning packages

FIGURE 8-12

and stimulate discussion on key questions. The responses given by students may be elaborated on by the teacher or merely summarized, depending upon the situation. Frequently, student responses will lead to the teacher or students asking questions which may lead into a meaningful discussion. Teachers who have mastered the following techniques of questioning are in a good position to effectively utilize the question-and-answer method and other teaching methods:

1. Begin each question with a word or phrase that calls for thought on the part of the students. Use words such as why, what, how, where, summarize, justify, trace, compare, describe, and analyze.

2. State questions in simple, straightforward language, and be as brief as possible yet complete enough to assure understanding.

3. Ask questions which challenge the student to apply knowledge rather than repeat facts. Questions should not be answerable with yes or no.

4. In most cases, limit questions to those within the students' experience and knowledge; however, questions that stimulate thinking with phrases such as "Let's estimate," "What would be your hunch," "Could you guess," and "Let's get your ideas," are excellent for stimulating discussion.

5. Organize the general sequence of planned questions around a thread or core and key them to the objectives of the lesson. A carefully planned series of questions provides an excellent springboard to launching a group discussion, buzz session, brainstorming session, role-playing situation, or a panel discussion.

6. Develop an attitude of student responsibility for answering questions from other class members, as well as those from the teacher.

7. Maintain an attitude during questioning which is natural, friendly, and conversational.

8. Precede each question by a situation thoroughly understood as the basis for the problem involved.

9. Allow questions to point up the important aspects of the lesson.

10. Give confidence-building questions to shy students.

11. Avoid questions so phrased that they give away the answers.

12. Avoid vague and general questions, like "What about display?" or "Are there any more questions?"

13. Encourage students to ask pertinent questions.

14. When practical, try to discuss students' questions when they are asked, rather than at some later time.

15. Do not hesitate to say "I do not know" in response to a student's question.

16. Avoid a pattern of calling on students in turn.

17. State the question; pause to give all students time to think on an answer before calling for a response.

18. Allow students time to answer without interruption.

19. As a rule, don't repeat questions.

20. Correct any misconceptions or inaccurate conclusions without antagonizing the class.

21. Reinforce concepts generated by answers to key questions, but avoid the practice of repeating or confirming every answer.

22. Accept any answer or part thereof which can be used by saying, "That's part of it, let's see if you can elaborate on it," or "Hold that a moment, we will use it later." Try not to tell a student he is wrong for fear of discouraging further contributions.

23. Draw out answers to questions by saying, "Do you agree?" "What do you think?" or "Can anyone add to what Jim said?"

24. Encourage students to give answers to the class, not the teacher.

25. Direct all teacher responses to questions toward the entire class and not to individual students who asked the questions.

The most common uses of the question-and-answer method are to:

1. Set the stage for group discussion, buzz sessions, panel or round-table discussion, role-playing, or other teaching-learning activities.

2. Determine progress of students in doing assigned work.

3. Identify student difficulties, interests, work habits, and levels of development.
4. Review previous instruction and prepare for examinations.
5. Pre-test to explore student background.
6. Secure and maintain student interest.
7. Draw upon student experiences in business.
8. Develop and reinforce concepts and generalizations.
9. Involve nonresponsive students in class activity.
10. Motivate students to do additional work.

Lecture. The major advantage of the lecture method is that it requires little prior student knowledge for implementation. The teacher can present new concepts and ideas in a relatively short period of time. Sometimes teachers tend to become overly anxious to present their students with a lot of knowledge and feel their students lack the experience to learn through other methods.

For this reason the lecture method of teaching on the secondary school level has been seriously overused. All too frequently, the lecture method is used because the teacher feels that when he is talking, the students are learning. Nothing could be further from the truth. The teacher who forces students to take notes may find that what really occurs is that facts are transmitted from his lesson plan to the notebook of the student, without passing through the mind of the student. It is very difficult to maintain interest over any extended period of time. Since the lecture method provides little opportunity for student participation or a check-up for understanding, it is almost impossible for the teacher to adjust for individual differences.

The "teacher-tell" method of teaching distributive subjects can be used most effectively if the following suggestions are implemented:

1. Lectures should usually be short. In most cases, any "tell" portion of the lesson should not last over five to ten minutes.
2. The language and vocabulary used in the lecture should be tailored to the class members.

3. Lectures should be related to students' backgrounds, knowledge, and interests.

4. The lecture should present new ideas and concepts not readily available to the students from other sources.

5. Lectures should be planned and organized so that they do not digress into a "talk session" for the teacher.

6. The presentation should be generously supplemented with examples, and both verbal and visual illustrations.

7. Lecture with enthusiasm both in terms of voice and in facial expression and body gestures.

8. The approach to the lecture should be informal and the contact maintained. Each student should feel as though the presentation is directed just to him.

9. The class should be watched and, at the first sign of fatigue, do something for a change of pace. Use an illustration, humor, move about, or ask a question to stimulate renewed interest.

10. The key points of the presentation should be summarized and the students given an opportunity to reflect upon what they have learned.

A short informal lecture can be used effectively for introducing a unit, presenting a problem for study, providing information which is difficult for students to find, motivating students, introducing an educational film, or in sharing one's own business experiences with students. The "teacher-tell" method of teaching on the secondary level is most effectively used when supplementing other teaching methods, such as demonstration, role-playing, group discussion, or case problems. It is important to remember that *talking is not teaching; listening is not learning.*

Group Discussion. Discussion is one of the most frequently used types of group work in teaching distributive subjects. In fact, it may be considered basic to other forms of group processes, such as planning, problem-solving, and evaluation.

The purpose of the group or class discussion method is to consider, examine, or investigate the various sides of a question, topic, or problem. It entails extensive student participation and creative thinking. Discussion implies a give-and-take between teacher and students, and among students themselves. It assumes a willingness to share points of view, to hold an open mind, and to weigh evidence. If properly used, the method provides an excellent opportunity for the teacher to check up on student understanding and attitude. Students are required to use two of the most important skills required of distributive workers—listening and speech. The testing of these two communication skills may be reason enough for distributive subjects teachers to use the group discussion method at regular intervals. The method also permits all students to participate and can be adjusted to serve individual student needs. One advantage which should not be minimized is that of changing student attitudes. Students who may have been skeptical about a subject have an opportunity to literally bounce their ideas off of the other class members during the give-and-take of a group discussion. Hopefully, desirable attitudes will prevail over undesirable ones in a majority of the group discussion sessions.

In effective group discussion each student directs his thinking toward the problem, topic, or subject being considered by the group. He feels a basic responsibility to help the group move its thinking forward as much as possible. Care must be taken so that discussions don't move too slowly or get side-tracked. Discussion follows one main line of thought, evolves a pattern of group thinking, and eventuates in clearly-defined ideas, sufficiently well organized that every individual is able to ascertain both the direction of thinking followed and agreements reached.

So far as possible, students should be seated in a face-to-face arrangement. The teacher occupies a most strategic and important position in planning and implementing the group discussion method. He usually initiates the discussion by posing the problem or formulating the topic for consideration. To facilitate discussion, he places the clearly defined topic, issue, or problem on an overhead projector transparency, flip chart, or chalkboard.

Distributive subjects teachers will find an almost unlimited number of topics, issues, or problems for stimulating a good group discussion, such as "How much profit is adequate?" "Do consumers really benefit from advertising?" "Cash vs. credit retail selling," "How to increase sales during the slack season," and "Are small businesses worth saving?"

Techniques such as the following have been used by distributive subjects teachers to guide group discussions:

1. Ask questions at the appropriate times: "What do you mean?" "Could you give an example or illustration?" or "Do you agree?"

2. Keep the discussion on target with comments such as: "Let's come back to the topic," "We seem to be wandering," "Perhaps we need a summary of what has been said up to this point," or "That is a very different matter."

3. See that all points of view are considered by making comments such as: "We seem to have overlooked . . .," or "Maybe we also should think about . . . in our discussion."

4. Guide the group to see more in the discussion than they would see individually with comments such as: "There are at least three other points that might be made," or "What does the author mean when he says . . . ?"

5. Summarize periodically to show the progress that has been made by saying: "Let's re-examine the ideas we have developed so far," or "Where do we stand now on this matter?"

6. Encourage all students to participate by asking non-contributing class members questions such as: "Jim, based on your experience, do you agree?" "Bob, would your employer want this to happen?" or "Jane, what does this point mean to you?"

7. Interpret clearly with the group the individual's contributions with comments such as: "Let's be sure we see what Jim means before we go on," or "If we accept what Julie says, it may change our earlier assumptions."

8. Clear up misconceptions and misinterpretations by asking questions, such as: "Did you all get the same meaning from the statement made by Mr. Roberts?" or "What proof can you offer to substantiate your belief?"

9. Record significant points as they are developed, using appropriate words to clearly express student ideas.

10. Help the group summarize the discussion and draw meaningful conclusions.

The group discussion should also be followed up and evaluated. The discussion may lead to individual, small or large group activities, such as field trips; reports based on library, business, or community investigation; research studies; or even long-term independent study projects.

A number of techniques can be used to evaluate a group discussion. However, answers to the following questions should be secured: "Did the group keep on the subject?" "Did the group accomplish the stated objective?" "Did all students participate?" "Were the class members objective?" "Were the class contributions based on facts and valid evidence?" "Did any students monopolize the discussion?" and "How did the discussion contribute to the growth of the students?"

The group discussion method should be used by distributive subjects teachers when the class is too small to divide into sub-groups; when for various reasons it is more desirable to keep the group as one unit; and when a total group needs to deliberate on ideas following a resource speaker, film, small group discussion, role-playing situation, or symposium. Units of instruction, such as careers in distribution, economics of distribution, human relations, business organization, salesmanship, advertising, and display, have excellent topics, subjects, and problems for launching a group discussion. For example, during a unit on salesmanship, the comments made by class members following the role-playing of a case problem involving a questionable statement made by the salesman led the teacher to believe that the class members would gain from a group discussion of the subject "Is the consumer always right?" While most of the topics selected for group discussion can be determined prior to initiating a unit, it is not always possible to do so while teaching distributive subjects. Frequently topics present themselves for which the students and the teacher have adequate background information and experience to initiate a group discussion. These group discussions should not be delayed unless for some reason the teacher feels additional study and planning is essential. Some of the most constructive group discussion sessions in distributive education classes are those which arise from real-life situations which one or more students are currently facing. Many teacher-coordinators of cooperative programs plan a specifically designated period of time each week for group discussion of student-centered job topics, problems, and subjects. This plan helps to provide an opportunity for the teacher to prepare himself, and the class members, well in advance for the topic to be discussed. If not properly planned for and implemented, the group discussion could become a "pooling of ignorance."

Panel or Round-Table Discussion. A panel or round-table discussion method can best be described as a speaker-audience technique in which approximately four to eight students carry on a discussion of a topic among themselves and the audience listens in on the discussion. It provides an element of suspense as to what will happen next. It creates interest and fosters participant involvement through fast moving questions and answers. There is a free exchange of ideas among the panel members. Several sides of an issue can be presented by either experts or student members. The presentations are presented in a much more informal method than those in a symposium or debate. However, the presentation of the topic is not a systematic one and many questions are left unanswered. Frequently, the discussion is based on opinion and not fact.

To be meaningful, the panel or round-table discussion must be carefully planned, although it is often difficult to get panel members together to discuss the proposed plan of action and clarify the topic in advance.

The chairman or leader is the key to an effective panel or round-table discussion. He may be selected by the class, the panel or round-table members, or the teacher. The selected leader starts the discussion by clearly stating the problem to be discussed. He then comments briefly on the topic for discussion and introduces the panel or round-table members. The chairman is responsible for both stimulating and controlling discussion among panel or round-table members. At a pre-determined time, the chairman either recognizes contributions from the audience or summarizes the panel or round-table discussion, and then asks for questions and discussion from the class. Usually panel or round-table members discuss the topic 20 to 30 minutes and allow for an almost equal amount of time for open discussion.

Distributive subjects teachers most commonly use the panel or round-table discussion method for introducing new materials, for motivating students during the unit, and for culminating a unit of work. Panel and round-table discussions can be effectively used for any of the distributive subject units where individuals may have differing opinions. For example, a discussion of "The need for an increased role of government in distribution," "Competition is wasteful," "Window displays are obsolete," "Advertisers are unethical," or "Salesmen are born, not trained" would all be possible topics for initiating, developing, or culminating a unit of instruction.

Buzz Sessions. Many variations and descriptive titles have emerged from what simply might be called a small group discussion. The short-term group, or "buzz group," usually functions for approximately five to thirty minutes. The "66" discussion session lasts for six minutes with six persons in a group. The progressive buzz session is quite similar to regular buzz sessions, except that at a pre-determined time, the groups rotate both sub-topic questions and contributions. The progressive buzz session allows each group to work on a number of different sub-topics and, at the same time, benefit from the written contributions of other class members. Buzz sessions and other small group discussion techniques can be easily modified to fit any teaching style.

To utilize the most common buzz group technique, the teacher divides the class into small groups, each group discussing a sub-topic and reporting back to the class. One student is selected to act as the leader of the group. Since the groups are smaller, the students feel freer to participate, sharing their ideas with the other members of the group. They learn to work with their peers in a life-like situation.

Some secondary school students are not disciplined enough to work independently. The effectiveness of the group may be lowered by the immature behavior of a few students. Therefore, the teacher who is planning to use buzz sessions should plan with care. Preplanning and a sense of timing are important ingredients for a good buzz session. First, the group must be prepared by the teacher, carefully explaining the purpose of the work they are to do, how they are to accomplish it, and in what period of time. Groups are designated and assigned a sub-topic to be discussed. Directions for group activity are provided, including the appointment of the leader and recorder by the teacher. Once the buzz groups, of 3-5 members, are assembled and begin their discussion, the teacher moves from group to group serving as a consultant. At a predetermined time, oral reports are given by the discussion leader or recorder. Questioning and discussing each of the group reports is common. Frequently group reporters are asked to get together later to summarize their findings and prepare a report on the topic discussed.

Because very little organization is required once the students learn how to "buzz," the technique can be used extensively by teachers. The purpose of the buzz session is exploratory. It sets the groundwork to get discussion started. Because buzz group members are merely expressing their opinions, the method has its widest application when dealing with controversial subjects, such as profit, competition, and ethics.

Brainstorming. Brainstorming is a technique for getting creative ideas through imagination rather than through reasoning. It promotes creative thinking, provides variety, and adds a zestful spirit of enthusiasm to the classroom. It is an excellent change of pace, and a technique which the future distributor should be able to use in business. The technique has been used extensively by business and industry to arrive at new product ideas and to determine names for products. When used properly, it can release individual potentialities in thinking up ideas. Frequently, students also learn to change their attitudes toward the ideas of others.

Initially some effort must be devoted to trying out the technique so that the students become accustomed to it.

It may take time for a class to really start producing new and original ideas. Brainstorming is often successful only with the more able students. If the class is reluctant to express their creative ideas verbally, individual brainstorming sessions can be used by asking students to list on a blank sheet of paper the numbers one to ten. Beside each number, they write each idea as fast as it occurs.

Four basic rules must be followed if the brainstorming session is to be successful: judicial judgment is ruled out, free wheeling is welcomed, quantity is wanted, and combination and improvement are sought. In addition to explaining the above four rules to the students, the teacher should explain that there are many ways ideas can be thought up, such as suggest other uses, adapt, modify, magnify, minify, substitute, re-arrange, reverse, and combine.

The technique is implemented by using the following procedure:

1. The teacher explains the brainstorming technique.
2. The carefully selected problem is stated.
3. Students offer suggestions one at a time.
4. The ideas are numbered and recorded.
5. The teacher or leader stimulates ideas and rings a bell when any student offers a criticism. (Ideally, no more than 10-12 students should be in each brainstorming group.)
6. The brainstorming session is terminated when ideas run out.
7. Ideas are then carefully examined through various techniques to arrive at the best possible solutions to the problem.

Brainstorming sessions have been used by teachers of distributive subjects to arrive at new ideas, approaches, and solutions to a problem. For example, the members of the local DECA (Distributive Education Clubs of America) chapter decide that they need to raise funds to finance their program of work. The members might then be split into two or three brainstorming groups for the purpose of arriving at a long list of possible fund-raising activities. The list of possible fund-raising activities then can be examined carefully by the DECA chapter executive committee or through an open discussion by all chapter members.

Role-Playing. Role-playing may be defined as a method of human interaction that involves realistic behavior in imaginary situations. It is a spontaneous technique, since participants act freely rather than from a script. It is a "make believe" kind of situation, where people act as though what they were doing was real. Role-playing takes advantage of peoples' natural desire to act and involves and interests everyone, even those not actually playing the roles. And, although it is harder to use than other techniques, it is one of the best devices for problem analysis.

Role-playing provides the students with an excellent opportunity to practice and develop skills in dealing with other people and to analyze others' points of view. By having several class members perform the same part, the group can examine and react to the different approaches and situations created by a single basic problem.

Role-playing can be a spontaneous device for putting an idea or discussion into practice. However, it is often used inappropriately. In some cases, a discussion, presentation of facts, or a direct question or problem may be more effective and take less time.

Role-playing has three major purposes in teaching distributive subjects: training, informing, and diagnosing or testing. All procedures with the objective of improving skills may be called *training*. For example, if a student role-plays a selling situation with the purpose of enabling him to actually sell in real life, this is training, he is "learning by doing." When students are observing and listening, and not role-playing themselves, role-playing is then used for *informing*, and role-players become living audio-visual devices. When the purpose of role-playing is to analyze and evaluate the role-player, then the procedure is done for *testing* or *diagnostic* purposes.

There are numerous techniques that can be tried in using the role-playing method. However, the following basic procedure is most commonly used:

1. Planning

   a. Determine desired outcomes of role-playing situation.
   b. Carefully structure the role-playing situation to achieve desired outcomes. Unless this is done, the group may become so involved in the technique that they forget the subject matter and content and place more emphasis on the acting than the problem involved.
   c. Describe the role-playing situation carefully so that players can be directed into the desired course of action. Unless role-players are carefully briefed, they may become embarrassed and the situation may backfire. However, be cautious of describing players so completely that actors can't do some of their own character construction.
   d. Make the role-playing situation typical of conditions and problems the students will face.

2. Implementation

   a. Describe the specific problem situation and the characters who are to be involved.
   b. If parts aren't well cast, people who really don't want to take part may be embarrassed. Therefore, select students by the volunteer method when practical.
   c. Prepare observers and participants for the role-playing situation. Each group may need some special instructions.
   d. When appropriate, provide the characters with large name cards and give them a little time for preparation.
   e. Describe the setting and let the role-players begin.
   f. Continue role-playing until the key characters have had a chance to respond two or three times or had an opportunity to make their positions clear.
   g. Stop the role-playing while interest and participation are still high.

3. Analyze and Evaluate

   a. Ask questions of the role-players or class members, such as "What happened?" "Why did it happen this way?" "What were the motives and feelings involved?" and "What variations would have produced other results?"

    b. In the discussion that follows, the group should propose various solutions to the problem and decide upon the best one.

Role-playing dramatizes a situation. If properly used, it should stimulate a considerable amount of discussion; however, care must be taken so that the discussion helps to achieve the desired outcome.

Unless effectively introduced, the students may resent the technique as a childish kindergarten approach to a serious problem. But role-playing is an excellent method for developing insight into human relations problems that might otherwise be heavily charged with emotions, or that the class members might feel guilty or embarrassed to discuss. It often will bring out feelings and attitudes which might not come out in regular discussion. It is also an excellent technique for helping students to look objectively at their own behavior, and test alternate methods of handling a situation. Distributive subjects teachers use the role-playing method extensively in teaching job interviews, sales, employee-employer relations, and similar people-centered competencies.

To increase participation during the role-playing, many distributive subjects teachers use what is referred to as team role-playing. In team role-playing, various class members are assigned as consultants or team members to each of the role-playing characters, and another group of class members is designated to serve as observers and evaluators. This technique is most useful when a role-playing situation may continue for an extended period of time. The consultants or team members, in addition to giving advice, may actually participate as role-players. Every member of the class has an important assigned function and, therefore, is actively involved.

Case or Incident Problem. The case problem method is increasingly being used by teachers of distributive subjects to add realism to their instruction. Teachers have found that the incidents which students describe or the cases which students themselves prepare are most effective in generating learning. Cases or incidents which the students contribute from their own employment experiences create much excitement and concern on the part of all the class members. Being able to solve real-life problems gives students a special sense of accomplishment. If properly used, the students have an opportunity to develop the ability to think clearly, enhance their own practical judgment, gain an appreciation of how facts can be used to make decisions, and are encouraged to do further study.

Care must be taken so that the cases or incidents presented are within the experience range of the group. Students may be so intrigued with the case method that too much time is consumed by problems irrelevant for the majority of the class. Careful pre-planning is essential for other than simple incidents and cases because, if the cases aren't presented in an organized form, students may waste time and "read" in conditions. A good case or incident should be genuinely interesting; should contain issues on which opinions may vary; should present events, objective facts, and opinions from the point of view of one or more people involved in the situation; provide no more information than persons in the actual situation possessed; and the proposed solution should contribute to the growth of the students.

Cases or incidents may be presented orally, in writing, or through role-playing. The teacher functions as a discussion leader, resource person, and judge of student performance once the case has been presented. The following steps are commonly used by teachers when a case is presented through role-playing:

1. Presents the case or incident, assigns roles, and has the case or incident role-played.
2. Directs student discussion so that the true problem is identified and then writes the problem on the chalkboard.
3. Divides the class into small groups with a chairman and recorder for each group or works with class as a whole for the purpose of arriving at the one best solution for the problem. If the class is divided into small groups, the chairman or recorder reports for each of the groups and then the class as a whole makes a decision on the best possible solution.
4. Summarizes the case or incident problem for use in future action.

The following five-step procedure is commonly used in arriving at both oral and written solutions to case or incident problems:

1. Identify the true problem.
2. Identify the important facts to be considered with this problem.
3. List several possible solutions.
4. Evaluate possible results if each solution is followed.
5. Determine what one solution is recommended, and why?

The case or incident method is most commonly used during the following units of study: human relations, job interview, advanced salesmanship, supervisory training, business organization, and economics of distribution. The method is ideally suited to explaining a wide variety of problems and actual situations rather than abstract principles. It can be used during any unit of study in which issues are discussed or in which opinions or practices may vary.

Conference Method. The conference method involves a group of people pooling ideas in order to solve their collective and individual problems. It is a valuable instructional activity because it promotes constructive and individual thinking and affords the student an opportunity to develop his self-confidence and judgmental skills which are considered a key to success in the distributive occupations. This teaching method is also valuable because students' attitudes or habits may be changed or modified as a result of their active participation in this instructional activity.

There is no standard procedure for handling a conference, but the following points must be considered before this method is selected:

1. The students should have a high apperceptive base.
2. The broad topic describing a specific situation should have one or more pertinent problems.
3. The students should be interested in solving the problems.
4. Judgment is needed in the solution of the problem.

All problems cannot be solved by use of the conference method. Caution should be used by the teacher who will act as the conference leader in the selection of appropriate topics for discussion. The success of the conference method in the classroom depends largely upon the teacher, how well he has mastered the skills of conference teaching, and how well he has prepared the class for this type of instructional activity. If the conference leader is weak, the ultimate objective may not be reached. Discussion may turn to argument and personal, private conversation may develop, or one group or individual may try to "show up" some student inside or outside the group. If this occurs, all possible solutions to the question may not be explored.

What are the responsibilities for the teacher as the conference leader? Much depends upon the ability of the conference leader. After the topic has been selected, it is his duty to properly introduce it and to motivate the group enough to start discussion. After the discussion is under way, the conference leader should:

1. Secure an even distribution of discussion.
2. Keep arguments from becoming personal or too "hot."
3. Refrain from pushing his own ideas and overlooking the contributions of the group.
4. Discourage private conversations and discussions.
5. Assist members in expressing their ideas.
6. Know and select proper conference devices.

    a. Use the overhead question.
    b. Restate a comment.
    c. Direct question to someone in the group.
    d. Use blackboard for emphasizing relevant points.
    e. Redirect discussion to another point.
    f. Make contributions.
    g. Summarize the discussion.
    h. Draw out conclusion of the majority of the group.

7. Direct attention to all angles of the problem.
8. Keep the ultimate objectives of the group in mind and direct the discussion in such a manner that they will be realized.

The conference method works best when students have background knowledge on the topic to be discussed. Most problems can be approached from the HOW, WHEN, and

WHY point of view. Such a pattern creates interest, discussion, and direction and makes it easier to get active student participation. Cooperation among students and an appreciation of other individuals' viewpoints are developed. The method is ideally suited for enabling students to work problems relating to youth organization activities, such as fund-raising, creative marketing research projects, other group competitive events, and the employee-employer banquet. Areas of classroom study, such as advertising, economics of distribution, and salesmanship, contain problems which are ideally suited to the use of the conference method, and the method provides an excellent means of student evaluation.

RESEARCH AND OPINIONS OF EXPERTS

What to Teach

E. Edward Harris, Chairman of the Research Coordinating Committee of the U.S. Office of Education, Region V, Distributive Education Program Planning Committee, conducted a study to determine the preferences and practices of employers and teacher-coordinators in working with cooperative distributive education.[6] A random sample of 1,086 employers was drawn from approximately 10,000 cooperating businesses in the states of Illinois, Indiana, Michigan, Ohio, and Wisconsin, together with 687 teacher-coordinators in the U.S. Office of Education, Region V.

Employers were asked to indicate the level of competency development and those personal characteristics that high school students need for employment as student/trainees in the distributive education program and as graduates of the program seeking employment. The employers indicated the preferred level of student development in the selected competency and personal characteristics areas using the following scale: 1 = extensive, 2 = acquaintanceship, and 3 = none. Teacher-coordinators used

---

[6] E. Edward Harris, *Employer Preferences and Teacher-Coordination Practices in Distributive Education* (New York: Gregg Division, McGraw-Hill Book Co., Inc., 1971), pp. 11-16, 31-34.

the same scale to indicate the competencies actually possessed by students who entered employment initially as distributive education students. It is important to note that in many distributive education programs, students have not had any formal school instruction in distribution and marketing before entering employment.

EMPLOYERS ASKED: What competencies should students possess upon entering employment as distributive education student/trainees?

COORDINATORS ASKED: What competencies do students possess upon entering employment as distributive education student/trainees?

N = 440 EMPLOYERS		COMPETENCY	N = 490 COORDINATORS	
Mean *	Rank Order +		Rank Order +	Mean *
1.224	1.5	Following directions	1	1.865
1.242	1.5	Acceptance and adherence to company policies	9	2.302
1.429	3	Working with people	2.5	2.023
1.489	4	Oral communications	2.5	1.961
1.687	5	Knowledge of products or services	9	2.315
1.801	6	Salesmanship	9	2.215
1.908	7.5	Public relations	14.5	2.448
1.924	7.5	Mathematics of business	5	2.137
2.025	9	Nonselling duties	9	2.372
2.139	10	Understanding of how goods and services get from producer to consumer	5	2.103
2.200	13	Decision making	14.5	2.500
2.218	13	Display	14.5	2.519
2.238	13	Written communications	5	2.135
2.260	13	Job opportunities in marketing and distribution	9	2.236
2.388	13	Distribution in the free enterprise system	9	2.247
2.564	16	Advertising	14.5	2.476
2.670	17	Buying	17	2.590

* Code for Mean Values: 1 = Extensive; 2 = Acquaintanceship; 3 = None
+ Two-Tailed T Tests Used to Determine Rank Order

FIGURE 8-13

Figure 8-13 shows the relationship between the competencies employers feel distributive education students should possess and those teacher-coordinators indicated their students did, in fact, possess. Data in the mean value columns show that employers desired students to have a higher level of proficiency in all competency areas except understanding of how goods and services get from producer to consumer, written communications, job opportunities in marketing and distribution, distribution in the free enterprise system, advertising, and buying.

The rank order data columns show that differences exist between the competencies students possess upon entering employment as distributive education students and those competencies desired by employers. The following competencies were ranked higher by employers: acceptance and adherence to company policies, knowledge of products or services, salesmanship, and public relations.

EMPLOYERS ASKED: What competencies should distributive education graduates possess for employment?				
COORDINATORS ASKED: What competencies are possessed by distributive education graduates?				
EMPLOYERS		COMPETENCY	COORDINATORS	
Mean *	Rank Order +		Rank Order +	Mean *
AVERAGE N = 375			AVERAGE N = 490	
1.125	1	Following directions	6	1.290
1.138	2	Acceptance and adherence to company policies and procedures	4	1.254
1.256	3	Working with people	1	1.129
1.332	4	Oral communications	8	1.326
1.375	5	Knowledge of products or services	6	1.290
1.479	6	Salesmanship	2	1.188
1.658	7	Public relations	11	1.500
1.688	8	Mathematics of business	12.5	1.541
1.798	9	Decision making	15	1.744
1.825	10	Nonselling duties	10	1.436
1.915	11.5	Understanding of how goods and services get from producer to consumer	3	1.232
1.947	11.5	Written communications	17	1.793
1.955	13	Display	14	1.563
2.163	14	Job opportunities in marketing and distribution	6	1.301
2.193	15	Distribution in the free enterprise system	9	1.389
2.254	16	Buying	16	1.765
2.315	17	Advertising	12.5	1.541

* Code for Mean Values: 1 = Extensive; 2 = Acquaintanceship; 3 = None
+ Two-Tailed T Tests Used to Determine Rank Order

FIGURE 8-14

Figure 8-14 displays the competencies that students should possess upon graduation from distributive education programs in the opinion of both employers and coordinators. The data shows that with the exception of following directions, acceptance and adherence to company policies and procedures, and working with people, the teacher-coordinators indicated their students possessed the 17 competencies at a higher level of proficiency than employers indicated students should possess them. Rank order data show that employers place higher priorities on the following competencies: following directions, acceptance and adherence to company policies and procedures, oral communications, public relations, mathematics of business, decision making, and written communications.

EMPLOYERS ASKED: What personal characteristics are desirable in distributive education students?

COORDINATORS ASKED: What personal characteristics are possessed by distributive education students?

EMPLOYERS		TYPE OF CHARACTERISTIC	COORDINATORS	
Mean *	Rank Order +		Rank Order +	Mean *
AVERAGE N = 215			AVERAGE N = 248	
1.046	1	Honesty	1	1.758
1.069	2	Dependability	6	2.169
1.152	3.5	Punctuality	6	2.169
1.159	3.5	Cooperation	2.5	1.931
1.221	6	Desire to learn	11	2.371
1.245	6	Neat appearance	2.5	1.940
1.275	6	Pleasant personality	4	2.077
1.400	9.5	Positive attitude	11	2.363
1.408	9.5	Initiative	11	2.456
1.410	9.5	Industriousness	11	2.403
1.455	9.5	Mental maturity	11	2.391
1.524	12	Tact	14	2.589
1.653	13	Self-confidence	11	2.423
1.774	14	Physical maturity	6	2.145

* Code for Mean Values: 1 = Extensive; 2 = Acquaintanceship; 3 = None
+ Two-Tailed T Tests Used to Determine Rank Order

FIGURE 8-15

Data in Figure 8-15 shows the relationship between the personal characteristics employers desire students to demonstrate and the personal characteristics teacher-coordinators believe that their students actually show. Data in the mean value columns show that employers desire all 14 personal characteristics at a higher level than distributive education students possess them. The rank order data columns show that differences exist between the personal characteristics distributive education students possess upon entering employment and those desired by employers. The following personal characteristics were ranked higher by employers than by coordinators: dependability, punctuality, desire to learn, and tact.

EMPLOYERS ASKED: What personal characteristics are desirable in full-time employees?

COORDINATORS ASKED: What personal characteristics are possessed by distributive education graduates?

EMPLOYERS		TYPE OF CHARACTERISTIC	COORDINATORS	
Mean *	Rank Order +		Mean *	Rank Order +
AVERAGE N = 182			AVERAGE N = 248	
1.022	1.5	Honesty	1	1.552
1.027	1.5	Dependability	4	1.746
1.086	3	Punctuality	4	1.742
1.125	7	Cooperation	4	1.706
1.153	7	Neat appearance	4	1.645
1.191	7	Desire to learn	14	2.040
1.196	7	Initiative	11.5	1.992
1.213	7	Pleasant personality	8	1.879
1.225	7	Industriousness	11.5	1.964
1.263	7	Mental maturity	11.5	2.000
1.279	7	Positive attitude	9	1.899
1.264	12.5	Tact	11.5	2.004
1.276	12.5	Self-confidence	4	1.723
1.588	14	Physical maturity	7	1.835

* Code for Mean Values: 1 = Extensive; 2 = Acquaintanceship; 3 = None
+ Two-Tailed T Tests Used to Determine Rank Order

FIGURE 8-16

Data in Figure 8-16 show that employers desire full-time employees to have all 14 of the personal characteristics at a higher level than that demonstrated by distributive education graduates. Rank order data show that employers place higher priorities on the following personal characteristics: dependability, punctuality, desire to learn, initiative, industriousness, mental maturity, and positive attitude.

Crawford identified the following 59 critical tasks for teaching distributive education:[7]

1. Relates classroom instruction to on-the-job situations or experiences.

2. Makes periodic coordination visits to businesses employing students enrolled for the purpose of gathering illustrative material.

3. Uses a variety of teaching techniques in classroom instruction for interest and effectiveness.

4. Recognizes individual differences of students.

5. Plans and develops teaching plans—with assignments, tests, and examinations tailored to individual and group needs—for D.E. classes sufficiently in advance to maximize teaching effectiveness.

6. Makes clear, definite, purposeful assignments to D.E. students.

7. Strives to help each student understand the content of lessons taught.

8. Provides students a number of participation experiences to develop the competencies needed to enter and advance in their chosen distributive occupations.

9. Has students give sales talks and demonstrations in class and has students suggest methods of improvement.

10. Provides instruction and experience that will measure the students' attitudes, initiative, ability, and insight.

11. Selects and procures reference texts and other instructional material for preparing lesson plans and for students' use.

12. Provides instruction to develop competency in one or more of the marketing functions to persons enrolled in distributive education classes.

13. Participates in the preparation, development, evaluation and revision of course outlines and subject materials for the high school D.E. classes.

14. Sets up, develops and maintains effective resource files.

15. Conscientiously evaluates work done by students.

---

[7] Crawford, *op. cit.*, pp. 39-44, 57.

16. Prepares each student for initial employment and/or advancement as quickly as student's development allows.

17. Up-dates teaching material and information through reading of current trade journals and other periodicals.

18. Brings qualified managers, supervisors, and other outside speakers into the classroom for demonstrations, observations, and talks on special class topics.

19. Develops in each student safe work habits, pride in his job, pride in himself, and a desire for advancement through additional skills and knowledge.

20. Prepares daily lesson plans including objectives, content, methods, and assignment.

21. Stimulates creative thinking through group and individual planning of projects and other activities.

22. Decides upon and arranges for interesting and instructive field trips when this experience will best achieve a particular objective.

23. Keeps adequate records for each individual student as evidence of competencies achieved either through projects completed or through occupational experiences.

24. Guides students in selection of appropriate individual projects related to the fields of marketing, merchandising, and management.

25. Maintains a library of periodicals in the field of distribution for pupil use.

26. Encourages students to contribute materials, information and teaching aids from their contact with these items in their training stations.

27. Uses DECA contests and activities as a teaching tool in developing competencies and in stimulating interest and developing a competitive attitude.

28. Establishes and maintains in the classroom an atmosphere wherein cooperative planning and working may take place.

29. When necessary, provides individual instruction for students.

30. Follows established school grading and record-keeping systems.

31. Cooperates with other vocational teachers, instructing in programs where both D.E. and other vocational services are involved.

32. Develops the problem-solving skill through the use of applicable cases.

33. Personally instructs adult classes when qualified to do so or secures and supervises adult instructors for the program.

34. Prepares an individual training plan for each student.

35. Evaluates the effectiveness of students' training and prepares periodic progress reports to be sent to parents of trainees.

36. Adjusts, when possible, outside assignments to the advantage of the student with regard to his schedule and proper use of library and other school services.

37. Helps student locate materials, literature, and information needed to successfully complete a project.

38. Encourages role-playing in the classroom for practice in applying information learned.

39. Prepares or secures audio and visual materials and devices needed for effective instruction.

40. Provides an opportunity for students to conduct research on market functions and/or products.

41. Encourages students to arrange with local merchants to borrow merchandise for use in display and selling demonstrations.

42. Enlists the aid of special teachers to help students with individual problems (remedial reading, English, school social worker).

43. Provides students with suggested list of possible projects related to various career goals in distribution.

44. Organizes and teaches short-term training courses for employment during the Christmas season, spring, and summer.

45. Assumes responsibility for securing training materials for adult classes.

46. Organizes and conducts pre-employment classes for graduating students.

47. Provides information concerning training films, books, trade journal articles of a specific nature, and other training aids to interested employers.

48. Uses the D.E. Student-of-the-Year contest as a "Standard of Excellence" by which each student's leadership development can be measured.

49. Consults with specialists to obtain background and technical information and know-how for teaching special units.

50. Maintains firm discipline and control in the classroom.

51. Applies basic learning principles and psychology in teaching.

52. Relates course content and learning activities to objectives.

53. Develops and relates DECA activities to course objectives.

54. Develops team teaching utilizing specialists in specific areas of distribution.

55. Utilizes such school activities as store, athletic events, and school lunch to supplement project method.

56. Holds orientation or reviews classes prior to school opening for all cooperative students.

57. Strives to maintain the amount of class time spent on DECA activities at an effective balance.

58. Evaluates individualized instruction materials in terms of specific jobs.

59. Designs learning activities involving students in mastering their own time.

Samson identified 127 critical requirements for secondary school distributive education teacher-coordinators.[8] Listed below are the 25 effective and ineffective critical requirements that were classified in the area of student discipline and control and the 39 coordinator requirements in the area of instructional activities:

STUDENT DISCIPLINE AND CONTROL

The *effective* distributive education coordinator:

1. Reminds students of regulations and of expected behavior in classroom.

2. Threatens lowering of grades or course failure to enforce desired behavior or compliance with program regulations.

---

[8] Harland E. Samson, "The Critical Requirements for Distributive Education Teacher-Coordinators" (Doctoral dissertation, University of Minnesota, 1964).

3. Warns students who violate program policy or who misbehave that they would be dropped from program.

4. Uses ego deflating techniques to maintain student control.

5. Enforces policy of not working at training station in afternoon if student-learner has not been in school that morning.

6. Refers students to school office for classroom misbehavior.

7. Uses detention or a demerit system to enforce assignments and behavior.

8. Temporarily removes students from training station to improve school work or enforce regulation.

9. Maintains school policy by enforcing tardy regulations, study hall passes, and other school regulations.

10. Drops students from distributive education program for violation of regulations or failure to do passing work.

11. Uses a firm personal appeal to keep class orderly.

12. Conducts private conferences with students who have conduct violations.

13. Conducts conferences with training sponsors, parents, and others on student-learner behavior.

14. Assigns extra homework or other activity for breach of conduct.

The *ineffective* distributive education coordinator:

1. Warns and threatens students, but does not follow through with action of any kind.

2. Gives extra work or written assignments to students who do not participate in class functions or who have poor classroom behavior.

3. Berates class or individual students in class for breaches of desired conduct.

4. Follows an illogical and inconsistent pattern of discipline or control.

5. Reduces student's grade for violation of program policy or personal misbehavior.

6. Makes no effort, ignores, or takes no positive action to maintain discipline in class.

7. Is unable to control emotions and may use profanity to attempt control of students.

8. Threatens suspension or expulsion from program for a variety of disciplinary causes.
9. Exhibits certain mannerisms or actions when class gets out of control.
10. Sends students out of class to school office for classroom misbehavior.
11. Allows students to get too far out of hand and then is unable to effectively regain control.

INSTRUCTIONAL ACTIVITIES

The *effective* distributive education coordinator:

1. Counsels with students and provides individual help on problems connected with jobs, training sponsors, or other related actions.
2. Gives special training to individual students, building up skills in necessary areas and providing suggestions on how to improve classwork.
3. Conducts individual conferences with students on their personal problems or behaviors (grooming, personality, attitude, etc.).
4. Counsels with students on educational plans, encourages them to continue their education and not to drop out. Assists in developing appropriate class schedule.
5. Uses a variety of teaching devices and techniques such as projects, case problems, tele-trainer, movies, and reports.
6. Works with entire class on job orientation, job problems, and technical content, uses suggestions from training stations and demonstrates techniques to class.
7. Allows students to assist in the planning and carrying out of in-classroom study and has students help each other on projects and problems. Uses students' experience as a basis for class study.
8. Explains to students employers' rating sheets and the grading system; then counsels with students when employers' ratings have been made.
9. Counsels with students who are inattentive or not doing well in D.E. and other classes and tries to help them improve.
10. Provides interesting lectures and gives clear and understandable explanations.

11. Arranges field trips to business firms and other establishments which can provide information appropriate to subject being studied.

12. Obtains and uses individual study manuals, work sheets, and merchandise manuals for job study and research.

13. Gives hard but appropriate assignments and expects them to be completed promptly and properly.

14. Impresses students with importance of work, especially in D.E. and keeps them busy in class on worthwhile assignments.

15. Uses resource people from community and from school for special units of study such as advertising, credit, store layout and parliamentary procedure.

16. Has students prepare displays at school, giving suggestions and help in planning and building the display.

17. Gives different types of tests, reviews before testing, and goes over completed tests with students.

18. Selects a variety of topics and units for class study and discussion.

19. Has students give sales talks and demonstrations in class and provides suggestions for improvement.

20. Uses illustrations and examples, and relates personal experience to get points across to class.

21. Varies and revises grading procedure, explains it to students and discusses grades with students.

22. Has students use a variety of reference sources for help on course work and projects.

23. Invites students to talk over problems and is willing to do so at any time.

24. Reviews and discusses personal grooming and social skills.

25. Adjusts assignments and examinations to fit students' schedules.

The *ineffective* distributive education teacher:

1. Gives heavy, short-notice assignments with little or no warning when projects will be called for, favors certain students, needlessly interrupts students who are working, overlooks needs of students and is inconsistent in classroom procedure generally.

2. Makes assignments, announces tests, or schedules activities, but doesn't follow through with plans, fails to check work, keeps putting things off, or forgets entirely about what was assigned or planned.

3. Uses poorly conceived tests, administers the tests in such a way that students easily cheat, and gives them at times when students are not apt to do well on them.

4. Covers material in class not related to D.E. and which has no connection with subject of the course.

5. Conducts little or no class discussion, and what is done is shallow and poorly handled.

6. Makes errors and is not entirely honest in grading or in relations with students.

7. Comes to class unprepared, unorganized, and does not seem to get much accomplished in class.

8. Talks or lectures all class period and has no discussion or question time.

9. Argues with students, criticizes their ideas, embarrasses them, and shows anger when students question assignments.

10. Gives assignments which are vague and instructions on how to do things are not clear or understandable and will not repeat or clarify.

11. Is unable to counsel effectively and students must take initiative when counseling is needed.

12. Attempts to cover too much material or gives so much work that students are often confused.

13. Provides content and instruction in class that doesn't help student on the job.

14. Uses same techniques day after day and makes no effort to get class working together as a group.

Harris identified 61 critical requirements for distributive education teacher-coordinators.[9] Listed below are the six effective and ineffective critical requirements that were classified in the area of discipline and control of students and the three coordinator requirements in the area of in-school learning activities.

---

[9] E. Edward Harris, *Requirements for Office and Distributive Education Teacher-Coordinators*, Monograph 115 (Cincinnati: South-Western Publishing Co., 1967), pp. 62, 66.

DISCIPLINE AND CONTROL OF STUDENTS

The *effective* distributive education coordinator:

1. Recommends to the administration that students who violate or continue to violate cooperative program rules and regulations be dropped from the course.
2. Secures the cooperation of training station personnel in helping students to improve their attitude, attendance, and performance in school.
3. Counsels with students or secures cooperation of other class members to help make them aware of their problems and how they can solve them.
4. Secures cooperation of guidance department or administrative staff members in dealing with student behavior problems.
5. Assesses a heavy grading penalty or detention for assignments that are late, improperly prepared, or not completed.

The *ineffective* distributive education coordinator:

1. Warns, threatens, or pleads with students in an attempt to gain a change of behavior.

DIRECTION OF IN-SCHOOL LEARNING ACTIVITIES

The *effective* distributive education coordinator:

1. Effectively utilizes the resources of local business establishments to supplement the instruction facilities of the school.
2. Secures guest speakers for his classes who are considered competent in the area being studied.
3. Provides students with guidance and direction in a variety of co-curricular activities.

Careful examination of the three studies pertaining to critical teaching tasks and requirements for distributive education teacher-coordinators shows that research has provided some significant guidelines for aspiring teachers. Hopefully, the identified teaching tasks and requirements will be carefully studied. Distributive education teacher-coordinators can use the critical tasks and requirements as a check list to evaluate their performance.

Teaching Beliefs

Crawford, in her monumental U.S. Office of Education funded study, listed the following belief statements concerning aims and objectives of the distributive education program: [10]

1. That preparation for gainful employment and for advancement in distributive occupation is the primary goal of the distributive education program.

2. That the distributive education program should engender an understanding and appreciation of the American private enterprise system as a cornerstone of the American democracy.

3. That the distributive education program should foster an awareness of the civic, social, and moral responsibilities of business to society.

4. That the distributive education program should encourage and promote the use of ethical standards in business and industry.

5. That the distributive education program should stimulate the student's interest in his chosen distributive occupational field by providing an understanding of the opportunities if offers him to be a contributing member of society.

6. That the distributive education program should prepare distributive personnel to analyze consumer demand and to satisfy the needs and wants of consumers intelligently, efficiently and pleasantly.

7. That the distributive education program should provide training that results in increased efficiency in distribution and marketing.

8. That the distributive education program should contribute to the improvement of the techniques in distribution and marketing.

9. That the distributive education program should be sensitive to changes in distributive and marketing practices and procedures as they are affected by societal, economic, technical, and educational developments, and adapt to such changes.

[10] Crawford, *op. cit.*, p. 20.

10. That the distributive education program should advance the objectives of the total education program.

11. That the distributive education program should strive to develop among employers, employees, and consumers a wider appreciation of the value of specifically trained personnel in distribution.

Crawford also determined the following to be beliefs that people in the field of distributive education could agree upon concerning curriculum: [11]

1. That the major portion of distributive education curriculum content is derived from functions of marketing.

2. That distributive education curricula should include, in addition to functions of marketing, the area of personal development, including human relations and occupational adjustment; the application of skills in mathematics and communications to distribution; appropriate product or service technology; and basic economic understandings.

3. That DECA, the youth organization for high school and post-secondary school students, should be co-curricular in that it should provide opportunities to further develop competencies normally learned in the classroom and on the job. It also provides opportunities to acquire additional competencies, such as leadership and social skills.

4. That vocational instruction in distribution and marketing should be based primarily on the local needs and trends in marketing, merchandising and related management. However, it should also take into account state, national, and world trade as well as such things as family mobility and occupational relocation.

5. That the development of competencies in distributive occupations involves both individual and group instruction.

6. That in most distributive occupations, judgment, human relations, and communication skills are predominant while manual skills are frequently less important.

7. That distributive education should provide for correlation with other subject areas such as English, social studies, economics, mathematics, and art, as well as with subjects in other vocational fields.

[11] *Ibid.*

8. That the *areas of study* concept of distributive education curricula provides for a flexibility in curriculum organization that makes the depth of instruction depend on occupational objectives and competencies needed by individual students and on their abilities.

Doneth determined the teaching beliefs and classroom methodology of selected project and cooperative plan distributive education teacher-coordinators.[12] Among the teaching beliefs "agreed" upon by the selected teacher-coordinators surveyed were these:

1. Each student enrolled in the distributive education program should be able to accomplish the general classroom goals.
2. Each D.E. student should receive instruction at his particular level of understanding.
3. An informal atmosphere in the D.E. classroom is essential for effective learning.
4. Occupational goals set by D.E. students themselves are desirable; however, students need assistance from the teacher-coordinator and counselor clarifying these goals.
5. The D.E. teacher should aid each student to make adjustments in individual learning problems and avoid assigning projects and tasks which are beyond the students' ability.
6. One role of the D.E. instructor is to assist the students in developing self-reliance so that they will be able to work independently.
7. Punctuality must be upheld as a responsibility by students and the teacher.
8. Grooming standards in a D.E. classroom must be exemplified by the businesslike appearance of the teacher.
9. Homework assignments in D.E. should be given three, four, or five days in advance because of the varied responsibilities of students.
10. Some degree of tension and frustration can be beneficial to learning.

---

[12] John R. Doneth, "Teaching Beliefs and Classroom Methodology of Selected Project and Cooperative Plan Distributive Education Teacher-Coordinators" (Doctoral dissertation, Northern Illinois University, 1969), p. 139.

11. Peer group pressure is more effective as a disciplinary action than teacher-imposed pressure.

12. D.E. teachers cannot relate classroom theory to business practices unless they have first-hand business experience.

13. Case studies based on hypothetical situations are not as meaningful as case studies based on real situations.

14. During teacher-student planned activities (e.g., DECA activities), the teacher is a member of the group, and his responsibility is as a resource person, sharing ideas and supplying materials when needed.

15. D.E. teachers need approximately 30 minutes per student, per week, of released time as part of the regular school day to develop, coordinate, and utilize community and school resources for occupationally-directed learning experiences.

16. Adequate individual records (*Project*—training record; *Cooperative*—training plan) must be maintained to illustrate students' accomplishments and evaluate student strengths and weaknesses.

17. D.E. students' written business reports, exams, and assignments should be graded on content, completeness, grammar, neatness, accuracy, and coherence.

18. In the classroom, discretion should be exercised in using specific store names when discussing strengths and weaknesses of distributive practices in the general locale.

19. D.E. laboratory equipment should, as closely as possible, duplicate the store equipment of the "downtown merchant."

20. Cooperative effort should be made to detect and modify conditions that interfere with the distributive education student's advantageous use of his educational and occupational opportunities.

21. Each student enrolled in distributive education should be made fully aware of the opportunities and careers in distribution and marketing that are available to him.

22. The distributive education program should reflect training needs and employment opportunities as evidenced by resources such as community surveys, business census and labor force reports, and advisory services.

23. Because of individualized instruction and the nature of the behavioral outcomes desired, the size of the distributive education class is an important factor.

Teaching Methods

Donaldson conducted an evaluative study of cooperative distributive education programs in the public secondary schools.[13] Several hundred students in Illinois rated a selected list of classroom activities. Donaldson used 5 as the highest rating and 1 as the lowest:

Value of Classroom Activities in Helping Students Learn	Average Score
1. Listening to talks by businessmen	4.7
2. Giving sales demonstrations before class	4.4
3. Viewing films related to the selling field	4.2
4. Directed class discussion of problems met on the job	4.1
5. Directed class discussion of text material	4.0
6. Field trips to other communities during class time	3.8
7. Field trips to businesses in local community during class time	3.8
8. Individual conferences with the teachers about job or other problems	3.6
9. Taking objective examinations	3.6
10. Observing sales demonstrations in class and giving constructive criticism	3.6
11. Putting window displays in classroom show window	3.6
12. Viewing sound-slide films	3.5
13. Putting interior displays in classroom display units	3.4
14. Studying individually during class period	3.4
15. Getting individual help from teacher on classroom assignments	3.4
16. Studying in small groups during class period	3.3
17. Preparing projects such as job manuals and merchandise manuals	3.3
18. Making analysis of store job	3.0

[13] LeRoy J. Donaldson, "An Evaluative Study of Federally Reimbursed Part-Time Cooperative Distributive Education Programs in the Public Secondary Schools of Illinois" (Doctoral dissertation, University of Iowa, 1958).

19. Doing research on individual topic and preparing written report on it 3.0

20. Listening to classroom lectures by teacher 2.8

21. Writing essay examinations 2.8

22. Listening to special reports by individual students 2.7

23. Participating in and listening to panel discussions 2.6

24. Preparing skits, plays, or other programs to be presented before school assemblies, over radio or TV, before service clubs or other groups 2.2

25. Participating in skits, plays, or other programs before various school and non-school groups, or over radio or TV 2.2

Weale surveyed New York State distributive education teacher-coordinators to determine the teaching methods they found to be most effective.[14]

Teaching Method or Device	Percent Very Effective or Effective	Percent Somewhat Effective	Percent Not Effective	Percent Do Not Use	Number of Replies
Demonstration	95.00	2.50	2.50	——	39
Discussion	90.00	10.00	——	——	40
Field Trips	80.00	10.00	——	10.00	40
Films	74.35	17.95	——	7.71	39
Oral Reports	64.09	30.76	5.15	——	39
Speakers	62.50	25.00	5.00	7.50	40
Project Manual	53.84	20.51	12.82	12.83	39
Case Method	50.00	31.58	5.26	13.16	38
Lecture	30.76	53.86	7.69	7.69	39
Workbooks	20.51	28.21	12.82	38.46	39
Work Diaries	15.79	23.68	21.05	39.48	38

FIGURE 8-17

Teaching techniques were suggested by 71 project and cooperative distributive education teacher-coordinators who participated in the study conducted by Doneth. The techniques were placed in the following categories by the

---

[14] W. Bruce Weale, "A Curriculum Guide for Distributive Education Students in New York State" (Doctoral dissertation, Columbia University, 1950).

researcher: survey, role-playing, school store, youth group activities, close-circuit television, manual, research projects, case problems, display preparation, advertising campaigns, unit reviews, continuing projects, simulated training programs, class discussion, business games, programmed instruction, career investigation and other suggestions.

Among the specific examples of techniques used by distributive education teachers in the Doneth study were these: [15]

Surveys: customer buying habits, impact of window displays, cost of living, food prices, and selling techniques.

Role-playing: salesmanship, job interviews, supervisory training.

School Store: bookkeeping, buying, selling, merchandising, and store personnel selection.

Youth Group Activities: fund-raising projects, direct selling businesses, fashion shows, management of school newspaper, open house displays, promotion of printed programs for school events.

Closed-Circuit Television: job interviews, salesmanship, and advertising.

Manuals: University of Texas distributive education manuals and merchandise manuals.

Research Projects: market potential of community, organization of a business.

Case Problems: published case problem materials, cases created by teacher-coordinators.

Display Preparation: displays in downtown store windows, window judging contest, window displays without actual merchandise.

Advertising Campaigns: planning of entire advertising contests.

Unit Reviews: team competition of various kinds.

Simulated Training Programs: students used to teach other students specific tasks, paper cash registers.

[15] Doneth, *op. cit.*, pp. 166-81.

Class Discussion: business topics, political events affecting consumers, personal business experiences.

Business Games: used for problem-solving, theory reinforcement.

Programmed Instruction: real estate units, markup, markdown, basic mathematics, and human relations units.

Other Suggestions: school attendance by advisory committee, reading and discussion of selected books, simulation of cashless society, personality discussions, investigation of data processing in the field of distribution, reading aloud to develop poise and self-confidence, extensive use of audiovisual equipment, field trips, buzz groups, panel discussions, committee reports, debates and guest speakers.

SUMMARY

Approximately one out of every three people is employed in the field of distribution and marketing. Education for distribution has received increased recognition in recent years because of the importance of distribution to the economic growth of our nation.

A quality program of instruction in distributive education cannot be achieved by merely assigning a few course titles, such as retailing, salesmanship, merchandising, marketing, distributive practices, DE I, or DE II. The curricula must be carefully designed to serve student and community needs. Once the competencies to be taught have been identified and the duration of the program determined, it is a relatively easy task to assign course titles. Hopefully, more and more school personnel will design comprehensive distributive education programs to serve the divergent needs of youth. A comprehensive distributive education program can match the resources of people with the demands for current and projected jobs.

SELECTED BIBLIOGRAPHY

Ashmun, Richard, and Roger Larsen. *Review and Synthesis of Research in Distributive Education.* Columbus, Ohio: The Center for Vocational and Technical Education, Ohio State University, 1970.

Business Education Forum, special Distributive Education issues (April of each year).

Career Information: Marketing and Distribution. Washington: American Vocational Association, 1971.

Changing Methods of Teaching Business Subjects, National Business Education Yearbook. Washington: National Business Education Association, 1972.

Contributions of Research to Business Education, Ninth National Business Education Yearbook. Washington: National Business Education Association, 1971.

Crawford, Lucy C. *A Competency Pattern Approach to Curriculum Construction in Distributive Teacher Education,* OE-6-85-044. Blacksburg: Virginia Polytechnic Institute, 1967.

Distributive Education & You. Washington: American Vocational Association, 1970.

Distributive Education Materials Directory. Washington: National Association of Distributive Education Teachers, 1971.

Donaldson, LeRoy J. "An Evaluative Study of Federally Reimbursed Part-Time Cooperative Distributive Education Programs in the Public Secondary Schools of Illinois." Doctoral dissertation, University of Iowa, 1958.

Doneth, John R. "Teaching Beliefs and Classroom Methodology of Selected Project and Cooperative Plan Distributive Education Teacher-Coordinators." Doctoral dissertation, Northern Illinois University, 1969.

Emerging Content and Structure of Business Education, Eighth National Business Education Yearbook. Washington: National Business Education Association, 1970.

Haines, Peter G. (ed.). *Readings in Distributive Education: The Project Plan of Instruction and Related Teacher Education.* East Lansing, Michigan: Michigan State University, Department of Secondary Education and Curriculum, 1968.

E. Edward Harris. "Distributive Occupations Career Objective." *Business Education for the Seventies.* Springfield, Illinois: Office of the Superintendent of Public Instruction, 1972.

—————. *Employer Preferences and Teacher-Coordination Practices in Distributive Education.* New York: Gregg Division, McGraw-Hill Book Co., Inc., 1971.

_____. *Requirements for Office and Distributive Education Teacher-Coordinators,* Monograph 115. Cincinnati: South-Western Publishing Co., 1967.

How to Teach Business Subjects, Business Education Publication No. 108. Sacramento: California State Department of Education, 1963.

Meyer, Warren G. "Outcomes in Developing Vocational Competence in Distributive Occupation." *New Perspectives in Education for Business,* First National Business Education Yearbook. Washington: National Business Education Association, 1963.

_____, and William B. Logan. *Review and Synthesis of Research in Distributive Education.* Columbus, Ohio: The Center for Vocational and Technical Education, Ohio State University, 1966.

Program Planning Guide for Distributive Education. New York: Gregg Division, McGraw-Hill Book Co., Inc., 1972.

Rose, Homer. *The Instructor and His Job.* Chicago: The American Technical Society, 1961.

Samson, Harland E. "The Critical Requirements for Distributive Education Teacher-Coordinators." Doctoral dissertation, University of Minnesota, 1964.

Sanders, Norris M. *Classroom Questions: What Kinds?* New York: Harper & Row, 1966.

A Selected and Annotated Bibliography Related to Cooperative and Project Methods in Distributive Education. East Lansing, Michigan: Michigan State University, Department of Secondary Education and Curriculum, 1967.

State curriculum guides and bulletins available from Distributive Education Service, Division of Vocational Education, Department of Education, in selected states.

Staton, Thomas F. *How to Instruct Successfully.* New York: McGraw-Hill Book Co., Inc., 1960.

U.S. Department of Health, Education, and Welfare, Office of Education. *Distributive Education in the High School,* OE 82019. Washington: U.S. Government Printing Office, 1969.

_____. *Post Secondary Distributive Education,* OE 82017. Washington: U.S. Government Printing Office, 1969.

——————. *Vocational Instructional Materials for Distributive Education Available from Federal Agencies.* Washington: U.S. Government Printing Office, 1971.

——————, and the U.S. Department of Labor, Manpower Administration. *Vocational Education and Occupations,* OE 80061. Washington: U.S. Government Printing Office, 1969.

Weale, W. Bruce. "A Curriculum Guide for Distributive Education Students in New York State." Doctoral dissertation, Columbia University, 1950.

Chapter 9

THE COOPERATIVE PLAN

BASIC PRINCIPLES AND CONCEPTS

Programs developed through the cooperation of business and education are not new. The apprenticeship system, which in many aspects is similar to present-day cooperative vocational education, was utilized by the ancient Hebrews. Jewish boys went to school in the morning, where they were taught by rabbis, and spent the afternoon learning a trade from their fathers.[1] From this prototype of the modern half-time in-school and half-time on-the-job plan, many modifications have been made in programs using learning-by-doing concepts.

The Educational Policies Commission, as a result of an extensive three-year study, made recommendations in regard to the value of work experience in the secondary school preparation of youth.[2] In its report, *Education for All American Youth*, the value of students having a period of productive work under conditions similar to adult working conditions was emphasized. Educators became increasingly aware of the fact that if the students' work experiences were to achieve their ultimate worth, supervision and planning were necessary. Many schools made arrangements to release teachers from part of their regular classroom schedule for job visitations to guide the experiences of young part-time

---

[1] Charles Alpheus Bennet, *History of Manual and Industrial Education Up to 1870* (Peoria, Illinois: Manual Arts Press, 1926), p. 13.
[2] Educational Policies Commission, *Education for All American Youth* (Washington: National Education Association and American Association of School Administrators, 1944), pp. 370-375.

workers. The World War II demand for workers made employment possible; but, frequently, without proper supervision, the work took an improper perspective in the eyes of the students and the employers.

As the relationship between business and education matured, educators felt the need for more definite understandings among the parties involved: the employer, the student, the home, and the coordinator. The Educational Policies Commission indicated that, with the formulation of advisory committees, studies of local and vocational requirements, qualifications of instructors, equipment, and curriculum offerings, cooperative education was strengthened.

Dewey cautioned educators against the misuse of the learning-by-doing principle when he said:

> The belief that all genuine education comes about through experience does not mean that all experiences are genuinely and equally educative. Experience and education cannot be directly equated to each other. For some experiences are miseducative. Any experience is miseducative that has the effect of arresting or distorting the growth of further experience. An experience may be such as to engender callousness; it may produce lack of sensitivity and responsiveness. Then the possibilities of having richer experience in the future are restricted.[3]

Early in the 1940's educators found that merely having a work program was not enough. They recognized that just giving students work experience had many inherent dangers. The following statement by Haskyn was typical of those made by many educators during the early 1940's.

> Work programs are not automatically real, practical, or anything else. They can be open to all the accusations ever leveled against the classics.
>
> An experience is not something which one simply goes out and has. It is not an entity shot into an individual like a quantum. The condition applies to the doing of work and to work programs as well as anything else. It is not possible simply to "give" young people work experience.[4]

---

[3] John Dewey, *Experience and Education* (New York: Macmillan Co., 1939), p. 28. (Used with permission of Kappa Delta Pi, an honor society in education.)

[4] F. P. Haskyn, "Work Experience: Basic Issues," *Curriculum Journal* (January, 1943), p. 24.

Between 1940 and 1970 a number of different types of "work-oriented" programs have emerged. However, with the development of these programs has come confusion. Businessmen, students, parents, administrators, guidance counselors, and other educational staff members frequently have little understanding of the various types of "work-oriented" programs. This confusion had indeed been unfortunate because there are just three basic types of "work" programs: cooperative vocational education, work experience, and work study.

Cooperative vocational education is an instructional plan which combines learning experiences gained through regularly scheduled employment in the community and vocationally oriented in-school instruction.

There are two different *work experience* programs—exploratory and general. *Exploratory work experience* is a program that emphasizes the occupational guidance of students by affording them an opportunity to observe and systematically sample a variety of work conditions. The main purpose of exploratory work experience programs is to broaden student occupational aspirations and opportunities. The program is not designed to develop salable skills. *General work experience* is a program designed to provide students with maturing experiences through employment that will help them become productive, responsible individuals. The part-time work need not be related to the occupational goals of the students, and they are paid for work performed.

Work study is a program designed to provide financial assistance, through part-time employment, to students who have been accepted for full-time enrollment in vocational training. The part-time employment is based on the financial need of the student and is not necessarily related to his career objectives.

Individuals without a sound background in cooperative education can easily become confused about the different types of "work-oriented" programs by reading the Vocational Education Amendments of 1968. Unfortunately, the use of terms such as "work study," "work experience," "cooperative work study," and "cooperative vocational education" by

Congress did more to confuse than to clarify program terminology.

Figure 9-1 should help clarify the goals and objectives of various "work-oriented" programs. The major purposes of general work experience are to provide social and maturing experiences for students which will enable them to gain emotional maturity and to serve as a means for the school to control the nature and extent of student employment.

COMPARISON OF STUDENT TARGET GROUPS AND PROGRAM OBJECTIVES FOR VARIOUS TYPES OF SECONDARY SCHOOL "WORK-ORIENTED" PROGRAMS

"Work-Oriented" Program Title	Major Program Goals and Objectives	Major Student Target Groups	Usual Grade Level
General Work Experience	1. Maturation experiences 2. Social experiences 3. Control employment 4. Emotional stability	1. Students who are potential drop-outs 2. Students who want to get out of school early 3. Students who want to earn money for various reasons	10-12
Exploratory Work Experience	1. Broaden occupational aspirations and opportunities 2. Aid in selecting occupation	Students who want or need assistance in selecting an occupational goal or objective	7-10
Work Study	Earn money to continue vocational training	Students who, because of financial need, must work to continue in presently enrolled vocational programs	11-12
Cooperative Vocational Education, i.e., Cooperative Office Education, Cooperative Distributive Education, Interrelated Cooperative Vocational Education	1. Develop competencies needed for employment in chosen occupational field 2. Motivation experiences 3. Social experience 4. Emotional stability 5. Broaden occupational aspirations and opportunities 6. Aid in selecting occupation 7. Earn money to continue education 8. Control employment	All students who want, need, and can profit from cooperative on-the-job training and vocationally oriented "classroom" instruction	10-12

FIGURE 9-1

The major purpose of exploratory work experience is to broaden students' occupational aspirations and opportunities so that they are better able to select vocations. The major purpose of work study is to enable students to earn money to continue their vocational training. Students enrolled in work study may also derive some of the same benefits as work experience students, but these benefits to students are more incidental and accidental than planned.

The diagram shows that cooperative vocational education is the only plan designed to enable students to develop the competencies needed for employment in their chosen occupational fields. It is a plan for implementing vocational education curricula in many occupational fields. A properly designed plan will enable a student to derive a majority of the benefits that are associated with work experience or work study type programs. In fact, it is the only vocational development program.

The purpose of this chapter is to provide guidelines for developing and implementing the cooperative vocational education plan in office education and distributive education. No attempt will be made to explain work experience or work study programs because, normally, these programs are directed by guidance or administrative staff members. However, a brief explanation of the role of short-term employment experiences in implementing "in-school" laboratory experiences plan programs is presented in Chapter 10.

Definition of Terms

A basic understanding of the following terms is essential for individuals working with cooperative vocational education programs in the fields of office and distributive education:

Advisory Committee: A group of persons, usually from outside the field of education, selected because of their knowledge and expertise in certain areas to advise educators regarding vocational education programs.

Cooperative Plan: Organizational pattern for preparatory instruction which involves regularly scheduled part-time employment that gives students an opportunity to experience theory in practice while developing competencies through supervised on-the-job training related to their occupational objective.

Cooperative Vocational Education: An instructional plan which combines learning experiences gained through regularly scheduled employment in the community and vocationally oriented in-school instruction.

Coordination: The process of integrating into a harmonious relationship the administrative, organizational, and instructional activities of the vocational program and directing them toward a common purpose.

Distributive Education: A program of instruction in the field of distribution and marketing designed to prepare individuals to enter, progress, or improve competencies in distributive occupations. Emphasis is on the development of attitudes, habits, skills, and understandings related to the performance of activities that direct the flow of goods and services, including their appropriate utilization, from producer to the consumer or user.

Distributive Occupations: Occupations followed by proprietors, managers, supervisors, or employees engaged primarily in marketing or merchandising of goods or services. Distributive occupations are found in such businesses as retail and wholesale trade; finance, insurance, and real estate; services and service trade; manufacturing, transportation and utilities; and communications.

Office Education: A vocational program for office careers through initial, refresher, and upgrading education leading to employability and advancement in office occupations.

Office Occupations: Those activities performed by individuals in public and/or private enterprises, which are related to the facilitating function of the office. They include such items as recording and retrieval of data; supervision and coordination of office activities; communication; and reporting of information regardless of the social, economic, or governmental organizations in which they are found.

Teacher-Coordinator: A member of the local school staff who teaches technical and related subject matter to students preparing for employment, and who coordinates classroom instruction and laboratory (on-the-job or project) learning activities of career oriented students.

Training Memorandum (or Agreement): A form prepared by the teacher-coordinator indicating the period of training, hours of work, salary, and other pertinent facts and information necessary to assure basic understanding of the student's position as a student-learner in the cooperative education program. This may be signed by coordinator, employer, student, and parents.

Training Plan: A written plan of experiences indicating what is to be learned by a specific student-learner, and when it is to be taught in the classroom (group or individual instruction) and in the laboratory (cooperative or project). The plan is derived from a realistic analysis of the tasks, duties, responsibilities, and occupational objectives of the student-learner. The plan includes a provision for evaluation and for recording achievement.

Training Sponsor: The individual to whom the student-learner looks for instruction and training in the cooperative or project plan laboratory. The on-the-job training sponsor may be the owner, manager, or responsible individual appointed by management.

Training Station: The business establishment where the student receives supervised experiences related to his occupational objective through part-time employment.

Cooperative Vocational Education in Action

Cooperative vocational education has successfully prepared young people for the world of work. More than 160,000 students currently are enrolled in some 4,800 different cooperative vocational programs in more than 3,000 high school and junior colleges.[5]

Dr. Rupert Evans, a member of the National Advisory Committee on Vocational Education, in commenting on the advantages of cooperative vocational education, reported that typical research studies show that more than 80 percent of the cooperative education graduates are placed in the occupations for which they were prepared.[6]

---

[5] Rupert N. Evans, "Cooperative Programs Advantages, Disadvantages, and Factors in Development," *American Vocational Journal,* Vol. 44, No. 5 (May, 1969), p. 19.
[6] *Ibid.*

In reporting studies in the economics of vocational education, he stated:

> Studies of the economics of vocational education show higher rates of return on investment in cooperative programs than in other types of vocational education. (Capital costs for schools are lower, and since the student is receiving wages for the on-the-job portion of the program, the costs for the individual are lowered.) [7]

Congress thought so highly of the record of cooperative vocational education in preparing persons for employment that it authorized Vocational Education Amendments of 1968 funds be used to extend this kind of training and instruction, particularly for those students in areas with high dropout and unemployment rates, so that the student will be able to develop and refine competencies needed for entry-level jobs and advancement in his chosen occupational field.

Figure 9-2 illustrates an organizational plan for cooperative vocational education programs. The following essential components of the cooperative program are highlighted: understanding and cooperative administrative personnel, a well-qualified and dedicated teacher-coordinator, competent training sponsors, a sound advisory committee, vocationally-oriented classroom instruction, carefully planned progressive on-the-job instruction and application, a youth organization that supplements instruction, and a comprehensive instructional program based on career objectives of students.

Considerable thinking and planning are required to develop and implement a quality cooperative education program. A majority of the cooperative vocational education programs, which have been most effective in serving student and community needs during the past three decades, have contained the following elements:

1. A well qualified and highly dedicated staff.
2. Written training agreements and individual student training plans that have been carefully developed and

---

[7] *Ibid.*

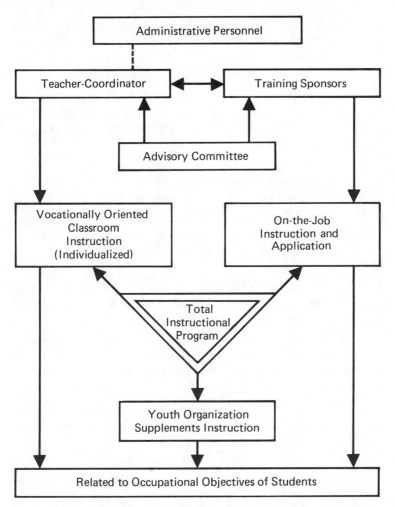

Administrative Personnel

Teacher-Coordinator

Training Sponsors

Advisory Committee

Vocationally Oriented Classroom Instruction (Individualized)

On-the-Job Instruction and Application

Total Instructional Program

Youth Organization Supplements Instruction

Related to Occupational Objectives of Students

Source: U.S. Department of Health, Education, and Welfare, Office of Education, *Curriculum Development in Distributive Education* (Washington: U.S. Government Printing Office, 1960).

FIGURE 9-2

agreed upon by the employer, training sponsor, student, and coordinator.

3. Adequate time in the teacher-coordinator's schedule to coordinate the classroom instruction and supervise on-the-job training (one-half hour per student per week).

4. On-the-job training supervised by a training sponsor who has been carefully prepared for his role by the teacher-coordinator.

5. Services of occupationally aware guidance and teaching personnel utilized in advising students concerning career choices and planning.

6. Students having a realistic career objective of which their present instructional program is an integral part.

7. Students selected by the teacher-coordinator on the basis of need, interest, and ability to profit from the instruction.

8. The classroom instruction phase of the cooperative program, which correlates with the on-the-job training preceded by a program of well-planned courses designed to assist in the occupational preparation of the student.

9. The vocationally oriented classroom phase of the cooperative program taught by the teacher-coordinator.

10. Enrollment in the vocationally oriented phase of the cooperative program determined by availability of adequate classroom facilities and teacher-coordinator time to provide individualized instruction.

11. The instructional program confirmed or changed by periodic analysis of the occupations for which the cooperative plan is being utilized.

12. An advisory committee including representatives from business, labor, and education to advise and assist in planning, developing, and implementing the cooperative plan.

13. A youth organization effectively developed and recognized as a co-curricular phase of the instruction phase of the program.

14. Adequate facilities, equipment, and materials to provide instruction related to the student's on-the-job experiences and career goal.

15. Students receiving pay for work performed and credit toward graduation for the on-the-job instruction phase of the program.

16. Training stations that comply with all state and federal laws regarding employment practices.

17. Home visitations and/or parental conferences, an integral part of the job of the teacher-coordinator, to assist in the total development of each student-learner.

18. Follow-up studies conducted regularly with the results of the studies utilized to improve the program.

19. The teacher-coordinator provided with an extended contract to develop training station personnel, conduct follow-up studies, make home visitations, develop training plans, up-date program records, and other program development activities.

Advantages of Cooperative Education

The benefits derived by the various participants involved in the operation of quality cooperative education will vary considerably from community to community and from school to school. The advantages listed in the publication *A Guide for Cooperative Vocational Education*, following the U.S. Office of Education Conference on Cooperative Vocational Education, are excellent.[8]

Greater Relevance of Curriculum and Instruction

Without doubt, the greatest current concern about education in general is the relevance of curriculum and instruction to the needs and interests of present day youth. Cooperative vocational education has some built-in features that almost insure relevant instruction when properly used. A few of the more salient points relating to the relevance of cooperative education are given below:

1. Students are placed on jobs that are in harmony with their abilities and interests.
2. Each student follows a plan of on-the-job experiences based on occupational requirements and individual student needs.
3. Students have the opportunity to learn skills on real jobs under actual working conditions.
4. Classroom instruction, on-the-job training, and student youth organization activities are articulated in the development of clearly identified competencies.

[8] *A Guide for Cooperative Vocational Education* (Minneapolis, Minnesota: University of Minnesota, College of Education, Division of Vocational and Technical Education, 1969), p. 8.

5. Students have an active role in the choice of content and methods because of their unique experiences which incite them to seek education for their developing personal needs.

6. The teacher is not the sole authority. His teachings are supplemented with the practices and ideas of employers and employees of the occupational environment.

7. Students can better evaluate the contribution of general and vocational education in terms of their own needs and aspirations.

8. Students are able to identify with the world of work in a meaningful way.

9. Students encounter daily situations in an adult environment which cause them to examine their values and reappraise their potential in occupational and social situations.

10. Students receive the guidance of trained teacher-coordinators who have been "through the mill" in the occupational field when making vital vocational decisions.

11. Students make the transition from school to work gradually under the skilled guidance of a teacher-coordinator, giving them time to comprehend the significance of the learning situation and the world of work.

12. Students receive direct on-the-job contact with professionals whose responsibility it is to stay up-to-date in their profession.

13. Curriculum revision is more rapidly reflective of current occupational requirements.

14. Cooperative vocational education enables the student to relate education to his occupational interests at a period in life when it is natural for him to look outside the school for learning and earning.

15. Cooperative education may provide the most influential means of coordinating the home, the school, and the world of work in behalf of the student.

Better Application of Learning

One of the most visible values of cooperative vocational education is the opportunity for better application of classroom learning to a real-life test. This value is particularly important in the development of the capabilities needed for good occupational adjustment. Simulated occupational environments rarely provide a laboratory of real-life customers or clients. Occupations vary widely in their reliance on job experience for learning the required technical competencies. Evidence concerning the better application of learning in cooperative vocational education follows:

1. Students are able almost immediately to test their occupational learning voluntarily and independently in a real-life situation.

2. The job usually functions as a learning laboratory in which structured assignments that do not interfere with production are carried out on the job. When they do interfere, arrangements may be made for special instruction outside of working hours.

3. Students apply their learning in a variety of job situations and return to the classroom for analysis and group discussions. Thus, they understand better and appreciate the difference in practices among employing organizations. Such variances in applications would not be possible in a simulated environment.

4. Students acquire a better understanding of problem-solving and the scientific method. Problems arising on the job or in school are investigated. Alternatives are explored and some are chosen. They are tried out on the job and observations are made. The action succeeds or fails and the cycle is dropped or repeated.

5. Well chosen training stations become rich learning sources and usually furnish more valid information than is available to learners through other means. Carefully prepared on-the-job training sponsors take a personal interest in the student's development and function as excellent laboratory instructors.

6. Under guided experiences on their jobs, and sometimes in unplanned situations, students are led to appreciate the values of general education.

7. The total physical and psychological job environment adds materially to the laboratory and teaching facilities available.

8. Frequent periodic applications of classroom learning to an employment situation remove artificial barriers to learning.

Balanced Vocational Capabilities

Vocational education has done a very commendable job of developing technical skills and knowledge in the traditional vocational fields. The same cannot be said of occupational adjustment and career development; studies show that a major portion of jobs are lost for reasons other than incompetency in the technical skills and that occupational tenure among vocational education graduates leaves much to be desired. Many vocational educators attribute this phenomenon to an inadequate training environment in the traditional vocational education setting. A few cogent points regarding balanced vocational capabilities follow:

1. Properly designed occupational experiences provide opportunities for exploration of the three major vocational capability areas: technical, occupational adjustment, and career development, through the employing organization's physical facilities and its human environment.

2. First-hand guidance information is available for the asking at the job training site. Chances are then, when properly solicited, such information will be more complete and accurate than could normally be communicated because of the bond between the student and the employing firm or organization.

3. Teacher-coordinators are likely to be more sensitive to the need for balanced instructional content than other vocational teachers because of the continuous feedback from training sponsors and other employees on the behavior of the student.

4. Continuous dialogue among the coordinator, the employer, and the student provides ample opportunities for a balanced viewpoint in formulating the student's individual curriculum.

5. The coordinator's regular contacts with employers, employees, and the student facilitate helping the student personally bridge the generation gap, as well as master the technical capabilities.

6. As wage earners, students develop an appreciation and respect for work and are aided in obtaining worthwhile jobs.

7. Students are able to observe and assess the importance of personal traits so necessary for employment: punctuality, dress, regular attendance, and responsibility for completing assigned tasks.

8. Cooperative vocational education provides many students with their most useful contacts with society outside the home.

9. Cooperative vocational education helps students clarify relationships between education and employment and earnings.

10. Cooperative vocational education adds breadth and depth of meaning to the student's studies.

11. Work periods offer opportunities for independent exploration of an environment providing for new knowledge, practices, and experiences.

Extension of Training to Additional Occupations and Students

Even with programmed instruction and computerized practices, the schools alone cannot provide adequately for the multitude of occupations which compose our labor force. Even if the technical training could be automated, it would not be possible to provide training in the personal and social capabilities needed in large numbers of behavioral-science-based occupations. In many occupations, however, cooperative vocational education can furnish the essential elements that complement classroom work and provide a reasonable training program.

Cooperative education is well-equipped to prepare students for new and emerging careers with some assurance that they will be gainfully employed. Students with wide ranges of ability can be accommodated more easily by cooperative education than by vocational education without occupational experience. It is also better able to provide for the needs of occupations which draw on more than one discipline than is vocational education, which is limited to classroom instruction.

Cooperative vocational education is a significant means of aiding low-income students, enabling those students to stay in school who would otherwise drop out to seek employment.

Finally, in these times of rising costs, educational institutions can utilize their staff and facilities much more effectively by shifting part of the cost of education to the employing community. This enables the school to provide for the expansion of occupational training.

Built-In Manpower Control

Congress is concerned about balancing the supply and demand of manpower. Reducing unemployment has been one of its major goals in recent years. Though the record has been favorable, Congressional concern remains. Hence, the manpower control feature inherent in cooperative vocational education appealed to Congress and will appeal to other groups dealing with manpower problems. Some of these features may be described as follows:

1. The number of persons training for an occupational field is limited to the number of available training stations (employing firms), unless an alternating plan is used in which two students hold one job.
2. Advisory committees representing both employers and employees are an essential feature of cooperative vocational education. These committees counsel the school on the manpower supply and demand problem.
3. Cooperative vocational education should be started only after adequate employment, demographic, and other essential data have been collected, analyzed, and a favorable report made.
4. Cooperative vocational education promises to have a stabilizing effect on the labor market because of its occupational tryout and guidance features.
5. Cooperative vocational education is equipped to help disadvantaged and handicapped youth become well-adjusted members of the labor force in quantities that can be absorbed.
6. Cooperative vocational education consistently yields high placement records, high employment stability, and high job satisfaction.

The Vocational Education Amendments of 1968 stress the use of the employment service, employers, labor and other community agencies and groups in identifying training opportunities. Extension of cooperative vocational education into new occupational areas, including disadvantaged and handicapped students both in and outside of school, thrusts new responsibilities on the community, and calls for new relationships between the school and community groups. These ties serve to strengthen the program.

A closer partnership between the schools and the occupational world is necessary in order to maintain the proper relevance of training and the basic subjects to support the occupational training. In cooperative education, the schools and the employing community are brought together on mutual educational problems that are within their power to understand and handle, resulting in a two-way working relationship which adds quality and distinctiveness to the school as a whole.

When employers engage in vocational education in their stores, shops, and offices, an appreciation of the school's problems is inevitable. The school also develops an understanding of the employer's problems. Student achievement is accelerated when academic and employment environments are combined as the experiences in one support and influence the experiences provided in the other. In addition, employers and students have a chance for a trial acquaintance before full-time employment.

Business and industry leaders who participate become spokesmen who provide the community with a vital understanding of education when they speak to civic clubs or participate in community activities. Participating employers can also readily see that, by becoming involved with educators who are working with young people through cooperative education, an excellent source of future employees may be developed.

Improved Vocational Guidance

Opportunities for improved vocational guidance abound during the period of cooperative employment when students can engage in occupational tryouts to see whether or not they are suited for the type of career in which they are gaining experience. Opportunities to investigate the way of life of persons engaged in an occupational field are much more favorable to a cooperative student than to students not in the program. Among the vocational guidance advantages and opportunities of cooperative vocational education are the following:

1. Cooperative vocational education provides career guidance in making suitable choices of a field of work. Students may receive the help of teacher-coordinators who have had successful occupational experience in addition to teaching, of regular vocational counselors, of employers, and of co-workers at their training stations.
2. Students who have the opportunities afforded in cooperative education are provided early occupational experiences which are vital in making immediate and long-range career decisions.
3. Cooperative vocational education encourages students to finish high school and enter employment or continue into higher education.
4. Cooperative vocational education students may try out a variety of work situations under trained teacher-coordinators before they leave school.
5. The ability to get and hold a job helps the young person bridge the gap between school and work. Alternated periods of school and work under guidance allow for gradual induction into the work world.
6. Cooperative vocational education provides the student with a wider range of possibilities for employment after graduation.

Teacher-Coordinator Requirements

It is important to remember that the key to the success of any cooperative vocational education program is the teacher-coordinator, who has been the subject of much discussion and a great deal of research during the past decade.

The notes and working papers from the National Conference on Cooperative Vocational Education listed the following essential competencies, understandings, and personal qualifications for teacher-coordinators: [9]

Essential Competencies of Teacher-Coordinators

1. Ability to communicate effectively with students, employers, labor groups, parents, and school personnel.
2. Ability to provide his students with guidance and inspiration as he helps them establish solid vocational foundations.
3. Ability to select and use appropriate learning materials and methods for effective teaching.
4. Ability to coordinate the youth club program.
5. Ability to write up appropriate reports.
6. Ability to integrate school, work and club learning experiences.
7. Ability to utilize appropriate public relations devices and media.
8. Ability to teach related classes.
9. Ability to help students make personal adjustments.
10. Ability to perform evaluation and follow-up activities.
11. Ability to keep up-to-date on business trends and developments.
12. Ability to help training sponsors plan and organize individual instruction to be provided students.

Essential Understandings of Teacher-Coordinators

1. Understanding of the requirements, demands, and atmosphere of the work situations of his students.
2. Understanding of the business point of view, as well as the needs of his particular students.
3. Understanding of Federal and state laws relating to vocational education and employment.

Essential Personal Qualifications

1. Sufficient occupational experience to earn and maintain the respect of the students, employers, school personnel

---

[9] National Conference on Cooperative Vocational Education, *Implications of the 1968 Amendments,* notes and working papers (Minneapolis, Minnesota: February, 1969), pp. 79-80.

and community and to perform the essential duties and responsibilities of an occupation in his teaching field.

2. Warmth and commitment to helping youth make the transition from school to the world of work. (Especially strong commitments are required of personnel who work with disadvantaged students.)

3. Public relations qualifications
   a. Enthusiasm
   b. Attractive appearance
   c. Ability to sell ideas

Teacher-Coordinator Job Description

A group of 200 selected participants representing business, industry, labor, education, government, and community interests from across the nation met in Minneapolis, Minnesota. One of the outcomes of the National Conference on Cooperative Vocational Education was the following job description of a teacher-coordinator: [10]

1. Guidance and selection of students:
   a. Describing the program to students
   b. Working with guidance personnel
   c. Providing occupational information
   d. Counseling students about entering the program
   e. Gathering information on students
   f. Programming and scheduling
   g. Helping enrollees with career planning

2. Placing students in training jobs:
   a. Enlisting participation of cooperating employers
   b. Selecting suitable training stations for each student
   c. Orienting employers, training supervisors and co-workers.
   d. Preparing students for job interviews
   e. Placing students on the job

3. Assisting students in adjusting to their work environment:
   a. Helping students on their jobs
   b. Dealing with job problems

---

[10] A Guide for Cooperative Vocational Education, op. cit., pp. 93-94.

c. Planning personal development with training super-visors and students

d. Evaluating job progress

4. Improving training done on the job:
   a. Establishing responsibilities on the job
   b. Developing training plans
   c. Consulting and assisting training supervisors
   d. Maintaining training emphasis

5. Correlating classroom instruction with on-the-job train-ing:
   a. Determining needed instruction
   b. Assembling instructional materials
   c. Preparing for instruction
   d. Teaching classes
   e. Directing individual projects and study
   f. Obtaining assistance from other teachers
   g. Advising training supervisors concerning applications of classroom instruction to be made on the job
   h. Evaluating learning outcomes

6. Assisting students in making personal adjustments:
   a. Aiding students in correcting poor personal habits
   b. Counseling students with personal and socio-economic problems
   c. Assisting students with educational problems
   d. Resolving behavioral problems

7. Directing vocational youth organization:
   a. Advising youth group
   b. Guiding students in organization of activities
   c. Participating in group activities

8. Providing services to graduates and adults:
   a. Providing guidance and placement services for gradu-ates
   b. Participating in the planning and operating of adult education programs

9. Administration activities:
   a. Planning program objectives
   b. Research and planning—surveys
   c. Organizing and working with advisory committee
   d. Planning curricula
   e. Communicating school policy

    f. Preparing reports

    g. Budgeting and purchasing

    h. Participating in professional meetings

    i. Consulting with manpower agencies, such as employment services and CAMPS

10. Maintaining good public relations:

    a. Planning the publicity program

    b. Preparing printed publicity

    c. Constructing displays and exhibits

    d. Contacting news media

    e. Maintaining communication with faculty, parents, community, employers, school administrators and student body

IN-SCHOOL INSTRUCTION

Educators have long recognized the importance of vocationally directed "classroom" instruction as a vital part of any program that uses cooperative on-the-job training. Career oriented in-school instruction is the heart of the total instructional program. Cooperative training in office or distributive education that has proven most successful in preparing youth for employment uses the business community as a laboratory to provide students with an opportunity to try out and apply what they have learned in school. To recognize the job as the center of the instructional program provides the possible danger of "locking" a student in a certain job, which may obstruct the way to future opportunities.

Suggestions and Generalizations

Kenneth Rowe, in a presentation made at the National Conference on Cooperative Vocational Education, listed the following suggestions for in-school instruction:

1. Instruction in the classroom should be related to the students' career interest area and to their on-the-job needs, both short-range and long-range.

2. Some content of the related instruction program should include occupational skills and job readiness instruction

so that the student can perform successfully certain tasks on the job.

3. To make related instruction meaningful the student should be able to see its purpose, its application, practice it, and discuss it with the coordinator or his training sponsor.

4. Related instruction should be both general and specific—concepts needed by all students and concepts, skills, and attitudes customized to the needs of specific career areas, training station demands, and/or individual student needs.

5. Related instruction should be timed to on-the-job application.

6. Competency development through the related instruction program must be realistic to the career needs of the students.

7. Students should be involved in the related instruction program by being given much responsibility for their training both on the job and in the classroom. They should be involved in the development of their training plan and the measurement of their growth and progress on the job.

8. The student should be encouraged to accept the responsibility for applying the group instruction in the classroom to his specific situation on the job.

9. Employers or training sponsors should be involved in the classroom instruction as resource people.[11]

The notes and working papers from the National Conference on Cooperative Vocational Education provide the following clear, concise explanation of the three aspects of instruction:

1. Nature of Content Materials
   a. Workers should be prepared to be flexible and able to adapt to new business procedures and industrial processes.
   b. The curriculum should be broad enough to equip the students to take advantage of a wide range of occupational opportunities.

---

[11] National Conference on Cooperative Vocational Education, *op. cit.*, p. 46.

c. Academic subjects should be made more meaningful and relevant to occupational preparation.

d. Desirable attitudes toward work and toward change should be developed as well as toward specific skills.

e. The teacher-coordinator should make provisions for special instruction and individual help for students who cannot read or lack the basic skills needed for occupational success.

2. Curriculum Flexibility

a. The schedule should be flexible to allow students a variety of patterns for obtaining on-the-job training and completing the related instruction and necessary general education.

b. Instruction should be adapted to the learning style of the individual. The director of learning must be able to identify the learning style most appropriate for each individual.

3. Characteristics of Instructional Methods

a. Related vocational instruction should be provided with the appropriate balance of technical competencies, occupational adjustment, and career development competencies. The balance depends on the occupations for which instruction is given and on the individual needs of the students.

b. A large portion of related instruction is of the individual type. Group discussions in which the students share their on-the-job experiences and discuss job-related problems are essential. Insofar as possible, group instruction should be given in homogeneous or occupational cluster groups in order to provide instruction relevant to the occupational fields for which students are preparing.

c. Teachers in related areas who can develop specific competencies, e.g., math for pricing, should be available to cooperative students who need special competencies in order to participate in cooperative training that is related to their career interest.

d. Vocational youth club activities should be conducted on school time only if activities have an instructional purpose and focus on occupational competencies.[12]

---

[12] *Ibid.*, pp. 81-82.

A Guide for Cooperative Vocational Education clearly explains the capabilities and competencies to be developed in the related in-school instruction.[13] The vocational capabilities to be learned may be classified as *specific skills* which are derived from an occupation, *occupational adjustment capabilities* which are needed to succeed in a work environment, and *career development capabilities* which are concerned with helping the learner find a satisfying occupational role. The emphasis given to each of these areas will vary with the purposes of the cooperative vocational education program, the occupations being taught, and the characteristics of the students. For example, regarding specific skills, in some occupations it takes much more time to learn the required technical information or to operate equipment than in others. In regard to occupational adjustment capabilities, some groups of students will require more instruction than others on how to get along with co-workers and their supervisors, and on how to learn a job. In regard to career development capabilities, the instruction focusing on career development will vary with the ages of the students and their previous experiences in exploring occupations. It is generally agreed that the three vocational capability areas are related and should be integrated, rather than organized in blocks of time or units of instruction.

Specific Skills

For each occupational field there are specific skills, knowledges, and attitudes required to progress in that field. The instruction is directed toward developing competencies in: manipulating tools or equipment; gathering, processing, communicating, or applying technical information; constructing, assembling, or combining elements; performing a service; or others drawn from the specific occupation.

Occupational Adjustment Capabilities

One of the outcomes of cooperative vocational education is the student's ability to adjust to work environments—

[13] *A Guide for Cooperative Vocational Education, op. cit.,* p. 46.

the plant, office, store, or institution. The intent is that by teaching him to interact effectively with fellow workers, supervisors, and the conditions under which he works in the cooperative training station, he will acquire capabilities which will persist as he progresses in his career and takes positions in other work environments. Occupational adjustment capabilities include: learning how to learn a job; interacting with co-workers, supervisors, and employers; participating in worker groups as a member and leader; developing desirable work habits and attitudes; making rational economic decisions; preparing for the jobs ahead; managing work and leisure time; keeping abreast of current occupational developments; and others drawn from the environments where the occupation is found.

Career Development Capabilities

Another expected outcome of cooperative vocational education is the student finding satisfying occupational roles in which he can get a sense of achievement and self-realization. The instruction focuses on learning about the occupational field and the lives of workers in the occupation and looking inward at one's own potential needs, abilities, and aspirations as they relate to occupations and careers. The capabilities would include: assessing and analyzing one's own needs, interests, abilities, and aspirations; assessing and analyzing the potential opportunities and satisfactions of an occupational field; predicting one's own chances of being successful and satisfied in the occupational field; and making decisions and plans to achieve goals and aspirations.

A System for Individualizing Instruction

Every year cooperative office education or distributive education teacher-coordinators are faced with the dilemma of how to best prepare each student for his chosen career. If all of the students in the cooperative office education program planned to become legal stenographers, or all of the students in the cooperative phase of distributive education program were pursuing careers as retail department store buyers, the teaching task would be greatly simplified.

The task of individualizing instruction could be more effectively concentrated on the various abilities and levels of student aspirations. Unfortunately, in most office or distributive education programs this homogeneous grouping of students by career objective does not exist.

How does a teacher-coordinator effectively individualize instruction for the 20-25 students who are normally enrolled? The teacher must begin with an attitude that he

TEACHER-COORDINATOR INSTRUCTIONAL ACTIVITIES

PHASE I	FORMULATION OF DESIRED LEARNING OUTCOMES	IDENTIFYING NEEDED COMPETENCIES PLOTTING COMPETENCIES ON MATRIX OR PLANNING GRID CLUSTERING OF COMPETENCIES THAT ARE COMMON TO MORE THAN ONE STUDENT IDENTIFYING STUDENT CAPABILITIES PREPARING INSTRUCTIONAL OBJECTIVES	
PHASE II	DEVELOPING AND DESIGNING LEARNING ACTIVITIES	Development and Preparation of: INSTRUCTIONAL MEDIA TEACHING TECHNIQUES STUDENT PERFORMANCE TESTS	Selection of: TEACHING TECHNIQUES INSTRUCTIONAL MEDIA DETERMINING WHETHER TO USE LARGE GROUP, SMALL GROUP, OR INDIVIDUAL INSTRUCTION CONDUCT INSTRUCTION ADMINISTER AND ANALYZE STUDENT PERFORMANCE TESTS
PHASE III	EVALUATION	COMPARE STUDENT PERFORMANCES WITH INSTRUCTIONAL OBJECTIVES COMPARE ACTUAL STUDENT ON-THE-JOB PERFORMANCE WITH EXPECTED EMPLOYER REQUIREMENTS	
		REFINE THE INSTRUCTION	

FIGURE 9-3

is willing to try to help each of his students develop or refine competencies for employment and, simultaneously, guide each student into a full and rewarding participation in society. To achieve these goals each student must acquire the necessary knowledge, skill, understanding, and attitude for the world of work.

Once this positive teacher-coordinator attitude has been established, the next task is to develop a system that will help each student achieve the desired patterns of behavior. Figure 9-3 illustrates the basic instructional system which will be presented in this chapter.

The three major phases of the system are formulation of desired learning outcomes, designing and developing learning activities, and evaluation.

Formulation of Desired Learning Outcomes

The key to any instructional system is the ability of the teacher to identify desired learning outcomes for each student. If a student desires to pursue a career as a bank teller, what does he have to be able to do? Or, to put this in educational terminology, what competencies must he possess to enter and advance in his chosen career?

Identifying Needed Student Competencies. How does a teacher-coordinator determine the competencies needed, for instance, by a bank teller? Ideally, the teacher-coordinator should conduct a task analysis as the first step. Task analysis is defined as the process of identifying and reporting significant worker activities, performance requirements, and environmental facts of a specific occupation. This technique can be used by the teacher-coordinator in the identification of tasks that comprise a specific occupation and the competencies (knowledge, understanding, skill, and attitudes) that are required of the worker for successful performance.

Experienced teacher-coordinators have found that they can have the outcomes of a task analysis and other needed information through the use of the following system of identifying needed student competencies.

DETERMINING NEEDED STUDENT COMPETENCIES					
E & TS +	AC +	T & PA +	CE & I +	SE & I =	C
Employer and/or Training Sponsor	Advisory Committee	Trade and Professional Association	Teacher-Coordinator Experience and Investigation	Student Experience and Investigation	Competencies Needed

FIGURE 9-4

A training plan which has been properly prepared by the teacher-coordinator, training sponsor, and student, will identify a significant number of the needed competencies. Hopefully, the input provided by the competent training sponsor will be almost equivalent to that gleaned from a task analysis.

The instructional program for vocationally directed individualized instruction cannot be completed until the competencies which have been identified for each student have been clearly stated. The training plan should contain many of these competencies, and others will be identified from the sources identified in Figure 9-4.

Care must be taken so that student capabilities are carefully identified. This care must be exercised in designing and implementing both on-the-job and classroom learning activities.

Plotting Competencies. To assist in the planning of instructional activities, experienced teacher-coordinators use a matrix or grid to plot the identified competencies for each of their students. Figure 9-5 is a copy of a portion of a matrix suggested by Harland Samson.[14] This portion of the matrix is for the social competencies area. The other matrices which Samson developed include economic, basic skill, marketing, and technological.

Obviously the competency areas at the top of the matrix will vary by type of instructional program.

Samson provides the following descriptions for the levels of study on the left hand column of the matrix in Figure 9-5:

---

[14] Peter G. Haines (ed.), *Readings in Distributive Education: The Project Plan of Instruction and Related Teacher Education* (East Lansing, Michigan: Michigan State University, Department of Secondary Education and Curriculum, 1969), pp. 43-54.

SOCIAL COMPETENCY

LEVEL OF STUDY	AREAS OF STUDY			
	INTER-PERSONAL RELATIONS	INTER-GROUP RELATIONS	OCCUPA-TIONAL RELATIONS	PUBLIC RELATIONS
Management Activities				
Operational Activities				
Basic Job Activities				
Fundamental Tasks				
Processes and Terminology				
Facts and Information				

FIGURE 9-5

1. Facts and Information. In this first level the student would become acquainted with facts, the various functions, and the definitions of simple terms.
2. Processes and Terminology. At this level he should learn the order of steps to be followed in routing activities, sequences in the process, and the association of terms with their generalized meaning.
3. Fundamental Tasks. This would include the carrying out of tasks assigned in either written or oral manner; the development of skill and accuracy in following a single routine; and, the ability to effectively replicate in a working condition demonstrated skills and procedures.
4. Basic Job Activities. This would require that the student identify elements within a task or steps within a process. He would be expected to solve, independently, basic job problems and would combine various fundamental activities into his behavior in order to perform all the tasks of a complete basic job or occupational position.
5. Operational Level Activities. At this level the student would be expected to draw conclusions from several incidents, and from these generalize to new problems or new job situations. Also, he would be expected to hypothesize

outcomes if certain procedures or actions were taken and make appropriate decisions. This level would require that he have fairly high degree of competence in functional, product, and social skills.

6. Management Level Activities. At this level, he would have to be able to make judgments, determine values, and perhaps extend these to fields outside that for which he had been prepared. The student would also be expected to interpret action and trends, and to project these into action or policy.[15]

Another matrix for planned instruction, called *A Unitized Model for Instructional System,* was designed by Peter G. Haines and is illustrated in Figure 10-7 on page 488.[16]

It is recommended that the time when the competency should be taught also be designated on either of the planning matrices. This time indication can be extremely helpful in determining the proper time for teaching each competency.

Once planning sheets or matrices have been developed for each student, they may be compared to see whether any, or perhaps all, of the students have to develop the same competency at the same level of performance. For example, examination of the prepared matrices may reveal that all students need to develop competency in human relations, while ten students need to be able to apply human relations to a new situation.

Clustering of Competencies. The following system can be effectively used in determining whether to use large group, small group or individual instruction to teach the identified competencies.

DETERMINING WHAT TO TEACH ON A GROUP BASIS				
NC —	PL & E —	PLLE —	PII =	NGI
Competencies Needed to Achieve Career Objective (See Figure 9-4)	Previous Learnings and Experiences (From occupational experience, courses, hobbies, etc.)	Planned on-the-job Laboratory Learning Experiences (From training plan)	Planned Individual Instruction (From training plan)	Needed Group Instruction (Small or large groups)

FIGURE 9-6

---

[15] *Ibid.*
[16] From a paper presented by Peter G. Haines at Oakland Schools, Pontiac, Michigan, November 1969.

The formula in Figure 9-6 can be revised to determine needed individual instruction if planned group instruction is already determined by the instructor.

DETERMINING WHAT TO TEACH ON INDIVIDUAL OR SMALL GROUP BASIS				
NC —	PL & E —	PLLE —	PGI =	NII
Competencies Needed to Achieve Career Objective (See Figure 9-4)	Previous Learnings and Experiences (From occupational experience, courses, hobbies, etc.)	Planned on-the-job Laboratory Learning Experiences (From training plan)	Planned Group Instruction (From course outline)	Needed Individual (and/or small group) Instruction

FIGURE 9-7

Identifying Student Capabilities. The importance of carefully identifying the capabilities and previous learning experiences of students has been emphasized throughout this chapter. The *for whom* aspect of the instructional program plays a crucial role in teacher-coordinator decisions concerning the selection and organization of content, selection of instructional materials, selection of teaching strategies, and selection of student performance assessment techniques.

Hopefully, students will have developed a number of competencies in other classes, from hobbies, and through previous business experiences. Experienced teacher-coordinators use a wide variety of written, oral, and performance-oriented techniques for assessing student capabilities. Information gleaned from these pre-tests is helpful in determining where the student should begin his learning experiences and in implementing the instructional program.

Preparing Instructional Objectives. Once teacher-coordinator decisions have been made concerning *what* competencies should be developed, by *whom,* and approximately *when* the knowledge, attitude, skill, or understanding should be taught, instructional objectives can be prepared. The achievement of the behavioral goal type instruction system requires effective student-teacher dialogue.

The student wants to know what performance is expected, under what conditions he will perform the task, and what the criteria is for successful performance. The student and teacher must agree on what is to be done to help the student in the attainment of his occupational objective, how it is to be done, and the level of performance. Once the student has been involved in setting goals and knows what is expected in what period of time, evaluation becomes a much easier task. Evaluative performance criteria measures are frequently based on quantity, quality, and time factors.

Chapter 2 contains a discussion of the techniques for preparing instructional objectives. It is important to remember that a meaningful instructional objective should satisfy three important criteria. The objective should identify:

1. Conditions under which the student will be expected to demonstrate or show his achievement of the objective.
2. Expected student performance, or what the student will be doing when he demonstrates that he has attained the objective.
3. Evaluative criteria, or the minimum standards of performance expected of the student.

The preparation of formal statements of objectives, describing desired behaviors and levels of performance, is essential for implementing and evaluating instruction. These behavioral objectives also provide students with learning goals, thus contributing to their motivation.

Developing and Designing Learning Activities

Once the teacher-coordinator has clearly formulated the desired student learning outcomes, he can devote his attention to developing and designing learning activities. The teacher has to determine how to aid the student in achieving his goals. The learning may consist of any and every teaching technique from lecture to role-playing, using the simplest of media created by teacher or student or the most complex computer-based programs.

Selection, Development, and Preparation of Learning Activities. The selection of the most appropriate instructional techniques and media is not a simple task. A myriad of decisions must be made. Figure 9-8 shows some of the techniques which are used for teaching in terms of the decisional factors that the teacher must make.

DECISIONAL FACTORS IN SELECTING INSTRUCTIONAL TECHNIQUES

Techniques *	Decisional Factors		
	Sensory Appeal	Relevant Learning Processes	Practical Advantages
Lecture	Sound, sight	Information, comprehension	Handle large groups. Fast way to cover large amount of material.
Group Discussion	Sound, sight	Information, synthesis analysis, evaluation	Involves students in decision-making.
Student Reports	Sound, sight, touch	Information, comprehension	Involves students.
Field Trips	Sound, sight, touch, smell, taste	Information, analysis, comprehension, synthesis, application, evaluation	Practical experience with real thing.
On-the-job Training	Sound, sight, touch, smell, taste	Information, analysis, comprehension, synthesis, application, evaluation	Practical experience with real thing.
Team Training	Sound, sight, touch, smell	Information, synthesis, comprehension	Allows for greater specialization and flexibility. Maximum efficiency.
Programmed Learning	Sound, sight, touch	Information, application, analysis, synthesis, evaluation, comprehension	Learner can proceed at his own pace. Immediate reinforcement.
Demonstration	Sight, sound, touch, smell	Information, analysis, evaluation, comprehension	See how to perform a given task.

* Additional techniques which may be developed are role-playing, buzz sessions, panel discussions, guest speakers, group leadership, debates, problem-solving, drills, question and answer periods, resource units, and brainstorming.

Source: William Reynolds, *A Research Model for Curriculum Development in Vocational/Technical Education* (Springfield, Illinois: Illinois Division of Vocational & Technical Education, 1970), pp. 40-41.

FIGURE 9-8

The techniques which are applicable to office or distributive education teacher-coordinators are discussed in Chapters 5, 7, 8, 10, and 11. Additional techniques will be presented in the latter part of this chapter.

DECISIONAL FACTORS IN SELECTING INSTRUCTIONAL MEDIA

Media *	Decisional Factors		
	Sensory Appeal	Relevant Learning Processes	Practical Advantages
Educational Television	Sight, sound	Information, comprehension	Dramatization. Enables teaching of values, attitudes and concepts.
Mock-ups	Sight, sound, touch, smell	Application, information, analysis, synthesis, comprehension	Spatial relations. Enables the study of dimensions.
Slides	Sight, sound	Information, comprehension	Regulates teaching speed.
Tapes	Sound	Information, comprehension, analysis, synthesis, evaluation	Individualized instruction. Can utilize human resources.
Wall Charts	Sight	Information, comprehension	Relationships seen.
Transparencies	Sight, sound	Information, comprehension, analysis, synthesis	Relationships seen. A self-teaching device.
Animated	Sight, sound	Information, comprehension, analysis, synthesis, evaluation	Self-teaching device.
Concept and Skill Trainers	Sight, sound, touch, smell	Information, comprehension, application, analysis, synthesis, evaluation	Self-teaching device.

* Additional techniques which may be developed are simulators, chalkboard, bulletin board, printed materials, computer-assisted instruction, computer games, single concept films, video tapes and teaching machines.

Source: William Reynolds, *A Research Model for Curriculum Development in Vocational/Technical Educational* (Springfield, Illinois: Illinois Division of Vocational & Technical Education, 1970), p. 42.

FIGURE 9-9

Figure 9-9 illustrates the decisional factors in selecting instructional media.

The effectiveness of various types of instructional media in achieving selected learning objectives has been carefully studied and researched. Even though the findings are not conclusive, Figure 9-10 is deserving of special attention.

Learning Objectives

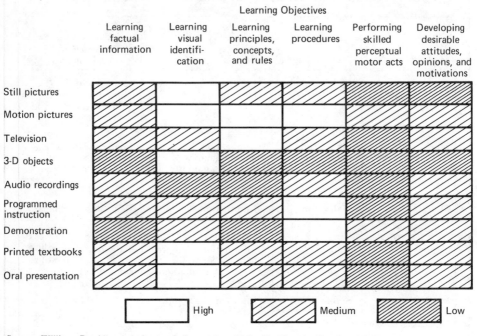

	Learning factual information	Learning visual identification	Learning principles, concepts, and rules	Learning procedures	Performing skilled perceptual motor acts	Developing desirable attitudes, opinions, and motivations

Still pictures
Motion pictures
Television
3-D objects
Audio recordings
Programmed instruction
Demonstration
Printed textbooks
Oral presentation

☐ High   ▨ Medium   ▨ Low

Source: William B. Allen, *Audiovisual Instruction,* Vol. 12, No. 1 (January, 1967), p. 28.

FIGURE 9-10

The selection of the technique and media should be considered concurrently in developing instruction. Three factors which must be considered in the decision-making process are characteristics of the learners, nature of the information to be presented, and principles of learning processes.

Determining Whether to Use Large Group, Small Group, or Individual Instruction. Figures 9-6 and 9-7 provide a sound basis for determining what should be taught on a large group, small group, or an individual instruction basis. The National Education Association, in their publication *Choosing Techniques for Teaching and Learning*, provides the following principles to guide the selection of teaching techniques:

1. If a student is involved in choosing the techniques, he will be more accepting of the resulting situation.
2. If the learning situation is a part of real life or seems real to the student, he will perceive the relevance and be more eager to learn.
3. If a student is participating, mentally as well as physically, his interest will be greater and achievement more rapid.
4. If there is ego involvement or *psychological ownership* in the learning situation (that is, the student has a personal interest in the success of the technique), motivation and learning are increased.
5. If the chosen techniques help a student to experience success, his self-esteem and motivation will be enhanced.
6. If a student finds pleasure in the learning situation, he is more likely to continue learning.
7. If a student develops skills for independent learning, he can continue to learn after his formal schooling is finished.
8. If a student sees usefulness in his learning activities, motivation will be increased.
9. If a student develops positive attitudes toward learning, he will be more likely to continue learning independently.[17]

Since teachers usually do not tutor one student at a time, they must find ways to work with groups. However, groups do not learn; *only individuals can learn*, although what and how each individual learns is conditioned by his group membership.

What we really mean when we speak of teaching a group is that we teach *individuals* within a group. What can individuals do in a group that is larger than 15 or 20? They can: watch or observe, listen, meditate, play certain games, read, write, vote, imagine, and participate in discussions.

Large groups can also divide themselves into smaller groups or teams. What can individuals do within a small

---

[17] Hazel Spitze, *Choosing Techniques for Teaching and Learning* (Washington: National Education Association, 1970), pp. 2-6.

group, a committee of two to five or a class of fifteen or less? They can do all of the things they could do in a large group, plus these additional ones: be more active participants in discussions of various kinds; lead discussion; plan; help create group designs; dramatize; practice in laboratory; experiment; demonstrate; carry out action projects; play additional types of games; and serve as recorders, summarizers, and evaluators.

Individuals working apart from the rest of the class can do much of the aforementioned, plus the following: do home projects and other individual projects and laboratory work, keep a diary and do other creative writing, interview and be interviewed, and pursue programmed instruction.

From the above admittedly partial list of what individuals can do to learn under varying conditions of group membership, we can conclude the following in regard to teaching techniques for classrooms:

> Fewer techniques are suitable for large groups than for small ones.
>
> Large group techniques do not usually permit active involvement of individual learners.
>
> If large group techniques are used, very large groups (50-100 or more) may be more economical than those of moderate size. Team teaching may increase flexibility in grouping.
>
> Large groups can be used as an audience to share the work of smaller groups and to increase feelings of unity.
>
> If we can accept that students do not all have to do the same thing at the same time in the same way in a large group (and the principle of individual differences surely dictates this as reasonable), then large classes can use small group and individual techniques much of the time by dividing into frequently changing committees, teams, or cells for various purposes.

Conduct the Instruction. The teacher-coordinator, in conducting the instruction, carefully considers: the students; the information gathered during the formulation of desired learning outcomes; and the decisions made during the selection, development, and preparation of teaching techniques and media. Figure 8-10 on page 365 illustrates a procedure for implementing instruction with steps for preparing the learner, presentation of material, application by the student, and follow-up.

Administer and Analyze Student Performance Tests. Cooperative plan teacher-coordinators have an opportunity to administer and analyze one type of student performance test that other office or distributive education teachers don't have. Student performance on a real life job situation is the ideal technique for evaluation.

The teacher-coordinator can observe the student on the job, discuss his performance with his training sponsor, or ask the student to describe, through oral or written means, answers to key questions.

Attitudes particularly can best be analyzed and evaluated through tests which permit a student to demonstrate overt behavior. Many of the key competencies in the field of business are not effectively measured with pencil and paper examinations.

Evaluation

Post-test or criterion examinations are designed to determine how well students perform. The concern of the instructor is in comparing each student's performance against pre-determined criteria. This principle determines how the performance tests are constructed. To accomplish this, test items are required that measure how well the student can perform in terms of behaviorally defined objectives. Student success is a primary goal.

Tests, which are used throughout the instructional program, are designed for: measuring competence of the student in relation to specific learning tasks; measuring the degree to which the learner has competencies necessary for mastering additional learning tasks; diagnosing the progress of the student so as to best accommodate the individual learner; assessing the progress of the student in order to make changes that will enable him to perform in the expected way; and, pointing out the deficiences in the instructional program.

If the comparison of student performance with instructional objectives is positive, the typical classroom teacher may feel satisfied. The regular classroom teacher has to wait for results from immediate post-exit and long-range follow-up studies to truly evaluate the effectiveness of his instruction. The immediate post-exit process takes place from one to two months after a student has completed his course of study. The primary purpose of the post-exit follow-up is to identify strengths and weaknesses of the program and to provide immediate feedback for use in defining new or modified curriculum objectives. The long-range follow-up, conducted on a continuing basis beginning several months after the student has completed a course of study, is necessary to provide up-to-date statistical data.

The teacher-coordinator of cooperative training can obtain immediate feedback, possibly even on a day-to-day basis if desired. Through the use of a carefully designed training plan and a properly prepared rating sheet, the teacher-coordinator can make refinements in the instructional system at the earliest possible date. Effective instructions should provide for the development of competencies commensurate with their potential, basic educational skills, abilities for functioning adequately in the social system, realistic self concepts, and decision-making skills required for implementing career strategies. Evaluation of the instruction is done by utilizing combined measurement data from all components of the instructional system.

Job-Oriented Instructional Techniques

The individualized instruction techniques which are presented in this chapter are not totally reserved for cooperative plan teacher-coordinators. Nor are these the only methods that should be used with cooperative office or distributive education students. Numerous techniques for teaching large and small groups of students are presented in Chapters 5, 7, 8, 10, and 11.

Job Study Guides. Job study guides of various types have been used extensively by teacher-coordinators as a technique for providing specific job learnings. Materials centers, departments of education, and individual business firms, are excellent sources of job study guides. Increasingly, job study guides are being set up in a programmed learning format. A distributive education student employed in a shoe store can benefit from studying the University of Texas *Shoe Manual,* while an office education student employed in a bank can profit from the learning activities provided in the University of Minnesota *Bank Officer Worker* job study guide.

The proper use of job study guides can provide maturation for student-trainees, both in school and in the on-the-job laboratory. However, the extent to which the following benefits are realized greatly depends on the techniques employed by the teacher-coordinator in using the job study guide method. The material learned if applicable to the student's on-the-job learning experiences frequently leads to favorable recognition by the employing officials, it enables the training sponsor to give assistance and encouragement in training the student, students enjoy working alone and are challenged by independent study, and the student sees what he is accomplishing and how it relates to his career goal.

The job study guide is just one of the methods which can be used for individualizing instruction. The student must be able to see clearly how the job study guide information is related to his occupational objective. Student time devoted to working on study guides must be carefully planned. Merely handing a student a job study guide to work on from cover-to-cover is not an effective approach to independent study.

Job Manuals and Fact Sheets. Teacher-coordinators use job manuals or fact sheets to assist student-trainees in learning about their training stations and the tasks performed. The information secured by the student-trainees in providing data required is, in effect, an orientation to business policy, procedures, organization, and practices, all of which every employee should know about the firm.

Job fact sheets or pages from a job manual are assigned to students at the appropriate time. The assignments are most meaningful when material learned in school can be related to on-the-job learning experiences. The completed assignments are filed in a notebook with other materials during the year to form a comprehensive guide for use by students in their chosen career fields.

Job manuals and fact sheets typically require that the students secure such information as facts about a business, rules and policies, duties performed, layout of training station, systems followed by business services, job analysis, and technical terms. Teacher-coordinators either develop their own job manuals or fact sheets by modifying those secured from other coordinators or use commercially prepared materials. Students tend to take a great deal of pride in a job manual when they can see that the work performed will help in their careers. If students feel that the teacher is merely giving busy work and can't see how the assignments are helping, the job manual will be an ineffective teaching method.

Job Reports. Teacher-coordinators use various types of forms for gathering data about student training job activities. Information, such as days absent, reasons for absence, hours worked per day, wages received, kinds of activities performed, new experiences, mistakes made, and improvements and progress made, provide an excellent basis for individual conferences with students. These conferences are particularly important for designing, assigning, and evaluating individualized job-related instruction.

Teacher-coordinators find it beneficial for all class members to periodically ask each student to report on his training duties and progress. These reporting sessions frequently turn into incident or case-problem-solving learning situations.

The information gleaned from both individual student and classroom discussion can be used by the teacher-coordinator to enrich large group, small group, and individual instruction. When this is done, student-trainees feel a sense of importance, and can better see the progress made toward career goals.

Other Techniques. Individual, small group, and chapter activities suggested by youth organizations have been carefully designed to assist students in developing needed competencies. Selected learning activities and projects contained in textbooks, workbooks, and manuals can be effectively used to achieve similar results. Increasingly, publishers are preparing instructional materials which can be used as self-contained units of instruction.

Magazines, films, filmstrips, books, and programmed instructions, which have been prepared by individual firms or trade associations, are used extensively for individualizing instruction. The teacher-coordinator, with the help of businessmen, can usually find training materials regarding any business activity which a student would need to perform.

ON-THE-JOB LABORATORY INSTRUCTION

John Smith, a junior at West High School, has completed two years of the three-year distributive education curriculum. He applies and is accepted for the cooperative laboratory phase of the distributive education program. John wants to become a manager of a supermarket, and plans to enroll in a post-secondary food marketing program following graduation from high school. During the first week in February, John complains to his teacher-coordinator that he has not learned anything new for the past three months. Is John's complaint justified? How could such a problem develop? What can the teacher-coordinator do to correct the situation?

This incident highlights one of the problems which can occur if the on-the-job laboratory phase of the office or distributive education instructional program is not carefully planned and implemented. Good on-the-job instruction is greatly dependent upon the ability of the teacher-coordinator to enlist the support, cooperation, and talent of employers and training sponsors.

It is easy for a teacher-coordinator to blame an employer or training sponsor for not providing effective on-the-job instruction. However, all too frequently the employers and training sponsors are not fully aware of their duties and responsibilities.

A group of experienced office and distributive education teacher-coordinators, enrolled in a graduate coordination techniques class, conducted interviews with the employers and training sponsors of their students to determine their understanding of the following responsibilities and conditions regarding training stations:

1. That the cooperative vocational education plan is a training program, not a school employment agency.
2. That the employer is considered a partner in the training and should assist the school by providing planned experiences and on-the-job instruction.
3. That a training station will provide, on the average, at least 15 hours of employment a week throughout the school year.
4. That a monetary wage will be paid all beginning trainees and that this amount should be increased proportionately with their productivity.
5. That candidates for part-time employment have vocational counseling at the school during which they have determined tentative career objectives.
6. That the trainee is enrolled in special classes at the school where he is receiving instruction directly related to his on-the-job activities and occupational objective.
7. That the trainee should have opportunities to move from one specific job activity to another in order to participate in various experiences leading to his occupational goal.
8. That the student-trainee should be placed in the same employment status as that of other part-time employees in matters of social security, insurance, vacations, and labor laws.
9. That the teacher-coordinator will visit the student-trainee, observe his job performance, suggest to the training sponsor some good methods of on-the-job training, and determine the job activities to which classroom instruction should be related.
10. That periodic ratings based on the job performance of the trainee will be made by the employer and/or training sponsor and reported to the coordinator.

The coordinators were amazed at how little the employers and training sponsors remembered of what the coordinators thought they had explained to them.

This part of the chapter will highlight five important aspects of the job of the teacher-coordinator in planning and implementing on-the-job laboratory instruction: selecting a training station, selling the employer on the training plan concept, launching the training plan, evaluating student performance, and training sponsor development.

Criteria for Selecting Training Stations

Training stations should be selected on the basis of their educational value to students and must be capable of providing the students with progressive on-the-job learning experiences which will contribute significantly to the development of their occupational competencies.

The time that is devoted to the careful selection of training stations will pay rich dividends. Employers and training sponsors are in fact the "administrators" and "faculty members" of the on-the-job laboratory phase of the cooperative program. They must be properly prepared for their roles, just as educational administrators and teachers are prepared for theirs.

The following criteria and factors, to be considered carefully in the selection of training stations, are listed in the guide from the National Conference on Cooperative Vocational Education: [18]

1. Training stations should have the potential to provide training for occupations that are challenging and worthy of the student's learning time and efforts.
   a. Compatibility of the occupations with the capabilities and the career interests of the student so that the job will be interesting and challenging.
   b. Sufficient learning content to be worthy of the time and effort to be expended in learning the occupation.
   c. "Susceptible to promotion and advancement."
   d. Relationships to existing and future career opportunities.

2. The policies and practices of the potential training stations should be such that the community will approve of

---

[18] National Conference on Cooperative Vocational Education, *op. cit.*, p. 87.

their participation in the program. The community will be critical if the participating firms do not have a good reputation.

  a. Wage scales in relation to those paid for similar occupations in the community.
  b. Relationships with labor groups and other employers, and with customers and clients.
  c. Work standards and efficiency of operation.
  d. Hiring, promotion, and dismissal practices.
  e. Working conditions and employer concern for well-being of employees.
  f. Credit record and financial stability.
  g. Support of community activities and welfare.

3. The management and the employees in potential training stations should be committed to the training objective and be willing to plan appropriate training and instruction for students.

  a. Employment of personnel responsible for planning and conducting training.
  b. Type and amount of training given to regular employees.
  c. Quality of facilities for training.
  d. Willingness of employer to participate in planning a training program for student(s) and agree to a written training agreement.
  e. Expertise of employees in performing their occupations.

4. The on-the-job training content should be matched to the capabilities and interests of students. A student is placed in a training station because of his interest in what is to be taught and because of the potential it offers for his growth.

  a. Amount of training required to perform the occupation.
  b. Opportunities for increasing responsibilities and upward occupational mobility.
  c. Applicability of the training content for future employment.
  d. Ability of the firm or organization to provide adequate instruction.
  e. Ability of the school to provide the necessary related instruction.

f. Attitude of on-the-job instructors (training sponsors) toward the training content.

5. It is essential that the training stations provide training sponsors who are competent in their occupations, who are able and willing to train students and who serve as worthy models for students to emulate.
   a. Technical competence in the occupation to be taught.
   b. Interest and attitude toward training and students.
   b. Ethics and habits which students can emulate.
   d. Ability and willingness to allot sufficient time and effort to training.
   e. Willingness to work with the coordinator in planning on-the-job learning experiences and related classroom instruction, and in evaluating student progress.
   f. Ability to adapt job instruction to the learning style and capabilities of the student.
   g. Competence in human relations and sensitiveness to student needs for recognition, guidance and direction.

6. The training stations should furnish work environments which are conducive to good health, to safety, and to the development of job satisfaction in students.
   a. Convenience of location with respect to students' being able to get there from school and home safely, and within a reasonable period of time.
   b. Healthful and safe working conditions.
   c. Hours of work which allow the student sufficient time to keep up with his school work, participate in some recreation, and get adequate rest.
   d. Adequate equipment and facilities to practice the occupation for which training is planned.
   e. Compliance with local, state, and Federal labor regulations regarding wages, hours, working conditions, insurance, and hazardous occupations.

Care must be exercised so that the teacher-coordinator does not become so anxious to "place" his students that he forgets to carefully qualify the training station. All too frequently, after a brief explanation of the program by the teacher-coordinator, the employer says, "I know all about these programs. I have had many students working for me during the past twenty years. You send me a couple of students and I'll take one."

Techniques for Selecting
a Training Station and
Selling the Training Plan Concept

Successful teacher-coordinators have developed a number of techniques for selecting a training station. Whenever possible, begin the selection process well in advance of the time when students are to be placed.

The first contact with the personnel manager of a potential training station is frequently a brief visit. However, many coordinators prefer to make an appointment with an employer through an advisory committee member or other contact person. The major purpose of the first visit should be to qualify the employer, not to sell the program. If an appointment has been made, arrive early, when appropriate, to carefully observe the business in operation and talk informally with employees. The meeting with the *owner* or *manager* of the firm should be centered on his business and his concepts for training personnel. Show interest in his business and methods, but do not be tempted to sell the program. Establish his confidence, so that on the next visit he will be willing to accept the cooperative plan. Make complete mental notes of the brief visit for later use in the presentation of the program. Before terminating the first visit, many coordinators prefer to leave a brochure explaining their program and make an appointment for a second visit.

The second contact with the employer who is considered a good prospect should take the form of a carefully planned presentation. Key points which the employer has mentioned should be capitalized upon in opening discussion and in making the presentation. Tailor the presentation to his business. Descriptive brochures or fact sheets should be used when appropriate. Various types of visual aids, such as pictures and documents endorsing the plan, can add to the effectiveness of the presentation if used properly. The following advantages of the cooperative distributive education or office education plan for the employer must be carefully explained:

1. The program is a source of loyal, competent employees.

2. The backing of the school insures that the employer will have the student-trainee for the entire school year, providing an opportunity to develop skills in greater depth.
3. Participating businesses make a civic contribution by helping the school and the student-trainee.
4. Employers have the assistance of the school and the coordinator in training a worker.
5. Workers are prepared for the entire industry, as well as for an individual business.
6. Workers have a career interest rather than just an interest in a part-time job.

The employer must also understand the benefits of a training plan for both himself and a student-trainee:

1. Employer Benefits: By rotating students, they become more knowledgeable about the many facets of business, in turn making more valuable employees. A method of rotation tends to sustain student interest and, the higher the interest level, the more the student will learn. A system of rotation tends to reduce employee turnover because the student is more likely to find stimulation in the business and will stay on the job longer.
2. Student Benefits: The more experience obtained by the student, the more he will learn and develop marketable skills. By experiencing many positions within a business the student will find what type of tasks he enjoys and from which he receives satisfaction. The student will have the opportunity to learn more about himself and will have a broader base from which to intelligently select a career. The student will retain his interest level at a high plane knowing he will receive numerous experiences.

A discussion-type atmosphere should be maintained during this visit. The coordinator must be careful not to do all the talking; employer comments and reactions should be secured whenever possible. Hopefully, the employer will see how plans for developing both his business and his personnel can be enhanced through participation in an office or distributive education program. The teacher-coordinator should be able to fully ascertain the attitude of the employer toward the goals and objectives of the program being presented. Willingness of the employer to give his support to the program may be indicated in a number of different ways. The teacher-coordinator may ask and make note of the training the employer feels his firm can give. Possibly the employer will just say, "I want to meet with my staff to decide how many students we want to train and have them prepare a list of the on-the-job experiences the students will receive." The teacher-coordinator should try to get the employer to at least indicate the broad types of experiences which he feels a student would receive with his firm.

Hopefully, at the end of the second or third visit, the teacher-coordinator will have the unqualified support of the employer. However, either the coordinator or the employer may desire additional dialogue before a final decision is made. Whether the teacher-coordinator has specific students in mind for the employer, or is just selecting a training station for use at a later date, may well be a determining factor.

The key role and qualifications of the training sponsor are constantly emphasized during the discussion with the employer. In smaller firms the employer may also serve as the training sponsor.

Assume the employer is willing to train a student, and the teacher-coordinator had just one student with an appropriate career objective. Then the training station selection process is almost completed. The teacher-coordinator will want to make sure that the employer has selected a training sponsor who meets the following criteria:

1. Technical competence in the occupation to be taught.

2. Ability to organize and conduct job instruction training.

3. Worthy personal traits and work habits which the student can emulate.

4. Ability to communicate and relate to superiors, co-workers, and subordinates.

5. Interest and attitude toward training and type of student who will be enrolled.

6. Specific skills or attitudes required in working with students having special needs (e.g., slow learner, or student who lacks confidence).

7. Willingness to work with school coordinator in planning instruction and evaluating student progress.[19]

A meeting with the teacher-coordinator and prospective training sponsor should be arranged by the employer. The teacher-coordinator should encourage the employer to briefly explain to the training sponsor the program and basic procedure that will be followed by the firm. Following the brief employer presentation, the coordinator will want to ask the training sponsor to indicate some possible on-the-job training experiences which he feels he would be able to give a qualified student-trainee.

These identified training experiences are carefully recorded by the teacher-coordinator for use in launching a training plan for the student-trainee.

The teacher-coordinator will want to make the training sponsor feel that he will be assuming a key role in the training program, and that he will have the assistance and support of both himself and the employer. The dialogue between the employer, training sponsor, and teacher-coordinator will set the stage for implementing an effective office or distributive education cooperative training program.

After this point has been reached, the teacher-coordinator is satisfied that a potentially sound training station has been selected that can assist his student in achieving his occupational objective. He is now ready to prepare the student for his job interview.

Launching the Training Plan

Once the student-trainee has been selected by the employer and training sponsor, the second of the five-stage procedure for launching a training plan can be implemented.

Stage one was accomplished when the employer and training sponsor indicated the broad areas of on-the-job experiences that they would be able to provide for a qualified student-trainee.

---

[19] *A Guide for Cooperative Vocational Education, op. cit.,* pp. 66-67.

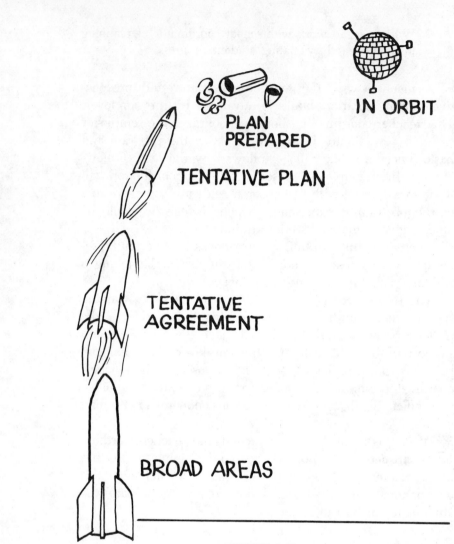

IN ORBIT

PLAN
PREPARED

TENTATIVE PLAN

TENTATIVE
AGREEMENT

BROAD AREAS

FIGURE 9-11

The meeting with the selected student-trainee, training sponsor, teacher-coordinator, and possibly the employer, should be held at the earliest possible date to work out a tentative agreement on the training the student will receive. The training sponsor relates for the second time, with some elaboration, what training will be given to the student. The teacher-coordinator can help stimulate the thinking of the training sponsor, but he must be careful not to dominate the discussion. Hopefully, the teacher-coordinator will have a sound basic idea of the experiences which a student with a career objective in a given field should receive. He may want to study previous training plans, but should not use them to tell the sponsor what training he should be giving. Also, student ideas and suggestions may be quite helpful in arriving at the tentative agreement.

The third stage of launching a training plan can be accomplished after the sponsor has worked with the student for a short period of time. Notes taken by the teacher-coordinator are carefully organized before making an appointment with the training sponsor. The purpose of this meeting is to design a tentative training plan. Competencies that the career oriented student must develop to achieve his occupational objective should be carefully identified. Also, on-the-job learning experiences, which will enable the student to achieve these competencies, should be carefully described.

Training sponsor recommendations concerning instructional materials available to aid in developing the identified competencies, which can be used at the training station or in school, should be solicited. The training sponsor should feel that he is a partner and teaching colleague of the coordinator in designing a plan to prepare a young person for his chosen career. The student should be directly involved in this stage of the development process, after the training sponsor and the employer have reached a basic agreement.

Stage four of the training plan sequence can be most effectively implemented if the teacher-coordinator has complete notes on the competencies needed for the student to achieve his career objective (see Figure 9-4), and the on-the-job learning experiences which will be provided by the training sponsor. The training plan may be prepared in detail for the total training period. However, many coordinators prefer to prepare the plan in detail for the first three or four months, briefly outlining the on-the-job learning experiences which will be developed later in the year.

Before the training plan is typed, the training sponsor should give his final approval. Copies of the training plan are made for the employer, training sponsor, student, parents, and teacher-coordinator. A portion of a training plan is shown in Figure 9-12.

TRAINING PLAN FORMAT

Student-learner (name, address, phone, social security number)

Firm and Training Sponsor (name, address, phone)

Career Objective (title, description, number, USOE code number)

General Areas of Student Experience and Learning
    I Selling
    II Display
    III Etc.

Specific Areas of Student Experience and Learning
    I Selling
        A. Suggestive and related selling
        B. Selling high fashion merchandise
        C. Etc.

SPECIFIC AREAS OF STUDENT EXPERIENCE AND LEARNING	TRAIN-ING STATION	SCHOOL		REFER-ENCE	TIME SCHED-ULE
		Group	Individual		
I. Selling					
A. Suggestive and related selling					
B. Selling high fashion merchandise					
C. Etc.					

FIGURE 9-12

Putting the plan into action is the key to the whole training plan concept. Can the coordinator work effectively with the training sponsor and the student to keep the plan functioning properly? The coordinator must plan his coordination calls carefully. Many successful coordinators plan calls approximately two weeks in advance. It is highly recommended that the coordinator keep an individual student coordination folder.

Evaluating Student Performance

The rating sheet which is used to evaluate student on-the-job performance should be carefully designed by the teacher-coordinator. The use of one prepared form to evaluate all students is not adequate. Each student should be evaluated on the job activities he performs in the process of developing his occupational competencies. The on-the-job learning experiences for any given period of time can be easily transcribed from the training plan to a rating sheet or an extra column added to the training plan.

The student needs to see that what he is doing in school and at his training station is relevant to his career aspirations. If he grasps this relationship, his attitude toward school and learning may be improved.

The following guidelines for evaluation of student-trainees are provided in notes and working papers from the National Conference on Cooperative Vocational Education:

> Both the school and the employer have the responsibility for evaluating the on-the-job performance of the student-trainee. In most cases, this is a joint venture between the coordinator and the training sponsor. A student should be evaluated according to the newly acquired experiences and to what level this new acquisition has been above and beyond that which he possessed before. Some considerations for evaluation are:
>
> 1. Competency acquirement and improvement as measured by the duties and tasks outlined in the training plan.
> 2. The student's ability to work with other individuals.
> 3. The student's response to supervision.
> 4. Personal development and adjustment.
> 5. Development of maturity and self-confidence.
> 6. Ability to handle the unexpected as well as the expected.
> 7. Comparing the student's performance with that of a fully trained worker or other beginning workers.
> 8. The growth rate of the student in terms of the progress he has made.
> 9. How well the student meets the expectations of the employer.
> 10. How well the student meets his own expectations and satisfactions.
> 11. The judgment of the student in making decisions.
> 12. Amount of initiative exhibited in looking for other things to be done.

13. Amount of information and help required before the student can understand and do what needs to be done.
14. Ability to grasp situations in which he has had little training or exposure.
15. Ability to solve the day-to-day problems that keep a business going.[20]

Training Sponsor Development

Increasingly, teacher-coordinators are recognizing the need for developing their training sponsors. Given below is one list of the responsibilities of a training sponsor:

1. Understand the goal of the training program.
2. Know units being studied in the classroom.
3. Know enough about the student-trainee to be able to teach him effectively.
4. Work in partnership with coordinator.
5. Give accurate information about the student-trainee to the coordinator.
6. Take time to be a teacher.
7. Provide "learning by doing" experiences.
8. Give support to the youth group.
9. Teach specific job competencies.
10. Teach business ethics, responsibility.
11. Teach policies, systems, methods of training agency.
12. Help student develop judgment and a mature outlook.[21]

Many teacher-coordinators have developed a checklist which they follow in helping the training sponsor carry out his teaching responsibilities. Listed below is a portion of the guide for training sponsor development prepared in the state of Virginia:

1. Develop a plan to follow in training the sponsor.
2. Make a training timetable for training the sponsor.
3. Set an appropriate place for training sessions with the sponsor.

---

[20] National Conference on Cooperative Vocational Education, *op. cit.*, p. 96.
[21] "Sponsor Development Program," from a report by the Richmond Professional Institute, Richmond, Virginia, 1956.

4. Get sponsor into adult classes on "How to Train" and "How to Supervise."
5. Develop a "clinic" for sponsors.
6. Keep the sponsor's training needs in mind during all co-ordination activities.
7. Invite the sponsor to club activities early in the year.
8. Develop and make available to sponsors needed materials:
   a. Unit sequence.
   b. Reports and records.
9. Review unit content throughout the year.
10. Develop projects in relation to job and class discussions.
11. Give personal data on the student-trainee with discretion.
12. Interpret school policies:
    a. Calendar (vacations, schedules, events).
    b. Regulations.
13. Suggest experiences student is ready for in the training agency:
    a. Give student an opportunity to learn by doing.
    b. Find ways for student to develop on the job assigned.
14. Suggest evidences of progress to look for in student's performance.
15. Suggest additional training directed towards promotional opportunities.[22]

SUMMARY

Teacher-coordinators of cooperative and office and distributive education programs are challenged to secure effective on-the-job learning experiences for their students. An individual who is able to identify and select quality training stations, sell the employer and training sponsor on the need for providing progressive on-the-job learning experiences, and design and implement a training plan is well on his way to becoming an excellent teacher-coordinator.

The training plan is the heart of the laboratory instruction phase of the cooperative plan in office or distributive education. Without it, the laboratory phase of the cooperative plan is, at best, an incidental or accidental learning

---

[22] *Ibid.*

experience. Students, employers, training sponsors, parents, and school officials can easily become critical of such an educational plan.

SELECTED BIBLIOGRAPHY

American Vocational Journal (May, 1969). Issue devoted to cooperative vocational education.

Banathy, Bela H. *Instructional Systems.* Palo Alto, Calif.: Fearon Publishers, 1968.

Bennet, Charles Alpheus. *History of Manual and Industrial Education Up to 1870.* Peoria, Illinois: Manual Arts Press, 1926.

Dewey, John. *Experience and Education.* New York: Macmillan Co., 1939.

Educational Policies Commission. *Education for All American Youth.* Washington: National Education Association and American Association of School Administrators, 1944.

A Guide for Cooperative Vocational Education. Minneapolis, Minnesota: University of Minnesota, Division of Vocational and Technical Education, 1969.

Harris, E. Edward. *Employer Preferences and Teacher-Coordinator Practices in Distributive Education.* New York: Gregg Division, McGraw-Hill Book Co., Inc., 1971.

——————. *Requirements for Office and Distributive Education Teacher-Coordinators,* Monograph 115. Cincinnati: South-Western Publishing Co., 1967.

——————, and Peter Johnson. *An Articulated Guide for Cooperative Career Education.* Springfield, Illinois: Division of Vocational and Technical Education, 1971.

Haskyn, F. P. "Work Experience: Basic Issues." *Curriculum Journal* (January, 1943).

Haines, Peter G. (ed.). *Readings in Distributive Education: The Project Plan of Instruction and Related Teacher Education.* East Lansing, Michigan: Michigan State University, Department of Secondary Education and Curriculum, 1969.

Huffman, Harry. *Guidelines in Cooperative Education.* Columbus, Ohio: The Center for Vocational and Technical Education, Ohio State University, 1967.

_____. *A Taxonomy of Office Activities for Business and Office Education.* Columbus, Ohio: The Center for Vocational and Technical Education, Ohio State University, 1968.

Reynolds, William. *A Research Model for Curriculum Development in Vocational/Technical Education.* Springfield, Illinois: Illinois Division of Vocational and Technical Education, 1970.

Levendowski, Jerry. *Cooperative Distributive and Office Education Programs.* Los Angeles, Calif.: University of California, Division of Vocational Education, 1969.

Mager, Robert F. *Developing Attitudes Toward Learning.* Palo Alto, Calif.: Fearon Publishers, 1968.

_____. *Goal Analysis.* Belmont, Calif.: Fearon Publishers, 1972.

_____. *Preparing Instructional Objectives.* Palo Alto, Calif.: Fearon Publishers, 1962.

_____, and Kenneth M. Beach, Jr. *Developing Vocational Instruction.* Palo Alto, Calif.: Fearon Publishers, 1967.

Mason, Ralph E., and Peter G. Haines. *Cooperative Occupational Education and Work Experience in the Curriculum.* Danville, Illinois: Interstate Printers and Publishers, 1965.

National Conference on Cooperative Vocational Education. *Implications of the 1968 Amendments,* notes and working papers. Minneapolis, Minnesota: University of Minnesota, 1969.

Richmond Professional Institute. "Sponsor Development Program." A report on training sponsor development, Richmond, Virginia, 1956.

Spitze, Hazel P. *Choosing Techniques for Teaching and Learning.* Washington: National Education Association, 1970.

U.S. Department of Health, Education, and Welfare, Office of Education. *Vocational Instructional Materials for Distributive Education Available from Federal Agencies.* Washington: U.S. Government Printing Office, 1971.

_____. *Vocational Instructional Materials for Office Occupations Available from Federal Agencies.* Washington: U.S. Government Printing Office, 1971.

—————, and U.S. Department of Labor, Manpower Administration. *Vocational Education and Occupations.* Washington: U.S. Government Printing Office, 1969.

Wallace, Harold R. *Review and Synthesis of Research in Cooperative Vocational Education.* Columbus, Ohio: Center for Vocational and Technical Education, Ohio State University, 1970.

Chapter 10

"IN-SCHOOL" LABORATORY INSTRUCTIONAL PLANS

One of the highest priorities in education today is individualized instruction to meet the needs of each student. Segregation of students by ability level has been tried, but even in such segregated groups there is much heterogeneity. Furthermore, students in segregated groups do not become acquainted with those outside their groups, and an important part of education for business is missed. Instruction can be individualized in heterogeneous classes if teachers reject the idea that all students in a class must do the same thing in the same way at the same time.

Educators in distributive and office education responded quickly to the opportunity and challenge presented by the passage of the Vocational Education Act of 1963 and the Vocational Education Amendments of 1968. Various types of programs were designed to prepare career oriented students for entry and advancement in the occupational field of their choice. While the goals of the career oriented programs are basically the same, different strategies and patterns for achieving the desired results have emerged.

BASIC PRINCIPLES AND CONCEPTS

Office education personnel developed two major strategies for individualizing instruction, the "block time" and the "intensified laboratory" approaches. Distributive education personnel have devoted their efforts to a strategy that is labeled the project plan. All three of the major instructional plans have been designed to provide an effective system for individualizing instruction.

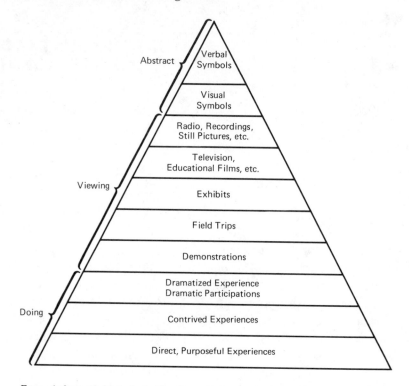

From *Audiovisual Methods in Teaching*, third edition by Edgar Dale. Copyright © 1946, 1954, 1969, by Holt, Rinehart and Winston, Inc. Adapted and reprinted by permission of Holt, Rinehart and Winston, Inc.

FIGURE 10-1

To implement each of the instructional plans, a number of teaching techniques are utilized which may be readily classified into the categories developed by Dale and shown in Figure 10-1. A significant proportion of the techniques used are in the contrived and dramatized experiences categories. The following are some methods which have merit: task simulation, business games, learning packages (UNIPAC's, LAP's, etc.), programmed instruction, audio-tutorial instruction, computer-assisted instruction, field interviews, field trips, field observations, role-playing, demonstrations, in-basket exercises, case problems, incident problems, personal conferences, youth organization activities, supervised study, learning by inquiry, and short-term directed occupational experiences.

Block-Time—Simulation Plan

Michigan State University developed the vocational office block-time—simulation program under a grant from the U.S. Office of Education. The following definition is included in Volume 1 of a comprehensive six-volume report on the block-time program:

> The block-time—simulation instructional system is a unique approach to teaching office education. The program uses a two- or three-period block of time to provide instruction that builds advanced skills, integrates realistic practice through projects in a simulated office environment, and allows for flexibility to meet individual student learning needs.[1]

Figures 10-2 and 10-3 illustrate the relationship between the various elements of the simulated office system and the total program of instruction and teaching methods utilized. The following basic concepts pertaining to the system for simulating office instruction were presented by Poland at the 1969 American Vocational Association Convention:

> Office simulation instruction can be a unique method and strategy of teaching the office skills and knowledges under simulated office conditions. A block of time can be utilized to effect individualized and group instruction, vocational guidance, task simulation, and job simulation. The office simulation can take the place of the traditional single-period approach to teaching the office skill courses usually offered during the senior year of high school. Once the longer time unit is in effect, it is possible to provide more intensive instruction in office skills. The educational challenge has been met by providing an instructional device, called simulation, which fits the office block-time units and allows for continued flexibility in student activities and individualized instruction.

---

[1] *Block-Time—Simulation: Individualized Office Instructional System* (East Lansing, Michigan: Michigan State University, Department of Secondary Education and Curriculum, 1969), p. 14.

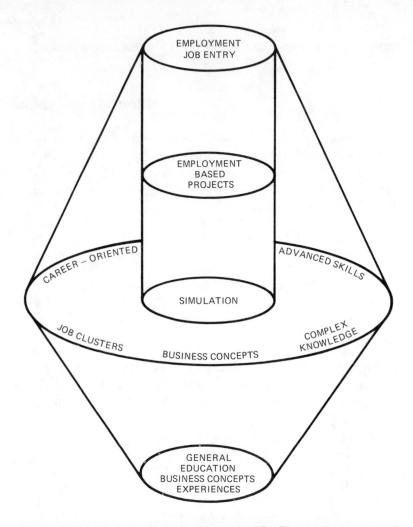

EMPLOYMENT
JOB ENTRY

EMPLOYMENT
BASED
PROJECTS

CAREER – ORIENTED

ADVANCED SKILLS

SIMULATION

JOB CLUSTERS

COMPLEX
KNOWLEDGE

BUSINESS CONCEPTS

GENERAL
EDUCATION
BUSINESS CONCEPTS
EXPERIENCES

Source: Robert Poland, "An Instructional System for Office Education," paper presented at the American Vocational Association Convention, Boston, Massachusetts, December, 1969.

FIGURE 10-2

In order to be employable in business, students must have an awareness of how they will be expected to perform in the world of work. If they are taught to type, use business machines, and are acquainted with business terminology, but have not knowledge of how to coordinate these skills, they have difficulty relating school-taught skills to on-the-job demands. A simulated environment enables students to use their knowledge and mechanical skills through application in a work situation closely resembling that which they will find in employment.

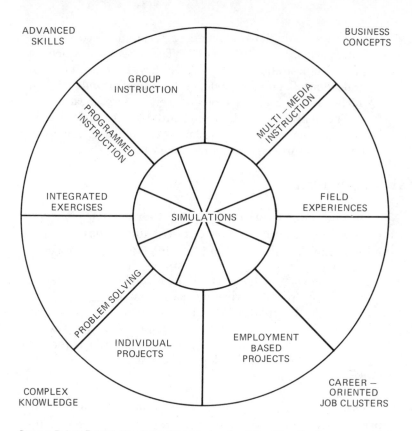

Outer ring labels (clockwise from top-left):
ADVANCED SKILLS — BUSINESS CONCEPTS — CAREER-ORIENTED JOB CLUSTERS — COMPLEX KNOWLEDGE

Ring segments:
GROUP INSTRUCTION
PROGRAMMED INSTRUCTION
MULTI-MEDIA INSTRUCTION
INTEGRATED EXERCISES
FIELD EXPERIENCES
SIMULATIONS
PROBLEM SOLVING
INDIVIDUAL PROJECTS
EMPLOYMENT BASED PROJECTS

Source: Robert Poland, "An Instructional System for Office Education," paper presented at the American Vocational Association Convention, Boston, Massachusetts, December, 1969.

FIGURE 10-3

The concept of simulation is based on the psychological premise that elements in two situations will provide for links in action by the individual who experiences both situations. Knowledges, skills, and attitudes which are encountered and learned in one situation, will have a tendency to reassert themselves whenever enough elements of the learning situation occur again. When transfer of training is the basis on which learning is to be constructed, as it is in the simulation approach, then the teacher tries to create learning situations in which the student will be expected to perform the learned skills. Thus, meaningful practice contributes to greater learning. The primary strategy in the office instruction program can center on simulation as the formal learning structure. The classroom becomes both a model office for simulated office experiences and a laboratory for creating additional simulations. Learning occurs as students participate in simulated office situations which involve demonstration of the skills they have learned and application of formal knowledge to individualized problems which have to be solved before work moves ahead.

The skills, knowledges, and attitudes learned in simulated situations must be constantly consolidated and maintained to ensure acquisition of new skills.[2]

Intensive Laboratory Plan

The state of Indiana is one of the states which pioneered the intensive laboratory concept. Adaline Jones provides the following definition of the intensive office laboratory:

> The intensive laboratory can be identified as an organization for instruction whereby each learner in this class receives final opportunity within the school to participate in those integrated and interrelated practical work experiences and related learning which are necessary for him in order that he may develop vocational competence for his chosen office career.[3]

Both the cooperative office education plan and the intensive office laboratory plan have the same ultimate aim: that of providing those practical occupational experiences and related learnings which will enable a student to develop vocational competence for his chosen career. The cooperative education plan has had a long record of success as a method for achieving this aim—not only in the area of office education, but in any branch of vocational education. The question is, "Can the intensive office laboratory approach the cooperative plan in the effectiveness by which the ultimate aim is achieved?"

If the intensive office laboratory plan is to be comparable to the cooperative office education plan, the learning experiences must be of three kinds for each student: laboratory experiences, field experiences, and related instruction. Excluding any one of these three seriously weakens the

---

[2] Robert Poland, "An Instructional System for Office Education" (From a paper presented to the American Vocational Association Convention, Boston, December, 1969).

[3] Adaline D. Jones, "The Enigmatic Intensive Office Laboratory," *The Balance Sheet*, XLIX (April, 1968), p. 384.

quality of the vocational education provided and threatens the achievement of the ultimate aim of the intensive office laboratory program.

Dr. Jones, in discussing teaching differences between the use of the intensive office laboratory plan and regular classroom instruction, noted:

> Perhaps the basic difference lies in the approach of the teacher to the instruction to be given. For the usual class, the approach is one of group instruction where objectives· are basically the same for all members of the group and there is an attempt to cause the levels of learning of all students to approach homogeneity. Limited attention may or may not be given to individual instruction for a student so that he will be able to participate more effectively in the group instruction.

> In the intensive office laboratory, on the other hand, the approach is completely one of individual instruction, where learning objectives are particular for each learner and thus are diverse among the members of the group; a limited attention may or may not be given to group instruction on common elements if such elements emerge from a comparison of the respective learning objectives of the students and the learning levels of the various members of the laboratory class.[4]

Blackstone, in commenting on various plans for operating office education programs, said:

> One of the most underrated programs in office occupations education is simulated office occupations education, which provides office occupations education "realism" under stringent education controls. This program uses the intensive block concept to give students some of the problem-solving experiences that are typically found in an office situation. A model office laboratory may be used so that the student is educated as a "whole office worker" by performing real office assignments.

> In many ways, the simulation program offers the greatest challenge to the office occupations education teacher. Because he can control both time and complexity of experience,

---

[4] *Ibid.,* p. 344.

he can eliminate much of the routine of the office and provide the "need to knows" more effectively than in an actual office.

By use of the "in-basket technique" the teacher can control the rate and nature of the input facing each student. Both typical and exceptional situations can be presented as students are ready for them. By rotating students "through the chair," everyone has the chance to be supervisor and employee and to appreciate the demands placed upon each.[5]

Fred Cook and the staff of Wayne State University initiated a three-year curriculum demonstration project, with the cooperation of the Detroit Public Schools, called Senior Intensified Programs.[6] The purpose of the program was to demonstrate that minimal essential business skills demanded by employers for entry into today's office and distributive occupations can be taught in a specifically developed Senior Intensified Program.

It is important to note that in Michigan State University's block-time—simulated plan, "classroom" and "laboratory"

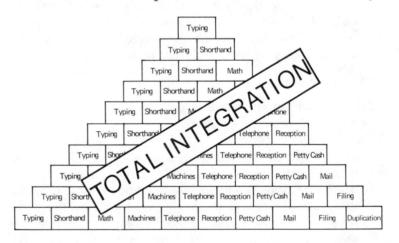

FIGURE 10-4

Source: Bill Radcliff, "Integrate—What?" paper presented at American Vocational Association Convention, Boston, Massachusetts, December, 1969.

---

[5] Bruce I. Blackstone, "VOE," *Business Education World*, L (January-February, 1970), p. 28.
[6] Frank W. Lanham and Fred S. Cook, "Preparing Students for Office and Distributive Occupations—the Intensified Approach," *The Emerging Content and Structure of Business Education*, Eighth National Business Education Yearbook (Washington: National Business Education Association, 1970), pp. 255-262.

instruction are totally integrated. Local conditions, such as student enrollments, availability of staff and facilities, and scheduling patterns, may make such an arrangement impossible. However, when feasible, all vocational programs should be planned so that "classroom" and "laboratory" teaching are effectively integrated. Blocks of learning time are important to the successful preparation of occupationally-oriented students.

Project Plan

The project plan concept in distributive education has been the topic of numerous local, state, and national meetings. Brown, in the U.S. Office of Education publication *Distributive Education in the High School,* defines the project plan as:

An organizational pattern of instruction which involves a regularly scheduled series of individually designed realistic learning activities or projects that give students an opportunity to apply theory in practice while developing competencies related to their occupational objectives.[7]

Chapter 8 presents a complete explanation of the basic, career development, and specialist job curricula in distributive education. The relationship of the project plan in the preparation of people for careers in distribution is illustrated in Figure 8-2.

Marx in discussing the similarities and differences in project and cooperative plan program designs, stated:

The goals of project and cooperative training are the same. No matter how instruction is organized, when it is identified as vocational distributive education, there are no differences in the results desired. Students are to be able to meet employment qualifications with the confidence and the competencies necessary to begin marketing and management careers. Employers are to compete to hire the graduates

---

[7] U.S. Department of Health, Education, and Welfare, Office of Education, *Distributive Education in the High School* (Washington: U.S. Printing Office, 1969), p. 11.

of distributive education classrooms. Teacher-coordinators are to fulfill their commitment by awakening the promise within each student.

Yes, the ends are the same and they evolve from beliefs basic to the achievement of the objectives of the distributive education program. Whether instruction is organized by cooperative plan or project plan, we believe that:

1. Vocational distributive education must be available when and where it can provide needed services,
2. Care must be exercised to make all learning activities vocationally significant,
3. Subject matter must be selected in relation to the level of the occupational purpose of the curriculum,
4. Enrollment must be open to all students whose potential and vocational purpose are compatible with the program of studies selected.

These are common beliefs which give validity to the goals of distributive education.[8]

Nelson, in discussing the impact of project plan instruction on education for distribution, stated:

We have, then, within our reach an enormously useful plan for instruction. Effectively supported by capable teacher-coordinators, project training will allow distributive education to exert a greater influence in satisfying the manpower requirements in distribution, to be more responsive to the needs of the people, to demonstrate more clearly to our public that the program is founded in theory rather than in method, and to satisfy training requirements without continuing employment.

By extending the capabilities of distributive education in this manner, we make the program available to all wishing to succeed in distributive employment. We make distributive education readily accessible to those students desiring to combine instruction offered in two or more vocational areas. We make distributive education flexible in organization by reducing or extending the amount of time

_____
[8] Peter G. Haines (ed.), *Readings in Distributive Education: The Project Plan of Instruction and Related Teacher Education* (East Lansing, Michigan: Michigan State University, Department of Secondary Education and Curriculum, 1968), p. 11.

needed to satisfy a level of performance. We make distributive education a useful instrument in our society.[9]

Common Elements

One underlying element is common to all three of the major plans for vocationalizing instruction in distributive and office education. Each plan emphasizes the need for developing realistic, occupationally oriented student learning experiences or projects. A *project* can be defined as any individually designed learning activity, which may include short-term work experiences, that has a behavioral objective related to an individual's occupational goal, and is to be accomplished in a specified length of time; an independent activity completed in a laboratory. These activities may be simulated in school and performed in the community or in employment.

The following basic guidelines should be given careful consideration when organizing a curriculum utilizing individualized instruction:

1. Services of occupationally aware guidance and teaching personnel are utilized in advising students concerning career choices and planning.
2. Students have realistic career objectives of which their present instructional program is an integral part.
3. Students are selected by the staff on the basis of need, interest, and ability to profit from the instruction.
4. Enrollment is determined by availability of adequate facilities and staff time to provide individualized instruction.
5. The instructional program is confirmed or changed by periodic analysis of the occupations for which instruction is provided.
6. An advisory committee, including representatives of both the school and the business community, advises and assists in planning, developing, and implementing the program.
7. The facilities in which the instruction is given provide an opportunity to simulate the facilities of the business world.

[9] *Ibid.,* p. 10.

8. An adequate budget is provided to update the instructional facilities and materials.

9. The local chapter of a youth organization is effectively developed and recognized as a co-curricular phase of the total instructional program.

10. Students receive credit toward graduation for time devoted to all phases of the program.

11. The staff has sufficient technical course preparation plus well-rounded current business experience backgrounds to enable them to realistically teach in the appropriate occupational field.

12. The staff has derived from their professionalized courses the diverse abilities required for the effective implementation of the program.

13. Individual student records have been carefully developed by the staff.

14. A minimum of one-half hour per week per student is provided for by the staff to effectively plan and correlate instruction.

15. Home visitations and/or parental conferences are an integral part of the job of the staff to assist them in the total development of each student.

16. Follow-up studies are conducted regularly and the results of the studies are utilized to improve the program.

17. Key staff members are provided with extended contracts to enable them to develop community resources, conduct follow-up studies, make home visitations, develop training plans, up-date program records, develop adult education programs, and execute other program development activities.

INDIVIDUALIZING INSTRUCTION

The image of modern education is not and can no longer be that of a teacher standing before 30 seated students and lecturing from a textbook. Technological innovations and new teaching theories have freed the teacher from ruts of tradition and dramatically expanded his capabilities. A new style of teaching has appeared across the United States, one destined to be adopted by more and more schools. This new style is based on the capabilities, goals, and aspirations of the students—individualized instruction designed to meet the greatly varied needs, capabilities, motivational drives, and growth patterns of different students by extensively utilizing the tools available.

Davis and Hanson provide the following basic outline of the steps involved in establishing the program in Roxana, Illinois: [10]

I. Planning—establish the overall objectives, guidelines, and requirements.

   A. Decide what business you want to simulate.

      1. Survey the area businesses.

      2. Find the type of office most prevalent in the community.

   B. Consider the equipment you have and the number of students enrolled in your course.

   C. Select a progressive business with which to work.

      1. Give the business a written idea of what you want to do after you have talked with them about it.

      2. Indicate how much of their time it will take for you to spend with their workers to find out what forms they use, what jobs they perform, etc.

      3. Get newspaper publicity concerning what you are doing and let the business you are simulating share in that publicity.

II. Make your data useful—don't just "collect." Be sure you understand what you have and how it is used.

   A. Decide how long the simulation will be carried out.

   B. Find out what type of training the students will have had before you get them.

   C. Decide what space you have available for the "office"—perhaps dividing the class and having two smaller office simulations would work better than one large one.

   D. Decide how unit will be evaluated.

      1. Evaluate quality of work turned out.

      2. Evaluate quantity of work turned out.

---

[10] Rose Ann Davis, "Hints on Office Simulation," from a workshop conducted by Dr. Garth Hanson, 1970.

3. Evaluate "mailable" letters.

4. Evaluate composition of work turned out.

5. Test skills on machines.

6. Test attitudes of workers toward their jobs and toward each other.

7. Test how students can work under pressure.

E. Decide what control will be used—this is handled through the simulator with the teacher out of the room as much as possible.

1. Create situations of stress (having work redone until perfect).

2. Create situations of pressure (deadlines amid interruptions).

III. Consider the above limitations and select student positions.

A. Have one large office simulation with vice president, office manager, executive secretary, sales manager and secretary, purchase manager and secretary, cashier, accounting manager and secretary, credit manager and secretary, receptionist, and duplicating operator, plus two simulators.

B. Divide the class and have two small offices. While one group carries out a simulation project, the other group works on regular class projects.

IV. Define the basic routines for each position.

A. Decide what kind of "input" will start each routine.

1. The mail, for example, might contain a letter of application, the bank statement, checks, the monthly Government forms to be completed, etc. In deciding on the basic routines, these might necessitate the use of various forms, and require action by certain members of the staff.

2. Telephone conversations (this might be for information on what your company has sent them, an applicant wanting a job, a request for information, etc.).

3. "Walk-in" customers paying bills, etc.

4. Interoffice memos or material sent from one department to another.

B. The jobs should be built for increasing complexity as the students become more proficient.

V. Make a positional flow diagram.

    A. Decide on paper what one student should be doing while another is performing another task. The simulator will initiate the work of the office, but you might decide approximately how long each task will take so that one person isn't overloaded while another sits idle.

    B. The students should be shown on paper what happens when a purchase requisition is received—where it should go, etc.

VI. Prepare job description manuals.

    A. At each position should be a list of duties that position covers. For example, in one procedures manual for vice-president, you are in control of the office. You will:

        1. Make all major decisions of the office.

        2. Handle all major complaints.

        3. Evaluate all executive personnel.

        4. Interview all applicants for office positions.

        5. Dictate executive and personal correspondence.

    B. Set up the procedures manual on tape at each position, as well as in writing.

VII. Develop a basic time schedule for the simulator so that he will keep the work of the office flowing smoothly. In other words, decide when, and in what order, he will make telephone calls, etc.

VIII. Develop a contingency list. This is a list of situations that will speed up or slow down the work in the office. For example, more purchase orders received in the mail if the workers seem to be idle, an unexpected caller, incomplete order blanks, duplicating jobs that are "rush," etc.

IX. Establish grading procedures.

    A. Decide what will be tested.

    B. How will it be tested?

X. How will debriefing sessions be conducted? At least once during each period of simulation, the whole office should be stopped and a discussion held as to things done correctly or incorrectly or methods that could be used for improvement. At this time the telephone calls that have been monitored can be played back for evaluation. This is a very important part of the simulation process. The students should not be allowed to continue doing jobs incorrectly. This is a good time to discuss the "human relations" elements that enter into any office situation.

XI. Decide what students will start where.

    A. For the first "run through" the biggest "ham" in the class should be the simulator because he will have to pretend to be the irritated customer, the applicant, the old college friend, etc.

    B. Have one of the best students in the class be office manager since he has control of the entire office staff.

    C. Have someone very good in shorthand for the executive secretary. (Getting the office started on the right "tone" will help or hinder the rest of the simulation period.)

XII. Go through at least three days in the same position before starting the office over again by switching the students to other positions. It is almost imperative that the class be two hours in length; otherwise, most of the time will be taken up by getting supplies out and putting them away.

The major portion of this chapter will be devoted to the instructional system having as its three major phases the formulation of desired learning outcomes, designing and developing learning activities, and evaluation. Figure 10-5 illustrates this system.

Formulation of Desired Learning Outcomes

It is essential that the teacher be able to identify desired learning outcomes for each student if an instructional system is to succeed. For example, what does a student have to be able to do if he is going to become a retail store salesman— what competencies must he possess to pursue his career successfully?

TEACHER-COORDINATOR INSTRUCTIONAL ACTIVITIES

PHASE I	**FORMULATION OF DESIRED LEARNING OUTCOMES**	IDENTIFYING NEEDED COMPETENCIES PLOTTING COMPETENCIES ON MATRIX OR PLANNING GRID CLUSTERING OF COMPETENCIES THAT ARE COMMON TO MORE THAN ONE STUDENT IDENTIFYING STUDENT CAPABILITIES PREPARING INSTRUCTIONAL OBJECTIVES	
PHASE II	**DEVELOPING AND DESIGNING LEARNING ACTIVITIES**	Development and Preparation of: INSTRUCTIONAL MEDIA TEACHING TECHNIQUES STUDENT PERFORMANCE TESTS	Selection of: TEACHING TECHNIQUES INSTRUCTIONAL MEDIA DETERMINING WHETHER TO USE LARGE GROUP, SMALL GROUP, OR INDIVIDUAL INSTRUCTION CONDUCT INSTRUCTION ADMINISTER AND ANALYZE STUDENT PERFORMANCE TESTS
PHASE III	**EVALUATON**	COMPARE STUDENT PERFORMANCES WITH INSTRUCTIONAL OBJECTIVES COMPARE ACTUAL STUDENT ON-THE-JOB PERFORMANCE WITH EXPECTED EMPLOYER REQUIREMENTS	
		REFINE THE INSTRUCTION	

FIGURE 10-5

Identifying Needed Student Competencies. The first step in determining needed competencies is to conduct a task analysis for the particular job in question. Conducting a task analysis means identifying and reporting significant worker activities, performance requirements, and environmental facts of a particular occupation.

TA & E	+	AC	+	T & PA	+	T-CE & I	+	SE & I	=	C
Task Analysis and Employers		Advisory Committee		Trade and Professional Association		Teacher-Coordinator Experience and Investigation		Student Experience and Investigation		Competencies Needed

FIGURE 10-6

One system of identifying needed student competencies is shown in Figure 10-6. The competencies of each student must be clearly identified before the instructional program for vocationally directed individualized instruction can be completed.

Plotting Competencies on Matrix or Planning Grid. Many experienced teachers use a matrix, or grid, to plot the identified competencies for each of their students. Figure 9-5 and the accompanying explanation on page 440 illustrate a matrix for the social competencies area suggested by Samson. Peter G. Haines has designed a grid for planned instruction, called *A Unitized Model for Instructional System.*[11] This grid is illustrated in Figure 10-7.

A UNITIZED MODEL FOR INSTRUCTIONAL SYSTEM

Level of Competence	Competency Area—A Sales Promotion					
	A-1-a	A-1-b	A-2	A-3	Etc.	B, C, D, etc.
1. Recognition/Recall						
2. Perceiving by example						
3. Applying to similar situations						
4. Applying to new situations						
5. Integrating with other problems						
6. Application to career goal						

FIGURE 10-7

---

[11] From a paper presented by Peter G. Haines at Oakland Schools, Pontiac, Michigan, November, 1969.

It is recommended that the time when the competency should be taught also be designated on the planning grids. This time indication can be extremely helpful in determining the proper time to teach each competency.

Once planning grids have been developed for each student, the process of comparing to determine whether any, or perhaps all, of the students must develop the same competency at the same level of performance may begin. For example, the examination of the prepared grids may reveal that all students need to develop competency in human relations at the recognition/recall level, while ten students need to be able to apply human relations to new situations.

Clustering of Competencies. The system shown in Figure 10-8 can be effectively used to cluster competencies common to more than one student and can also be used as a basis for determining whether to use large group, small group, or individual instruction to teach the identified competencies.

The formula in Figure 10-8 can be revised to determine needed individual instruction if planned group instruction is already known by the instructor. Figure 10-9 is one example.

DETERMINING WHAT TO TEACH ON GROUP BASIS				
NC —	PL & E —	PLLE —	PII =	NGI
Competencies Needed to Achieve Career Objective (See Figure 10-4)	Previous Learnings and Experiences (From occupational experience, courses, hobbies, etc.)	Planned on-the-job Laboratory Learning Experiences (From training plan)	Planned Individual Instruction (From training plan)	Needed Group Instruction (Small or large groups)

FIGURE 10-8

DETERMINING WHAT TO TEACH ON INDIVIDUAL OR SMALL GROUP BASIS				
NC —	PL & E —	PLLE —	PGI =	NII
Competencies Needed to Achieve Career Objective (See Figure 10-4)	Previous Learnings and Experiences (From occupational experience, courses, hobbies, etc.)	Planned on-the-job Laboratory Learning Experiences (From training plan)	Planned Group Instruction (From course outline)	Needed Individual (and/or small group) Instruction

FIGURE 10-9

Identifying Student Capabilities. As maintained throughout this chapter, it is important to identify the capabilities and previous learning experiences of students so

BUSINESS ENGLISH AND COMMUNICATION

Inventory Test (Including Key)

Name —————————————— Date ——————————————

This inventory of your communication skills is to be taken before beginning your work in this course. The results will tell you a great deal about what you know and what you need to learn if you are to be an effective speaker and writer. (Note: This Inventory Test is divided into four sections. There is a total of 100 items; score one point for each correct answer.)

Section I: SPELLING

Directions: In each of the following groups of words, one word is incorrectly spelled. In the answer column, write the letter that precedes this word.

				Ans.	Scoring
0. a. Wednesday	b. guard	c. merchandise	d. truely	d	0.——
1. a. definite	b. compel	c. conceding	d. repetition	a	1.——
2. a. losing	b. disappoint	c. ocassion	d. fulfill	c	2.——
3. a. pleasant	b. recomend	c. license	d. realize	b	3.——
4. a. admissible	b. privilege	c. article	d. occurence	d	4.——
5. a. apologize	b. argument	c. cipher	d. paralell	d	5.——
6. a. nineth	b. assistant	c. surprise	d. coolly	a	6.——
7. a. February	b. fourty-four	c. doesn't	d. pastime	b	7.——
8. a. committee	b. comparative	c. accomodate	d. field	c	8.——
9. a. conferring	b. conveinience	c. courtesy	d. seize	b	9.——
10. a. renumeration	b. conscious	c. control	d. safety	a	10.——
11. a. criticism	b. indelible	c. preceed	d. excellent	c	11.——
12. a. efficient	b. identical	c. instill	d. greatful	d	12.——
13. a. liberally	b. insolvent	c. accross	d. reducible	c	13.——
14. a. proceed	b. volumn	c. resources	d. deceit	b	14.——
15. a. alterred	b. securities	c. weird	d. visible	a	15.——
16. a. valleys	b. releive	c. underwear	d. transferred	b	16.——
17. a. tariff	b. seperate	c. transmitted	d. seige	b	17.——
18. a. extention	b. solely	c. recollect	d. reference	a	18.——
19. a. registered	b. remittance	c. untill	d. receptacle	c	19.——
20. a. sense	b. piece	c. nickel	d. perserverence	d	20.——

Source: *Block-Time—Simulation: Individualized Office Instructional System* (East Lansing, Michigan: Michigan State University, Department of Secondary Education and Curriculum, 1969).

FIGURE 10-10

that the teacher-coordinator can make decisions concerning the selection and organization of instructional content, materials, strategies, and student evaluation techniques.

A number of competencies will have been developed by students from other classes, hobbies, and previous business experiences. The competent teacher-coordinator will use many written, oral, and performance-oriented techniques in determining at what level the student should begin his learning experiences and in implementing the instructional program set up specifically for him.

Participants in the Michigan State University Block-Time—Simulation Program have complete data sheets and files on each student. Data was also obtained from interest and aptitude tests, autobiographies, guidance counselors, and teachers. The participants also used pre-tests, such as the one shown in Figure 10-10.

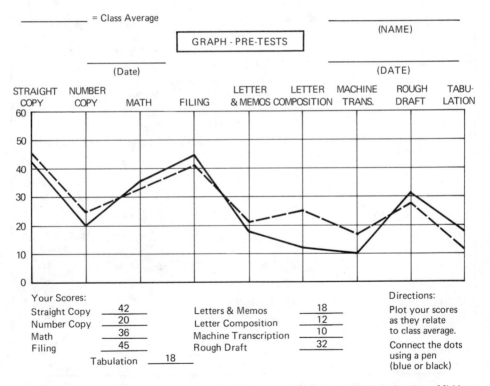

Source: *Block-Time—Simulation: Individualized Office Instructional System* (East Lansing, Michigan: Michigan State University, Department of Secondary Education and Curriculum, 1969).

FIGURE 10-11

Scores were then plotted on the pre-test graph shown in Figure 10-11.

Student checksheets were used to assist the students in evaluating their current level of performance. The completed checksheets were used to prepare a profile sheet in each competency area for every student. A copy of directions given to the students, a checksheet for evaluating human relations responsibilities, and a profile sheet are presented in Figures 10-12, 10-13, and 10-14.

Name ————————————

CHECKSHEET BOOKLET

Using the following classifications, please indicate your present capabilities regarding your ability to successfully complete the following business activities by circling an appropriate number:

1. I have little interest in this area of business activity and have, therefore, *made little use of available information and training.*

2. In order to complete this business activity satisfactorily, I feel I *would need more training, experience, and close supervision.*

3. I feel I could carry out this phase of business activity sufficiently *some of the time, but would need additional supervision and experience.*

4. I feel I could carry out this phase of business activity sufficiently *most of the time, with short intervals of supervision.*

5. I feel I could *at all times adequately* carry out this phase of business activity with my own judgment, skills, and knowledge.

AREAS TO BE CHECKED:

BANKING	MACHINE	COLOR CODE:
COMMUNICATION	MAIL	1st Time—Pen
DICTATION AND TRANSCRIPTION	RECEPTIONIST	2nd Time—Red Pencil
DUPLICATING	RECORD KEEPING	3rd Time—Pencil
FILING	REFERENCE	
HUMAN RELATIONS	TELEPHONE	
JOB APPLICATION & INTERVIEW	TRAVEL	
LETTER WRITING	TYPING	

Source: *Block-Time—Simulation: Individualized Office Instructional System* (East Lansing, Michigan: Michigan State University, Department of Secondary Education and Curriculum, 1969).

FIGURE 10-12

HUMAN RELATIONS RESPONSIBILITIES

PERSONAL APPEARANCE

1 2 3 4 Health habits and cleanliness—body and clothing.
1 2 3 4 Attractiveness—basic, smart business dress.
1 2 3 4 Posture and poise—businesslike, mature, intelligent.
1 2 3 4 Continual maintenance—never let down your standards in the above.
1 2 3 4 _____
1 2 3 4 _____

PERSONALITY AND ATTITUDES

1 2 3 4 Accurate—do the job, check it, correct, and recheck it.
1 2 3 4 Good judgment—concentrate, analyze, decide, act.
1 2 3 4 Follow through—implied requests, assigned requests (in time).
1 2 3 4 Resourcefulness—think clearly, widely into all possibilities.
1 2 3 4 Initiative—awareness and enactment of all situations.
1 2 3 4 Consideration—awareness and enactment of all situations.
1 2 3 4 Tact—speech, actions, attitude.
1 2 3 4 Discretion and loyalty to yourself, your boss, and your company.
1 2 3 4 Objectivity—critical analysis without personal involvement.
1 2 3 4 Promptness—in arriving *at* work and going *to* work.
1 2 3 4 Dependable and trustworthy—always there, doing what you should.
1 2 3 4 Well organized—the day in general, each particular job.
1 2 3 4 Conscientious—use of company's time, supplies, and equipment.
1 2 3 4 Cooperative—an effective member of the "team."
1 2 3 4 Ability to follow instructions.
1 2 3 4 Ability to accept criticism from those with whom you work.
1 2 3 4 Ability to get along with others.
1 2 3 4 Pride and interest in your job.
1 2 3 4 _____

THE BEWARE AREAS OF H.R.

1 2 3 4 The gossip column.
1 2 3 4 Social office etiquette.
1 2 3 4 The overbearing co-worker.
1 2 3 4 The confidential information.
1 2 3 4 Spelling and pronouncing customers' names correctly.
1 2 3 4 Answering the telephone after it rings off the wall.
1 2 3 4 Hanging up *only* after the customer has.
1 2 3 4 Exchanging clever repartee with friends in the presence of callers.
1 2 3 4 Proper and warmly poised introductions versus stiff and stumbling.

Source: *Block-Time—Simulation: Individualized Office Instructional System* (East Lansing, Michigan: Michigan State University, Department of Secondary Education and Curriculum, 1969).

FIGURE 10-13

HUMAN RELATIONS PROFILE of ————————————————

This specific profile will be used as a basis for determining the performance and rating on the MASTER PROFILE.

	Minimum	Average	Good	Superior
Ambition				
Cooperation				
Dependability				
Expression				
Initiative				
Judgment				
Leadership				
Loyalty				
Manners				
Mental alertness				
Persistence				
Respect				
Self-control				
Social attitudes				
Tact				
Voice & speech				

Source: *Block-Time—Simulation: Individualized Office Instructional System* (East Lansing, Michigan: Michigan State University, Department of Secondary Education and Curriculum, 1969).

FIGURE 10-14

Preparing Instructional Objectives. Instructional objectives which are appropriate for each student can only be determined after the teacher-coordinator has made decisions relating to what competencies should be developed, by whom, and when the knowledge, attitude, skill, or understanding should be taught. It is imperative that student-teacher dialogue be present if the behavioral goal type instruction system is to be effective.

Students obviously want to know what level of performance is expected, what conditions will be present when performing the task, and what the criteria are for successful performance. If the student is involved in setting appropriate goals and knows what is expected, evaluation becomes easier. Quality, quantity, and time factors are frequently used as measures for evaluating performance.

Techniques for preparing instructional objectives were discussed in Chapter 2. Meaningful instructional objectives should contain the conditions under which the student will be expected to show achievement of the objective, expected student performance, and what the minimum standard of performance will be.

Developing and Designing Learning Activities

After the desired student learning outcomes have been researched and formulated, the teacher-coordinator can turn his attention to developing and designing those learning activities that will aid the student in reaching his goals.

Selecting, Developing, and Preparing Learning Activities. It is a difficult task to select the most appropriate instructional techniques and media needed to reach the desired learning outcomes. Decisions must be reached relative to the nature of the sensory appeal, the learning processes involved, and the advantages of the particular technique used. Figures 9-8 and 9-9 on pages 444 and 445 illustrate some of the decisional factors involved in selecting the appropriate technique and media.

The effectiveness of various types of instructional media in achieving selected learning objectives has been carefully studied and researched. Even though the findings are not conclusive, Figure 9-10 on page 446 is deserving of special attention.

The selection of the technique and media should be considered concurrently in developing instruction. Three factors which must be considered in the decision-making process are: characteristics of the learners, nature of the information to be presented, and principles of learning processes.

Levendowski has developed the self-assessment form on page 497 to be used by teachers in making instructional strategy decisions.[12]

Determining Whether to Use Large Group, Small Group, or Individual Instruction. Figures 10-8 and 10-9 provide a sound basis for determining what should be taught as large group, small group, or individual instruction. The National Education Association, in their publication *Choosing Techniques for Teaching and Learning*, provides the following principles to guide the selection of teaching techniques:

1. If a student is involved in choosing the techniques, he will be more accepting of the resulting situation.
2. If the learning situation is a part of real life or seems real to the student, he will perceive the relevance and be more eager to learn.
3. If a student is participating, mentally as well as physically, his interest will be greater and achievement more rapid.
4. If there is ego involvement or *psychological ownership* in the learning situation (that is, the student has a personal interest in the success of the technique), motivation and learning are increased.
5. If the chosen techniques help a student to experience success, his self-esteem and motivation will be enhanced.
6. If a student finds pleasure in the learning situation, he is more likely to continue learning.
7. If a student develops skills for independent learning, he can continue to learn after his formal schooling is finished.
8. If a student sees usefulness in his learning activities, motivation will be increased.
9. If a student develops positive attitudes toward learning, he will be more likely to continue learning independently.[13]

---

[12] J. C. Levendowski, "Individualizing Instruction," from a paper prepared for a workshop at Northern Illinois University, 1971.
[13] Hazel Taylor Spitze, *Choosing Techniques for Teaching and Learning* (Washington: National Education Association, 1970), pp. 2-6.

INDIVIDUALIZING INSTRUCTION

This learning activity is designed to facilitate an assessment of the instructional strategies which you currently are using. Listed below are nineteen questions. Answer each question with yes or no, and add as much qualifying information as you wish. This learning activity may be conducted as a self-assessment or, if you wish, someone else can assist you by observing in your classroom.

First identify three students in one of your classes; try to select a "high," an "average," and a "low" achiever. Then respond to the following questions for each of the three students by placing a "yes" or a "no" in each of the spaces provided.

High Aver. Low

_____ _____ _____ (1) Are your students permitted to progress at their own unique rates of learning?

_____ _____ _____ (2) Do you pre-test students?

_____ _____ _____ (3) Are any of the three students which you identified for this assessment studying the same assignment and using the same materials/media?

_____ _____ _____ (4) Does the organization of your learning materials help students relate themes, generalizations, theories, principles, and concepts to the structure of the content which you teach?

_____ _____ _____ (5) Are your students given materials and techniques which encourage them to consciously and individually examine values and the processes of valuing?

_____ _____ _____ (6) Are your students provided opportunities to select from print, non-print, and human resources for learning (media of all types)?

_____ _____ _____ (7) Do the materials and techniques which you use help your students learn the modes and processes of investigation employed in your discipline(s)?

_____ _____ _____ (8) Are your students given opportunities to use inquiry, discovery, and inductive procedures in their learning activities?

_____ _____ _____ (9) Are your students provided with performance objectives to guide them in their learning?

_____ _____ _____(10) Is there always a specified sequence of learning activities which all students must follow?

_____ _____ _____(11) Are your students allowed to follow alternative paths in their learning sequences based on their personal interests and motivation?

_____ _____ _____(12) Have you incorporated games and/or simulation techniques and materials into the learning activities employed by your students?

_____ _____ _____(13) Are your students provided opportunities to select from learning materials aimed at a variety of difficulty levels?

_____ _____ _____(14) Are texts which are written at different reading difficulty levels available to your students?

_____ _____ _____(15) Do the learning materials provided for your students contain content which are discussed at differing depths of sophistication or abstractness?

_____ _____ _____(16) Do the learning materials provided for your students contain topics which are discussed from opposing or divergent points of view?

_____ _____ _____(17) Do your instructional strategies provide for individual differences in student self-initiative?

_____ _____ _____(18) Do your instructional strategies provide for individual differences in student self-direction?

_____ _____ _____(19) Do your instructional strategies help students to increasingly value self-responsibility?

FIGURE 10-15

Teachers must find ways to work with groups of students since they usually do not tutor one student at a time. It must be remembered, however, that what and how an individual learns is conditioned to some degree by his group membership. Those in groups larger than 15 or 20 can watch, listen, meditate, play certain games, read, write, vote, imagine, and participate in certain kinds of discussion. Those in smaller groups can be more active participants in discussions, plan, help create designs, dramatize, experiment, demonstrate, serve as recorders, and engage in other similar activities. Individuals working alone can do much of the above and the following: home projects and other individual projects, keep a diary, do creative writing, conduct interviews and be interviewed, and pursue programmed instruction.

From the above discussion, it can be concluded that: fewer techniques are suitable for large groups than small groups; large groups do not usually permit active involvement of the individual members; very large groups (50-100 or more) may be more economical than those of moderate size; large groups can be used as an audience for the other members of the group; large classes can use small group and individual techniques by dividing into frequently-changing committees, teams, or cells for various purposes.

Conducting the Instruction. Figure 8-10 on page 365 can serve as a procedure for implementing instruction after the teacher-coordinator has carefully considered each student, studied the information gathered during the formulation of the desired learning outcomes, and made decisions regarding the selection, development, and preparation of teaching techniques and media.

Administering and Analyzing Student Performance Tests. Student performance in a real life job situation is the ideal technique for evaluation. The teacher can observe the student, evaluate and discuss his performance, and ask the student to describe through oral or written means answers to key questions.

Attitudes, particularly, can best be analyzed and evaluated through tests which permit a student to demonstrate overt behavior. Many of the key competencies in the fields of business are not effectively measured with pencil and paper examinations.

Evaluation

The purpose of post-test or criteria examinations is to determine how well students perform in relation to predetermined criteria and in terms of behaviorally defined objectives. Throughout the instructional program, tests of various kinds are used to determine the competency of the student in relation to specific learning tasks. They are also used to measure the degree to which the student possesses competencies necessary to master additional learning tasks, to make diagnoses concerning the progress of the student in order that needed changes be made to enable him to better perform, and to point out any deficiencies in the instructional program.

The results of post-exit and long-range follow-up studies are not immediately known to the teacher. The immediate post-exit process takes place from one to two months after a student has completed his course of study with the purposes of identifying strengths and weaknesses of the program and providing immediate feedback. The long-range follow-up, conducted on a continuing basis, begins several months after the student has completed his course of study and is used to provide up-to-date statistical information.

Carefully designed training records and properly prepared rating sheets enable the teacher to obtain immediate feedback. As a result, refinements can be made in the instructional program almost immediately. Effective instruction considers each learner's competencies and potential, and provides for development of basic educational skills, social development, realistic self concepts, and decision-making skills. Evaluation of instruction utilizes the combined measurement data from all the components in the instructional system.

INSTRUCTIONAL TECHNIQUES

The individualized instruction techniques which are presented in this chapter are not totally reserved for implementing block-time, intensive laboratory, or project plan programs. Nor are these the only methods that should be used. Numerous techniques for teaching business and distributive education are presented in Chapters 5, 7, 8, and 9. It is assumed that the instruction will take place in various kinds of school and community laboratories.

Community laboratories will be provided by businesses so that students are able to have periods of short-term occupational experience. The school book and supplies store and various offices in the educational facility will be available as in-school laboratories. Model offices, marketing laboratories, and model stores have been carefully designed to facilitate instruction. A number of the publications listed in the bibiliography have excellent illustrations and suggestions for designing, equipping, and supplying "laboratory" facilities.

The purposes of an office or marketing laboratory facility vary in degree of emphasis, time, and depth of subject matter. However, the following purposes are worthy of consideration:

1. To simulate previously learned competencies.
2. To evaluate previously learned competencies.
3. To develop responsibility in performing tasks.
4. To develop the ability to work cooperatively in completing assigned tasks.
5. To determine the need for further training.
6. To explore and develop career patterns.
7. To further develop occupational competency.
8. To aid the student in evaluating his total performance.
9. To form correct work habits and attitudes.
10. To develop and/or advance decision-making processes.
11. To prepare students for job entry.[14]

---

[14] *Block-Time—Simulation: Individualized Office Instructional System,* op. cit., p. III-43.

Task simulation, in-basket exercises, and business games are just three examples of teaching techniques utilizing simulation. The simulation activity blends two or more competencies into a realistic business activity. The complexity of the activities depends upon the students' stage of development and their acquisition of necessary information. The activities should not be unreasonably complex, but should be of such a nature that the students must make decisions and apply what they have already learned. An increasing number of published activities are available which the teacher may adapt to his classroom situation. It may be necessary, however, for the teacher to develop additional simulation activities.

Sabin has identified the following three kinds of office simulations:

> The first is the model office, and this is the form that is currently attracting the greatest attention. A model office is typically based on a real operation, it contains a number of work stations that reflect a realistic office organization, and it permits a realistic flow of work. As input comes into this office (in the form of orders, payments, inquiries, and so on), it generates a flow of work through the various job stations so that at each stage some form of output is produced. While the individual jobs within the model office may be limited in scope, the fact is that all the jobs, taken in aggregate, cover the full range of objectives for a well-trained office worker from A to Z. Therefore, the office education student who rotates through all of the jobs in the model office and performs them satisfactorily demonstrates beyond question that he has achieved the behavioral objectives that were established for him.

> The second kind of simulation focuses on just one of those job stations. Although it does not typically allow for interaction, it does permit you to simulate the way input comes in on the job, the conditions under which the job will be performed, and the standards of quality and quantity that would be applied on the job.

> The third kind of simulation does not attempt to simulate a total job; it deals only with the decision-making process

that the student must go through in resolving problems that will occur on the job. These may be problems that involve a management decision, they may be human relations problems that can occur between people on staff, or they may involve problems of communication with people outside the company. They may be presented in the form of case problems or as role-playing situations. In either case, the student must go through a certain process of analysis to arrive at a decision—which is the output in this instance.[15]

A properly designed simulation activity must clearly state what kinds of tasks a student should be able to do, and what kinds of behavior he ought to demonstrate. A simulation should exhibit the following characteristics:

1. It should simulate the way input comes in on the job. In an office simulation, this means that the input should be provided in a realistic variety of written and oral forms (incoming letters and memos, incoming phone calls, conversations with visitors, oral directions and dictation from the boss, computer printouts, and so on). Moreover, the input should come in a realistically unorganized fashion, as it would on the job.

2. It should simulate the conditions under which the student will be expected to perform on the job. That is, the simulation should replicate the work flow and the procedures the student would encounter on the job. It should make available to the student the kinds of records, reference materials, files, and other resources he'd have access to on the job. It should make available to him the kinds of equipment he'd be expected to use on the job.

3. It should simulate the standards of quality and quantity by which his work would be judged on the job.[16]

Although people think of a practice set as a form of simulation, most practice sets do not meet the foregoing criteria. First, practice sets do not typically provide for random input in a variable sequence such as one would encounter each day in an office job. Here the input is

---

[15] From "Simulation in the Seventies: An Overview," by William A. Sabin, Editor in Chief, Office Education, Gregg Division, McGraw-Hill Book Company, in *Business Education World,* Vol. 52, No. 1, pp. 5-7, September-October, 1971. Reproduced with permission of McGraw-Hill, Inc.

[16] *Ibid.,* p. 5.

typically provided in a fixed sequence defined as Job 1, Job 2, Job 3. Second, the typical practice set does not afford the student a chance to sort through the daily mess of papers on his desk, organize them, and set priorities as he would have to do on the job. Finally, the typical practice set does not provide for the kinds of realistic files and the realistic records of previous transactions that a worker would have access to on the job.

The role of simulation in vocationalizing instruction must be given careful consideration. An experienced office education teacher offers the following advice for teachers considering simulation:

Whatever type of simulation you choose, keep in mind that the business you operate becomes the means of carrying your program through the school year. With proper design of your entire year, you may drop in any type of simulation you choose. In your overall plan for the year, you might attempt to sketch a chart that would establish, in order, the year's lesson plan. (See Figure 10-16)

First, you might start with pretesting so that you will know what skills and knowledges your students actually bring to your class in September. If you will plot class averages for each of the pretests, students may then plot their own scores as they relate to the class average. This graph will point up the individual weaknesses of each student—this information to be used later in the year in choosing certain units of instruction for the students in training classes.

Presimulation follows pretesting. Your presimulation will be built according to the equipment, tasks, and documents that you will be operating in your laboratory and model office.

Interviewing and employment testing begin just prior to the opening of your agencies/branch offices and parent company/main branch. Your year's chart will end with the closing of agencies/branch offices and parent· company/main branch and posttesting.

The actual operations of your company should be depicted in flow-chart form that you will prepare in conjunction with your resource people. A section of the agency flow chart dealing with supplies is shown in Figure 10-17.[17]

---

[17] Beverly M. Funk, "A Blueprint for Successful Simulation," *Business Education Forum,* 24 (February, 1970), pp. 22-23.

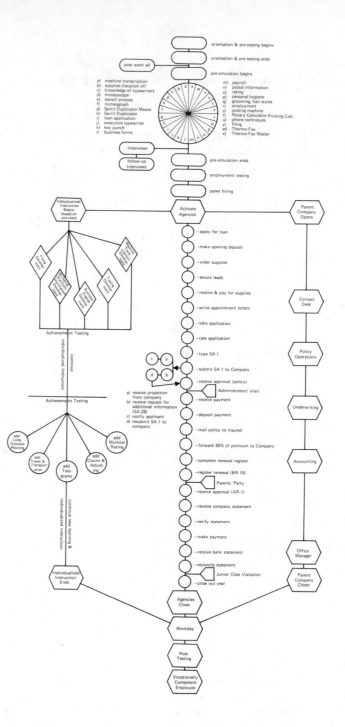

Source: Beverly M. Funk, "A Blueprint for Successful Simulation," *Business Education Forum,* 24 (February, 1970), pp. 22-23.

FIGURE 10-16

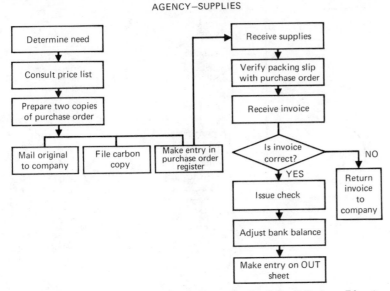

Source: Beverly M. Funk, "A Blueprint for Successful Simulation," *Business Education Forum*, 24 (February, 1970), pp. 22-23.

FIGURE 10-17

Figure 10-18 is one example of a model office organizational chart for a simulated office, while Figure 10-19 shows a portion of a sales order chart.

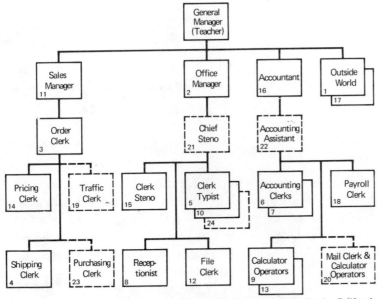

Source: Robert Fuller, "The Simulation Office," Clovis High School, Clovis, California, 1970.

FIGURE 10-18

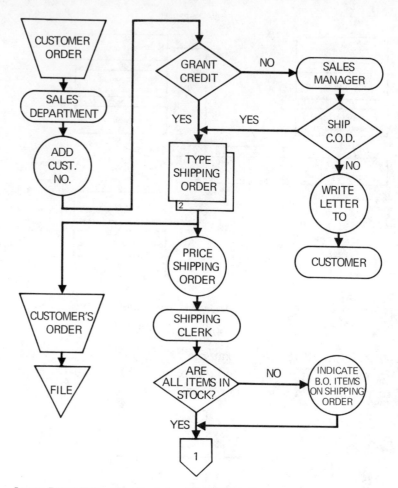

Source: Robert Fuller, "The Simulation Office," Clovis High School, Clovis, California, 1970.

FIGURE 10-19

A typical office task simulation activity is described below:

The students are working for the Audio Condenser Company and are expected to complete a series of sequential tasks which are necessary when a purchase order is received by the Sales Department. The tasks are to write an acknowledgment letter to the purchaser, to write three interoffice memos to three departments, and to make a follow-up card for the order. Students are expected to perform the tasks without interruption in an assumed office-like atmosphere. All tasks are to be completed in 45 minutes, provided the letter is dictated or given on machine transcription. One hour will be allowed if the student is expected to write the letter. The letter must be proofread and ready for the manager's signature, complete with envelope and ready for mailing. The interoffice memoranda must be composed, proofread, and ready for signature. A record card must be filled out and ready for filing in the Sales Department office. The following subjects and competency areas are integrated into this exercise: typewriting, transcription, composition, problem-solving, record keeping, shorthand (possibly), business English, and spelling.

Figure 10-20 shows a form for recording office task simulation activities. This form aids the teacher in reviewing his teaching techniques and content with the aim of improving classroom operation and effectiveness.

The in-basket exercise provides training which approximates or "simulates" experiences, forming a bridge between training and performance on the job. It consists of confronting an individual or small group of students with materials, such as a supervisory or administrative official might find in an in-basket on a given day, and requiring each member to decide how he would handle it. The items in the in-basket present a variety of realistic operating situations ranging from the simple to the complex.

This technique is most commonly used for small group instruction, but can also be adapted for individual student use. The in-basket exercise provides specific experience in individual decision-making and problem-solving because some of the items are connected in various ways, requiring students to discover interrelationships. Also, some of the items are considerably more urgent than others, making it necessary to determine the relative importance of various matters. Time is short, requiring that it be used in the most efficient manner.

The in-basket exercise produces a vivid realization that supervisory and administrative problems do not have a single answer. A student may feel quite content with his answer, until someone else not only comes up with a different answer, but also presents a good case. Students also

```
+--------------------------------------------------------------+
|              TASK  SIMULATION  RECORDING  FORM               |
|                                                              |
|      SUBJECT MATTER AREAS _____           |
|      DATE(S) USED _____           |
|                                                              |
|                            EVALUATION  COMMENTS              |
|   OBJECTIVE(S)              |   OBJECTIVE(S)                 |
|                            |                                |
|                            |                                |
|   CONTENT                   |   CONTENT                      |
|                            |                                |
|                            |                                |
|   METHOD (Techniques)       |   METHOD (Techniques)          |
|                            |                                |
|                            |                                |
|   MEANS OF EVALUATING       |   EVALUATION  COMMENTS         |
|   ACTIVITY (Include tests and|                               |
|   all other evaluating schemes)|                            |
|                            |                                |
|   SUGGESTIONS AND/OR  GENERAL  COMMENTS (Use                 |
|   other side if necessary)                                   |
|                                                              |
+--------------------------------------------------------------+
```

Source: *Block-Time—Simulation: Individualized Office Instructional System* (East Lansing, Michigan: Michigan State University, Department of Secondary Education and Curriculum, 1969).

FIGURE 10-20

discover that they may have overlooked a factor, or that they have given different emphasis to the factors involved. Also, requiring the students to select the individual who will best carry out an action brings out the importance of getting things done through people.

Student instructions for an in-basket exercise might read something like this:

> You are Jim Smith, department supervisor, Jones Supply Company. When you arrive at work, your boss calls, says he is ill, and won't be in today. He wants you to serve in his position. You must examine each item in the basket, decide what should be done with it, and write a letter or memorandum whenever action is indicated. You may write to anyone, including yourself, but everything must be committed to writing. Write down also the reasons behind the action you took, as well as additional observations that you make about the problem.
>
> You will be given 100 minutes to write down for each item the action you took and the reason the action was taken. Then you will have an opportunity to discuss the appropriateness of your actions.

The in-basket exercise has been used in business and education to train leadership personnel. Teachers have adapted business-developed materials with some success. Teachers can either secure actual copies of letters or descriptions of situations that face business personnel or develop their own situations. They can be prepared in letter or memorandum form. A letter from a customer complaining about service, a memorandum from an employee who is planning to resign because of low wages, or a copy of a discussion between an executive and employee can be prepared as a series of in-basket exercises.

Business games have been used for a number of years in the training of management personnel. A business game may be defined as a sequential decision-making exercise, structured around a model of a business operation, in which participants assume the role of managing the simulated operation. Participants make believe they are operating a company in a hypothetical industry. Some business games involve all aspects of a business, while others are restricted to one particular phase. Games have been devised for computer or non-computer application.

Teachers have adopted a number of games, originally designed for training management personnel in business, for use in secondary and post-secondary classes. The

Arizona Distributive Education Clubs of America has produced and distributed two business games.[18] The Arizona *Business Simulation 1 & 2* includes instructor, player, and reference instructions and forms to be used by the teacher and 25 students. Instructor recommendations on the use of business game number one are presented below:

Instructor Directions

RECOMMENDATIONS ON THE USE OF BUSINESS SIMULATION #1

1. Introduction and Period 1: Use group discussion technique and fill out all forms for Period 1 in class. The instructor should predetermine the decisions for this period and have his form (or key) completely filled out so that each company's figures can be checked quickly. Price changes are to be made in increments of $1.00 only. It is suggested that the retail price be set at either $11.00 or $12.00 for this period. This may keep discussion away from such things as lowering prices in order to increase volume. REMEMBER—THIS TECHNIQUE IS DESIGNED TO DEVELOP DECISION-MAKING ABILITIES OF THE STUDENTS . . . INSTRUCTOR MUST NOT "LEAD" DECISION. ACT AS A REFEREE ONLY.

2. Periods 2, 3, and 4: Each team (company) will make their decisions independent of the other "competing" companies. Allow 15 to 25 minutes for them to enter their decisions on Form A, using their analysis of Cash Available (Form B) and the Income Statement (Form C). *Collect all forms.* The instructor will now follow the "referee instructions" in computing the results of the company's decision. This may be done in time for class the following day.

3. A fifth class period should be used to present the final standings of the companies. Below are suggestions for this "critique" session:

   a. Post the following on the chalkboard as a basis for discussion:

      1. Total sales
      2. Total gross margin

---

[18] Arizona Distributive Education Clubs of America, *Business Simulations 1 & 2* (Phoenix, Arizona, 1967).

3. Total operating expenses
4. Total net income
5. Average % of Net Income to Total Sales
6. Ending inventory

   b. A demand curve might be placed on the chalkboard comparing each company's sales volume for each period. Have students analyze this in regard to:

1. Sales volume vs. price
2. Volume vs. profits
3. Other factors that might increase volume without necessitating a rise in retail prices

   c. Discussion should be conducted on techniques used by the students in arriving at decisions. The notes of the company recorders are to be used as a basis for this discussion.

   d. Other points of discussion that you or your students feel are important during this critique session.

The Western Publishing Company, Inc., New York, produces the following games: *Consumer, Economic System; Life Career; Generation Gap; Ghetto Democracy; and Community Disaster*. The Avon Hill Company, Baltimore, Maryland, publishes *Management* and *The Stock Market Game*. Milton Bradley Company produces *The Game of Life. Sales Management* magazine publishes, as a regular service, games which have been used by distributive education teacher-coordinators. Sometimes games produced by teachers and students add interest to the instructional process.

In judging games as teaching techniques one might consider, in addition to the general criteria for judging all techniques, the following questions:

1. Is the time required to play the game reasonable in terms of expected learnings?
2. Is the game itself subordinate to the learnings, i.e., not "gimmicky."
3. Does the game create interest, excitement, enjoyment of learning?
4. Is the structure of the subject matter carefully preserved in the game, i.e., no misinformation implied or wrong

implications drawn because of omissions, oversimplification, etc.?

5. Is it complicated enough to be interesting and challenging, but simple enough for the rules to be understood quickly?
6. Is it flexible enough to be adapted for students of different ability levels and for different purposes?
7. Does winning the game require knowledge rather than *luck*?
8. Is the "paraphernalia" for playing the game reasonable in cost, storage requirements, etc.?
9. Does the competition remain friendly? Team competition may be better than individual so that cooperation is also involved.
10. Does the game require high levels of cognitive behavior? Foster good relationships among students? Aid in skill development? Improve attitudes toward learning? Help clarify values? [19]

In using games in the classroom the teacher should be sure that objectives are clear to the students; materials are ready, reducing confusion and avoiding wasted time; and precaution is taken so that losers are not embarrassed. If games are varied and require different skills and abilities, the same students will not always be the winners. The "handicap" idea may be incorporated into some games to reduce the unfair advantage of some students. Amount of handicap could be based on a pre-test given without revealing its purpose, or on previous game scores if the game is played several times. If several students can be declared winners, so much the better for motivation.

Resource Persons

Teachers frequently use the services of individuals having expertise in a particular area, community members with practical knowledge, or faculty members and students from other areas. The contributions that resource personnel make vary considerably from community to community, from school to school, and from teacher to teacher. They may give

---

[19] Hazel Taylor Spitze, *op. cit.*, p. 20.

a lecture or talk, take part in panel discussions, act as consultants, give demonstrations, take part in informal classroom discussions, serve as judges for youth organization activities, be interviewers, or provide materials for developing simulation activities.

Resource people can often contribute new and vital ideas which enrich and motivate learning. Students develop more respect for out-of-school people; developing, at the same time, a keener appreciation of the community. In reverse, the resource person carries a new understanding of the business program back to both his job and the community.

Advisory committee members can be asked to serve as resource people or to recommend appropriate individuals. Teachers in distributive education have found that businesses have complete display, inventory control, sales promotion plans, and other materials which can be used to make instruction more realistic. One teacher secured enough merchandise from various retail, wholesale, and manufacturing firms to equip a complete marketing laboratory. Office education teachers have secured forms, flow charts, consultant services, and general know-how regarding the operation of a company in order to set up simulated offices for various types of businesses. Many large companies and trade associations have complete instruction kits for training office and marketing personnel which can be borrowed or purchased.

Resource personnel may be invited to the school by the teacher, individual students, or a committee of the class. The teacher should, however, clear all invitations with appropriate school officials. The resource person may be asked to contribute his services as a part of the regular instructional program or in conjunction with youth organization activities.

Careful planning is necessary. Personnel who are competent in their field and can communicate with students should be selected. If a presentation is to be made, assist the resource person by providing a list of key questions to answer or an outline of the topics that should be covered. Verify the date a day or two before he is to appear. The students should be carefully prepared so that they can ask intelligent questions. A follow-up thank-you letter is in order, and is most appropriately written by members of the class or youth organization.

Field Observations and Interviews

The educational value of students going into the business world to observe and interview has never been challenged. Field trips, field observations, and field interviews provide students with an opportunity to gather information firsthand about objects, places, people, or processes; to enrich, extend, validate, or vitalize information from printed or other sources; or to try to uncover entirely new data. This may not be "real life experiencing," but the dimensions are near real life. Students see and observe things, places, people, and process in life situations; they see objects in true size and in their natural setting. Field experiences are good motivators because students are given an opportunity to observe firsthand how business is conducted. (See page 321 for a discussion of the field trip as an instructional technique.)

The field observation can be made by one or more persons: three students working on a general merchandise display project might evaluate a series of window and interior displays; an indivdual working on a bank teller project may be required to observe a teller in two different types of financial institutions.

Field interviews provide one or more students with the opportunity, on an informal basis, to secure opinions and facts related to a problem. Career information and competency development projects can be pursued, both requiring data which can be secured through field interviews.

Teachers who use field interview or field observation techniques to individualize instruction have found that students must be carefully prepared. The following steps should be followed in helping students prepare for a field observation:

1. Make sure the student knows what he is to observe.
2. Help determine where he is to do the observing.
3. Help determine when he is to observe.
4. Help the student design information recording sheets.
5. Help determine how the student will report the observed data.
6. Help the student make any necessary arrangement for the observation.

The following student-teacher steps for using the field interview technique should be considered:

1. Determine the goals of the field interview.
2. Select the interviewees.
3. Determine when to interview.
4. Determine what to ask the interviewees.
5. Design information recording sheets.
6. Conduct practice interview sessions.

The location of the school, maturity level of students, individual local or school board of education policies, and provisions made for staffing and scheduling field experiences help determine the extent to which teachers can use field trips, observations, and interviews. Many observations and interviews can be arranged during out-of-school time periods, such as over weekends or during vacations.

Short-Term Directed Occupational Experiences

Learning activities may be designed which include a provision for employment in business. Firms can be contacted by the teacher to determine peak employment requirements, and a plan designed to serve students and employer needs. Students preparing to become salesmen may sell during peak hours or days of the week and during vacation periods. A student engaged in receptionist training may actually serve as a receptionist in a firm.

The same care exercised in using any other methods must be taken when planning an activity which includes occupational experience. Employers can be of major assistance in helping to develop all projects. However, their cooperation in developing the occupational experience portion of any learning activity is essential.

Demonstrations

A demonstration may be given by the teacher, a student, a resource person, or a team of any or all of these. Its purpose may be to present ideas or processes or to provide opportunity to experience attitudes and feelings. Hence, it may be useful in all three domains of educational objectives: the cognitive, the effective, and the psychomotor.

Demonstrations by students may serve as evaluative devices to show understanding or skill development, or to reveal attitudes. Careful planning to assure that all needed materials are at hand, that sufficient time is available, and that the physical arrangement permits all to see and hear will enhance the effectiveness of the demonstration. As in other techniques, distractions should be eliminated as far as possible—written material distributed during a demonstration may be such a distraction.

The usual procedure of explanations by the demonstrator along with the action can be varied by either a silent demonstration with questions prepared to guide careful observation and a follow-up discussion or a repeat demonstration by a student to see if the process was understood; or a demonstration in which the demonstrator asks with each step of the action "What am I doing?" and "Why am I doing it?" The demonstrator may precede each step with "What shall I do next and why?" Another variation, which might be called "monkey see, monkey do," has students repeat each step of the demonstration as it is being given.

Some teachers have students analyze and classify procedures during the demonstration. For example, in a foods demonstration students could be asked whether a procedure is for sanitation, accuracy, efficiency, etc. Some teachers tell students to watch for errors and then deliberately make some.

Demonstrations can stimulate interest and make teaching clearer, since two senses are involved as students watch and listen. When the objective is skill development and process learning, the technique is particularly needed and should usually be followed immediately by an opportunity for all the students to practice the process with supervision.

The technique of demonstration, in which a process is performed, should not be confused with a lecture, in which products are shown in various stages of the process. The students do not, in the latter case, see the *action* involved in making the product.

The Look Ahead

The vast majority of the techniques and media discussed in this book have been used successfully for a number of years in educational institutions and should continue to be important components of various instructional systems. For example, role-playing, learning by inquiry, programmed instruction, skits, case problems, case incidents, and discussion are teaching methods which can be used to individualize instruction in the "in-school" laboratory program. During the past few years a surge of activity in educational technology has been witnessed which has tremendous potential for developing and implementing individualized learning systems. While many of these technological developments have not been fully implemented in education, many business teachers have had an opportunity to experiment with them. The following expanding instructional resources and media will increasingly be produced by various agencies and integrated into the teaching styles of business teachers: computer-assisted instruction; computerized resource listings; new "write-on" surfaces; telewriter and telelecture; sound slides and filmstrips; audio projection component systems; school and regional distribution systems; closed-circuit, 2,500 M-C television; airborne distribution systems; teaching kits; single concept films; film cartridge projections; student response systems; commercial educational television; simulator kits; and information storage and retrieval.

The computer in education for business will play an increasingly major role. Computer-assisted instruction will make greater use of simulation and gaming in curriculum areas now characterized chiefly by linear presentations of facts to be learned. The computer terminal is now being used for the following five educational purposes: laboratory calculating device, record keeper and retriever of student information, problem solver or model simulation device, homework monitor or recitation receiver, and tutor.

A number of experimental studies and projects are now being conducted to determine the best methods of using the computer in instruction. Literature from the following studies should be carefully examined: Stanford-Brentwood Computer Assisted Laboratory, Programmed Logic for Automated Teaching Operations (PLATO), Edison Responsive Environment (ERE), and Program for Learning in Accordance with Needs (PLAN).

New systems for computer-assisted instruction are constantly being developed. The following are advantages and disadvantages of some of the newer systems:

Advantages of the System

1. It is useful as a tutor—it can be used with study guides.
2. It can accommodate students' questions.
3. It has tutorial and remedial advantages.
4. It possesses the capability to branch, accelerate, etc.
5. Forty hours to program one hour of instruction results in a carefully constructed program.
6. It is useful for problem solving segments of teaching.
7. It can accommodate learners with different needs.
8. It is applicable for adaptive education and the decision-making process.
9. Course writing is not excessively difficult—computer symbol system can be learned with a few weeks instruction.
10. A users group can form to produce programming and share equipment.
11. There are unlimited gadgets you can interlock to the computer, e.g., tape recorder—at random access.
12. There are no limitations on transmissions over long distances.
13. The cathode ray tube is best for instructional purposes.

Disadvantages of the System

1. Compatibility between different brands of equipment does not exist to a great degree. (Manufacturers have not standardized.)
2. Preparation of programs is necessary, time consuming, and expensive.
3. It is difficult to get users group to agree on a framework for curriculum making.
4. Cost prohibits many users—$136,000 one year rental for a 32 terminal computer. It presently costs $15-20 per student terminal-hour—it is reducing.
5. Technicians are needed to operate equipment.
6. It is difficult to anticipate student questions.
7. There is a problem in scheduling students.
8. Lecture notes cannot be directly translated to course writing.
9. It is difficult to anticipate trouble spots in lessons.
10. It is difficult trying to adapt business machines to processes of education.
11. The typewriter as a teaching device is slow.[20]

SUMMARY

Viable education programs in the field of education for business require new and additional kinds of insight. Harold Howe II, former U.S. Commissioner of Education, in discussing the role of technology in education, said:

> We know from research carried on during the last decade or so that we have barely scratched the surface of man's ability to learn, and that there is a vast potential for change at every stage in education—nursery schools, elementary and secondary schools, colleges and universities, adult education, vocational training, and rehabilitation.
>
> What we have seen so far in the production of teaching aids is only a trickle compared with what is likely to come when we find the answers to some fundamental questions. . .[21]

---

[20] Calvin J. Cotrell and Edward F. Hauck (eds.), *Education Media in Vocational and Technical Education* (Columbus, Ohio: The Center for Research and Leadership Development in Vocational and Technical Education, Ohio State University, 1967), pp. 124-125.

[21] Harold Howe II, "The Realities of the Learning Market," *Educational Technology* (April, 1967), p. 40.

SELECTED BIBLIOGRAPHY

Banathy, Bela H. *Instructional Systems.* Palo Alto, Calif.: Fearon Publishers, 1968.

Bjorkquist, David. *What Vocational Teachers Should Know About Individualized Instruction.* Columbus, Ohio: The Center for Vocational and Technical Education, Ohio State University, 1972.

Block-Time—Simulation: Individualized Office Instructional System. Vol. I, *Guide to Organizing and Operating the Block-Time—Simulation Program.* Vol. II, *Teacher's Manual and Curriculum Guide for the Block-Time—Simulation Program.* Vol. III, *Integrated Projects and Supplementary Materials for the Block-Time—Simulation Program.* Vol. IV, *An Office Simulation—Teacher and Student Kit for the Block-Time—Simulation Program.* Vol. V, *100 Case Problems for the Block-Time—Simulation Program.* Vol. VI, *A Guide for Designing, Using, and Evaluating Office Simulations for the Block-Time—Simulation Program.* East Lansing, Michigan: Michigan State University, Department of Secondary Education and Curriculum, 1969.

Blackstone, Bruce I. "VOE." *Business Education World,* L (January-February, 1970), p. 28.

Business Simulations 1 & 2. Phoenix, Arizona: Arizona Distributive Education Clubs of America, 1967 and 1972.

Changing Methods of Teaching Business Subjects, Tenth National Business Education Association Yearbook. Washington: National Business Education Association, 1972.

Cotrell, Calvin J., and Edward F. Hauck (eds.). *Education Media in Vocational and Technical Education.* Columbus, Ohio: The Center for Research and Leadership Development in Vocational and Technical Education, Ohio State University, 1967.

Davis, Rose Ann. "Hints on Office Simulation." Paper developed from a workshop conducted by Dr. Garth Hanson, 1970.

Emerging Content and Structure of Business Education, Eighth National Business Education Association Yearbook. Washington: National Business Education Association, 1970.

Funk, Beverly M. "A Blueprint for Successful Simulation." *Business Education Forum,* 24 (February, 1970), pp. 21-22.

Guidelines for Implementing the Project Plan of Instruction in Distributive Education in the Schools. East Lansing, Michigan: Michigan State University, Department of Secondary Education and Curriculum, 1968.

Haines, Peter G. (ed.). *Readings in Distributive Education: The Project Plan of Instruction and Related Teacher Education.* East Lansing, Michigan: Michigan State University, Department of Secondary Education and Curriculum, 1968.

Howe, Harold, II. "The Realities of the Learning Market." *Educational Technology* (April, 1967), p. 40.

Huffman, Harry. *A Taxonomy of Office Activities for Business and Office Education.* Columbus, Ohio: The Center for Vocational and Technical Education, Ohio State University, 1968.

Impellitter, Joseph, and Curtis Finch. *Review and Synthesis of Research on Individualizing Instruction in Vocational and Technical Education.* Columbus, Ohio: The Center for Vocational and Technical Education, Ohio State University, 1972.

Jones, Adaline, D. "The Enigmatic Intensive Office Laboratory." *The Balance Sheet,* XLIX (April, 1968), pp. 344-7, 384.

Kibler, Robert J., Larry Barker, and David Miles. *Behavioral Objectives and Instruction.* Boston: Allyn and Bacon, Inc., 1970.

Mager, Robert F., and Kenneth M. Beach, Jr. *Developing Vocational Instruction.* Palo Alto, Calif.: Fearon Publishers, 1967.

Poland, Robert. "An Instructional System for Office Education." Paper presented at American Vocational Association Convention, Boston, December, 1969.

Popham, W. James, and Eva I. Baker. *Establishing Instructional Goals.* Englewood Cliffs, N.J.: Prentice-Hall, Inc., 1970.

_____. *Systematic Instruction.* Englewood Cliffs, N.J.: Prentice-Hall, Inc., 1970.

Sabin, William A. "Simulation in the Seventies: An Overview." *Business Education World,* LI (September-October, 1971), p. 6.

A Selected and Annotated Bibliography Related to Cooperative and Project Methods in Distributive Education. East

Lansing, Michigan: Michigan State University, Department of Secondary Education and Curriculum, 1967.

Spitze, Hazel Taylor. *Choosing Techniques for Teaching and Learning*. Washington: National Education Association, 1970.

U.S. Department of Health, Education, and Welfare, Office of Education. *Distributive Education in the High School*. Washington: U.S. Government Printing Office, 1969.

_____, and U.S. Department of Labor, Manpower Administration. *Vocational Education and Occupations*. Washington: U.S. Government Printing Office, 1969.

Writing Performance Goals: Strategies and Prototypes. New York: Gregg Division, McGraw-Hill Book Co., Inc., 1972.

Chapter 11

YOUTH ORGANIZATIONS

"Don't let the tail wag the dog," "I can't get my students to do anything," or "How do you fire up your students?" are common reactions when the topic of youth organizations is introduced. These and similar questions indicate the need for teachers to develop competencies in planning and implementing youth organization activities.

In this chapter, youth organizations in education for business will be presented as a technique or method of instruction. It will be assumed that the techniques themselves are more important than the goals of specific youth organizations. This assumption is essential because numerous youth organizations in business are now operating on local, state, regional, and national levels. Likewise, it is assumed that the techniques which are appropriate for advisors of one youth organization are applicable for chapter advisors of other youth groups in education for business. A listing of several national organizations, together with the current addresses of the headquarters' offices, is presented in the bibliography at the end of the chapter.

EDUCATIONAL VALUES OF YOUTH ORGANIZATIONS

Why would 20 members of a youth organization devote over 1,000 hours of their free time to planning, conducting, and reporting upon a research project? Why would a student spend every minute of her free time for six months in study and preparation of a 200-page business report? Why would a group of 100 students in a youth organization give over 200 hours of their time to assist a community organization which needed help? Why would students go door-to-door in cold weather selling candy to raise $700? Answers to these questions can be provided by the students in a midwestern high school who performed these and other similar achievements.

Students participating in youth organizations throughout the country are continually amazing educators with their achievements. Not all students respond in the same manner to youth organizations; the techniques which may be successful with one group of students may not be as effective with another group. However, teachers who have been most effective in working with youth organizations in education for business do have similar beliefs. They believe that: (1) the youth organization is an activity which complements, supplements, and strengthens the instructional program; (2) combined with classroom and laboratory instruction, the youth organization gives greater scope and depth to the total instructional program; and, (3) the youth organization provides an avenue for the enrichment of the instructional program through activities planned by students under the teacher's guidance. These three statements emphasize the fact that a youth organization in education for business is an integral part of the instructional program. It contributes to the development of such competencies as leadership ability, professional attitude, cooperation, economic understanding, citizenship responsibility, and social growth.

The program for a youth organization should be carefully designed and planned so that maximum educational benefits can be achieved. While it is impossible to identify all of the specific purposes of a youth organization, a number of educational values are important. The youth organization can:

1. *Satisfy basic psychological needs that are not wholly satisfied in the formal program of instruction.* Classroom

instruction is primarily concerned with a body of knowledge which applies in part to the total field of business and in part to the immediate occupational goal of each student enrolled. School and community laboratories provide a means of trying out the concepts learned in the classroom. The youth organization rounds out this classroom and laboratory instruction by providing a controlled method for participation in activities which are of particular interest to the members of the organization. Each student has an opportunity through the youth organization activities to satisfy psychological needs, such as a desire to excel, to belong, to self-ascertain, to be identified, and to be recognized.

2. *Stimulate higher student standards of performance.* Classroom standards are generally prescribed by the teacher; school and community laboratory standards, by the teacher and the employer. In youth organization activities, standards become the joint decision of the students and the teacher-advisor. In the youth organization atmosphere, a student feels he is being judged by standards set by peers. Hopefully, each student will be motivated and stimulated to reach his maximum potential.

3. *Clarify, dignify, and glorify a tentative career choice.* Contacts that a student makes with key business leaders on local, state, regional, and national levels can have a major impact on his career choice.

4. *Establish dialogue with the teacher that is not possible in the formal program of instruction.* The relationship between a student and the teacher-advisor is on more of a player-coach basis than the typical student-teacher relationship. This relationship develops naturally with the planning and implementation of youth organization activities.

5. *Afford freedom of expression.* Students have an opportunity to design, plan, and implement their own program of work under the guidance of the teacher-advisor. This type of learning atmosphere is particularly conducive to free expression. Each student has an equal voice in making decisions.

6. *Enable each student to develop competencies needed for entering and advancing in business.* Activities are carefully planned so that they complement, supplement, and strengthen the instructional program. Emphasis is given to vocationally oriented large-group, committee, and individual projects which help to develop competencies needed for employment.

7. *Enable students to develop a knowledge and appreciation of employment opportunities and the requirements for entering and advancing in the world of business.* Opportunities for students to meet formally and informally with businessmen can be arranged by either the teacher-advisor or the students. Activities, such as field trips, use of resource personnel, field observations, field interviews, and youth organization conferences on an area, state, regional, or national level, can assist the student.

8. *Enable each student to understand his civic and social obligations.* Reading to people in a retirement home, working with the League of Women Voters to get out the vote, conducting a fashion show, or holding an employee-employer appreciation banquet are examples of activities which help a student to understand his civic and social obligations. The opportunity to associate with recognized leaders in community activities is often an important plus for the student. Frequently, the student learns more during the planning stage than the implementation stage of the activities.

9. *Enable students to develop a sense of individual responsibility and self-respect.* When a student is placed in an environment where he is assuming and implementing major or minor assignments as a part of the work of a youth organization, significant changes in behavior are noted. The student finds that he is a responsible person and gains self-respect.

10. *Contribute to the student's mental and emotional stability.* "Nothing breeds success like success" may be a trite expression, but it vividly expresses one of the major educational contributions of a youth organization. All too many young people go through school being rated

average or below average by their teachers. As a result, they lose confidence in themselves. Youth organization activities are planned so that each student has an opportunity for success. Each student has an equal opportunity for acceptance by and identification with members of his peer group through carefully designed youth group activities.

11. *Provide an opportunity for both leadership and followership to be developed by all students.* In the youth organization, the student accepts both the position of leader and that of follower. This not only lends itself to the development of leadership abilities, but also, what is just as important, lends itself to the development of followership abilities. The structure and activities of the youth organization are designed to achieve maximum student participation.

12. *Enable students to develop important personal qualities, such as cooperation, dependability, and a sense of humor.* An opportunity to learn how to become a cooperative and dependable member of a business or community organization is provided through a well designed program of youth activities. The student learns the importance of cooperation and dependability while assuming both leadership and followership roles. He learns about the importance of a good sense of humor while working with peer group members in general sessions and committee meetings.

13. *Enable students to understand the American economic system.* Classroom-oriented activities, laboratory learning experiences, and youth organization projects can all make a contribution to the economic literacy of young people. Through participation in youth organization activities, such as fund raising, field trips, guest speakers, and competitive events, basic concepts are further developed and applied in different situations.

THE ROLE OF THE ADVISOR

The youth organization should be student-centered and student-directed. It is recognized, however, that while young people are capable of planning and implementing their own activities, it is essential that they have the counsel of a teacher-advisor. In order to function as a youth organization advisor, the teacher should be aware of the potential values of the youth organization and should understand the educational values which are inherent in youth organization activities. The advisor should provide guidance and counsel for youth organization members, develop interest and support of adults, and assume responsibility for the total youth organization program.

As a Counselor

The youth organization advisor's first concern should be the educational development of each individual student-member. His relationship with youth organization members should be that of a counselor. He should provide students with maximum opportunities to conduct their own program. The advisor should realize that the typical young person lacks sufficient maturity to organize and carry out a youth organization program. He should sense when assistance is needed, stimulate student participation, and channel student efforts into activities which have educational benefits.

There is a correlation between the enthusiasm students have in the youth organization program and the interest of the advisor. In introducing the program to the students, the advisor must demonstrate an understanding of the purposes of the youth organization and the benefits that will accrue to the students. Seldom do students develop vision, understanding, and imagination through a superficial presentation. The depth of understanding demonstrated by the advisor will do much to create a youth organization program which will reflect the enthusiastic devotion of the students.

After the youth organization concept has been presented, the advisor should encourage a student-centered relationship. The enthusiasm of the students may tend to encourage activities which are not in keeping with the basic goals of the youth organization and the objectives of the instructional program. The advisor must, of necessity, channel this enthusiasm into those activities which retain the enthusiastic interest of the students and still fall within a program of sound educational values.

Educational and business leaders in the community can be of immense value to the youth organization advisor. They can inform the advisor of acceptable practices and methods, lend assistance to youth organization operations, and add their support to the overall program. Such resource people can be used continually as consultants to further the youth organization program.

Parents represent a group which has the educational interests of the students at heart. They can provide many services of real value to youth organization activities and, through this involvement, can develop a better understanding of the total instructional program and an appreciation of the opportunities which the program offers their children.

The youth organization advisor should see that interested individuals and groups are properly recognized for their contributions to the success of the program. Courtesy demands that appreciation be shown for assistance. Furthermore, the interest of those in a position to help the youth organization program can be maintained and cultivated further only if their time and efforts are properly and appropriately rewarded. Introductions at meetings, mention in publicity releases, words of thanks in private conversations, and honorary memberships can stimulate continued support of the youth organization and the instructional program it represents.

As a Leader

The youth organization advisor is the teacher-leader in the program. Various activities may be the responsibility of the youth organization officers who in turn delegate these responsibilities to student members, but it is the responsibility of the youth organization advisor to see that all activities are conducted within educational objectives.

This responsibility includes protecting the educational interests of students participating in youth organization activities. Proper orientation and constant supervision will assure constructive and wholesome youth organization learning experiences. The advisor must see that all functions are properly chaperoned and must assume full responsibility for students attending functions wherever they may be conducted. The advisor may on occasion delegate certain responsibilities in connection with the youth organization program to some other adult. However, the advisor, in the final analysis, is responsible and should assure himself that whatever responsibilities he has delegated to other adults will be properly assumed and executed.

Students can reap a harvest of values by participating in youth organization activities. They are influenced, however, by the interest the youth organization advisor takes in the program. The advisor who stimulates the students and who assumes the proper role of responsibility deserves a full measure of credit for the growth and development of students in the local youth organization program.

The following list, published by the Distributive Education Clubs of America in their *Chapter Management Aids Handbook,* can easily serve as a guide to aid the chapter advisor in his role: [1]

1. Initiate the organization of the DECA activities by the chapter.

2. Become thoroughly versed in the history, principles, constitution provisions, ceremonies, typical activities, parliamentary procedures and other essentials of the organization.

3. Assist in the plans for securing an efficient group of officers. Set up criteria for candidates (grades, attendance, etc.). Let candidates know of the responsibilities of each office.

4. Instruct newly elected officers concerning their duties and give all members leadership training.

5. Assist members in planning a calendar of events. Set dates of events early in the school year. See that they get on the school calendar early.

6. Plan programs that are adequately financed and funds properly protected. Help set up adequate DECA Chapter records and accounts.

---

[1] Distributive Education Clubs of America, *Chapter Management Aids Handbook* (Falls Church, Virginia, 1971), p. 16.

7. See that DECA Chapter meetings are held regularly and conducted in a businesslike manner.

8. Help new DECA members to take part and get into the spirit of the DECA activities.

9. See that every DECA member has a part in the work, accepts the responsibility and tries to do his or her share. Here is an opportunity for leadership training through youth activities.

10. Encourage the procurement of the standard minimum DECA Chapter equipment. See that it is used and protected.

11. See that a DECA Chapter library is set up and read.

12. Conduct DECA Chapter Executive Committee meetings to assist officers with chapter business.

13. Counsel individual members and committees on problems and activities.

14. Encourage participation in district, state, regional and national conferences. Help students prepare for leadership activities and contest participation at all levels of competition.

15. See that all ceremonies, initiations, public performances, and displays are carefully planned and creditably executed.

16. Keep school administration and the public posted on activities and developments.

17. Keep abreast of new developments in DECA and call them to the attention of the members.

18. Utilize the DECA Chapter as a leadership training device by impressing the membership that it is their organization. You should see that they perform the necessary functions to keep the DECA Chapter improving in its opportunities for widening the scope of the learning situations that may be developed.

ORGANIZING A LOCAL YOUTH ORGANIZATION

The steps which should be followed in organizing a local youth organization will necessarily vary from community to community and from school to school. Before making an effort to generate student interest in a youth organization, the teacher should determine local school policy. If school policy permits or encourages cocurricular youth organization activities, the following steps may be helpful in organizing a local chapter:

1. Determine and identify the educational values of the proposed youth organization in terms of serving individual student needs.

2. At the first meeting:

   a. Discuss the history, development, educational values, and typical activities of the proposed youth organization with the students.
   b. Discuss the characteristics of a good member.
   c. Determine student interest.
   d. Request that students volunteer to serve on the constitution, program, and nominating committees.

3. Prior to the second meeting, the following tasks should be accomplished:

   a. The program committee should meet to carefully plan the second meeting and develop a list of possible activities for the next month. Guidelines for selecting activities, which are discussed later in this chapter, should be followed.
   b. The constitution committee should study various constitutions and be prepared to propose one to the membership.
   c. The nominating committee should meet to carefully study and discuss qualifications, duties, and characteristics of various officers and prepare a slate of candidates for leadership roles in the youth organization.
   d. The members of all three committees should meet as a group several times as a coordinating committee. This group will also elect a temporary chairman, secretary, and treasurer to serve until officers are elected.

4. At the second meeting:

   a. Copies of the proposed constitution are distributed and voted upon.

b. Members of the nominating committee discuss the characteristics, duties, and responsibilities of a good officer.

c. A proposed slate of officers is distributed and the meeting is opened to nominations from the floor.

d. A report is presented by the program committee and ideas are solicited from chapter members.

e. The group votes on activities for the next month.

5. At the third meeting:

a. Collect local, state, and national dues.

b. Elect officers.

c. Have program activity which was selected by the members.

6. Instruct officers, individually, on what is expected of them.

7. Hold executive committee meetings to make plans for work and budget programs.

8. Submit the applications for charter and appropriate state and national forms for paying dues.

9. Submit proposed work and budget programs to the membership as developed by the executive committee.

10. Appoint committees to carry out programs of work.

11. Help officers learn how to develop an agenda and conduct meetings using correct parliamentary procedures.

KEEPING YOUTH ORGANIZATION ACTIVITIES ON TARGET

The value of any local, state, or national youth organization must be measured in terms of educational benefits. Activities which enable students to develop or refine skills for employment, and simultaneously guide each student into a full and rewarding participation in society, should be planned. Students have to be effectively prepared for the world of work in the most efficient manner. The youth organization activities to which they devote their time and effort must make a positive contribution to their occupational preparation.

Successful teacher-advisors have found that a carefully designed program of activities, correlated with classroom and laboratory instruction, is an essential device for planning youth organization activities.

A professional teachers association in one state recommends the following plan to develop a program of activities for a youth organization:

1. Establish an annual program of activities:
   a. It is an outline of activities covering a definite period.
   b. It includes specific goals, ways and means of reaching them, and adequate provision for checking on accomplishments.
   c. The plan should be well thought out and carefully worded.
   d. It should be based on the needs of the members, the organization, the school, and the community.
   e. It should represent the thinking of a majority of members.
   f. Although new youth organizations should not undertake an overly elaborate program the first year, it should be one that presents a challenge to the members.

2. Steps for building a program of activities for a new youth organization (or a youth organization that has not previously set forth a program of activities):
   a. Review, as a total youth organization, the possible activities in which the organization might participate.
   b. Secure copies of programs of activities of other youth organization chapters and review them for ideas. Materials sent from the national office of the youth organization can suggest many ideas.
   c. Decide on several activities that will definitely be undertaken.
   d. Appoint a Program Planning Committee (with subcommittees for each section of the program) and turn over to the committee all of the preliminary materials on hand. It should be the duty of this committee to further survey and check needs, study suggestions already offered, and set up a tentative program of work, including goals and ways and means.
   e. Have the program committee report back to the youth organization; discuss their reports in open meetings

and have them re-worded as necessary until they are in satisfactory order.

   f. Put the total program of activities in writing.
   g. Check the program of activities with school authorities and others concerned.
   h. Adopt the program when satisfactory, appoint permanent committees for each major division, assign duties, and set to work.

3. Steps for building a program of activities for an established youth organization:
   a. Review last year's program of activities at youth organization meetings. Try to find out why certain items were successful and others were not. Discuss also the present needs of the club, its members, and the community.
   b. Select from last year's program the items to be continued for the present year. Add new items suggested by members.
   c. Follow the outline presented in steps (c) through (h) above.

   To aid students in planning the program of activities, a matrix or grid is provided by the teacher-advisor. (See Figure 11-1.) Across the top of the matrix are the goals of the youth organization which are contained in the local constitution. Down the side of the matrix, the teacher-advisor lists the planned units of group instruction or competencies to be developed, together with proposed teaching dates. A large piece of paper or poster board can be used effectively as a planning matrix.

   The program planning committee then begins its task of planning youth organization activities. Once the committee has planned the activities, the planning board can be kept in place or stored for future reference and use. Copies of the schedule or calendar of activities, showing all of the planned events for the year, are duplicated for distribution to members. One state association recommends using a program of activities form, in addition to a schedule of events, to facilitate the planning of the executive committee. This form contains the activity, beginning date, goal, responsible committee, ways and means, accomplishments, and date completed.

YOUTH ORGANIZATION ACTIVITIES PLANNING MATRIX

Units of Instruction or Competencies to Be Developed	Goals of Youth Organization						
	Civic Consciousness	Social Intelligence	Leadership Development	Vocational Awareness	Vocational Competence	Etc.	
Orientation Dates ———							
Human Relations Dates ———							
Communications Dates ———							
Economics Dates ———			WHICH YOUTH ORGANIZATION ACTIVITIES WILL COMPLEMENT, SUPPLEMENT AND STRENGTHEN THE INSTRUCTIONAL PROGRAM?				
Mathematics Dates ———							
Public Relations Dates ———							
Supervisory Training Dates ———							
Etc.							

FIGURE 11-1

The DECA *Chapter Management Aids Handbook* gives the following examples of youth group activities, how they relate to teaching-learning activities, and how to evaluate each one: [2]

1. To develop progressive leadership in the field of marketing and distribution that is competent, aggressive, self-reliant and cooperative.

   Through competitive events and activities relating to the DECA program of work, students participate in experiences that groom them to assume leadership responsibilities in marketing and distribution.

   Example: The Student of the Year event is a significant project which encourages the highest degree of individual student achievement in all program activities in the student's total school program and in service to his community and business community.

2. To develop a sense of individual responsibility.

   The individual acceptance of responsibility is a trait of prime importance in the student's development into an effective personality. Projects pertinent to the following activities give reinforcement to this trait development and aid the student in gaining vocational competence.

   Example: Individual Studies in Marketing, Area of Distribution and Merchandise Information Manual, and committee assignments regarding professional and social chapter activities.

3. To provide opportunities for intelligent career choice in the field of marketing and distribution.

   Selected DECA activities become useful projects helpful to students choosing significant career goals in marketing and distribution.

   Example: The Merit Awards Program.

4. To allow practical application of the principles of marketing and distribution through competitive activities.

   Competitive involvement in competitive events provides opportunities to apply knowledges, skills and abilities

---

[2] *Ibid.*, pp. 12-14, 58.

and motivates the student to refine these skills which aid him in being successful. Ultimately this refinement makes the student's skills more marketable.

Example: Sales Demonstration, Advertising, Manual Projects.

5. To encourage use of ethical practices in business.

An insight into the practices and policies used by business is attained by the investigations and observations required for some projects.

Example: Creative Marketing, Advertising, Sales Demonstrations.

6. To provide for mental and physical health through satisfactory social and recreational activities.

The need for mental and physical health through DECA activities is reflected in the personality and physical qualities which permit personnel in marketing and distribution to function effectively. A variety of DECA activities is instrumental in developing these qualities.

Example: Leadership conferences, chapter recreational activities, sponsoring and staging of a fashion show or a good grooming clinic.

7. To develop a respect for education in marketing and distribution which will contribute to vocational competence.

Personal competition and completion of written studies require a descriptive vocabulary and the ability to communicate clearly. These activities illustrate to the student the need for clear thinking, persuasive thinking, forceful speaking, and effective writing—hallmarks of a successful person.

Example: Public Speaking, Job Interview, Sales Demonstration, Individual Studies in Marketing, and other written manuals.

8. To engender an understanding of, and an appreciation for, our free, competitive enterprise system.

As DE students are refining their occupational goals and beginning to learn about the field of distribution, a substantial part of the curriculum may be spent in learning about job opportunities and distributive activities in a free enterprise system. Many chapter activities and competitive activities lend themselves to understanding how distributive projects affect the individual in a free, competitive economy.

Example: Public Speaking, Creative Marketing Projects, Studies in Marketing, Sales Projects, professional speakers and field trips, civic projects.

9. To develop an appreciation of civic and social obligations of those engaged in marketing and distribution.

In both his class and chapter work, the student learns to recognize his obligations to the community in which he lives through studying community needs and planning civic improvement.

Example: Community service projects, various marketing projects.

Through social events held during the year, the DECA member is given an opportunity to develop poise and to gain a knowledge of the social graces necessary in our society.

Example: Employer-employee functions, recreational activities, appearances before civic or trade groups, inviting business representatives to speak at chapter meetings.

10. To serve as a means of interpreting the instructional program to businessmen, faculty, parents, and other students.

By involving businessmen and faculty as judges and advisors of competitive events as part of student projects, the student is afforded the opportunity to interpret the instructional program of Distributive Education. The student may interpret the instructional program in school through assemblies and other various media. Parental involvement should be solicited throughout the school year as guests as well as participants.

Example: Public Speaking, Studies in Marketing, Creative Marketing Projects, DECA month, civic appearances and field trips.

Listed on page 541 are examples of youth organization chapter activities.

EVALUATION CRITERIA FORM

Activity Evaluation of	Much	Some	Little
A. Evaluative Criteria:			
1. Does DECA Chapter activity contribute to meeting the goals of the DE program			
a. by offering instruction in distribution and marketing			
b. by aiding in the improvement of techniques of distribution			
c. by developing a broader understanding of the social and economic responsibilities of those engaged in distribution			
2. Does the chapter activity provide educational experience in distribution			
a. by experiences contributing to the overall instructional program			
b. by experiences contributing to the professional development of the individual student of distribution			
3. Is the activity the best method of providing the desired educational experiences in distribution			
a. does the activity serve to enrich the classroom instruction			
b. does the activity serve as a supplement to job instruction			
c. does the activity provide educational experiences in distribution that cannot be provided through classroom or job instruction			
4. Does the activity provide for maximum student participation			
a. Do students participate in every phase of activity:			
(1) creating the idea			
(2) planning the activity			
(3) conducting the activity			
(4) evaluating the activity			
b. Do all students have equal opportunity to participate in the activity			
c. Does the advisor serve as a counselor and guide			
(1) encourage student participation			
(2) serve as a "helper" rather than a "doer"			
5. Does the activity contribute to the improvement of the position of distribution in the school and the community			
B. Application of the criteria to the needs of the program:			
1. Extent to which this activity should comply with the criteria			
2. Extent to which the activity should relate to instruction			
a. direct relation to instruction			
b. indirect relation to instruction			

FIGURE 11-2

Films	College Orientation
Field Trips	Election of Officers
TV Program	Needy Family Project
Fund Raising	Professional Meetings
Fair Exhibit	Savings Club Program
Fashion Show	Installation of Officers
Radio Program	Local Publicity Releases
Parents' Night	Initiation of New Members
Guest Speakers	Employer-Employee Banquet
Contest Program	"Good Citizenship" Project
Boss Breakfast	"Get-Out-the-Vote" Project
Assembly Program	Creative Business Projects
Regular Meetings	Sponsor "Clean-Up" Project
Alumni Activities	State Leadership Conference
Social Activities	Executive Committee Meetings
Civic Appearances	"Student Day" at Local Business
Panel Discussions	Studies in Business Projects
Homecoming Parade	National Leadership Conference
Chapter Newsletter	"Careers in Business" Observances
National Youth	Reception for Prospective Members
Organization Week	Scholarship Fund Campaign
Faculty Recognition	

Additional ideas for youth organization activities can be found in handbooks provided by the national headquarters of each youth organization, state vocational education departments, and professional teacher organizations. The table of contents from a publication prepared by the Illinois Secondary Marketing and Distributive Education Association is a good example of what is contained in the youth organization handbooks from various sources.[3]

Chapter I   Introduction to the Illinois DECA Program

General Information, Organization of DECA, The Local Chapter, The Area Level, The National Level, What is DECA, Purposes of DECI, Why Join DECI, DECA Colors, The DECA Emblem, The DECA Creed, The National DECA Handbook, DECA and DECI

---

[3] Illinois Secondary Marketing and Distributive Education Association, *Handbooks of Distributive Education Clubs of Illinois* (Springfield, Illinois, 1971).

Terminology, Sources of Instructional and Reference Materials for Distributive Education, Responsibilities of the Local Advisor, How to Organize a DECI Club, Sample Chapter Charter.

Chapter II   Hints on Holding DECA Chapter Meeting

Conducting the DECA Chapter Meeting, Procedure in a Typical Meeting, Opening Ceremony for DECI Chapter Meetings, Closing Ceremony for DECI Chapter Meetings, Parliamentary Procedure, Chapter Committees, Committee Assignment Sheet, Committee Report Form, Resolution Covering a Change in the Local Chapter Constitution, DECA Chapter Secretary's Book, Information and Instructions, DECA Chapter Membership Roll and Record, Attendance Record, Sample Minutes of DECA Chapter Meeting, DECA Chapter Treasurer's Book, Member Dues and Fees Record, Chapter Cash Receipts and Disbursements, DECA Chapter Financial Summary.

Chapter III   DECA Officers

The DECA Officer, Characteristics of a Good Officer, Characteristics of a Good Member, Duties and Responsibilities of Chapter Officers (President, Vice President, Secretary, Treasurer, Reporter and/or Historian, Parliamentarian), Helpful Hints for Chapter Officers, Duties and Responsibilities of State Officers (President, Vice President, Secretary-Treasurer, Parliamentarian, other officers), State Executive Officer Qualification Form, Responsibilities of National Officers.

Chapter IV   Review on Leadership

What is a Leader?, What Are the Qualities of Leadership?, Characteristics of Leaders, How Do I Rate Myself?, Self Analysis Form, What Abilities Do You Need to Develop?, Activities Which Provide Leadership Training, Participating in a Group Discussion,

Leading a Group Discussion, How to Get More Out of Conferences, The Group Members as the Leader Sees Them, Human Relations and the DECI Chapter Member.

Invitation Committee, Reception Committee, Decoration Committee), Songs and Skits for DECA Social Events, Assemblies and Other Entertainment.

Once the major activities for the chapter have been planned, the advisor works with individuals and small groups of students to help them implement the appropriate youth organization projects and events.

A beneficial, well-rounded program of youth activities does not "just happen," it must be developed. Its development requires sound thinking and careful planning. "What," "when," "where," "who," and "how" are important questions which must be considered well in advance. In order to get a broad view of the whole proposed program, it is necessary that the entire plan be put on paper.

One very effective way to get the youth activity program down on paper where every member can see it is to begin by making a listing of the regular and proposed special meetings for the year. The number of regular meetings would, of course, be governed by the rules and regulations of the local chapter by-laws. Special meetings would be determined by looking ahead to specific and seasonal school, community, and business activities.

After the over-all schedule of meetings for the year has been agreed upon, at least as far as can be determined, it becomes necessary to decide the "what," "when," "where," "who," and "how" of regular and special meetings falling within the various months. Here is where the actual "shaping-up" of the program of work begins. At this stage specific committee and individual assignments should be made and plans developed for following through on the assignments.

Any program of youth activity developed and put into action by the local chapter should be planned in keeping with the needs of its members and in harmony with available human and community resources. Too often, the local chapter overlooks or bypasses many fine and beneficial sources of aid available right in its own community.

SUMMARY

A good youth organization must have the following essential elements:

1. A challenging program of work.
2. Capable officers and leaders.
3. Interested members.
4. Distributed responsibility shared by all members.
5. Proper equipment and records.
6. A knowledge of organization on the part of every member.

The program of work carried on at the local level is the most important phase of the entire chapter structure. Both the state and national organizations originated from the grass roots of isolated, individual local chapters. It is at the local level that the greatest amount of member participation takes place.

SELECTED BIBLIOGRAPHY

Distributive Education Clubs of America. *Chapter Management Aids Handbook.* Falls Church, Virginia, 1971.

Illinois Secondary Marketing and Distributive Education Association. *Handbooks of Distributive Education Clubs of Illinois.* Springfield, Illinois, 1971.

Organizations

Distributive Education Clubs of America, 200 Park Avenue, Falls Church, Virginia 22046.

Future Business Leaders of America, National Business Education Association, 1201 Sixteenth Street, N.W., Washington, D.C. 20036.

Future Secretaries Association, The National Secretaries Association, The International Secretaries Association, 1103 Grand Avenue, Kansas City, Missouri 64106.

Junior Achievement, Incorporated, 51 West 51st Street, New York, New York 10019.

Office Education Association, P.O. Box 4287, Madison, Wisconsin 53711.

INDEX

C

Calling-the-throw drills, 94
Career development capabilities, 436
Case problem method, 300, 382
Chalkboard illustrations, with lecture, 289
Class report, 308
Classroom organization, in basic business, 263; in office practice, 193, 194; in shorthand, 129; in typewriting, 72
Classroom procedures, in office practice, 189; in shorthand, 122, 151, 168; innovations in, 332
Community resources, 294
Competencies, identifying, 438, 487
Competency areas, distributive education, 346
Complete-cycle approach, advantages, 241; in accounting, 224; 234; problems, 237-240; review, 242; teaching suggestions, 236; testing, 242
Composing, at the typewriter, 74, 102
Computer-assisted instruction, advantages, 518; disadvantages, 519; in business education, 517
Cone of Experience, 472
Conference method, 384
Control, in typewriting, 88-91, 109
Control and criteria sheets, in office practice, 206-208
Cooperative education, in office practice, 200
Cooperative plan, in distributive education, 342; in office practice, 192
Cooperative vocational education, 413; advantages, 421, 458; application, 422; basic principles and concepts, 411; benefits, 459; career development capabilities, 436; community relations, 427; definition of terms, 415; evaluation, 449, 464; guidance, 428, individualizing instruction, 436; in-school instruction, 432; job manuals, 451; job reports, 452; job study guides, 450; learning activities, 443; learning outcomes, 438; manpower control, 426; occupational adjustment capabilities, 435; on-the-job instruction, 453; planning, 418; specific skills, 435; teacher-coordinator, 428; techniques, 450; training plan, 461; training sponsor, 460, 466; training station, 454; work experience programs, 413; work study, 413
Curriculum, construction, 348; guidelines for organization, 481; in distributive education, 401; levels, 356

D

Daily planning, 44
Data processing, in accounting, 254; in office practice, 212
DECA, 346
Debate, 330
Democracy in the classroom, 72
Demonstration, 516; in accounting, 223, 231; in basic business, 292; in office practice, 198; in shorthand, 124; in typewriting, 82
Dictation, office-style, 138, 164; selecting material for, 131
Directed occupational experiences, 515
Discussion, 372; duties of leader, 273
Display boards, 324
Distribution, 340
Distributive education, adult programs, 345; advantages, 347; basic beliefs, 340; basic concepts, 361; brainstorming, 378; buzz sessions, 377; case problem, 382; competency areas, 346; competency development, 386; conference method, 384; constructing curricula, 348; cooperative plan, 342; curriculum, 401; DECA, 346; defined, 340; discipline, 394; group discussion, 372; high school programs, 342; instructional activities, 396; lecture, 371; methods, 367, 404; objectives, 400; panel discussion, 376; planning instruction, 357; post-secondary programs, 343; principles and concepts, 339; project plan, 342; question-and-answer, 367; role-playing, 380; teaching tasks, 391; teaching techniques and procedures, 360
Distributive Education Clubs of America, 537

E

Economic reading report, 311
Education, modern, 2-5
Emotional factors, in basic business, 270
Equipment, in office practice, 210; physical layout and, 194
Evaluation, control sheet, 282; in accounting, 229, 245; in advanced typewriting, 77; in basic business, 277; in beginning typewriting, 71; in cooperative vocational education, 449, 464; in in-school instruction, 499; in office practice, 187, 202; in shorthand,

132, 149, 154; in typewriting, 98-99, 110; of teacher, 277; summary sheets, 98-99
Evaluation criteria form, 540

F

Fact sheets, 451
Field interviews, 514
Field observations, 514
Field trips, 321
Filmstrips, 314
Forms, typing on printed, 77, 105

G

Gaming, 323
Generalization, 275
Gestalt approach, in accounting, 224; in office practice, 187; in shorthand, 130
Goal setting, 39
Goals, relationship to abilities, 40
Grading plan, in shorthand, 159
Group discussion, 372
Guest speakers, 294
Guidance, in cooperative vocational education, 428

H

Handwriting, in accounting, 228
High school programs, in distributive education, 342
Human Relations Profile, 494
Human Relations Responsibilities, 493

I

In-basket exercise, 507
Incident problem, 382
Incident process, 300
Individual differences, in shorthand, 147; in typewriting, 67, 84
Individualizing instruction, 436, 482
In-school instruction, 432; aspects of instruction, 433; basic principles, 471; block-time—simulation, 473; business games, 509; computer-assisted instruction, 517; curriculum construction, 481; demonstration, 516; evaluation, 499; field interviews, 514; field observations, 514; in-basket exercise, 507; individualizing instruction, 482; intensive laboratory, 476; learning activities, 495; learning outcomes, 486; occupational experiences, 515; office simulation, 473; project plan, 479; resource personnel, 512; simulation, 501; suggestions, 432; techniques, 500
Instructional activities, in distributive education, 396

Instructional films, 313
Intensive laboratory, 476

J

Job description, teacher-coordinator, 430
Job Instruction Sheet, 196-197
Job manuals, 451
Job reports, 452
Job study guides, 450

K

Knowledge of progress, in shorthand, 121, 122; in typewriting, 70, 110

L

Laboratories, in distributive education, 500; in shorthand, 171; purposes, 500
Learning, concepts of, 33; defined, 33-34; in an office atmosphere, 185; psychological guides to, 35; setting the stage for, 38
Learning activities, 443, 495
Learning blocks, in shorthand, 127
Learning plateaus, 78
Learning process, 33
Learning stages, in typewriting, 77
Lecture, 371; straight, 287; with chalkboard illustrations, 289
Lesson plan, 44, 249; format, 49-51
Letters, typing, 76, 104

M

Machines, knowledge of, 184
Mailable copy, elements of, 162; in shorthand, 137; standards, 162
Manpower control, in cooperative vocational education, 426
Materials, presenting new shorthand, 148
Media, selecting, 445
Methods, of teaching accounting, 230-249; of teaching basic business, 284-332; of teaching distributive education, 367-386, 404; of teaching office practice, 188-208; of teaching shorthand, 143-166; of teaching typewriting, 81-105
Motivation, 59; in basic business, 272; in office practice, 195; in shorthand, 126, 143; in typewriting, 68
Multiple-job projects, in typewriting, 103

N

Notebooks, 310

O

Objectives, general and enabling, 52; in distributive education, 400; in office practice, 181; in shorthand, 129, 132, 157; in typewriting, 67, 86; specific behavioral, 53

Occupational adjustment capabilities, 435

Office machines, knowledge of, 184

Office practice, advance planning, 181; assignments, 183, 197; battery plan in, 192; classroom layout, 193; classroom procedures, 189; control and criteria sheets, 206-208; cooperative plan, 192; course objectives, 181; data processing in, 212; demonstration, 198; drill, 186; equipment, 210; evaluation, 187, 202; fundamental principles, 179-188; Gestalt approach in, 187; job instruction sheet, 196, 197; learning in an office atmosphere, 185; methods of teaching, 188-208; motivation, 195; participation, 195; performance review guide, 215; personal factors, 201; physical facilities, 182, 194; planning, 189, 208; rotation charts, 211; rotation plan, 189, 210; rotation schedules, 190; routines and procedures, 182; simulated office plan, 192; standards, 214; work experience, 200

Office simulation, 473

Office-style dictation, 138, 164

On-the-job laboratory instruction, 453

Overhead projector, 316; in accounting, 232

P

Panel discussion, 298, 376

Participation, in basic business, 267; in office practice, 195

Performance review guide, 215

Personal factors, 201

Physical facilities, in office practice, 182

Physical factors, in basic business, 262

Planning, in office practice, 208

Planning and organization, in accounting, 249; in basic business, 262, 265; in in-school instruction, 481; in office practice, 189; in shorthand, 151, 168; in typewriting, 65, 72, 81; in transcription, 140

Planning instruction, 40; daily, 44; in cooperative vocational education, 418; in distributive education, 357; in office practice,

189; objectives, 51; skill learning factors in typewriting, 106; unit, 41

Planning matrix, 536

Post-secondary programs, in distributive education, 343

Practice set audit sheet, 247

Practice sets, in accounting, 246

Priming the pump, in shorthand, 129; in typewriting, 111

Principles, of teaching accounting, 221-230; of teaching cooperative vocational education, 411; of teaching distributive education, 339; of teaching office practice, 179-188; of teaching shorthand, 117; of teaching transcription, 140; of teaching typewriting, 65, 75

Problem-solving, 291

Procedures and routines, in office practice, 182

Procedures and techniques, in teaching accounting, 230-249; in teaching basic business, 284-332; in teaching distributive education, 360; in teaching office practice, 188-208; in teaching shorthand, 143; in teaching transcription, 140; in teaching typewriting, 81-105

Production typewriting, 74; basic principles and guidelines, 75; letters, 76; multiple jobs, 76

Progress, knowledge of, in shorthand, 121, 122; in typewriting, 70, 110

Project, defined, 481

Project method, 318

Project plan, 479; defined, 479; in distributive education, 342

Proofreading, 73, 101

Psychological guides to learning, 35

Q

Quality, in typewriting, 71, 99, 111

Question-and-answer method, 290, 367

Questioning, in basic business, 269

R

Reading, in shorthand, 120, 146, 167

Reading Control Sheet, 273

Record, typewriting progress, 110

Resource personnel, 512

Resource unit, 42

Role-playing, 305, 380

Rotation plan, in office practice, 189, 210

Rotation schedules, in office practice, 190

Round-table discussion, 376
Routines and procedures, in office practice, 182

S

Scrapbooks, 310
Self assessment form, 497
Self-evaluation, in basic business, 283; in shorthand, 149
Shorthand, assignments, 129, 169; basic principles, 117; classroom organization, 129; classroom procedures, 122, 151, 168; comparison with plates, 168; demonstration, 124; evaluation, 132, 154; evaluation sheet, 155, 156; first-day procedures, 130; Gestalt approach, 130; grading plan, 159; individual differences, 147; knowledge of progress, 121, 122; laboratories, 171; learning blocks, 127; learning new material, 121; mailable copy, 162; motivation, 126, 143; objectives, 129, 132, 157; office-style dictation, 138, 164; presenting new material, 148; procedures and techniques in teaching, 143; reading, 120, 146, 167; rectangle, 152; rules, 131; selecting material for dictation, 131; self-evaluation, 149; spelling, 129, 170; success in, 119, 145, 167; writing, 127, 166
Shorthand Rectangle, 152
Simulated office plan, in office practice, 192
Simulation, 323, 501; characteristics, 502; types, 501
Skill-building, three factors in, 59
Skyline Drive, 91
Slides, 314
Specific skills, 435
Speed, development in typewriting, 109
Speed-building, devices, 91-98; in typewriting, 69, 88-90
Spelling, in shorthand, 129, 170
Standards, in advanced typing, 112; in office practice, 214; in transcription, 138, 161; in typewriting, 107
Straight lecture, 287
Success, in shorthand, 119, 145, 167; in typewriting, 71

T

Tape recorder, 325
Task Simulation Recording Form, 508
Teacher-coordinator, job description, 430; requirements, 394, 428
Teaching tasks, in distributive education, 391

Teaching techniques, 366
Teaching unit, 42
Techniques, in teaching accounting, 230-249; in teaching basic business, 284-332; in teaching co-operative vocational education, 450; in teaching distributive education, 360; in teaching in-school instruction, 500; in teaching office practice, 186; in teaching shorthand, 143; in teaching transcription, 142; in teaching typewriting, 81-105; selection, 444, 447, 495
Techniques and procedures, brainstorming, 302, 378; bulletin boards, 324; business games, 509; buzz group, 303, 377; case problem, 300, 382; class report, 308; conference method, 384; debate, 330; demonstration, 292, 516; discussion, 273, 372; field interviews, 514; field observations, 514; field trips, 321; filmstrips, 314; gaming and simulation, 323; guest speakers, 294; in-basket exercise, 507; incident process, 300; instructional films, 313; job manuals, 451; job reports, 452; job study guides, 450; lecture, 287, 371; lecture with illustrations, 289; notebooks, 310; occupational experiences, 515; overhead projector, 316; panel discussion, 298, 376; problem-solving, 291; project, 318; question-and-answer, 290, 367; resource personnel, 512; role-playing, 305, 380; scrapbooks, 310; simulation, 501; slides, 314; straight lecture, 287; tape recorder, 325; television, 327; term papers, 330; transparencies, 314
Television, 327
Term papers, 330
Testing, in accounting, 242, 248
Training plan, 461; benefits, 458; format, 464
Training sponsor, criteria, 460; development, 466
Training station, responsibilities, 454; selection, 455
Transcription, factors in, 139; introduction, 134; introductory techniques, 159; mailable copy, 137, 162; materials, 136; office-style dictation, 139; principles, 140; rating chart, 164; standards, 138, 161; teaching, 134, 171; time factors, 135
Transparencies, 314, in accounting, 233
Typewriting, accuracy, 90; advanced standards, 112; assignments, 73, 101, 111; basic con-

cepts, 63; basic principles and guidelines, 65, 75; calling-the-throw drills, 94, 96, 97; classroom organization, 72; composing at the machine, 74; control, 88; demonstration, 82; developing control, 69, 88, 90, 109; developing speed, 69, 88, 91, 109; evaluation, 71, 77, 98, 110; first-day procedures, 65, 81; first year objectives, 67; in today's schools, 64; individual differences in, 67, 84; interest-generating devices, 87; keyboard, 106; knowledge of progress, 70, 110; letters, 76, 104; motivation, 68; multiple job efficiency, 76; multiple-job projects, 103; objectives, 86; on printed forms, 77, 105; production, 74; proofreading, 73, 101; quality, 71, 99, 111; speed and accuracy development, 69, 88, 109; speed-building devices, 91-97; standards, 107; success in, 71; teaching techniques and procedures, 81-105; TV and the teacher, 81

Typewriting progress record, 110

U

Uniform Answer Sheet, 199
Unit, 42
Unit planning, 41

V

Vocabulary, in accounting, 227
Vocational Education Amendments of 1968, 12, 14-20

W

Writing, shorthand, 127, 166
Work experience, in office practice, 200; programs, 413
Work study, 413

Y

Youth organization, activities, 533; advisor, 527; educational values, 523; evaluation of activities, 537; organizing, 531; planning matrix, 536
Youth organization advisor, 527; as communicator, 529; as counselor, 528; as leader, 529; responsibilities, 530